THE POLITICS OF WORK

Studies in Australian History

Series editors:
Alan Gilbert, Patricia Grimshaw and Peter Spearritt

Sharon Morgan   *Land Settlement in Early Tasmania*
Stephen Nicholas (ed.)   *Convict Workers*
Pamela Statham (ed.)   *The Origins of Australia's Capital Cities*
Jeffrey Grey   *A Military History of Australia*
Alastair Davidson   *The Invisible State*
James A. Gillespie   *The Price of Health*
David Neal   *The Rule of Law in a Penal Colony*
Audrey Oldfield   *Woman Suffrage in Australia*
Paula J. Byrne   *Criminal Law and Colonial Subject*

THE POLITICS OF WORK

Gender and Labour in Victoria 1880–1939

Raelene Frances

SCHOOL OF HISTORY, UNIVERSITY OF NEW SOUTH WALES

To the memory of my maternal grandmother,
MAY HANSFORD (born May Hovenden)

Published by the Press Syndicate of the University of Cambridge
The Pitt Building, Trumpington Street, Cambridge CB2 1RP, UK
40 West 20th Street, New York, NY 10011-4211, USA
10 Stamford Road, Oakleigh, Melbourne 3166, Australia

© Cambridge University Press 1993
First published 1993

Printed in Hong Kong by Colorcraft

National Library of Australia cataloguing in publication data
Frances, Raelene.
The politics of work: gender and labour in Victoria, 1880–1939.
Bibliography.
Includes index.
ISBN 0 521 40199 2.
ISBN 0 521 45772 6 (pbk.).
1. Labor – Victoria – History. 2. Industry and state – Victoria –
History. 3. Victoria – Social conditions. 4. Victoria – Economic
conditions. 5. Victoria – Industries – History. 6. Victoria – Industries
– Case studies. I. Title. (Series: Studies in Australian history
(Cambridge, England)).
331.09945

Library of Congress cataloguing in publication data
Frances, Rae.
The politics of work: gender and labour in Victoria 1880–1939
Raelene Frances.
   p.   cm. – (Studies in Australian history)
Includes bibliographical references and index.
ISBN 0-521-40199-2
1. Working class – Australia – Victoria – History. 2. Work
environment – Australia – Victoria – History. 3. Sexual division of
labor – Australia – Victoria – History. I. Title. II Series.
HD8849. V532F73 1993
331.25–dc20   93-15133
                                                    CIP

A catalogue record for this book is available from the British Library.

ISBN 0 521 40199 2 hardback
ISBN 0 521 45772 6 paperback

Contents

Illustrations, Tables   vii

Note on currency   viii

Acknowledgements   ix

Abbreviations   xi

Introduction   1

Part I   Before the Wages Boards   13

1   The advent of machines and women: the clothing industries, 1880–1896   22

2   An age of grim adversity: the boot industry, 1880–1896   43

3   Drawing the line: the printing industries, 1880–1900   58

Part II   Under the Wages Boards   73

4   No more Amazons: the clothing industries, 1897–1919   81

5   The workers baffled: the boot industry, 1897–1910   100

6   Educating the girls: the printing industries, 1901–1925   116

Part III The Era of Federal Wage-fixing   131

7 Diplomacy and guerilla warfare: the clothing industries, 1919–1939   137

8 The Cinderella of the skilled trades: the boot industry, 1911–1939   151

9 Marginal matters: the printing industries, 1925–1937   169

Conclusion   180
Appendix: Selected Employment Statistics, Victoria, 1880–1939   193
Notes   207
Bibliography of works cited   244
Index   261

Illustrations

1 Proportions employed in the clothing industries, 1891   24
2 'The advent of machines and women' in tailoring, 1874   27
3 *Punch's* response to the tailoresses' strike, 1883   33
4 Early mechanised stitcher for bookbinding, 1890s   62
5 Woman bookbinder at work, 1891   62
6 Binding room, Government Printing Office, 1911   64
7 Sewing Room, Government Printing Office, 1891   64
8 Advertisement for a linotype in the journal of the typographers' union, 1908   70
9 Advertisement for United Shoe Machinery Company, 1905   101
10 The Rex pulling-over system in the boot trade, 1905   102
11 Early steam-powered paper-box making machinery, 1895   118
12 Women and the Clothing Trades Union, 1948   140
13 An advertisement for the Clothing Trades Union, 1941   141
14 Stitching and clicking departments, Edwards' 'Crown' boot factory, 1908   156
15 Victorian executive of the Australian Boot Trade Employees Federation with the union banner, 1915   157

Tables

1 Areas of employment by gender, Victoria, 1881–1901   18
2 Percentages never married in selected age groups, Victoria, 1889–1901   19
3 Areas of employment of female workforce, Melbourne, 1901–1933   79
4 Number of shirt and dress factories of various sizes, Melbourne, 1909–1910   90

Note on currency

In the currency used during the period dealt with in this book, there were 12 pennies (d) in one shilling (s), and 20 shillings in one pound (£).

The sum of 10 shillings and 6 pence could be written as 10s 6d or as 10/6. A guinea was £1 1s.

When Australia changed to decimal currency in 1966, $2 was equal to £1.

Acknowledgements

A number of people have contributed in different ways to the production of this book, which began as a doctoral thesis. I am greatly indebted to my supervisors at Monash University, Marian Aveling and Graeme Davison, who provided expert criticism and support. Lenore Layman was also generous and helpful, patiently reading and criticising earlier drafts. I am also indebted to my thesis examiners, Ann Curthoys and Stuart Macintyre, for their constructive and encouraging comments. I would like too to thank Janet Mackenzie and the staff at Cambridge University Press, especially Phillipa McGuinness and Robin Derricourt, and the series editors, for their help and support.

Fellow postgraduates and staff members at both Monash University and the University of Melbourne provided a stimulating and supportive environment in which to research and write. I wish to thank all those people who shared ideas and material with me, especially Verity Burgmann, Eddie Butler-Bowdon, Joy Damousi, Mimi Colligan, Bradon Ellem, Jane Elliott, Charlie Fox, Diane Kirkby, Marilyn Lake, Jenny Lee, Mandy Leveratt, Sara Maroske, John Mathews, Melanie Raymond, Julie Wells and Evan Willis.

This project would not have been possible without the rich deposits of union records available, and I am grateful to each of the unions which granted me access to their records. The staffs of the State Libraries of Victoria and Western Australia were always co-operative and helpful, as was Marian Letcher at the Carringbush Regional Library. Archivists at the University of Melbourne Archives and the ANU Archives of Business and Labour gave service well beyond their official duties. Dick Curlewis, archivist for the Printing and Kindred Industries Union, was likewise generous with his time and assistance.

The research for the thesis was funded by a Commonwealth Postgraduate Research Award and Monash University. Needless to say, I am grateful to both the Australian Government and to Monash.

On a more personal note, I wish to thank the following people who have in different ways helped me during this project: Maryon Allbrook, Giselle Byrnes, John Cook and Nancy Lane, Suzanne Cross, Karina and Mehmet Adil, Trish Crawford, 'Tucky' Davidson, Margaret and Ivor de Souza, Diana Elliott, Cheryl and Patrick Farrell, Christine and Bob Fleming, Jan Gothard, Denise Hill, Violet Jeffkins, John Leckie, Margaret McClure, Barry Reay, Athina Tsoulis, Hans and Sarah Van Dyk, Shayleen Thompson and Margaret Steadman. Eddie Scates came to my rescue on several occasions with emergency grandchild-care and my sister, Janice Anderson, now deceased, was always supportive. My children, Alexandra and Bill, could have been much worse!

Three people deserve special thanks for their sustained and unstinting help. My mother, Frances Anderson, put aside her own life and helped me out after the birth of my two children, both born during this time. She also helped us move house/country more times than any of us care to count. My father, Ray Anderson, was likewise ever ready to help in countless ways.

Finally, words cannot express my debt to Bruce Scates. Suffice to say that his emotional, intellectual and practical support both at home and at work gave me the time, space and strength essential for writing. Perhaps even more importantly, he has given me faith in Lane's vision of men and women as 'mates, not enemies'.

Abbreviations

General

ACTJ	*Australian Clothing Trades Journal*
ADB	*Australian Dictionary of Biography*
ALJ	*Australian Leather Journal*
AM	*Australian/Australasian Manufacturer*
ABTEF	Australian Boot Trade Employees Federation
ANL	Australian National Library, Canberra
ANUA	Australian National University Archives of Business and Labour
ATR	*Australasian Trade Review*
BBHF	Boot Wages Board History File
BBM	Minutes of Australian Bookbinders and Paper Rulers Consolidated Trades Union, Victorian Branch
BM	Minutes of Victorian Operative Bootmakers Union; Minutes of Victorian Branch of Australian Boot Trade Employees Federation
Boxmakers' Minutes	Minutes of Cardboard Box and Carton Employees Association (Melbourne)
CCCA	Commonwealth Court of Conciliation and Arbitration
CIFR	Reports of Chief Inspector of Factories, Workrooms and Shops
CTG	*Clothing Trades Gazette*
CTU	Clothing Trades Union: applied to the Federated Clothing Trades Union of Australia (Victorian Branch) and (after 1921) the Amalgamated Clothing and Allied Trades Union of Australia (Victorian Branch)

HF	History File
LTL	La Trobe Library, Melbourne
ML	Mitchell Library, Sydney
MPA	Master Printers' Association
MUA	Melbourne University Archives
PIEUA	Printing Industry Employees Union of Australia
Pressers' Minutes	Minutes of Victorian Pressers' Union
PM	Minutes of Victorian Branch, Printing Industry Employees Union of Australia
PTJ	*Printing Trades Journal*
Tailors' Minutes	Minutes of Tailors' Trade Protection Society
THC	Trades Hall Council
Typographers' Minutes	Minutes of Melbourne Typographical Society (later Victorian Typographical Society)
Typo. Jn.	*Australasian Typographical Journal*
USMC	United Shoe Machinery Company
VGG	*Victorian Government Gazette*
VOBU	Victorian Operative Bootmakers Union
VPD	*Victorian Parliamentary Debates*
VPP	*Victorian Parliamentary Papers*
VPRO	Victorian Public Record Office
VPRS	Victorian Public Record Office Series
WB	Wages Board
WBHF	Wages Board History File
Women BBM	Minutes of Women Bookbinders and Stationery Employees Association

Official inquiries
(See Bibliography for fuller listing)

1883–84 Factory RC	Royal Commission on Factories Act, Minutes of Evidence, *VPP*
1883 Tariff RC	Royal Commission on the Tariff, Minutes of Evidence, *VPP*
1890 Sweating Report	Report of Inquiry into Sweating, *VPP*
1893 Factories Inquiry	Minutes of Evidence and Reports of Board of Inquiry into the working of the Factories and Shops Act 1890, *VPP*
1895 Tariff Inquiry	Board of Inquiry into the Effect of the Fiscal System of Victoria upon industry and production, *VPP*
1901 Factory RC	Royal Commission on the operation of the Factories and Shops Law of Victoria, *VPP*

INTRODUCTION

Technology can only be understood as the aggregate of a series of social choices made in the past; it therefore carries the scars of past struggles and compromises.[1]

Writing the history of work is a political exercise. How we understand the past shapes our behaviour in the present and our strategies for the future. John Mathews, quoted above, is concerned to explore appropriate trade union responses to new technologies and innovations in the labour process. He looks to history for guidance on the outcome of previous strategies and responses. Nor is he alone in this project. Trade union officials and workers before him have also looked to history in this way.

Conversely, while employers have been less inclined to look to history for guidance, they have attempted to construct the past in such a way that it legitimises their own position. The portrayal of improved wages and working conditions as the outcome of employer-initiated technological innovation is one example.[2] By denying the creative role of workers' struggles over work and its remuneration, employers hope to vindicate the reorganisation of production as beneficial to workers whilst negating the importance of workers' responses. History becomes an ideological weapon in the 'struggles and compromises' which determine the nature of work.

Given the reality of these issues, this is no time to abandon 'labour process theory', as some critics have advocated.[3] Rather, historians need to respond to the challenge to explain and interpret changes to the way in which work is performed and organised by grounding theory in more empirical research. Harry Braverman's influential book, *Labor and Monopoly Capital*, published in 1974, suggested the possibilities of such analysis by charting the deskilling, or 'degradation', of craft work in the late nineteenth and early twentieth centuries. The interest generated by the so-called 'Bravermania' and its critics

1

has already produced a plethora of case studies. But despite all this work, the labour process debate is, as Richard Price put it, still in the exploratory stages. Although monographs and case studies have proliferated, they have often been undertaken in isolation from each other.[4] And while it is now generally admitted that Braverman's thesis is flawed, few attempts have been made to improve it. We still need to know in more detail *how* work has changed and, even more importantly, *why* it has changed. What factors can be identified as determinants of the nature of work? The historian is well placed to offer answers to these questions, since a perspective of changes over time is essential to unravel the dynamics at work. It is to these questions which this book is addressed.

Building on insights from other writers in the debate, I propose a multi-faceted explanation of change in the labour process. Rather than seeking a single factor which can account for labour process formation, this book argues that such formations are produced by the operation of a set of factors. Thus, labour and product markets, technological developments and the availability of capital all directly affect the labour process to varying degrees in different historical circumstances. In a more general way, the activities of organised labour and capital, the state, and racial and gender orders (ideologies and practices) also influence the way in which work is designed and performed. None of these factors is, however, the *determinant* of the labour process. It is not possible to accord theoretical primacy to any single factor; the precise weighting of each contribution can only be established empirically. The resolution of this problem will be a central task of this book. Nevertheless, it can be argued that each factor interacts with the others and, most importantly, is mediated by the social relations at the point of production. Although the operation of these factors structures the options available at any given point, the outcome is determined by the decisions of management, with greater or less input from workers. In the final analysis, work is shaped by people.

Within this general framework, there are a number of specific theoretical points in the labour process debate which require clarification. Braverman contends that industrial work in capitalist societies since the Industrial Revolution has involved the degradation of traditional craft skills, and with this degradation has come a 'real subordination of labour' (in the Marxian sense). He links these changes with the development of capitalism towards monopoly capital, and the quest by the capitalist to control the labour process, the variable part of capital. According to Braverman's analysis, this quest for control led to three major processes. Firstly, by dividing the processes involved in any task and having these performed by different individuals, the skill of the worker was thereby degraded. This ultimately reduced the bargaining power of workers who could no longer rely on their monopoly of skills as a lever in bargaining, while at the same time standardising the way in which tasks were performed.

Secondly, the introduction of what became known as scientific management meant increased control over every detail of the work process. Thus conception and execution were separated, and knowledge and discretion were removed from the worker. Workers performed the manual work while mental tasks were reserved to management.

Thirdly, the development and use of new forms of technology increased direct control of management over production by tying the work process to particular machines. In the twentieth century Braverman points to the adoption of Frederick Taylor's theories and methods for factory management as the embodiment of capitalist logic and the major element in the process of deskilling of the mass of industrial operatives. Taylor was the most prominent and influential exponent of 'scientific management' in the United States during the Progressive era.

Subsequent analysis has suggested six major flaws in this argument. Firstly, the deskilling thesis has been criticised as being too sweeping. Rather than a continuous, even transformation, it is claimed that the process was in fact much more uneven, involving reskilling as well as deskilling. Braverman's notion of the 'traditional craftsman' is also criticised as being too romantic. Real subordination, it is argued, was possible without the destruction of craft skills.[5]

At a more fundamental level, the notion of 'skill' itself is now understood as having ideological and political dimensions as well as a technical one. That is, skill is socially constructed in the workplace by the exercise of strategic power by particular groups of workers. Any discussion of 'deskilling' must specify what concept of skill is being employed. Is work 'deskilled' when the operatives lose their status or when the technical content of the work is simplified? For instance, in one sense female bookbinders were deskilled over the period 1750 to 1800 in that initially their work had been a recognised apprenticeship trade, with a seven-year period of indenture. After 1780, however, the status of bookbinding as a skilled trade was undermined by the use of trainee labour taught on the 'learner system' rather than through an apprenticeship. There had been no corresponding change in the actual work performed.[6]

Conversely, in some cases workers can be recognised as skilled workers where the technical content of their work is of a routine nature. Machine minders in the British printing industry, for instance, were called 'machine managers' and paid a 'skilled' rate, while people performing similar work in other industries were regarded as unskilled.[7] Are machine minders therefore deskilled?

These cases complicate the more usual application of the term to male craft work which has been subdivided and mechanised, with or without loss of status and pay for the worker. Beyond this, there is a major problem in distinguishing between work which has become 'specialised' as opposed to that which has been 'fragmented'. The former term refers to the situation where a worker brings a more general expertise to bear in performing a narrower range of tasks. Fragmentation, on the other hand, refers to a part of a formerly unified process, performance of which requires no knowledge or experience of the process as a whole. Thus, bricklayers who spend their time exclusively constructing elaborate towers would be considered specialists. The labourer who carries the bricks would be performing fragmented work.[8]

The distinctions, however, are not always so clear. Some workers can successfully claim fragmented work as specialised (and therefore more skilled) by insisting on a general period of training before being allocated to a subdivided process. On the other hand, workers who bring a general training outside the workplace to performance of a particular task might not have this general training recognised as skill. For instance, women who acquire expertise at sewing in the home then enter paid work sewing shirts or underwear have not been regarded as specialists. Similarly, when such work is subdivided it is regarded unequivocally as fragmented because of the inability of

workers to define it otherwise. As Cora Baldock has pointed out, 'the issue of deskilling
. . . needs to be seen in the context of the power invested in the position'.[9]

These issues have particular relevance for any discussion of women's work. Feminist
writers have noted the 'gender bias' of definitions of skill.[10] Men are able to claim their
work as skilled while women are not. It is indisputable that historically women have
been largely confined to low-paid, low-status, so-called unskilled work. What is less
clear is how far this work is technically less skilled than men's or how far it is merely
defined as less skilled because women perform it. Discussions of feminisation accompanying deskilling become confused and misleading unless this issue is resolved, as do
more general attempts to explain the historical development of the sexual division
of labour.

To resolve this difficulty it is necessary to arrive at some objective definition of skill,
apart from its social construction. Attempts to formulate objective evaluations of work as
skilled have stressed the importance of task range and worker discretion as key criteria.
Thus, a skilled worker has a knowledge of materials, tools and methods, and applies
these as appropriate to a variety of jobs.[11] Such knowledge and judgement require a considerable period of training and it is this training period which gives skilled workers their
main weapon in collective bargaining. By restricting entry to training they can secure a
monopoly of knowledge and judgement. Any campaign by employers to break this monopoly has to be of a very protracted kind, lasting at least as long as it takes to educate
new workers.

While I would agree with much of this argument, I think it underestimates the importance of manual dexterity in the whole process. Skills take time to acquire in the manufacturing context because they involve practice as well as education. Thus, a compositor
needs time to learn about principles of balance and spacing, different typefaces,
divisions of words, spelling and grammar, and so on, but time is also needed in order to
become adept at picking type and setting it quickly.[12]

This dimension of technical skill is important since it explains in part why women's
skills are devalued in the market place. Manual dexterity, although often considered a
'natural' female attribute, in reality is acquired by large numbers of women in the course
of their training at home and school. Thus, as Chilla Bulbeck has observed, if a skill 'is
widely held in the workforce, it is less likely to command high status and rewards,
because it confers less bargaining power on those who have that skill'.[13] The fact that
manual dexterity is not generally considered an integral part of skill reflects the common
equation of skilled work with men's work. Their skills are acquired through formal
on-the-job training.

For my purposes, then, an objective definition of skilled work in the manufacturing
context refers to work which involves a variety of tasks, an element of judgement and a
degree of special dexterity (speed, accuracy and particular technique). Work is more or
less skilled to the extent that it embodies these features in greater or lesser degree.[14]

A second area of debate concerns Braverman's treatment of Taylorism and scientific
management. Tony Elger's critique draws our attention to Braverman's failure to explain
the timing of the adoption of scientific management. Such dramatic changes were, he
argues, precipitated by 'crises of valorisation', or serious difficulties (from the capitalist's

point of view) in extracting surplus value from production. Or, as Eric Hobsbawm explains: 'It was safer if less efficient to stick to the old ways, unless pressure of profit margins, increased competition, the demands of labour or other inescapable facts forced a change.'[15] It was the depression of the late nineteenth century, combined with growing working-class demands, which precipitated the movement to intensify labour in the United States of America.

Others challenge Braverman's assertion that Taylorism expressed *the* management logic of monopoly capitalism. Subsequent writers emphasise other strategies employed by management to minimise the opportunities for collective worker opposition. Friedman, for instance, points to the adoption of 'responsible autonomy' by managements anxious to overcome the contradictions produced by scientific management's tendency to monopolise conception. This attempted monopoly, argues Friedman, produces an inevitable worker resistance. In order to cope with this new form of insubordination, managements were forced to adopt alternative strategies, namely 'the maintenance of managerial authority by getting workers to identify with the competitive aims of the enterprise so that they will act "responsibly" with a minimum of supervision'.[16]

Bryan Palmer argues that Braverman's account of Taylorism emphasises its direct control features to the neglect of its more subtle, ideological aspects. Taylorism, he suggests, along with the 'efficiency movement' in general, undermined the populist conception of the worker as creative agent and transformed him/her to a passive factor of production. At the same time, welfarism and 'personnel' initiatives developed alongside Taylorism to strengthen and sustain capitalist hegemony beyond and within production.[17] Littler likewise emphasises the changing nature of Taylorism as it became allied with industrial psycho-physiology (industrial psychology and fatigue studies) in the years between the two world wars.[18] As an extension to these arguments, Beechey draws attention to the importance of the state in affecting the labour process. She criticises Braverman for failing to distinguish between the strategies of individual capitalists in organising the labour process and the strategy of capital in general, 'represented in state apparatuses which are involved in organising the general conditions of production and accumulation and in regulating the supply and conditions of labour'.[19]

This point is particularly pertinent in the Australian context where state wage-fixing bodies played a key role in constructing and reinforcing definitions of work. Australian feminists have begun an examination of the role both of state wages boards and of federal arbitration in defining the sexual division of labour.[20] Peter Cochrane has looked more particularly at the role of arbitration in affecting workers' responses to technological change. He argues that 'the arbitration system also militated against any ideas about workers' power'. The industrial courts were, he points out, empowered to deal only with 'economist' issues (wages and working conditions) and had no mandate beyond this to interfere with the rights of capital to run business in its own way.[21] But while the scope for the arbitration system to be used as an arena of struggle over the labour process was thus limited, arbitrators still had considerable influence. In fact, argues Cochrane, between the wars, 'progressive' arbitrators pressed Taylorist ideas on 'sluggish manufacturers', contributing to the 'important part' played by the state in popularising scientific management amongst Australian employers.

Richard Edwards acknowledges the range of strategies employed by capital in the period coinciding with the emergence of monopoly capitalism. He argues, however, that all these attempts failed. There was, he maintains, a shift to structural forms of control through bureaucratic and technical means. Most importantly, dual labour markets were created in a strategy to 'divide and conquer' worker opposition.[22] As this idea is expressed in the later work by Edwards, Gordon and Reich, large firms 'aimed to divide the labour force into various segments so that the actual experiences of workers would be different and the basis of their common opposition would be undermined'.[23]

The work of Hagan and Fisher on Australian coalminers and compositors suggests a variation of this 'divide and conquer' theme. They argue that different methods of payment encourage different levels of class consciousness. In the case of coalmining and printing, 'piecework acted to diminish the chance of the union members developing a loyalty to a large entity like the working class'.[24]

Different methods of payment clearly do have different effects on workers' attitudes to each other and to their employers. However, it is important to note that it is not possible to deduce these effects in any direct way. For instance, in some circumstances workers can combine in defence of the independence associated with piecework. (Indeed, the evidence from Hagan and Fisher also supports this contradictory aspect of the system.) Similarly, persistent cutting of piece rates can engender an enhanced sense of collective exploitation amongst workers. Nor is it necessary for workers to be paid by the piece for them to recognise a degree of self-interest in the prosperity of the industry which employs them.[25]

When discussing methods of payment it is important to bear in mind Hobsbawm's warning about the dangers of generalisation, 'especially in view of the incredible complexity of the industrial scene'.[26] The ramifications of any particular method depend very much on the circumstances and conditions under which it is implemented. There are many factors, such as quality control; regularity of work; the need for careful use of machines and materials; ease of accounting; the necessity of supervision; flexibility in working hours; the existence of outwork; the need for apprenticeship training; the imposition of tasks for time work, and how these are decided; methods of determining levels of piece rates; whether pieceworkers are paid for waiting time and compensated for other difficulties in the physical working environment; the sex of the workers; and the effects of government regulations. All these can affect whether or not a particular scheme is advantageous to either employees or management. With these qualifications in mind, it is nonetheless true that methods of payment do have the potential to enforce greater intensity, or speed-up, in the workplace and can thus be seen as a method of control over labour.[27] And they also have the potential in some circumstances to deflect worker opposition to management into competition with other workers.[28]

Michael Burawoy also investigates the ways in which potential worker opposition to management is deflected into conflict or rivalry between workers. He shows how workers' methods of adaptation to work can produce acquiescence in the capitalist system itself. He points in particular to 'games' constructed by workers, such as speed competitions, which legitimise the labour process. As Burawoy says, 'one cannot play a game and question the rules at the same time; consent to rules becomes consent to capitalist production'.[29]

Several British writers have investigated other ways in which workers' techniques for adapting to industrial work can serve the interests of management. Paul Willis has shown how definitions of masculinity which emphasise performance of 'tough' work help to reconcile male workers to heavy, dirty, noisy, boring factory jobs.[30] Anna Pollert's study of tobacco workers shows how feminine cultures also serve the interests of capital. The world of romance, brides and babies imported into the factory with female workers helps them cope with the rigid format, supervision and general tedium of modern factory work. At another level, firms draw on family ideology and patterns of hierarchy in an attempt to bolster the authority of employers over employees with the patriarchal authority of men over women and older workers over younger workers. Thus, 'class control was mediated by patriarchal control'.[31]

What all these writers share is an emphasis on the inadequacy of Taylorism alone as a method of securing control of labour. This relates to a third area of criticism of Braverman: his failure to allow for the strength of workers' resistance in the shaping of the labour process. Numerous writers have shown how important such resistance was, as was the opposition of overseers and middle-level managers.[32]

While workers' resistance was often important, it is wrong to assume that the workforce will always be oppositional. To assume that conflict is always the major characteristic of the relationship between labour and capital is misleading. This relationship is ambivalent and interdependent. There is potential for co-operation and compromise as well as conflict. What is of interest to historians is the particular set of historical circumstances which affect the balance between these tendencies at any given time.

One can apply the same argument to the critique of participants in the labour process debate who argue for the primacy of either control or exploitation as the source of conflict between workers and management over the labour process.[33] For example, at one extreme are writers such as Storey who argue for 'control' and 'resistance' as the dialectic in the development of the labour process. Thus,

> ... a key structural element of management is control. But because perceived interests are thereby potentially threatened, workers do in varying degrees resist this control both individually and collectively, passively and actively. This dynamic of contestation constitutes the basis for a dialectical interplay between control and resistance.[34]

At the other extreme is Sheila Cohen's assertion that workers' struggles within the labour process 'are not about "control" but about exploitation; not about "bossing" but about the relationship between effort and reward, labour intensification and work measurement'.[35]

I would suggest that it is not theoretically necessary to choose between control and exploitation in this way. From the workers' point of view, some struggles are about control, particularly those which involve craft workers conscious of their traditions and status as artisans. One could also hypothesise that 'bossing' itself would become an issue where workers felt they were being exposed to unreasonable or offensive authority. The case of female workers subject to the closer scrutiny of male overseers is one obvious situation where conflict would be about bossing rather than exploitation of labour. On the other hand, exploitation would appear to be the most likely cause of friction when changes in production methods clearly resulted in workers having to work harder for fewer rewards. This would seem to be more applicable to semi-skilled workers where subdivision and mechanisation are more obviously aimed at intensifying labour rather than undermining control. And, in a sense, the distinction between control and exploitation is a false one: loss of control usually implies greater exploitation. It is generally impossible to struggle against one without struggling against the other.

The issues from management's point of view are likewise not amenable to such reductionism as the dichotomy between control and exploitation implies. The capitalist imperative to extract increasing levels of surplus value is clearly the major reason why capitalists seek innovations in the work process. But the motive to effect changes as well as the ability to carry out such plans is often closely related to the question of control in the workplace. For instance, capitalists may introduce machinery and subdivided work processes as a strategy to undermine or co-opt the power of skilled workers who are resisting employer efforts to reduce their wages. For such employers, securing additional control over the labour process is essential to increasing the rate of valorisation. The issues of exploitation and control are thus often inseparable for employers, as they are for workers.

The final relevant area of criticism of Braverman's thesis is that provided by feminists. We have already noted the connections made between patriarchy and capitalism in the context of the 'control' debate. We have also seen how feminists, along with others, have questioned definitions of skill which do not allow for its 'social construction'. This is related to the question of 'feminisation' of occupations which had been predominantly male. Thus, any discussion of women entering 'male' jobs which have been deskilled must be sensitive to the possibility that such jobs are not so much technically deskilled as, rather, redefined as unskilled because women do them.[36] Or, as Beechey puts it, when discussing feminisation, 'it is important to investigate the extent to which it is the same occupation which is being "feminised", or whether the process of deskilling results in the creation of a new occupation or function within the collective labour process'.[37]

I would also add that it is important to determine the extent to which women are entering existing jobs previously performed by men, or whether they are performing new work created by changing technologies and market requirements. Thus, women entered the Australian meat-processing industry in large numbers in the 1950s and 1960s via packaging departments. This was new work created by the growing demand for boned meat packed in cartons for the US market rather than the export of whole carcasses.[38]

Feminists have also drawn attention to the importance of the inter-relationship between the position of women as wage-labourers and as domestic labourers within the family in affecting changes in the labour process. Thus, state policies, male trade union exclusivism and ideological assumptions about women's place affect the sexual division of work in ways which cannot be understood by reference to Braverman's models of family transformation under capitalism.[39] Braverman posits the destruction of the social and productive roles of the family under capitalism, leaving only an expanded role as a unit of consumption.[40]

One can question whether the family under capitalism has been stripped of its social functions. And while, in general, the trend from production to consumption is true, it overlooks the continuing role of the family in the daily reproduction of labour power and the biological reproduction of the species. This oversight underestimates the continuing amount of domestic labour performed in the home, in addition to the 'labour of consumption'. And as this labour falls mainly on women, their role in the paid workforce is inevitably affected.[41]

The importance of this qualification is that it helps explain why it is women who occupy the lower-paid, lower-status jobs in the workforce. As Curthoys expresses it:

> the sexual division in the labour market . . . is neither a simple reflection of earlier pre-industrial, household divisions, nor something independently generated within the workplace or the labour market. Rather, it arises from an interaction between bio-cultural tradition and practices, on the one hand, and the specific institutions of individual capitalist production on the other. [It] is the product of a fundamental contradiction between the continuation of a family household structure and capitalist relations of production.[42]

Thus, the biological and cultural association of women with childbirth and child-care placed them at a disadvantage in the labour market. Their lower participation rates meant they were in a weaker position to bargain for high wages and the recognition of skills than were male workers. Their lower wage rates in turn provoked exclusionary tactics from male workers (supported by some women) in defence of higher male wage rates which were often used to support women as unpaid labourers in the home. These tactics were reinforced by the state through protective legislation and the decisions of wage-fixing tribunals, as well as through educational services which channelled workers into different occupations according to sex. The sexual segmentation of the paid workforce then reinforced the sexual division of labour in the home as women, restricted to low-paid work, were unable to challenge men's position as family 'breadwinners'.

Analyses by other writers offer variations on this theme, with the major disagreement being over the extent to which male worker exclusivism was a defence of male patriarchal privilege or of the 'working-class family'.[43] This is an issue which can be illuminated by historical research, bearing in mind that there was always more than one version of 'the family' in the working class. Households headed by women were not unusual. One must ask whether they were also defended by such strategies.

Work such as that by Cynthia Cockburn also indicates that the stakes were more than monetary. The erosion of job segregation by sex was a challenge to men's sense of masculinity as well as to their capacity to earn high wages.[44]

The emphasis on the connections between family and paid work also feeds into analyses of the 'reserve army of labour'. Originally posited by Marx as a category undifferentiated by sex, the idea was taken up by Braverman. He argued that women formed part of the 'floating and stagnant' sectors of an industrial labour reserve, drawn into the workforce by the inadequacies of the male wage. They formed a pool of labour which could be drawn on in times of economic expansion and repelled in times of recession.[45]

Feminists, however, have criticised this analysis as being sex-blind in the same way that Marx's was.[46] Braverman's concept fails to take account of the sex-segregation of the labour market which prevents women's labour from being interchangeable with men's except in extreme circumstances (for instance, in wartime). Some would therefore argue for its rejection altogether as a useful category of analysis.[47] I would argue, however, that the concept is a useful one, but that it is more appropriate to conceptualise women as a pool of potential wage-earners who can be provided for the labour market under certain circumstances. This concept emphasises changing factors in the supply of female labour rather than fluctuations in demand alone. Combined with a notion of household economic strategies, it can explain shifting levels of female workforce participation in terms of shifting requirements for the labour of women (both married and unmarried, mothers or not) as unpaid labourers in the home.[48] Thus, patterns of fertility, shifts in household production and domestic technology, and fluctuating male incomes determine whether a woman's labour is of more value to the household unit in the home or in the workforce. And the decision for women to enter paid work outside the home is mediated by the strength of ideological prescriptions about 'woman's place'.

A focus on the labour process can illuminate these processes. It can also provide a new angle of vision on other aspects of social history: on the changing role and status of women within industry and society as a whole; on definitions of masculinity and femininity; on the role of the state in constructing and reinforcing sexual divisions both in the home and in the paid workforce; on the quest for social justice for workers, both male and female; on the relationship between radical ideologies (such as anarchism, socialism, communism, syndicalism and feminism) and the workplace.

This study focuses on the years between 1880 and the outbreak of World War II. This period coincides with the rise of Victoria's manufacturing industry as an important part of both the Victorian and Australian economies. Victoria led the way in the establishment of manufacturing industries in the period between 1860 and 1890. Even when New South Wales overtook it in terms of total manufacturing output in the 1890s, Victoria continued to be the leading employer of female labour and the most important centre for the production of clothing and footwear. The time-span covers periods of expansion, depression and war. It was in this period that industrial capitalism was both established and tested. Over the same time, workers became organised and governments entered the industrial arena in an unprecedented way, not only fixing tariffs but also regulating the price and conditions of labour and, in some cases, directly engaging in manufacturing. And, while paid work was being transformed under these influences, domestic labour was changing. As the birth rate fell, domestic production increasingly moved into the factory. In short, these were formative years in the development of Australian urban society and culture. The time-span thus offers a broad field of view in which to observe the historical unfolding of patterns of change.

The industries selected as case studies also offer a range of types and experiences. First there is the clothing industry, with its overwhelming female workforce (over 85 per cent), labour intensity, multiplicity of productive units, and an extremely varied and highly protected product market. In sharp contrast is the printing industry, traditionally a male industry but increasingly employing females (one-third were women by the 1930s), increasingly capital-intensive, a smaller number of firms, a relatively homogeneous product market and little import competition. The boot and shoe industry falls somewhere between the two: a recognisably male trade but one which employed a significant number of women (between one-quarter and one-half of workers); and a combination of both extensive capital investment and labour intensity. It shared the clothing industry's features of numerous product units and a varied and highly competitive product market, although—with the exception of the level of competition—these features were not as marked as in clothing manufacture.

The nature of work in each of these industries also varied. This variety offers, I believe, ample scope to test my contention that the structure of work arose out of the interplay between product and labour markets, capital supply, technology, racial and gender orders and the activities of the state.

The book is divided into three broad sections according to the level of state involvement in wage-fixing. Thus, the first section covers the period of unregulated wages before the establishment of the wages board system in the wake of the 1896 Shops and Factories Act. The second section covers the years during which the industries operated exclusively under these state wages boards. The third section embraces the period of federal wage-fixing under the Commonwealth Court of Conciliation and Arbitration. Within these broad sections, the industries are examined separately. The exact time-span covered by each chapter varies slightly, depending on when each board was formed and when the first case was brought before the Arbitration Court.

Sources for this study are varied, allowing a focus on work from many perspectives: that of the employer, the union official, the factory inspector, the consumer, the Arbitration Court judge and, not least importantly, the worker. This variety allows consideration of the importance of human agency whilst giving due recognition to real structural restraints. To paraphrase Marx, we can see people making their own history and also the conditions which constrain them.

PART I

Before the
Wages Boards

The stirring tale of Melbourne's rise to wealth and glory in the wake of the 1850s gold-rushes, and its subsequent decline in the depression of the 1890s, has been told and retold.[1] The three industries examined here rose and fell with the general economic tide, so a brief account of the context is necessary to situate the detailed discussion of individual industries which follows.

The goldrush immigrants brought with them more than their optimism to Victoria: they also provided the basis for a thriving industrial colony. As consumers, workers, entrepreneurs and financiers, the new population contributed immeasurably to the growth of Victoria's urban centres in the 1860s and 1870s. In the 1880s their children continued the process of urbanisation. With urbanisation came manufacturing to satisfy the demands of the towns for food, clothing and shelter. The development of farming areas in the Wimmera, North-East and Riverina in the 1870s provided additional markets for the produce of the factories, and improved communications, especially by rail, ensured the speedy transport of goods to these markets.[2]

Victorian manufacturing in the 1860s and 1870s was thus based on a building boom and import-replacement industries such as engineering, food processing and clothing. The infant industries were nurtured initially by protective tariffs, and the economy as a whole benefited from the injection of government expenditure on public works.[3]

Despite the overall expansionary trend in these decades, it would be misleading to paint the period from 1860–90 as one of sustained and uniform growth. The economy as a whole grew more slowly, for instance, in the first half of the 1860s and second half of the 1870s than it did in the periods of rapid growth, 1871–74 and 1880–83.[4] Individual industries also experienced periods of fluctuating growth which did not always correspond to general trends. Employment and production in the metal and printing trades, for instance, rose steadily in the late 1870s, whereas in footwear they increased sharply between 1874 and 1881 and in clothing at a slightly later period (1880–82).[5]

The golden age of 'Marvellous Melbourne' in the 1880s was a similarly complex decade economically. While the economy as a whole was buoyed by the spin-offs from the building boom and high wool prices, many consumer industries stagnated. These import-replacement industries had, by the middle of the 1880s, saturated the local market. The tariffs which had protected them from competition in the early years now acted as a barrier to the expansion of markets into neighbouring colonies, as some of these colonies retaliated. Victorian manufacturers also lost ground in southern New South Wales where reduced rail charges benefited their Sydney competitors. The competition from overseas imports also became more intense, as lower ocean freights reduced the price of these goods on the Melbourne market. Rising labour costs in these labour-intensive industries also took their toll, but the cruellest irony of all was the effect of protective tariffs which raised the cost of imported producers' materials. This was particularly felt in the clothing and footwear industries which depended to a large extent on imported woollen cloth and leather.[6]

The collapse of the land boom in 1888 was the first in a series of crises which culminated in the severe depression of 1892–95. The maritime strike followed in 1890 and, even more disastrously, foreign investment dried up and export prices plunged from early 1891. This turned recession into depression. The series of bank failures in 1892–93 acted like shifting ballast on an already sinking ship.

Manufacturing industries were caught up in the general economic crisis, although some were harder hit than others. As Davison has aptly expressed it, 'the higher they rose the further they fell'.[7] Those industries which had stagnated in the late 1880s, like clothing, boots and food, were less dramatically hit than the construction, consumer-durable and related industries (including printing).[8] In fact, those industries which competed with imports made relative gains in the 1890s as consumers bought more of the cheaper local product in preference to expensive imports. Local manufacturers were able to keep their costs to a minimum because of the general fall in wage rates. These industries also benefited from new markets in Western Australia and were among the first to recover after 1894, along with renewed gold production and new industries such as dairying, frozen meat, coalmining and wheat farming.[9]

Within these general fluctuations there were three important changes in manufacturing in the late nineteenth century: the subdivision of work, mechanisation and feminisation. Although Victoria's industrial revolution lagged behind that in Britain and the USA and never achieved the heights or depths of the northern hemisphere experience, the changes that occurred between the 1850s and the 1890s were nonetheless dramatic.[10] The three-storey clothing factory of the 1880s and 1890s, employing upwards of 200 women on sewing machines, bore little resemblance to the small group of male tailors and apprentices, helped by the occasional female vest or trouser hand, which represented the usual clothing establishment of the 1850s. Mechanisation of spinning and weaving, brewing and food processing accompanied the capitalist intrusion into formerly small-scale domestic production. And while printing had long been mechanised to some extent, the application of steam power to drive presses in the 1870s and 1880s signalled the erection of the imposing daily newspaper office with its hundreds of workers and expensive machinery.[11]

The process of mechanisation and the growth of the factory system was, however, very uneven. In the shadow of the new mechanised factories, production continued in more or less traditional ways in under-capitalised workshops and workers' homes. Indeed, despite the emergence of larger factories in the 1880s, the average size of the production unit actually declined in labour-intensive industries such as clothing.[12] In some ways this represented the survival of pre-industrial methods alongside modern factory production. The blacksmith's shop, and the engineering factory, for instance, continued in their different ways to make many similar products.[13] Likewise, a needlewoman working at home might cut and sew garments from material supplied by a draper, while a large factory would make the same items of clothing from materials supplied by a warehouse. In other cases, however, factory production and small workshop and home production were more interconnected, with some parts of the manufacturing process being carried on in a factory and others outside it. Garments and boots, for example, were often made up in mechanised factories with the hand-finishing being done by outworkers.[14] However, the association between homework and benchwork was not always clear. Most notably, in the sewing trades, workers using treadle machines employed technology as sophisticated as that employed in most large factories at the same time.

Nor was there a clear correlation between mechanisation and either feminisation or subdivision of work processes. Those areas which experienced the greatest transformations in technology—ironworking, engineering and brickmaking—did not employ significant numbers of women.[15] The dramatic increase in the female manufacturing workforce in the 1860s and 1870s occurred mainly in the garment industries. Garment workers constituted about 90 per cent of female manufacturing workers by 1881. (See Appendix, Table A2.)[16] And while it is true that the use of sewing machines on ready-made men's clothes hastened the existing trend toward female labour in that branch of the trade, the overwhelming proportion of female garment workers were involved in the largely unmechanised dressmaking section which was traditionally a female preserve.

Females as a percentage of total manufacturing workers did not increase in the 1880s. However, in the 1890s, the percentage of workers in registered factories who were female increased from 25 in 1890 to 37 per cent in 1900.[17] This did not mean, however, that women were displacing men from traditional male occupations. Most of the increase can be explained in terms of greater levels of unemployment in male trades connected with building and rural industry (such as brickmaking, engineering, agricultural implement making, sawmilling). (See Appendix, Table A1.). The industries of the 1890s which experienced the most pronounced technological changes (bootmaking and sections of printing) showed no significant increase in female employment.[18]

The association between mechanisation and subdivision of the labour process was similarly complex. Subdivision of the tailoring trade into the making of individual garments predated mechanisation. In bootmaking, however, the division of the old shoe-maker's craft into clicking, making and finishing was precipitated by the introduction of machinery on the making process.[19] Subsequent subdivision of both garment and bootmaking processes occurred both in association with machinery and independently of it. In the 1880s for instance, as Davison points out, 'most complaints of subdivision of labour and dilution of skill [in these trades] come not from huge mechanised factories but small backyard workshops'.[20]

Whether subdivision was associated with mechanisation or not, it was clearly an increasing feature of Victorian industry in the 1880s and 1890s. The breakdown of the apprenticeship system was symptomatic of this trend away from craft production, and this in turn was accompanied by the increasing employment of unindentured juveniles in place of trained adult workers.[21]

The entry of women into the Victorian paid workforce was related more closely to demographic changes than changes in industrial technology and work processes. The high population growth of the 1860s was the result both of births and of female immigration, and it was these women who provided the supply of cheap labour for the developing consumer industries.[22] In fact, women in nineteenth-century Victoria had few alternatives: the paid labour market was so rigidly sex-segregated that for most women the choice was between factory work and domestic service, either in one's own home or someone else's.[23] After 1881, domestic work represented the largest female occupational grouping, followed by industrial employment. (See Table 1.) And as we have seen of the industrial occupations, the overwhelming majority of women and girls were engaged in the production of clothing.

The market for female labour did not, however, remain static over the period from the 1860s to the turn of the century. On the contrary, the kinked age distribution of Victoria's population as a whole had peculiar effects on the supply of female labour.[24] The girls who worked in the clothing, boot and food factories in the 1870s had, by the 1880s, reached marriageable age.[25] While as couples they contributed to the building boom of this decade, as wives and mothers their role was rather different. No longer available to work in factories, many were still prepared to combine paid work in their own homes with their domestic duties to help the family economy as a whole. Many factories felt the loss of their most experienced workers very keenly, and were only too willing to give them work to do at home. For instance, the Chief Inspector of Factories reported in 1889 that there was a shortage of skilled female hands in the boot trade, particularly machinists and flowerists. He attributed this to the shortage of apprentices, and the fact that many employees were leaving to get married. The latter had often been 'induced' to do outwork for the factories: 'Some are making as much as two pounds a week, and considered it a great compliment to do the work at all.'[26] It was these same women, by this time burdened with young children, who contributed to the growth of outwork in the 1890s, when reduced family incomes as a whole made their contributions more vital. In 1893, for example, Edward Bartlett told the Factories Commission that his clothing factory employed 120 hands inside and 200 hands outside. 'The bulk of the hands working out of the factory', he explained, 'are those who were in the factory before, who have got married or have met with misfortunes.' Others were able to return to factory work. Another clothing manufacturer gave evidence at the same enquiry about 'four or five young women' working in his factory, 'doing it for the sake of their husbands and children'. He explained that 'they have been in tolerably comfortable circumstances after working for me as young girls for some years'.[27]

The shortage of apprentices referred to by the Chief Inspector of Factories was also partly the result of the skewed age distribution, but as a factor in the overall supply of female labour it needs further explanation. Sinclair has suggested that the participation of single women in the paid workforce bore an inverse relationship to the general level of economic prosperity. That is, when male breadwinners' earnings were high, daughters contributed their labour directly to the household in the form of domestic help rather than as paid factory workers. By the same token, in times of high male unemployment,

Table 1   Areas of employment by gender (percentages), Victoria, 1881–1901

Year		Professional	Domestic	Commercial	Industrial	Primary production
1881		5.4	28.3	1.5	22.3	40.4
1891	Women	9.5	41.4	9.0	28.0	10.6
	Men	4.7	5.6	23.8	36.9	30.1
1901	Women	11.2	40.7	13.4	24.8	19.0
	Men	5.3	3.4	24.6	56.0	36.3

Source: Victorian Census, 1881, 1891, 1901.
Note: Figures for men for 1881 have not been included because the categories used in the Census are not comparable.

as in the 1890s, it was more important for daughters to contribute financially to the family economy, whether by factory work or outwork.[28]

The 1890s saw not only an increasing proportion of single 'girls' in paid work, but also an increasing percentage of the female population remaining single. Table 2 illustrates the significant increase in the proportion of unmarried women in all age groups between the Censuses of 1891 and 1901.

It was thus a combination of these factors—the marriage of the female goldrush child-cohort, the changing rate of workforce participation among unmarried women, and the increasing percentage of women remaining unmarried—which together account for the relatively short supply of female factory labour in the 1880s and the increased participation of women in both outwork and factory work during the depression.[29] Sinclair estimates that the proportion of all women engaged in paid work increased from 36.5 per cent in 1891 to 40.7 per cent in 1901.[30]

The market for male labour was much more varied than that for females, both in terms of the range of occupations and the range of industries. They were found in significant numbers in almost all categories of employment. Agricultural and pastoral pursuits still accounted for the bulk of male labour in the late nineteenth century, although large numbers were also found in mining and building. (See Appendix, Table A1.) In manufacturing, men were concentrated in the 'heavy' industries, such as machinery, tools, carriages and metalwork. The exact proportions varied with the fluctuations in each particular industry, but none of these occupations was ever seriously challenged as adult male domains at this time. (See Appendix, Tables A4, A5.) As we have seen, this was not the case in some of the lighter factory work, where the craftsman's status and skill were being undermined by cheaper juvenile labour employed on subdivided work.[31] This was especially so in those consumer industries which faced a cost-price squeeze in the latter half of the 1880s and were therefore more than usually anxious to cut labour costs. Some employers also turned to female labour as more efficient and tractable than the notoriously undisciplined colonial youths.[32]

The prevalence of outwork in the boot and clothing industries in particular also undermined the position of workers in the trade as a whole, as outworkers were not amenable to trade union organisation in the same way that factory workers were. The problems presented by females, juveniles and outworkers compounded the difficulties created by the seasonal fluctuations in the general labour market. In an economy so dependent on rural produce and construction, the weather played a crucial role in determining the availability of work, making worse the situation of those already disadvantaged by skill,

Table 2   Percentage never married in selected age groups Victoria, 1881–1901

Year	Males			Females		
	20–24	25–29	45–49	20–24	25–29	45–49
1881	87.9	57.2	19.5	67.9	33.0	4.5
1891	89.5	60.5	19.1	69.3	38.3	7.4
1901	91.6	66.1	19.0	77.8	50.8	12.9

Source: P. McDonald, *Marriage in Australia*, pp. 112, 134.

gender and/or ethnicity. The summer peak and winter trough experienced in these industries produced far-reaching effects within the economy as a whole, from the transport industry to services and manufacturing. Indeed, recent work suggests that intermittency and underemployment were so significant in the nineteenth-century economy that even the conventional characterisation of the 1880s as the 'long boom' or 'The Workingman's Paradise' needs major modification. Wage rates may have been high, but real earnings were often seriously eroded by the casual and unreliable supply of work.[33] Manufacturing was not exempt from these violent fluctuations in demand for labour. This was partly a response to seasonal variations in the rest of the economy, but was also the product of factors specific to particular industries. For instance, the changes in the weather affected the demand for clothing, producing sharp demand for labour in spring and autumn preparing the new season's stock, and equally dramatic slumps in winter and summer. Mantle makers, perhaps the worst affected, were idle for three to four months of the year because of the shortness of the seasons in the context of a limited colonial market.[34] The spring social season leading into Christmas was a busy time for clothiers, whilst providing additional demand for services, such as printing and tourist facilities.[35]

Even before the depression of the 1890s low wages, long hours, poor conditions and large numbers of juveniles characterised those industries associated with female labour and led to a series of legislative enactments. The Shops and Factories Act of 1873, the first of its kind in Australia, was mainly directed at the general physical standard of working conditions (for instance, ventilation and overcrowding), and at limiting the hours of female workers. Although in theory women were not permitted to work more than eight hours per day, in practice the regulation had little effect. Pieceworkers were exempt from this restriction, as were workers in factories employing fewer than ten people. As these categories covered the majority of clothing workers, the main targets of the legislation, the gains for workers were minimal. Furthermore, factory workers could apply for exemption from the eight-hour limit, and this was granted to the entire textile industry.[36]

The 1885 Act attempted to remedy some of these defects, but with limited success. The size of a factory as covered by the Act was reduced from ten to six employees, but many employers evaded this provision by reducing the number of inside hands and sending work out. The employment of juveniles was regulated so that girls under thirteen years and boys under twelve were forbidden to work in factories; boys under fourteen and girls under sixteen were not permitted to work at night (between 6 p.m. and 6 a.m.); persons under eighteen were forbidden to work in certain dangerous and noxious trades. The Act also provided for the registration and inspection of factories to ensure they met certain stipulated health and safety standards, but when breaches were discovered local boards of health would not prosecute the offenders. More than one-quarter of Victoria's manufacturers escaped the provisions altogether because the Act did not apply to shires, which included large towns like Beechworth and Kyneton. Furthermore, all factories in existence before March 1886 were exempt from key provisions of the Act. Although employers were supposed to keep records of all outside workers, there was no provision for compulsion and employers proved very uncooperative. Probably the only real gains were in relation to safety, where better standards regarding gas and steam engines and the fencing of dangerous machinery were achieved.[37]

Despite amendments to the Act in 1893 which provided for female inspectors, no major changes were made until the 1896 Act which provided for the setting up of Wages Boards to regulate certain 'sweated' trades. Until that time, there was no government intervention in the contentious areas of men's hours, wage rates, limitation of apprentices and the control of outwork, nor was there any effective remedy to the deficiencies contained in the 1885 Act. If anything, government surveillance became less effective in the 1890s, with an increasing amount of work being done outside registered factories, and a reduction in the staff in the Chief Inspector's Office in 1892.[38]

It would be easy, however, to overstate the failure of this early legislation. Although it certainly achieved few of the tangible benefits intended, the fact that the workplace was recognised as an appropriate arena for state activity was in itself significant. The creation of a separate office to administer this legislation in 1886 provided a core of experienced and dedicated public servants who monitored the industrial situation and played an important part in the creation of more far-reaching legislation in the 1890s.

Clearly, however, factory legislation played a small role in determining developments in the labour process. More important was the general level and nature of economic activity and the peculiarities of the Victorian labour market. The labour market in turn was the product of both demographic features and a gender order which assigned women the primary role in child-care. The effect of these factors on the nature of work is illustrated in the case studies of individual industries.

1

THE ADVENT OF MACHINES
AND WOMEN:
THE CLOTHING INDUSTRIES, 1880–1896

The three most important structural factors affecting the nature of work in the clothing trades were the limitations of the colonial market, the suitability of clothing manufacture for home production and the sex of the workers—or, to be more precise, the sex of the workers in the context of the prevailing gender order. As the ensuing discussion will show, these factors were closely intertwined. The gender order affected the general price of female labour, which was further lowered by outwork. The cost of labour affected the extent of the market for any particular product. The market demand for cheap products in turn put a downward pressure on wages, and the gender order limited the ability of female workers to resist the pressure. It was the combination of labour costs and length of production runs which structured employers' choices about methods of manufacture.

The gender order affected the price of female labour in the clothing industry in three ways. Firstly, the sexual division of labour in the home, whereby men were regarded as breadwinners and women as dependent housekeepers and child-rearers, justified lower wages being paid to women. They were not usually dependent on their earnings for their own support or that of others. As one employer explained, 'a boy could not earn his salt at trousers and vests', because the piece rates were women's rates.[1] The assumption was clearly that women's 'salt' cost them less. This assumption was true of enough women to lower the wages of all, so that even when women did the same work as men, as in some tailoring firms, they were paid less.[2]

The sexual division of labour in the home lowered female wages in another way. Women's primary responsibility for child-care (and the care of the sick and elderly) made many of them unable to leave home for extended periods of work in factories. Those who needed to earn money to contribute to the upkeep of their families found outwork an attractive option. Home labour was usually cheaper labour because of the ease with which employers could cut rates without fear of collective resistance from individuals isolated from each other in their own homes. As Duncan Blythell concluded about out-work in nineteenth-century Britain, 'so long as there are women who find it hard to make ends meet as they strive to run their homes, there exists a cheap and docile labour force for anyone who wishes to use it'.[3]

The cheapness of outside labour inevitably lowered the wages of factory workers or reduced the amount of work available.[4] Gender also affected the wage earnings of inside workers in a more direct way by curtailing unionisation and militancy. Ray Markey points out that female labour faced all the problems of organisation common to 'unskilled' workers. 'Without the strategic monopoly of skills which the craft unions possessed', he argues, 'unskilled labour could be easily replaced during disputes with employers.'[5] In a sense he is correct, although I would argue that it was the fact that the skill of sewing was general in the female population which made workers easily replaceable, rather than that the work was technically unskilled. As the report of the official enquiry into shops and factories found in 1893, even the lowest-paid work in the clothing trade involved a degree of skill: 'To call them "unskilled" is not quite correct, for the work of "finishing" often requires the possession of expertness and ability on the part of the operative which can only be acquired after long practice.'[6] However, because the sexual division of labour assigned women the domestic task of sewing, large numbers of the female population did have the 'long practice' which made them experts.

Other aspects of women's roles within the family impinged on their position in the paid workforce.[7] All three sections of the clothing industry (tailoring; dressmaking and millinery; shirts, underwear and whitework) contained large numbers of young, single women. Figure 1 shows relative numbers in each section. In fact, only in the tailoring trade did adults (over the age of twenty-one years) outnumber juniors. (See Appendix, Figure A3.) Such workers, more preoccupied with their futures as wives than as paid workers, were poor material for a strong union which could fight for higher rates of pay.[8] And while even working-class girls were influenced by the expectation of marriage as an escape from the poor pay and conditions of the factory, the presence of many girls from more well-to-do families in the millinery and dressmaking sections further depressed wages. As a factory inspector, Margaret Cuthbertson, pointed out, 'there are so many girls who take it up, not with the idea of earning a living, but because they do not like housework'.[9] Such girls would 'rather work for nothing than stay at home'.[10] While it is true that the skills these girls acquired no doubt contributed to the family budget (whether by the small amount they earnt or by the amount they saved through making their own dresses), the fact was that they did not depend on their earnings. As Harrison Ord, the Chief Inspector of Factories, observed: 'While it is very difficult to object to young girls learning to make their own dresses, it is very hard on those who have to earn a living in the trade to see the wages lowered by their better-off sisters.'[11]

This was less of a factor in tailoring, where girls do seem to have been interested in acquiring marketable skills. The daughter of Hinrich and Catherine Meyer, for example, was apprenticed to tailoring because her parents believed the possession of a trade was the best protection against poverty for men and women alike. Their attitude is probably representative of other nineteenth-century working-class parents.[12]

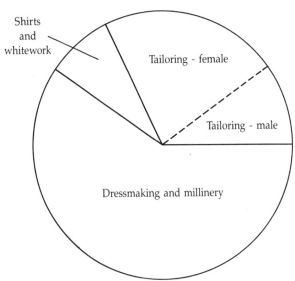

1 Approximate proportions of workers employed in each section of the clothing industries, 1891.
Victorian Census, 1891, Occupations of the People.

Nevertheless, the initial stopgap nature of employment for most girls resulted in high labour turnover which in itself presented a practical problem for a union trying to keep track of its membership and deterred workers from paying their dues in advance.[13] Furthermore, the 'genteel', feminine image of dressmaking and millinery workrooms attracted a disproportionate number of girls and women with 'respectable' aspirations.[14] Such workers were unlikely to see unionism as a 'ladylike' pursuit.[15] Often socialised into a passive, retiring femininity, these young women were reputedly unwilling to assert their rights in the workplace, or to appear in court as witnesses for breaches of the Factories Act.[16] Speaking of women, especially young women, employed in the sewing trades, Cuthbertson maintained that 'those people had no idea of looking after themselves. Men are always better able to look after themselves.'[17]

Older women workers, for whom personal misfortune had exposed the realities of this feminine model, were potentially more militant in regard to wages and conditions. Barbara Taylor has observed of 'mothers of families' in eighteenth- and nineteenth-century Britain, 'Far from being a conservatizing influence, here the responsibilities of motherhood drew women out of their homes to act and speak in ways shocking to upper-class observers, used to associating mothering with passivity and domestic confinement.'[18] The activities of women such as Mrs Ellen Cresswell, Mrs Warsaw, Mrs Jane McLeod, Mrs Helen Robertson and Mrs Bryant on behalf of the Tailoresses' Union support this conclusion for colonial mothers as well. Married women were certainly disproportionately prominent during a crisis such as the strike of 1882–83.[19] The same factors which made them militant, however, also made them more vulnerable and desperate and limited their regular union activity. Women with dependents, working a double shift of paid and unpaid labour, had little time, opportunity or energy to spare for unionism.

Mature women without dependents, who were to form the backbone of twentieth-century women's unionism, were less common in the nineteenth-century workforce, and understandably daunted by the task which faced them.[20] This clearly contradicts the conclusions reached by Johanna Brenner and Maria Ramas who argue that 'where young single women made up the majority of the workforce, the chances of organised struggle were improved'. The case of the various sections of the clothing trades suggests that the reverse was true.[21]

These three factors—the fact that women were not usually breadwinners; the prevalence of outwork; and the low level of worker organisation—arise from the colonial gender order. Each contributed to the cheapness of female labour, which in turn was the major determinant of the labour processes adopted in the various branches of the clothing industry.

As only the very cheapest house frocks and sunhats were made ready-to-wear, most dressmaking and millinery was done for individual customers in small workrooms conducted by women proprietors, who did their own cutting and fitting. (The 1881 Census recorded only one man engaged in this branch of the clothing industry, compared to 11,517 women.[22]) Although a few individual workers were paid exceptionally high rates, in the late 1870s and early 1880s most experienced workers earned between 15 and 25 shillings weekly, and up to 30 and 40 shillings in the busy periods.[23] Treadle machines were used, but much fine handwork was a feature of the best work. Dressmakers and milliners thus depended on a supply of cheap labour: in dressmaking this was employed finishing (sewing on buttons, etc.) the garments made by experienced dressmakers; in millinery the milliner's assistant prepared the basic work and she did the 'artistic' last stage.[24] Most of this labour was provided by juniors, who usually worked for at least six months without payment of any kind, and in some establishments they were required to pay premiums of up to £20 whilst 'learning'.[25]

The shirts, underclothing and whitework branches of clothing manufacture were likewise labour-intensive. The more elaborate end of the trade which produced the stiff-fronted white dress-shirts and collars was catered for by large factories like the new Braeside Shirt Factory in Richmond, but most of the colony's shirts were made by an army of female outworkers from cut pieces of cloth supplied by contractor, draper or warehouse.[26] The sewing involved in these shirts was relatively straightforward, as was the making of basic underwear, pillowcases, tablecloths, and so on. The treadle sewing machine was, in most cases, the only mechanical aid to manufacture.

In such a labour-intensive industry, the size of the wages bill was an important element in the level of profits. In order to remain competitive in a contracting market, such as that of the later 1880s and 1890s, employers of female labour found further mechanisation an unviable method of cutting costs for most employers. Thus, 'many machines which were profitable to use when they displace labour at a shilling an hour were hardly worth investing in when hand labour cost but sixpence'.[27] It was more economical, and certainly much easier, to cut the rates paid to workers. And as we have seen, the existence of outwork and the low level of unionisation made this a simple proposition in the economic climate of the 1880s and 1890s.

In the tailoring section, however, the effect was slightly different. This was a traditionally male occupation: female labour had become a significant part of the workforce only from the 1820s, when women were employed in England in the ready-made section of the trade, initially to make vests. As cloth merchants diversified into the production and sale of these 'slop' garments, they contracted much of the actual sewing to tailors who did the work in their own homes. The competition amongst these outworkers led them to look for cheaper labour, so women were employed to perform some of the simpler kinds of making, particularly trousers and vests. Initially, male tailors were helped by their wives and daughters but, as their orders increased, they also employed other women in the neighbourhood.[28] The subdivision of work in the making of a suit of clothes into its three individual garments (trousers, vest and coat) was part of the process of using cheaper, less skilled workers: a worker could learn to make one of the garments adequately much more quickly than the whole three. And while the cheapness of female labour encouraged the subdivision of suit-making into individual garments, it also encouraged the subdivision of the tailor's craft into its three processes: cutting, pressing and sewing, with men employed on the first two and increasing numbers of women doing the sewing. This represented a classic application of Charles Babbage's principle of dividing labour into its various parts and thus cheapening labour on the separate sections. As Babbage put it: 'the manufacturer, by dividing the work to be executed into different processes, each requiring different degrees of skill and of force, can purchase exactly that precise quantity of both which is necessary for each process'.[29]

The more expensive male labour was mainly employed on the more expensive tasks (those which required more specialised training) of cutting, pressing and coat-sewing. Cheaper female labour was employed on the cheaper processes of machining, or sewing one only of the garments, especially trousers and vests. The cost of labour on all the divided parts was cheaper because workers became more expert through concentration on one aspect of the craft. As J. R. Blencowe, manager of Melbourne's largest clothing factory, explained: 'It is not advisable for a girl to learn coats, trousers and vests, she cannot get along so quickly. By doing the one they get more expert.'[30]

And in the case of female labour, the savings were even greater because it was only half the price of male labour from the outset. Thus, when the clothing industry was established in Victoria in the wake of the goldrushes, many of the English practices were transported to Australia. As in England, women had entered tailoring in significant numbers from the middle of the century. By 1881 they comprised about 65 per cent of the workforce.[31] This percentage increased further to reach almost 80 per cent in 1886, and fluctuated for the rest of the century between 70 and 80 per cent. (See Appendix, Figure A1.) A Melbourne tailor described the process as similar to that which occurred in England, with home tailors employing their wives. The influx of women to the trade, he argued, was 'made worse by the introduction of machines'.[32] There was still an important distinction between the work made to order by tailors for individual customers, and the growing trade in ready-made, or slop, articles. The latter were usually made under contract to the large city warehouses, either by substantial factories or by the small 'backyard' enterprise.[33] Drapers and other retailers, such as department stores, were also involved in manufacturing ready-made clothing, some directly engaging in factory

2 'The advent of machines and women': the ready-made outfit manufacturing room at Messrs Sargood, Son and Company's factory in Melbourne in 1874 shows the revolution which machines and female labour brought to tailoring. A handful of male tailors can be seen 'sitting on the board' in the foreground. These men were still required for the fitting and hand-sewing. They were greatly outnumbered, however, by the female machinists and table-hands. The sketcher has obviously eliminated much of the clutter which would have been present in this scene.
Illustrated Australian News, 4 November 1874, p. 189. (State Library of Victoria)

production whilst others had the work done by contractors.[34] And the expansion of the slop trade coincided with the introduction of treadle sewing machines, almost invariably operated by women.[35]

Given the dramatic savings in using women instead of men, the question arises as to why they were not also employed on cutting, pressing and high-quality order work. The explanation for this is partly to be found in the nature of these occupations which allowed male workers (in co-operation with many employers) more control over who entered them. More specifically, all three tasks were most efficiently performed within a factory or workroom rather than in the worker's own home, thus enabling organised resistance by the men against the employment of women. Cutting, for instance, was more easily done close to the supply of cloth. Carrying pre-cut garment pieces between warehouse and home was one thing; carting the heavy bolts of cloth was quite another. Cutters also used long tables to lay out pattern pieces on the cloth before cutting, and most workers' cottages could not accommodate such a large piece of furniture. The advantages of factory cutting were even more evident when mass-produced items were cut in bulk, with up to eighty layers of cloth spread on the table to be cut with a knife or, more rarely, with a cutting machine.[36]

Pressing, in the days of flat irons and coke ovens, was also more economically performed in a central location, with one oven heating the irons for dozens of pressers. This also minimised the chances of the work being spoiled before reaching its final destinations. In the case of quality order tailoring, the work required supervision which was more easily achieved within a factory or workroom.

So long as these processes were kept out of the hands of outworkers, the men had a reasonable chance of keeping women out of them. These men were helped by the fact that none of these processes seemed to offer much scope for female labour. Cutting, for instance, was considered too heavy for women, who were believed to be unable to lift the bolts of cloth or to cut through as many layers of cloth with a knife. The calculation of the most efficient layout of the various pieces before cutting required considerable experience, another factor which militated against the shorter-term female workers. Pressing, too, was heavy work, requiring the manipulation of irons weighing up to 32 pounds (14.5 kg). Pressing was also considered unhealthy work, involving work in steamy conditions so bad that 'at times you can hardly speak'.[37] Like cutting, the pressing of most garments did not lend itself readily to further subdivision, especially where the garments were actually sewn together by outworkers before reaching the presser in the factory. Moreover, it was said to require a long period of training before acceptable levels of competence in shaping garments could be achieved. This long period of training was also a major deterrent to employing women on high-class tailoring, and some employers maintained that women could never perform these tasks as well as men, regardless of training. John Clark, a representative of the firm of Sargood, Butler, Nicol and Ewen, maintained that 'a woman could not cut out trousers under any circumstances'.[38] Employers also had other reasons for restricting entry to the occupation of cutting, as we will soon discover.

In the provincial cities of Geelong, Ballarat and Bendigo, women were employed more extensively on such 'male' tasks. The reason for this seems to be that the male workers abandoned these fields without a fight. William Corbauld, a Ballarat clothier, attributed the scarcity of men in the town to the reluctance of lads to be apprenticed.[39] If this was indeed the case, it would have been virtually impossible for the male tailors to prevent females entering the trade. It seems, in fact, that the fate of tailoring in these provincial centres represents a classic case of 'contagious effeminacy', with males deserting this occupation for more 'manly' trades.[40]

In general, then, the availability of cheap female labour encouraged subdivision of tailoring. It also helped popularise alternatives to the traditional made-to-order suit—garments sold ready-made and the 'slop-order' suit. As we have seen, slop garments were becoming increasingly popular from the 1820s. The 'slop-order' item, however, was a product of the 1880s and represented a breakdown in the traditional division between the ready-made and order sections of the trade. This breakdown was made possible by the customer's use of self-measurement cards, with the measurements being passed on by the draper or wholesaler to so-called 'slop-order factories' for making into suits.[41] The order trade was then divided into a higher class, or 'legitimate' trade, carried on in the traditional way in tailoring shops with mostly male hands, and the cheaper class of trade carried on in factories with predominantly female labour and more use of sewing machinery. By 1893, for instance, one of Melbourne's larger order factories employed ninety women to sew garments and only one man.[42] It is unlikely that slop and slop-order garments would have achieved such an easy acceptance had it not been for the fact that female labour made their price so much lower than the tailor-made article.

The questions of cheap labour and further subdivision, however, overlap with the influence of product markets. The demand for an individual type of clothing limits the extent to which subdivision is economical. Where demand is limited, production runs of any particular item are short. To subdivide work to any extent would involve extra calculation and handling at the supervisory level and would not produce significant cost savings in greater speed on the part of workers; by the time the workers had reached a sufficient level of speed to justify the extra costs of subdivision, the order would have been complete. However, the division of suit-making into the three garments, each with three main processes (cutting, pressing, sewing), and the employment of women on many of these subdivisions, made ready-made garments cheaper. This cheapness expanded the demand for such clothing, which in turn made further subdivision practical. Thus, by the early 1880s three of Melbourne's ready-made tailoring factories were employing 'the division of labour that is properly understood'—dividing the making of each garment into two or three divisions.[43] By the early 1890s it was standard practice to sew garments in three stages (machining, tacking and buttonholing) and by the end of that decade a few manufacturers had taken the process as far as seven.[44]

Product markets were in general, however, a serious check on the subdivision of labour. Raphael Samuel makes this point about mid-Victorian industry in general, but the uncertainty of markets and the variability of production runs were exaggerated in the colonial context.[45] The colonial market for consumer non-perishables such as clothing was restricted by the size of the colonial population. This meant both short production runs and short seasons, both of which discouraged economies of scale. James Wyeth, a mantle manufacturer, was amongst the worst affected. As he explained, 'we lie idle from three to four months and a half in the year. It is because the seasons are shorter than at home . . . the limited market'.[46]

Competition from imports exacerbated this trend, as did local methods of retailing. The Busy Bee factory, for instance, was typical of many workrooms which took cloth from drapers to be made up into specified quantities of different articles. Such an order might include 100 pairs of women's knickers in various sizes and fifty bodices in different styles and sizes. Clearly, any degree of subdivision was not viable under such circumstances. Fashions in clothing also contributed to limited demand for standard items.

Women's clothing in particular was extremely varied and changeable, with customers seeking individuality in style and fit even in ready-made garments.

Those factories which did experiment with power-driven machinery and subdivision of labour were those for whom the generalisations about cheap outside labour and short production runs were less applicable. Most notably, manufacturers of high-quality stiff-front dress-shirts, such as the Braeside and Acme factories, could not resort to out-workers to cheapen production because the nature of their product required strict quality control. Moreover, the starching and ironing, which were a large part of the labour involved, were more economically done inside a factory.

These products were, however, fairly standard items and some of the processes (the starching and ironing, for instance) were the same regardless of the slight variations in the style of the shirt. Subdivision enabled these employers to employ less experienced juvenile labour, in conjunction with 'all the latest machinery and appliances'.[47] At the Braeside factory, one of the largest shirt factories in Victoria, over half of the workers in 1895 were girls employed on wages of two shillings and sixpence per week.[48]

Manufacturers of higher-quality ready-made and slop-order trousers also used mechanisation and subdivision to a greater extent than other clothing makers. In 1893, Foy and Gibson's tailoring factory had 185 sewing machines driven by gas engines at the rate of 1700 stitches a minute.[49] Longer production runs of standard sizes and styles made use of cutting machines (such as that used at Beath and Schiess from 1883) more practical. Their expense was justified when large orders required cutting out up to seventy layers of cloth in one batch.[50] Like the shirt factories, makers of high-class men's clothing could not cheapen production by giving work out because of the problems this created for quality control.[51]

Factories such as those operated by Foy and Gibson and Beath and Schiess had an added advantage in that the vertical integration of manufacturing and retailing or ware-housing provided them with more stable contracts and enabled a greater degree of 'rationalisation'. The size of these factories, like those in shirtmaking, also provided economies of scale in easier access to capital and the use of powered machinery. Henry Blomfield, a manufacturer in a smaller way, maintained that he wanted to install a gas engine but he could not out of his own earnings 'erect a gas-engine and plant necessary for driving all the machines . . . and independently of that the employing of a man at £2 10s a week [to operate the machine]. It costs me from £2 to £3 a week for expenses and gas to run this thing.'[52]

As Jenny Lee and Charles Fahey point out, there was a 'chronic shortage of capital' for Victorian manufacturing.[53] Large companies were more likely to attract what limited funds were available from outside sources, as well as having greater reserves in the form of accumulated profits. And the statutory requirement for a qualified engineer to attend to the gas engine was less of a burden on the wages bill when the engine was driving hundreds rather than dozens of machines.

The minority of large tailoring and shirt factories which had the means to mechanise and the economic rationale to do so were, however, constrained in their innovation by the limitations of available technology. The question of motive power was the most serious. Clothing factories were slower than many to use power-driven machinery because of the difficulty of finding a suitable motive power for the light, high-speed machines.

The usual steam engines were not suitable, so it was not until gas engines became commonly available in the 1880s that some factories used them to drive sewing machines, and even fewer to drive continuous band-knives. Gas engines, however, did not come into general use until the late 1890s. The advantages of gas-powered sewing machines to the manufacturer were limited by the fact that they did not go much faster than treadles and cost a good deal more to provide than female leg-power, especially given the compulsory employment of a qualified attendant.[54] Finishing machines, introduced for buttonholing, button-sewing and felling in the 1890s, were also of limited appeal. The machines 'were not expert enough' for any but the lower-quality slop work—the work which was done so cheaply by outworkers.[55] With such cheap labour available, the extra investment in this machinery was hardly warranted, particularly as it only reduced the finishing time for trousers from three hours to two.[56]

At the other end of the factory scale, small operators were encouraged to stay that way, or to reduce the size of their workforce, by state regulations. Thus, the 1873 Factories Act encouraged employers to keep the number of inside hands below ten in order to evade the provisions of the Act which dealt with hours of work and safety standards. The reduction in the number of employees to six in 1885 reinforced this trend toward the proliferation of small workshops.[57]

Such were the broad conditions which affected individual employers and employees in their relationship to the labour process. These were not, however, static, immutable structures. Collective action by groups of manufacturers and workers could, and did, affect the particular shape of the structures. In a labour-intensive industry such as clothing manufacture, the major way in which workers and employees could affect the work process was by collective action which raised the price of labour. Although such collective action is usually thought of as the province of workers, in some cases employers too have an interest in restricting entry to key occupations in the trade. Market forces then generally ensure that this scarcer labour is paid more. Take the case of the tailor's cutter. Both employers of cutters and employed cutters had an interest in limiting the total number of trained cutters in existence. From the employees' point of view, extra cutters represented competition for jobs. From the employers' viewpoint, they represented potential business rivals, since cutters were well-placed to become proprietors in their own right. Both agreed to limit the numbers of males admitted to apprenticeship and to keep girls out of the occupation altogether.[58]

The case of first-class milliners was similar. By charging expensive premiums on apprenticeships, employers restricted the number of expert hands in the business. Only a limited number of girls would have been able to afford the ten or twenty pounds charged in Victoria before the Factories Act of 1896 made the practice illegal. This restricted entry explains the high rates paid to first-class hands.

The corollary of high wages for the small number admitted to the elite of 'experts' was lower wages to the mass of workers engaged on tasks requiring less training and judgement. As Inspector Cuthbertson explained, millinery firms 'have one good milliner to whom they will pay anything from 30 shillings a week up to £2, perhaps £4 . . . but then they have a lot of poorly paid, or low paid, employees working under this milliner preparing work for her; she does the artistic work herself'.[59]

In tailoring, a similar dichotomy existed between the salaries of the cutters and the wages of machinists. However, the general level of machinists' wages was considerably higher than that of the milliners' assistants. Initially, this difference was due to the fact that tailoring was a recently subdivided trade. Prior to the 1830s, the cutter was also the tailor and presser, and the maker of trousers was also the maker of vests. With subdivision into garments and processes and the employment of women, tailors were no longer able to restrict entry into the sewing of men's clothing and employers had no interest in doing so; a worker would not start a workroom of his or her own without cutting skills, and so long as entry to cutting was still restricted it did not matter to employers how many entered the sewing workforce—much of which operated from the workers' homes. The oversupply of female labour, together with the ideology of females as dependents, depressed wages for the sewing process. However, female wages in tailoring were, for the average worker, up to 20 per cent higher than those in millinery. This was partly because females employed in tailoring were initially replacing men. Female wages were so much lower than men's (about 50 per cent), that considerable savings in total labour costs occurred without cutting rates to the levels paid in female branches of the clothing trade. Male unions ensured that their members' rates were kept at an agreed level.[60] However, as competition in tailoring increased, employers did attempt to cut female rates of pay. But in this case the collective opposition of female factory workers prevented unrestrained reduction in wages.

Victorian tailoresses had been facing piece-rate reductions throughout the 1870s. Ellen Cresswell, widowed with three young children in 1860, complained that ever since she had started as a trouser-hand in Melbourne in 1870 there 'had been an endeavour to pull prices down'.[61] This situation became acute in the late 1870s and early 1880s as numbers of ex-employees set up as manufacturers. Butlin has estimated that the number of clothing and textile factories in Victoria increased from 71 to 234 over the period 1871–81.[62] The intense competition this caused resulted in a crisis of valorisation, whereby employers tried to cheapen production in order to attract customers. At first the tailoresses had tried to defend themselves in each workplace but, as Cresswell found, such attempts were easily defeated by employers who could get plenty of unorganised labour to replace the agitators. Cresswell herself had been victimised after a strike in 1879.[63]

The situation reached a crisis of exploitation—from the workers' point of view—in 1882. In their quest for ways to cheapen labour, employers were attacking workers' earnings in new ways. In addition to simple rate-cutting, some manufacturers were having order work made up in factories at slop rates of pay. Because the order goods had to be made 'more accurately and slowly' this had the result of 'diminishing their wages by 50 per cent'.[64]

The tailoresses again went on strike against this renewed form of exploitation. However, on this occasion they formed themselves into the Victorian Tailoresses' Union. With considerable support from the Trades Hall Council, the *Age* newspaper and the majority of the large manufacturers, the tailoresses of Beath and Schiess' factories succeeded in broadening the strike to all the major Melbourne factories. By the end of February most of the factories had returned to work, having agreed to a compromise log of rates arrived

THE TROUSER FAMINE.

WHAT IT MUST COME TO IF THE TAILORESSES CONTINUE MUCH LONGER ON STRIKE.

3 *Punch's* response to the strike highlights the extent to which trouser-making had become the preserve of tailoresses, as well as indicating the success of the strikers in closing Melbourne's factories. *Melbourne Punch,* 1 March 1883.

at in negotiation between the Tailoresses' Union and the newly-formed Clothing Manufacturers' Association.[65]

The strike was significant at a number of levels. Its immediate importance was its role in drawing public attention to the fact that even if Victoria was the 'Workingman's Paradise', it was certainly no paradise for working women. So far as the strike was effective in this, it was also useful in the campaign to extend the powers of the Shops and Factories Royal Commission.[66]

In the context of Victorian trade union development, the strike was significant in that it marked the first occasion on which the Trades Hall Committee had acted to finance and control a strike. The fact that the strikers were women is particularly important here, although to date historians have neglected the role that gender played. Individual male trade unions were generally jealous of their own independence, and unwilling to concede power to a body such as the THC. Women, on the other hand, were accustomed to the direction of men, and inexperience in industrial matters made them more likely to accept the help of the men at Trades Hall. In the 1880s, when women had no right to vote and experienced a range of other legal disabilities, it was unusual for them to participate in public affairs.[67] As the *Age* pointed out: 'Men under similar circumstances can hold indignation meetings, and publicly make their grievances known; women cannot. They can only depend upon friends to champion their cause.'[68]

Without funds of their own it was important that these 'helpless girls', as the *Age* called them, secure support from the male union movement and preferably the public at large. Flouting conventional codes of female behaviour by attempting to organise an entirely female-run campaign was considered less likely to be successful than 'placing themselves entirely in the hands of the Trades Hall Committee'.[69] They thus provided the opportunity for the THC to demonstrate its effectiveness at co-ordinating industrial action by one of its affiliates, and this precedent was soon followed by others and contributed to a general expansion in the role of the THC in the labour movement.[70]

Within the tailoring trade, the strike exposed the changing nature of industrial relations. The growth of the slop trade in the 1870s and, with it, the number of large factories, provided the physical preconditions for united worker action. Assembled in numbers of up to 500 workers under one roof, workers became more likely to organise. At the same time, such large factories created division between employers, giving rise to the possibility of strategic alliances between workers and groups of manufacturers. The most obvious divisions occurred between large-scale producers and the small 'backyard' operators and order tailors. Albion Walkeley, proprietor of the Phoenix Clothing Company, commented on the antagonism between the new-style entrepreneurial manufacturers and the craftsman-turned-working-proprietor: 'Some years ago, when there was a meeting of the clothing manufacturers called, I attended the meeting; but when I found it was principally cutters and tailors and that sort of thing, I withdrew from the meeting.'[71]

In the 1870s, the large clothing manufacturers, John Parry and Frederick Sargood, joined with trade unionists to agitate for factory legislation.[72] In the 1880s, Beath, Schiess and Company encouraged the formation of a union amongst the tailoresses as a way of limiting the cut-throat competition between manufacturers for cheaper labour.[73] Initially, they were supported by most of the larger manufacturers, who saw a common interest between themselves and their workers in preventing the endless price-cutting of their small competitors.[74] This enthusiasm cooled only when the difficulty of drawing up a uniform log caused problems between these larger manufacturers and their own workers.

The directions which the industry had taken in the late 1870s and early 1880s produced other, more unexpected, alliances, notably that of the so-called 'middlemen' with the tailoresses. The sixteen major middlemen who took work on contract from warehouses and distributed it to outworkers expressed their desire to join with the tailoresses in establishing uniform rates of pay.[75] Usually cast as the villains in the sweating scenario, the middlemen drew attention to the need for an organisation of warehousemen to regulate the prices paid for contract work so as to restrict the price-cutting at its source. So long as warehouses played one contractor off against another, they argued, the earnings of both middlemen and their workers would suffer. The middlemen and the union failed, however, to secure the co-operation of the warehousemen, and the non-union outworkers proceeded to undercut wages by taking out work below the log rates.[76]

While the development of a union of tailoresses prompted a more united stand amongst some employers, as the strike progressed the limits to this co-operation were also revealed. In the highly competitive atmosphere of the 1880s, manufacturers found it difficult to trust each other and differences in methods of work also produced divisions.[77] The main lines of division in the early 1880s were exposed in the negotiations over the log. The manufacturers who were also warehousemen (such as Beath and and Schiess and Banks and Company) were divided from the rest.[78] Because they used their factories to make up garments to order, they were more concerned with the quality of work than its cheapness, and consequently were prepared to pay up to one-third more in piece rates than their fellow manufacturers who were restricted to the slop trade. Beath and Schiess continued to pay the higher price after the Manufacturers' Association had negotiated the lower rate, because they were paying for a different class of work.[79]

A further rift appeared between those manufacturers who divided the work into garments and those who also subdivided the making of individual garments. The difficulty in framing a log to meet these different methods of manufacture resulted in the extension of the strike at the innovative factories for a further two months after the settlement with the Manufacturers' Association. It is possible that the continuing problem of inflexibility in the tailoresses' log discouraged manufacturers from experimenting with subdivision and risking further conflict with the union.

After the major strike was over, the rifts between the manufacturers evident in the negotiations over the log remained, and caused continuing suspicion within the Manufacturers' Association. Individual factories began to give out increasing quantities of work at below-log rates.[80] Attempts to reduce factory rates were met with resistance by the unionists, who had the advantage of union funds to back them.[81] The sporadic, spontaneous tactics, which had characterised worker resistance before the union was established, became strategic, co-ordinated and relatively effective resistance in the context of the solidarity of the Tailoresses' Union. These tactics ensured the payment of log rates or better in the major Melbourne factories and virtually eliminated the practice of taking working home at night.[82] In the long-term, however, the economic collapse of the 1890s brought temporary defeat to the Tailoresses' Union, as it did to the male unions in the clothing trade.[83]

The emergence of the Tailoresses' Union also reflected (and possibly contributed to) a changing definition of femininity in the 1880s and 1890s. Although the majority of female garment workers may have still aspired to the helpless, docile and retiring stereotype, the tailoring factories seem to have attracted and fostered a more outspoken and independent type of woman. Many, of course, were forced to reject the dominant stereotype, finding, as did Cresswell, that it was of little use to a widow with young children. It was not that these women were any less 'respectable' than their more genteel counterparts in dressmaking, but that they had a different standard of virtue. Indeed, most employers were at pains to maintain the moral tone of their factories and women were said to be unwilling to give evidence to the 1883–84 Royal Commission on the Factories Act as long as it met in an hotel.[84] The 'new women' of the trade union movement left the shelter of their homes to engage in picket duty outside the factories, reportedly using 'violent language and threats' to deter would-be strike-breakers.[85] Employers found such women, or 'girls' as they were usually called, 'very difficult to deal with' in that 'they have no consideration except for themselves' and 'have no faith in what you say'.[86]

The growth of the union encouraged this spirit, so that by the late 1880s the Chief Inspector of Factories reported that 'the factory work girl would appear to be a very difficult person to deal with', who was 'as a rule able to take care of herself'.[87]

The Tailoresses' Union and the spirit of resistance it fostered succeeded, at least in the 1880s, in raising the average level of earnings for Melbourne tailoresses.[88] It did this by increasing the rates paid to the 'lower-class' hands and by insisting that slop-order work be paid for at a higher rate than regular slop work.[89] Indirectly, the wages of factory workers probably also curtailed further erosion of outwork piece rates, since employers could pay higher rates yet still be undercutting the tailoresses' log for inside work.

By forbidding the taking home of work by factory workers for completion after hours, the union also made the 48-hour week more of a reality for tailoring workers.[90] This is an interesting instance of the agency of workers in contributing to the separation of home and work, or 'work' and 'life'.[91] Instead of this separation being something which is imposed on workers for the convenience of industrial capitalism, it is clear that in this case at least such a separation was the price workers had to pay for shorter working hours. So long as work was taken home at night, there was no way of demarcating the working day.

Ironically, however, the success of the Tailoresses' Union in maintaining the price and improving the conditions of factory labour encouraged employers to embark on other strategies to cheapen labour which gradually eroded the union's victory. Outwork became even more attractive when cutting rates to indoor workers was no longer an option. This was not a new strategy, since outwork had played an important role in Victorian garment-making from the establishment of the industry: the Inspector of Factories for the City of Melbourne estimated that half the clothing trade in Melbourne was carried on outside factories in the 1870s and early 1880s.[92] Employing outworkers had numerous advantages for manufacturers. It relieved them of the expense of providing factory buildings, as well as the cost of equipment and fuel. Because outwork drew on the labour of isolated and often desperate workers, the piece rates paid were usually well below those demanded by factory workers. The marked seasonal variations in demand for clothing also meant that manufacturers did not have to bear the burden of plant and equipment lying idle during the off-season. In this sense the advent of the sewing machine in the 1850s had increased the burden on outdoor workers, who had to supply their own machines instead of merely a needle and thread. Nor did the worker receive any benefits from the increased speed these machines allowed. The *Internationalist*, a Melbourne secularist journal, summed up the position: 'The sewing machine has not abolished ill-paid work, nor has it diminished considerably the length of the day's toil.'[93]

The increasing competition amongst manufacturers as the market for Victorian clothing stagnated after the early 1880s meant that more and more work was being given outside, and the tailoresses' strike contributed to this trend by raising the price of factory labour. However, as Fry points out, it is very difficult to make any definitive statements about the extent of outwork because of the lack of detailed business or official records for this period. I disagree with his guess that it was 'probably decreasing' during the 1880s, for several reasons. Firstly, the general expansion of the industry was not matched by an expansion of markets, increasing the pressure on employers to cheapen production.

Secondly, the supply of female labour for factory work was not increasing as rapidly as the supply of outworkers because of the marriage of the children of goldrush immigrants. In 1889 the Chief Inspector of Factories reported that 'so great is the demand for female labour that the factories go to the employees rather than that they should lose the chance of the employees coming to them'.[94] Factory employment figures support this observation: the number of females employed in factories with more than five employees declined from 4948 in 1886 to 4525 in 1890. The number of men in factories increased over the same period from 1322 to 1499. It seems reasonable to assume that part of the fall in female factory employment was the result of an increase in homeworkers. The trend established in the 1880s towards increasing use of outworkers was intensified in the 1890s under the pressures of general economic depression. Even the most modern and efficient firms could not compete with the goods made by the cheap labour of outworkers. Banks and Company's modern three-storey factory became a monument to this process. Built in 1884 to accommodate 300 workers, it was by 1892 standing idle, its hands discharged and its work transferred to a myriad of outworkers.[95]

This move by firms such as Banks, who had previously paid the union rates, signalled the demise of the Tailoresses' Union. Clearly, the union's failure to tackle the outwork issue was the major cause of its downfall. Why it did not do so is not entirely clear. The initial log proposed by the union certainly showed an awareness of the problem: it proposed a separate scale of piece rates for outworkers which was consistently higher than the scale for indoor work.[96] The revised log, arrived at in negotiation with the Clothing Manufacturers' Association, omitted the outworkers' log altogether. It is possible that this was considered a strategic concession on the part of the union in order to prevent further compromises on the log for inside work. It also seems to have reflected a deep hostility between factory workers and homeworkers. Cresswell referred to 'people who would not acknowledge themselves to be tailoresses [who] are carrying it out on the quiet. They take it out from our places far below our prices and then they laugh at us.'[97] Such was the depth of this hostility that outdoor workers who sought to join the union were rejected. John Wing, the union's secretary, reported that the members 'classed them [outworkers] as sweaters, and they thought if they joined the union it would bring prices [piece rates] down'.[98] This seems a curious logic, especially given that the tailoresses acknowledged the existence of 'large numbers of people who must work out'. Mrs Jane McLeod, a representative of the union, explained that she did not object to such people working at home, only to the fact that they were underpaid.[99] It is not clear how excluding them from the union could have helped raise their rates of pay.

The relationship of the factory tailoresses to outworkers was, however, representative of the general state of worker organisation in the tailoring trade. The craft exclusiveness which helped win higher wages for this section of the clothing trade also acted as a brake on a more unified worker organisation. The existence of six separate unions covering tailoring workers alone was symptomatic of this narrowness. Order workers preferred not to combine with stock workers, and male inside workers were also reluctant to admit those working outside.[100] Cutters, pressers and tailors also maintained their own organisations.[101]

Furthermore, men refused to form common associations with women. As one disgruntled tailor put it, 'Oh let the women look after themselves, they have taken our jobs.'[102]

When a union of Outside Tailors was formed in 1890, the Tailors' Society noted with satisfaction that 'they are also anxious to work with us to suppress female labour'.[103]

The fact that some tailors did help manage the tailoresses' unions was the result of a broader conception of strategy held by a few individuals rather than a widely felt sense of common cause among the tailors as a whole.[104] This sectionalism was to leave the workers divided in the face of the unrestrained price-cutting of the 1890s, their craft status cold comfort alongside the hunger and poverty accompanying low wages or none at all. As the *Australian Leather Journal* put it, 'in the broad principles of business there is no charity'.[105] Like many other unionists in the 1890s, workers in the clothing trade saw no hope in unionism, but turned once more to the legislature to alleviate their lot.

The few employers who continued to operate large factories sought to reduce their costs by experimenting with new technologies (such as gas-powered machinery and new machines for cutting and finishing) and new work processes (such as greater subdivision).[106] Although the initiative for these innovations clearly came from management, there is no suggestion that workers opposed them. Indeed, the evidence suggests that, initially at least, workers welcomed power-driven machinery as a way of reducing the physical stress of the treadles and of increasing their earnings. Henry Blomfield, proprietor of a slop-tailoring factory, reported how his workers responded to his proposal to introduce a gas engine on condition that they accept a 10 per cent reduction in piece rates:

> I made them [the] proposition, not being able to do it out of my earnings, to erect a gas-engine and plant necessary for driving all the engines, and I put it to them in that way that if I did that it would entail certain expense, and independently of that the employing of a man at £2–10s a week . . . I put them in the position to earn more money than they could twelve years ago, if working fulltime.[107]

The catch, from the workers' point of view, was the condition 'if working fulltime'. This became apparent only after they had agreed to the reduction. As Blomfield reported, 'they thought that this gas-engine was overrated'.[108] To quell their dissatisfaction, Blomfield organised a demonstration using one of the machinists to show how much more exhausting it was for workers to perform at high speed using the treadle rather than the gas engine. While the workers were apparently convinced by this exercise, it is unlikely that they had really made a good bargain in the short-term. In the environment of the 1890s, few factories worked full-time and those that did had greatly reduced staffs. The secretary of the Tailoresses' Union estimated that in 1893 the average tailoress was earning only 12 shillings a week because of short-time, compared to about 21 shillings for a full week's work.[109] Blomfield's own workforce had been reduced from 150 hands to 25. Even with this reduction, the five men (three tailors and two pressers) were working on average three days out of six.[110] The gas engine might have allowed the machinists to work at high speed for a longer period, but with limited orders for work this was of no advantage to them, collectively or individually. Blomfield, on the other hand, got his work done more cheaply.

Nor is there any suggestion that workers opposed the subdivision of labour, although, as the last few months of the 1882–83 strike showed, tailoresses were keen to have sectional work paid at rates comparable to other rates.[111] The concern here was clearly a desire to reduce exploitation rather than to maintain 'control' of the work in process *per se*.

In the 1890s, work in tailoring factories was increasingly fragmented, with workers employed on the table system performing increasingly simpler, repetitive finishing tasks. Sarah Muir, a tailoress with twenty-three years' experience, described the 1890s version of the table system, where a journeywoman had eight or nine apprentices working with her: 'some were kept at turning out the sleeves; some were turning over the edge of coats; some were taking out the tacking, or sewing on buttons or sewing on tickets'.[112] While there is little evidence that workers opposed this process in general, there was clearly an awareness that subdivision of labour acted as a check on greater homogenisation of the workforce with factory production. As John Wing, secretary of the stock Tailoresses' Union, reported, the subdivision of labour undermined the union because 'only one branch suffers a reduction at a time, and the others not affected are not in sympathy with those suffering the reduction, and they each distrust each other'.[113] Wing, however, was not anxious to do anything about the situation. He said he had not made himself prominent in 'stirring up' the tailoresses because he did 'not believe in making the water muddy'.

Workers were, however, concerned about alterations to the method of payment. Paying by the piece was the traditional method of payment in the clothing trade. As Hobsbawm explains, payment by results (or the piece) was a 'degenerate form of the price which the formerly independent artisan had been paid for the sale of his product'.[114] (Hence the common reference to piece rates as 'prices'.) In the 1880s custom still prevailed, with only cutters and some machinists and finishers paid time rates. In the case of cutters, the practice seems to have arisen with the development of ready-made clothing. With cutters working on numerous layers of cloth at once, a slip of the knife became a very costly mistake. By paying cutters for their time rather than their output, employers encouraged greater care. From the cutters' point of view, this was a step forward. They did not have to work quickly in order to be the highest-paid workers in the tailoring industry, and the fact that they were paid salaries marked them off from other workers. As one employer explained, 'their salaries are a matter of private negotiation and not to be made publicly known. They have their reputations to consider.'[115]

It is not clear why machinists were paid weekly wages rather than piece rates. Probably it was because employers hoped to retain all the benefits arising from the faster production made possible by the machines.

As competition amongst manufacturers increased in the late 1880s and 1890s, some employers sought to extend the weekly wage system as a means of avoiding union rates for piecework. As with the case of the taking home of work by tailoresses, this is an instance of workers' actions precipitating changes to the structure of the working day and the management of industrial time. Strategies to defend piecework earnings thus inadvertently led to counter-strategies by employers, and it was these counter-strategies which led ultimately to the move from task-based payment to time payment in some sections of the tailoring trade. As Richard Whipp has pointed out, and as these clothing industry cases demonstrate, 'Time in relation to work is for management and employees a potential commodity which has to be created and its control and disposal negotiated.'[116]

The move to put pressers on weekly wages was successfully resisted by the Pressers' Union in 1889, but in the depressed conditions of June 1892 the workers agreed to the change.[117] Other employers extended the practice to female table hands as well as machinists. Edward Bartlett, for instance, told the 1893 Factories Inquiry that he paid by the week 'to avoid the log price for each garment'.[118]

While weekly wages were gradually replacing piece rates in ready-made tailoring, there is no evidence that this was happening in order tailoring or in the other sections of the clothing trade. For employers in these sections piece rates had the advantage of simplicity for accounting purposes. It was much easier to compute a worker's earnings by counting trousers or dresses made than by calculating how much time he or she had actually worked. Piecework also solved the problem of discipline to a large extent: if workers did not work they did not produce and did not get paid. Employers thus saved on the costs of supervision. Piecework had an additional advantage in that it enabled the payment of outworkers on a convenient basis. And in the order trades, piece rates absolved the employer of the responsibility of paying hands for idle time while they waited for work. Even in relatively prosperous times, the demand for bespoke services was extremely uneven.[119]

In the unorganised sections of the clothing industry employers also had less incentive to experiment with new forms of payment for labour: less subtle ways of reducing the wages bill were still open to them. Of these, the employment of cheaper juvenile labour in place of adults was probably the most popular strategy in the 1890s depression. Speeding up of workers was also common, either in conjunction with new machinery or under the older hand methods.[120] Tactics for ensuring maximum effort on the part of the employees varied. Some employers used abuse to maintain discipline. Edward Bartlett, for instance, a clothing manufacturer employing between 100 and 350 workers, told the 1893 Factories Inquiry that, yes, he did swear at the 'girls', but, 'I offer apologies, and we are the best of friends, it is merely a *lapsus linguae*. I never do any one any injury.'[121]

Others were more subtle, drawing on notions of family and co-operation to lead rather than to drive workers. The Busy Bee factory in Ballarat is a useful example. As the company historian expressed this ideology: 'The "Busy Bee" girls were indeed not so much hired helpers as an extension of her [the proprietor's] family, working beside her and her daughters on a common project.'[122] This attitude was common amongst nineteenth-century manufacturers who drew on authority patterns within the family to reinforce factory discipline. Wherever possible, younger workers were supervised by older workers, and females by males. As George Denton, clothing manufacturer and previously manager of Banks and Company's factory, explained: 'As far as my experience goes, women would rather be looked after by men for foremen and so on. I would sooner employ men to look after women.'[123] The employment of members of the same family within one factory often made this process easier. The relatively small scale of most Victorian clothing factories and prevalence of working-proprietors also made this style of authority easier to maintain than it would have been in larger, more impersonal establishments. The latter sometimes took advantage of the limited liability legislation to offer their supervisory staff shares in the company in the hope of infusing them with a sense of personal investment in the success of their employer's business.[124]

The success of patriarchal-style authority was, however, limited by the strength of such relations within Victorian working-class families. Nor should one be tempted to romanticise the more personal style of management which prevailed in the smaller factories. Relations between employers and employees varied, with the more fortunate approximating the happy family of employer rhetoric. Not so lucky were those who worked in workrooms like this dressmaking business in West Geelong, reported on by a factory inspector in 1896:

> As an instance of how the girls are treated, I have been informed, a girl fainted some weeks ago, and some of the girls went to render her some assistance. She [proprietor] ordered them back to their places, stating she would soon come round; and for the half-hour or so, before she recovered, she made her work an extra half hour to make up the time lost.[125]

Probably the most effective form of discipline was, however, the fear of unemployment. The depression of the 1890s intensified this fear and made workers more vulnerable to ill-treatment at the hands of their employers. With the unions in retreat, collective action was ineffective in checking these abuses in the workplace. Collective action took on a more political meaning, with workers looking to the Factories Act of 1896 as a way of regulating the arbitrary authority of employers in the workplace, as well as providing them with reasonable wages.

Both workers and employers attempted to influence the nature of work by affecting government regulations relating to industry. Specifically, they hoped to protect their interests by high tariffs to restrict import competition, and legislation to restrain 'unfair' exploitation of workers by some employers. As earlier noted, campaigns on these issues often involved alliances of workers with groups of employers. Large proprietors, in particular, were keen to co-operate with unionists to enforce their own standards of wages and conditions on their local rivals—the 'sweater' employing outworkers and the 'unscrupulous' employer paying substandard wages.[126] Many manufacturers, especially those not also involved in importing, were anxious to co-operate with unions to achieve a high level of tariff protection for the clothing industry so as to ensure steady profits and regular wages at acceptable levels for all.[127].

The success of these strategies is less clear than their motives. The move for protective tariffs, for instance, had contradictory effects. On the one hand tariffs made the local product relatively cheaper, but at the same time they increased the price of imported cloth and machinery (except sewing machines).[128] The duties on imported machinery may have discouraged some manufacturers from buying newer technology and making the accompanying changes to the organisation of their factories.

Similarly, as we have seen, the factory legislation of the late nineteenth century provided incentives to manufacturers to use outworkers in preference to inside labour. Both the Factories Acts of 1873 and 1885 were intended to prevent the exploitation of female labour, but ironically they encouraged the growth of small workrooms and homework where rates of pay and conditions were at their worst. Such legislation might have afforded some relief to female workers had a factory been defined as a place employing two persons, as proposed in the original Bill. Modifications in both Houses, however, raised the size to ten in the first instance and reduced it to six in 1885. Rather than helping eliminate cut-price labour, this legislation encouraged the small workroom and outwork, as employers sought to evade the provisions of the Act which applied to registered factories only.[129]

Renewed agitation in the 1890s to expose 'sweating' and amend the factories legis-lation was in the short-term also unsuccessful. The advertisement given to the low rates paid by some firms encouraged competitors to reduce their rates as well. Harrison Ord, Chief Inspector of Factories, reached the conclusion in 1895 that the campaign had in fact been counter-productive:

> For nearly ten years now the workers in the clothing trade have been questioned, and have supplied information, so that amending legislation might be introduced to ameliorate their lot. Inquiries have been made by a board and a committee and yearly reports issued from this office. The benefit to the workers has, however, been worse than nil, since some employers who were paying higher prices have lowered them.[130]

It remained to be seen whether the culmination of this agitation—the Factories and Shops Act of 1896—would prove any more successful than its predecessors in dealing with 'the sweating evil'.

2

AN AGE OF GRIM ADVERSITY:
THE BOOT INDUSTRY, 1880–1896

In contrast to the clothing industry, the actions of organised workers in the boot trade played a major role in precipitating mechanisation and subdivision of the labour process. The boot industry shared many features with garment making: it was labour-intensive, its product was highly portable and suitable to domestic production, and its product market was also seasonal and vulnerable to import competition. The footwear and clothing industries also experienced similar patterns of growth and stagnation. It differed in one major respect: most of the workforce (between 70 and 75 per cent) was male. (See Appendix, Table A4.) It is this fact which accounts for the very different pattern of worker involvement in the shaping of work.

Because men generally did not have domestic duties tying them to the home, their options in the paid workforce were wider. Men were able to adopt industrial strategies which were not viable in female-dominated trades, as the history of the boot industry in the 1880s and 1890s will show.

As the first Victorian contingent set forth for the Boer War in 1899, it was only fitting that they were shod in Bedggood boots. Bedggoods' was the first boot factory in Melbourne, built in 1854, and for almost half a century had been the leading Victorian manufacturer of footwear.[1] The boots the soldiers wore to South Africa were similar in style to the earliest products of the Richmond factory—strong boots made for hard work and long wearing. But apart from the style, these military boots had little in common with the handmade article found upon the feet of the army of goldrush immigrants in the 1850s.[2] The boot turned out of the major Melbourne factories in the 1890s was the product of 'the march of the machine', which wrought a radical transformation in the nature of bootmaking.[3] As the *Australian Leather Journal* noted in 1899, 'There is scarcely an operation which was done long ago with pleasure to the doer which is not now performed by the iron fingers of the machine.'[4]

The widespread introduction of specialised machinery into Victorian factories in the early 1890s imposed regular hours, set tasks and other kinds of factory discipline on a group of male workers who possessed recognised skills and a high degree of independence. Chummy Fleming, one of these 'workers of the old times style', recalled the 'devil-may-care' lives led by the 'Knights of St. Crispin' in the 1880s: 'We seldom worked on Mondays. We worked as we pleased; no one feared the boss, for we lived free lives.'[5] John Bedggood recalled that in the 1880s many operatives worked only five or six hours a day by choice.[6] Bootmakers were also notorious for honouring 'Saint Monday'. As the *Age* commented: 'For some occult reason most of the general hands connected with boot and shoe making will not work on the second day of the week.'[7]

This independence evaporated in the 1890s under the combined effects of economic depression, mechanisation, subdivision of labour processes and the substitution of weekly wages for piecework. In sharp contrast to the carefree ways of the 1880s (allowing for some exaggeration on Fleming's part), workers at Whybrow's factory in 1895 were discharged if they could not complete the task set by Arthur Whybrow.[8] Perhaps even more significant was the report to the Bootmakers' Union in the same year that 'Mr. Whybrow still continued to discharge men if they were caught speaking to their shopmates.'[9]

This tightening of factory discipline was symptomatic of the general erosion of job control experienced by bootmakers in the nineteenth century. This erosion was certainly accelerated in the economic storms of the 1890s, but the process had been under way since the middle of the century. Even the largely handmade boot made in Bedggood's first factory passed through a number of different pairs of hands, so that subdivision of the shoemaker's craft was part of factory production from the very beginning of the Victorian trade.

The making of a shoe involved three major processes: the cutting out of the leather, the shaping and joining of these pieces, and then the trimming and final preparation of the finished shoe (including buffing, colouring and coating the surface of the leather). In the hundreds of bespoke (or order) bootmakers' shops which sprang up in Melbourne in the 1850s, these processes were performed by hand, often by the same person. The male hand-maker was frequently helped by members of his own family or apprentices. Where women were employed, they usually sewed the uppers, particularly of women's shoes. Apprentices helped out with the 'uncommonly *fidgety* work' of sewing round, as it was described by 'An Oldster'.[10]

There were over 300 such workshops in Melbourne in 1861, employing between two and twenty workers each, and catering mainly for the well-to-do market. Bedggoods was one of the few local manufacturers making work boots, as most of this class of footwear was imported from Britain.[11] With the imposition of a tariff on imported footwear in 1866, local manufacturers became competitive and the bespoke workshops were increasingly replaced by primitive factories to increase production for the ready-made market.[12] In these factories machinery was used to roll the leather prior to cutting (clicking), but the cutting was still done by hand. The actual making, stitching and finishing were given to workers who did the work in their own homes. As one nineteenth-century manufacturer recalled, at that time a 'boot factory consisted of little more than a clicking room, a skin room, a rough-stuff room, and an office'.[13]

As was the case in clothing manufacture, subdivision of bootmaking into its various processes (clicking, making, stitching, finishing) preceded mechanisation. Like garment making, it was a product of the growth of wholesaling and its demand for a mass-produced article, rather than new technologies.[14] And as with the clothing industry, this subdivision was initially accompanied by an expansion of outwork, and with it an expanded role for women as upper stitchers.[15]

The major change away from homework occurred in the 1860s with the introduction of treadle sewing machines to stitch the uppers. These machines were too expensive for the average worker to buy, so their use drew women into factories which made the capital outlay.[16] The use of the Blake (or McKay) sole-sewing machine from 1876, meant that the male clickers, stuff-cutters, sole-cutters and the female upper machinists were joined inside the factory by increasing numbers of male makers, who shaped the upper and fastened it to the sole.[17] With the help of a 15 per cent tariff on imported footwear and duty-free imports of upper leather, these Victorian factories flourished in the second half of the 1870s and captured the home market for all but the high-quality lines, with the export of local produce increasing from 58,000 pairs in 1876 to 157,000 in 1880.[18] (See Appendix, Figure A4.) In 1879, Whitten's boot factory in Ballarat, occupying a large weatherboard building equipped with the latest machinery, employed fifty men in its making room and twenty women in the preparation and sewing of uppers. Machinery was used for some of the work in both sections, as it was in the cutting out of uppers, soles and heels.[19] There were no machines, however, for finishing, and the greater output of the factories meant an increasing number of men employed finishing outside the factories.[20] These outworkers were supplied by an army of lads who swarmed over Melbourne, Fitzroy and Collingwood, pushing barrow-loads of boots in various stages of construction.[21] Nor were the manufacturers anxious to bring the finishers inside the factories as they took up valuable space and were considered a 'nuisance, trouble and expense as they must have gas burning'.[22]

Despite the advances of the late 1870s, the technology in Victorian boot factories was fairly unsophisticated. Power-driven machinery was unusual, and the capital outlay on new factories minimal. It was still possible in the 1870s for an enterprising bootmaker with a few hundred pounds to set up as a manufacturer, and with the increased tariff on imported footwear in 1879 more and more bootmakers were encouraged to do so.[23]

But the 1880s were not the years of unlimited expansion that many anticipated. At the same time as the 1879 tariff changes gave an additional 5 per cent protection against imported footwear, a duty of 7.5 per cent on imported calf and kid leather increased production costs. The increased capacity of Victoria's boot factories was not matched by an expansion of markets. In fact, in the 1880s, imports of footwear increased whilst exports decreased. (See Appendix, Figure A4.) The result was fierce competition amongst local manufacturers for the remaining markets, and a quest for ways to cut prices and production costs.[24]

This highly competitive market produced a crisis of valorisation for employers in the boot industry. In response, manufacturers sought to reduce their labour costs by intensifying the work inside factories with the installation of gas engines to drive the machines. By 1890, 30 per cent of registered boot factories used motive power, compared to only 12 per cent in 1880.[25] At the same time, employers attempted to reduce the costs of their hand labour—the large numbers of finishers working outside the factories—by reducing piece rates. These attempts led to a strike and lockout in 1884–5 over the issue of outwork. This strike or lockout, like the tailoresses' strike two years previously, was the product of deteriorating industrial relations since the late 1870s. The good feeling between masters and men which accompanied the expansion of the boot trade in the 1860s and 1870s could not survive the more competitive atmosphere which existed after the market had been saturated. Many of the 'self-made' men continued to amass fortunes by using cheaper boy labour and outside labour; the widening economic gap between employers and employees became a symbol for the workers of the 'greed' of these 'mushroom capitalists'.[26] To add insult to injury, it seemed to the workers that the manufacturers were deliberately deceitful in their dealings with the Operatives' Union, agreeing to certain terms whilst in practice ignoring them.[27]

For their part, the manufacturers had become more and more exasperated with the demands of the operatives, and particularly with the 'objectionable and dictatorial manner' of their 'paid agent', W. E. Trenwith.[28] Men who prided themselves on their 'grit' and 'independence' resented what they saw as interference with the running of their businesses by the proposed Board of Conciliation.[29] Many expressed surprise at the militancy of their employees, blaming it all on Trenwith's demagoguery in the workplace.[30] Trenwith, with his buggy and top-hat, assumed monstrous proportions in the imaginations of these manufacturers, and securing his defeat seemed to justify any tactics.

But the manufacturers, being hardy individualists, were divided amongst themselves. As each sought to maintain his share of the market, the suspicion they felt for each other was often greater than their sense of shared class interest. This produced wages and conditions which varied enormously from factory to factory, with no two manufacturers paying the same price (piece rate).[31]

It was in this atmosphere of mutual fear, suspicion and chaotic piece rates and practices that the Bootmakers' Union (VOBU) resolved to act. Established in 1879, by 1883 it had recruited over 1000 members and had accumulated a substantial bank balance.[32] Nevertheless, members were reluctant to strike, hoping to secure the co-operation of the manufacturers to establish some order in the chaos.

The employers were likewise wary of confrontation, having no association of their own until October 1882. Both sides agreed to a Board of Conciliation consisting of nine representatives from the workers and nine from the employers, with an independent chairman (in this case James Ferguson, MLA). After a laborious thirty-six meetings extending over many months, the board agreed to a uniform log of prices, a limit to the number of apprentices and a set proportion of hands on weekly wages to those on piece rates in order to limit the use of weekly wages.[33]

Within days of the agreement between the union and the Manufacturers' Association, three employers began to flout the log by putting their workers on weekly wages and by cutting the prices paid to the largely non-union outworkers.[34] The 1883 agreement had said nothing about outwork, so in mid-1884 the union attempted to persuade the manufacturers to bring their outworkers inside the factories to help prevent price-cutting. Unfortunately, the Manufacturers' Association had withdrawn from the Board of Conciliation, saying its membership had fallen away to an unrepresentative number.[35] So the union waited on the employers individually and, by August, had secured the agreement of almost all of them to end outwork by October the same year (1884).[36] At the same time, the union was also engaged in a struggle over weekly wages being used to evade the log prices.[37]

The bootmakers, raised on piecework and its relative independence, in general had a horror of weekly wages. Their stated objection was that it usually meant working to a task, and was thus a concealed form of sweating.[38] Less openly stated but probably just as real was the fear of factory discipline this implied, a discipline which bootmakers had successfully evaded despite the erection of large factories and the installation of machinery. In the Victorian manufacturing context, weekly wages also usually meant subdivided labour, a phenomenon which bootmakers were anxious to avoid as it too implied a loss of control over the work process.

This is an instance of the difficulties in identifying the issue in dispute as either control or exploitation. Clearly, the workers saw it as both. Weekly wages meant working to a task (or quota) which meant both greater exploitation and loss of control over one's working rhythms. Both of these implied a collective defeat for the workers. Trenwith's explanation of the issue captures this inextricable connection: 'Later it became known that the manufacturers were going to crush the union, if possible, by introducing what they call the weekly wage system, but what in reality is a most pernicious system of piecework at reduced prices—that is to say, what is commonly known as task work.'[39] To maintain piecework as the method of payment in boot factories, the union engaged in 1884 in two bitter strikes with the leading employers of weekly wage hands, Mair and Company and McGan's. Mair and Company capitulated after a short struggle, but McGan, treasurer of the Manufacturers' Association, held out for ten weeks before giving in.[40] It seemed the union had triumphed, but just at the point where its funds had been depleted by strike pay, the Manufacturers' Association took the offensive over the issue of outwork.

The issue was further complicated by the formation of a union amongst the workers at the non-VOBU factories, which attempted to affiliate with the THC and claimed it stood for 'weekly wages and the Eight hour day'.[41] The employers hoped to exploit this division amongst the workers for their own advantage. As a meeting of manufacturers resolved to reject the agreement with the union about outwork as early as August, it seems they were waiting to choose the most favourable time before confronting the Bootmakers' Union.[42]

On 17 November 1884, a manifesto was posted in most Melbourne factories announcing the manufacturers' intention of 'reverting to the old system' of giving work outside. It also proclaimed their intention to accept only those workers presenting certificates of discharge from their last employer—a move interpreted by the union as designed to victimise 'agitators'. The manifesto declared the employers' determination to prevent access of union officials to their workplaces and to refuse to negotiate with anyone 'not directly engaged in the trade', a thinly veiled reference to Trenwith.[43]

The union retaliated by boycotting factories requiring certificates, banning overtime and outwork by its members and insisting on negotiations by the union's officers. The members also placed a 15 per cent levy on their earnings to build up their funds for the expected strike. Significantly, the union expected the first confrontation at Mair and Company, which was again trying to extend the weekly wage system.[44] But the employers acted first, locking out 300–400 men on 19 November, with more being discharged as they completed contracts on hand.[45] Within days 1400 men were locked out from sixty factories, and a further 700 female workers were unemployed due to the absence of male operatives to perform the other parts of the manufacturing process.[46]

Both sides stood firm, the employers apparently determined to break the power of the union, and the union equally convinced of the need to defend itself.[47] The union's funds were not exhausted as quickly as employers anticipated, as Ballarat workers continued to pay the 15 per cent levy and funds flowed in from other unions who saw the principle of unionism itself on trial.[48] Even after the Ballarat employers were persuaded to aid their city counterparts by locking out their own workers, the strike fund still managed to pay 1400 men their allowance every Saturday. A number of the strikers formed a co-operative boot factory and supported themselves, thus easing the burden on the union's funds.[49]

This deadlock lasted for thirteen weeks, the unionists defending the picket lines with vigilance and sometimes violence.[50] By the end of January it was clear that the union's funds were not drying up, whereas many manufacturers faced ruin. Negotiations in early February, mediated by Mr Mirams, MLA, and Andrew Lyell, accountant, resulted in a compromise.[51] Employers agreed to forgo the discharge certificates, adhere to the eight-hour day and to the limitation of weekly hands. On the crucial issue of outwork, the employers agreed to the union demand to bring their outside workers into the factory, but the union allowed them almost a year in which to arrange for the extra accommodation necessary. The union conceded the right of entry of its officials, agreeing that they would not enter factory premises during working hours.[52] On 11 February 1885, the boot factories of Melbourne and Ballarat again opened their doors, but for men and masters alike it was an uneasy peace, marked by even greater suspicion, tempered only by a greater enthusiasm for conciliation after the bitter experiences of the previous months.

The costs for both sides had been high: the union had paid out over £9000 in strike pay, while the manufacturers lost valuable contracts and intercolonial markets.[53] The 700 women and girls thrown out of work were probably the worst affected, although they fail to rate a mention in the existing accounts of the strike.[54] Indeed, it appears to have taken contemporaries three months to notice that these non-unionised females and their dependents were without any financial support, having no access to the strike pay issued to male unionists.[55]

The ramifications of the lockout were far-reaching, affecting both industrial relations and the organisation of work in the footwear industry. Most importantly, once the finishers were brought into the factories the whole climate of employer–employee relations altered. Inside the factories, it was a relatively easy matter to unionise the workers, whereas in their own homes they had been beyond the reach of organisation. The employers were only too well aware of this, and the defeat of 1885, combined with the prospect of even greater worker solidarity, encouraged them to work more closely with each other than they had previously done.

The restrictions on outwork also narrowed the options of employers still facing the over-competitive local market. Since large-scale, cheap outwork was no longer possible, manufacturers looked for ways to cheapen production inside their factories. Many began to experiment with new machinery and greater subdivision of labour, hoping thus to reduce their labour costs. The introduction of machinery also weakened the union.[56] As unemployment rose in the boot trade in the late 1880s, these strategies began to pay off and, one by one, the factories abandoned the 1884 log until by 1892 only a few adhered to it.[57] The stage was set for the large-scale mechanisation undertaken by boot manufacturers during the depressed years of 1892–95.

The most obvious targets for mechanisation were the processes of lasting and finishing, so far untouched by the technological innovations which had been introduced in England and the USA, and the only branches of bootmaking still done exclusively by hand.[58] With more of the finishing being done inside the factories, this incentive was even stronger. Many proprietors did insist on their workers paying for the gas they used to keep their pots of pitch warm, but from the manufacturers' point of view having them on the premises was still an additional and unnecessary expense, particularly as factory workers demanded higher piece rates than outworkers.[59]

The move to modernise Victoria's boot factories began in earnest in 1891 when Smalley and Harkness installed that 'most wonderful of machines', the Goodyear welter and chain stitcher.[60] Other manufacturers followed suit, taking advantage of the leasing facilities offered by the United Shoe Machinery Company.[61] Between 1892 and 1895 lasting and heeling machines arrived in the major factories, and were accompanied by an immediate subdivision of the making process and the use of weekly wages instead of piecework.[62] The final blow to handwork came in 1893–95 when leading firms such as Bedggoods bought the newest American finishing machines, which saved over 50 per cent of the labour in finishing. These machines did everything from shaping the instep to buffing the finished product.[63] Thus the boots which came out of the twenty or so large, modern factories in Melbourne in the late 1890s were entirely machine-made, passing through about twenty different pairs of hands in the process of conversion from cut leather to footwear.[64] Factories making strong work were slower to mechanise, but by the turn of the century they too were installing more machinery.[65]

This rapid mechanisation in Melbourne's leading boot factories in the 1890s had a number of effects on the structure of the industry as a whole. Firstly, the saving of hand labour displaced hundreds of male factory workers, whose occupations disappeared virtually overnight.[66] The last of the processes to be mechanised were in many ways the most difficult, and most highly paid. As one old bootmaker put it, these shoemakers 'lost half their work and their high consideration in one blow'.[67] Arthur Whybrow, a 'modern' manufacturer who had himself risen from the bench, described the process whereby machines displaced skilled men:

> In the making and finishing of a boot the most particular parts that require the most skill are done by machines now. Take the operation of lasting, getting in the toes, which was a most difficult

operation—that is all done by lasting machines, and one man will do as much in a day as perhaps 30 men could under the old conditions, and the other men have to do work which requires not much skill at all; therefore a man who could earn very high wages because he was exceptionally skilful— his occupation is gone.[68]

Men displaced by the machines were forced to take whatever unskilled work they could pick up, or attempt to eke out an existence as cobblers, repairing the machine-made boots. Others swelled the numbers of outworkers competing for the work given out by those factories unable to afford the latest technology.[69] The improved productivity of the mechanised factories as a result of the greater speed of the machines and the speeding-up of labour under the team system (subdivision plus tasks), made the old-style factories increasingly less competitive. In an effort to avoid being squeezed out by the large firms, these manufacturers reduced piecework rates again and again, but many businesses failed anyway.[70] The increasing price of leather in the second half of the 1890s added further to the problems of the less productive factories, and large numbers of smaller factories turned their workers out and closed their doors forever.[71] Others, such as the Ballarat factories, joined the trend toward mechanisation rather than face extinction.[72]

Secondly, the increased capacity and speed of the mechanised factories led, on the one hand, to over-production and, on the other, to an intensification of the seasonal variations in trade.[73] As one contemporary commentator remarked, 'the dreary gaps between cheerful busy seasons are ever growing longer'.[74]

Inside the mechanised factories, the impact of all the new machines had a profound effect on the atmosphere of the workshop. In the modern factories of the late 1890s,

everywhere one meets with rapidly whirling wheels, revolving knives and spinning brushes. Leather shavings fly from the knives, and what with the thumping of the presses, the grating of the rollers, the roar and rattle and clanking of various machines . . . in the near future speaking trumpets will form part and parcel of a boot factory's 'kit'.[75]

The men who worked the new machines were still exposed to the health risks, especially tuberculosis, caused by the particles of dust and the vapours associated with bootmaking, but they also had to work at greater speed.[76] Gone were the days when forty men would be kept hanging about the factory playing draughts 'simply at the convenience of the employer'.[77] With the new regime of weekly wages the employers made sure all workers were well-supplied with work, and any man not completing his quota was discharged. In the mid-1890s there were at least three men waiting to take the place of every unemployed hand, so the pressure was more than an idle threat.[78]

In addition, the new machinery sometimes meant new risks. Apart from the added dangers of physical entanglement with machinery, some machines produced symptoms akin to those now recognised as being the result of repetition strain injury. Men holding their work with both hands against a polishing wheel, for instance, developed injuries produced by the force and the vibration.[79]

The subdivision of bootmaking,'by which each operator contributes an exceedingly small portion towards the building of a boot', also made it easier for employers to use inexperienced labour in place of trained men.[80] Boys, in particular, were cheap and easily trained in the new methods.[81] Boot operative Thomas Richards reported:

> I can quote a shop where, in the finishing department, they used to average from 12 to 16 men. With machinery, that department is turning out the same amount of boots with really only two journeymen in it. They are doing the amount with the machines the 15 or 16 men were doing before. They crowd the boys into that department.[82]

The whole apprenticeship system, already under threat in the 1880s, was abandoned in most factories. If a lad wanted to learn to make a boot throughout in order, for instance, to 'make and mend boots with simple appliances in country towns', he would not acquire such knowledge in a factory.[83] Before the widespread use of machinery, apprentices in factories were lined up on a bench under the supervision of the most competent journeyman, and taught their trade. With the use of machinery and consequent subdivision of processes, an apprentice would be employed on one process only, 'with nobody to tell him whether he is right or wrong'.[84] Under such conditions, a lad in a modern factory had in most cases, 'literally to pick up his trade'.[85] The result was that apprentices, or 'improvers', learnt very little beyond one particular process, and when they became eligible at twenty-one for an adult wage were discharged in favour of fresh youths.

Workers had contributed to the reorganisation of the work process and of the industry as a whole in the 1890s, just as they had in the 1880s. The very fact that so many outworkers had been brought inside the factories and the apparent boost this gave to the union influenced employers in choosing strategies to deal with the valorisation crises of the depression. But in general the initiative shifted in this decade to the employers who seized every opportunity to capitalise on the workers' weakness in a period of high unemployment. And whereas the trials of the bootmakers in the 1880s had been tempered by triumph, in the 1890s their experience was one of unmitigated 'grim adversity'.[86] The decade began badly, with employers taking the offensive again by sacking union hands. The ensuing strikes were lost because of the availability of blacklegs—a sad defeat for the union leaders who cherished fond memories of the solidarity of 1884.[87] This was a serious reverse for the union and, with their funds depleted by assistance to the maritime strikers, the workers were badly placed to cope with the trials of the depression.[88] The failure of the union's attempt to establish a branch in Geelong was also ominous, as it provided a pool of non-union labour close to the Melbourne market.[89]

Over the early years of the depression, from 1890 to 1892, more and more factories abandoned the 1884 log despite repeated strikes against reductions. The union was forced to renegotiate this log, and conceded reductions amounting to about 12 per cent on all lines except strong work. To a large extent, the 1892 log reflected the change in factory organisation from a 'primitive' to a 'modern' system which had occurred since the mid-1880s.[90] The rates devised for the 1884 log reflected custom rather than costing, paying work on the basis of the quality of the work rather than the time taken in its making.[91] Strong work was therefore paid less than fine work, even though it took longer.[92] In contrast, the 1892 log was based on the more precise costing methods being employed along with new machinery and labour processes.[93] Despite the general 'modernisation' of the log, however, the union refused the manufacturers' request to recognise formally the weekly system of payment and subdivision of work.[94] The timely imposition of a new tariff averted even greater concessions on the union's part.[95]

Although the 1892 log was in general considerably lower than the 1884 'statement', it was still not low enough for some manufacturers. Those producing strong work in particular either gave up this line, introduced machinery or paid less than the union rate. As strong work was well-suited to outwork, being still predominantly a hand process, it was a simple matter to contract the work out at cut rates.[96] Within the factories the prices were also gradually whittled away until, by 1894, few were paying the 1892 log rate. The larger firms who had paid the log introduced more machinery to cope with this competition.[97]

It would be misleading, however, to portray the union in these years as completely defeated. Although membership had fallen away, funds were running low and unionists were discharged at many factories, the members who remained carried on a continuous campaign to resist reductions which succeeded in at least modifying the proposed rates.[98] Even when these efforts were totally defeated, the resistance was by no means token. The strike against outwork at the Hotham boot factory in 1893, for instance, lasted several months before being defeated by the use of scab labour.[99] And although by 1894 only fifteen out of about sixty-five factories in Melbourne still adhered to the union agreement, these included the major manufacturers in the colony.[100] The year 1894 saw an increase in strike action against non-statement employers, but it was not on sufficiently large or systematic a scale to influence the general trend in wages.[101] By late 1894 the union employers were complaining of the unfair competition of the non-statement shops, and urged the union to mount a more thorough-going campaign.[102] Although the union was not optimistic of success, the campaign began on 3 September 1894.[103]

By November the number of 'statement' shops had been increased from fifteen to fifty-six, a clear majority of the trade. Of the 1050 men originally on strike, 775 had reportedly returned to work on the union's terms.[104] But although the initial victory belonged to the union, the war was far from won. The non-union shops held out for over six months by sending their work to the non-unionised workers in Geelong.[105] The strikers eventually lost faith in victory and abandoned their picket lines. Others went back to work, unable to carry on once the union's strike pay had run out. A few battled on regardless of their isolation, but by May 1895 they too had surrendered.[106] One of the strike leaders, J. W. Billson, was boycotted by the manufacturers and forced to leave the colony in search of work.[107]

The year 1895 was therefore the darkest one the union had ever experienced. The membership, numbering more than 1000 in 1890, was down to about 400. Many of these were on short-time, so that the flow of dues diminished to a mere trickle.[108] Whereas Trenwith had enjoyed a fee of three pounds per week for his services, his successor had to make do with one pound.[109] Thus weakened, the workers faced another threat: the substitution of weekly wages for piecework and the subdivision of their work.

From the employers' point of view, weekly wages were clearly seen as a way of obtaining a more disciplined and diligent workforce. One of the leading advocates of 'modern methods', Arthur Whybrow, explained the difference between the two systems as he saw it:

The weekly wage system has elevated the men, and we have no St. Crispin's Monday now like we used to under the piecework regime. The men have to be in the factory at eight o'clock in the morning, and they have to stay there till five o'clock. The new conditions have made better men of them altogether.[110]

Although couched in terms of the betterment of the workers, it is clear what benefits accrued to employers. Having invested in so much expensive machinery, they were not prepared to see it stand idle whenever pieceworkers decided it did not suit them to work. And the workers' suspicion that weekly wages entailed working to a task or quota was well founded. There would have been no point in having men in the factory all day if they were allowed to work at their own pace. 'We gauge the capacity of the staff in the room', said Whybrow,'and we have work given out in accordance with that capacity . . . The foreman sees that every man does his fair share.'[111]

The union's objections to weekly wages in the 1890s remained the same as those expressed during the 1884 lockout: the system was a way of speeding up workers and cutting rates of pay by working to a task. Weekly wages were 'but the means of getting work done cheaply'.[112] However, in the harsher economic circumstances of the 1890s, the men were forced to compromise on this issue, as they were on the general question of mechanisation.

The mechanisation drive of the 1890s was met with apprehension by the workers, fearful that the machines would cause additional unemployment. The union made careful enquiries of their counterparts overseas to find out what impact they had had on the workers abroad. The responses were encouraging: the English union reported that the lasting machinery available in the early 1890s was not very fast and had not displaced many men. On this assumption, then, the union did not oppose its introduction in Victoria.[113]

By 1895, however, newer models were available and these did affect the employment of workers, particularly finishers. But by then the union was powerless to resist. The situation was made worse by the bad harvest and increasing price of leather, which retarded the recovery of the industry as a whole.[114] Accepting the inevitable, the union resolved to oppose any innovations in the work process not connected with the machinery. In particular, it was opposed to the subdivision of hand labour and the use of weekly wages except in conjunction with machinery.

For instance, when in 1894 the employers' association first suggested subdividing hand-finishing into four steps in order to compete with the speed of the machines, a majority of the members sided with Anarchist, Chummy Fleming, and voted to reject the subdivision of labour without machinery.[115] The meeting also rejected an amendment to this motion, proposed by the union president, J. W. Billson, to allow for subdivision providing that 'present prices should be paid'.[116] The question of subdivision thus continued as a major issue between unionists and employers. In January 1896, one manufacturer reported that 'we have had more friction with the operatives as to subdivision of labour than as to price'.[117]

Experience over the following years confirmed the men's suspicion that weekly wages meant working to a task, a situation akin to slavery in the mind of the bootmaker. Robert Solly, union secretary, recalled Whybrow's attempt to introduce this system:

On one occasion a man stood behind me with a watch, timing me while I was doing a boot. I said to him—'I am not going to work under that system. I am prepared to do a fair day's work, but I am not going to be a slave.' I had that spirit within me that I would not knuckle down to a man like that.[118]

The union had managed to prevent the general use of subdivision of hand labour in early 1894, but by 1895 independence of spirit was not enough on its own to overcome the obstacles to the union's continued success: lack of funds and excess labour.[119] Whereas militantly anti-union firms like Marshall's of Port Melbourne had for many years employed the 'team system', in 1895 they were joined by some of the supposedly friendly employers.[120] Two of the biggest firms, Whybrow's and Thomson's, announced their intention to use subdivision and weekly work after the failure of the union to enforce the 1892 log. A strike and lockout at Thomson's factory lasting several months became the test case for the 'team system', and the union's defeat encouraged other employers to follow Thomson's lead.[121] Meanwhile, Whybrow's had also introduced a system of discharging recalcitrant and slow workers and replacing them with faster, more docile men.[122] In their determination to introduce the new system, the manufacturers brought out a number of workmen from England who had experience of the newest methods and machinery.[123] Sporadic resistance to both the team system and wage reductions continued throughout the remainder of 1895 and 1896.[124]

This resistance had limited success in modifying some of the more objectionable aspects of the task system. At Whybrow's, for instance, the stopwatch disappeared from the shop floor. 'We do not record what each individual does', reported Arthur Whybrow in 1904.[125] Nevertheless, the foreman saw that every man did 'his fair share'. One of the virtues of the team system, from the manufacturers' point of view, was that it made identification of individual 'slacking' a simple matter. The 'test is that if there is a block at a machine or elsewhere we know there must be something wrong'.[126]

On the other hand, the system also had potential for collective regulation of output; the workers' successful opposition to time-and-motion studies no doubt made such pacing a more viable strategy of resistance to increased exploitation. Given the men's record of solidarity, it is highly likely that they adjusted their output to what they considered a 'fair' day's work. And this standard of fairness, as Hobsbawm has pointed out, varied according to a complex range of physiological, social, technical, moral and historic considerations.[127]

In the context of general defeat in the face of the employers' campaign to cut rates of pay and subdivide work, however, this was a small victory. For the most part the union abandoned the struggle and bided its time, hoping for relief from the Factories Act where industrial action had failed.[128]

The case of the Victorian bootmakers in the 1880s and 1890s shows very clearly how workers' initiatives and responses can have a deciding impact on the shaping of work. The tragic irony is that the impact was not the one the workers intended or would have wished for. Had the workers not succeeded in the 1880s in eliminating outwork by finishers, the employers would have responded quite differently to the economic crises of the 1890s. Faced with dwindling profits, it would have been far simpler to cut the costs of their labour by reducing wage rates. Where outworkers were the norm, this was quite an easy matter. Besides, had finishing continued as an outwork process it is less likely that manufacturers would have considered putting in new machinery as this would have meant extending their buildings. Had it not been for the 1884 lockout, the boot industry in the 1890s would most probably have adopted the same course of action as that followed in the clothing trades: extension of the outwork system on ever-decreasing piece rates. It was because this alternative means of extracting surplus value had been closed to them that employers adopted mechanisation as a last resort. Victorian boot manufacturing in the 1890s thus replicated a pattern which occurred in Britain in the mid-Victorian era.[129]

The question of gender played an important part in the bootmakers' success in limiting outwork. Unlike female clothing outworkers, male boot workers were not usually tied to the home by their domestic duties within the family. The sexual division of labour in the home in fact encouraged the absence of the male 'breadwinner', making the men's move to the factory both possible and acceptable. Because clothing outworkers were usually women, a strategy of abolishing homework was not considered, nor would it have succeeded.

The trade-off made by the male boot workers in 1884 in sacrificing the independence of the outworker in order to maintain their earnings had much greater long-term effects than anticipated. The bootmakers hoped to resist factory discipline and the degradation of their skills by opposing weekly wages and subdivision, but their earlier action in encouraging the extension of the factory system was to place them at the mercy of the employers and their machines. The other concession they made in agreeing to the use of weekly wages and subdivision in conjunction with machinery was also counterproductive, as it too encouraged the installation of even more machines, and opened the way for less skilled labour, mainly boys, to be employed in place of tradesmen. And as the decade following the 1896 Factory Act would show, this 'boy-labour' was to have very serious consequences.

Unlike some industries, however, there was no attempt in the twenty years before the 1896 Act to use female labour instead of male labour in boot factories, although 'men outside the union' allegedly had 'their wives and families to assist them' with outwork.[130] Mechanisation affected women's work in the boot trade much less than men's. They were still largely restricted to the sewing of uppers, although within this occupation there was now a more noticeable division between those who prepared the work (fitters) and those who sewed it (machinists).[131] Since the 1880s more factories had also installed gas engines to drive the sewing machines, and, as in the men's departments, there were complaints of untrained juveniles displacing adult women. Apart from these changes, little had altered since the 1860s.[132] A few women were employed in the packing department, supposedly because the 'work appeals to the artistic talent latent in so many women', where boxmaking, gold-stamping and embossing machines had been installed in more modern factories.[133] Buttonholing and eyeletting machines had also speeded up these tedious operations.[134] Women did not suffer unemployment to anywhere near the extent that men did as a result of mechanisation and subdivision, but there was no alteration of the sexual division of labour accompanying mechanisation.[135]

The main reason why employers did not attempt to replace male with female workers seems to have been the boot factory's lack of appeal to female workers. Even in the depressed years of the 1890s, there was reportedly 'no excess labor in females'.[136] Boot factory work was 'generally not considered a very desirable life for the girls'.[137] For employers, the question of female labour was more a matter of obtaining enough women for 'female' work than extending it to 'male' occupations. To this end, they offered higher starting wages to girls than other manufacturing industries. Where girls in the clothing trades started out on two shillings and sixpence per week or, in many cases, nothing at all, boot workers began on five shillings. Employers were at pains to dispel the 'low' image which their factories had. John Cairns, for example, had males and females starting and finishing work at different times: 'We do not like the two sexes to mix, to give the factory a bad name', Cairns explained.[138] The sexes were also kept rigidly segregated inside the factories. Whitten's boot factory in Ballarat took the added precaution, in the interests of respectability, of posting a sign in the upper room which read: 'Notice.— Smoking strictly prohibited by the girls.'[139] Placing females alongside males in the workshop was therefore temporarily impractical and would have been detrimental to the employers' interests in the long term.

A further reason why employers would have been reluctant to experiment with female labour in the 1890s was the attitude of the females themselves. They had a record of solidarity with male workers whenever attacks were made on men's wages or conditions.[140] Since women had struck against victimisation of male unionists and reductions in male rates of pay, it seems unlikely that they would have agreed to do men's work at cheaper rates.

Women were less militant on their own behalf. Although a Female Boot Operatives' Society was formed in 1890, it had a chequered existence in the subsequent six years. In February 1893 the male unionists of the VOBU considered it desirable to co-operate with Sydney socialist-feminist, Rose Summerfield, in 'reorganising the Machinists'.[141] These efforts were apparently not very successful, as the task of re-forming the union had to be undertaken again in 1894 and again in 1896.[142] And although during these years the women were involved in at least half a dozen strikes, all of these were in support of men. On one occasion, in 1894, women were reportedly dissatisfied with 'the very low wages paid' and 'seemed determined to better their Condition', but nothing seems to have come of this resolve either in increased wages or strike action.[143] The result of this inertia was that they were 'underpaid', a fact which even employers admitted.[144] In the 1880s, the average adult female could earn only fifteen to twenty shillings per week.[145] In the year before the Wages Board Determination, only 233 out of 1265 received twenty shillings or more.[146] The low wages paid to female boot workers had an effect on the labour process similar to that of low wages in the clothing trade. With the cost of labour so cheap, employers had little reason to experiment with 'labour-saving' machinery in the uppers department.

It is not entirely clear, however, why the fitters and machinists were so much more militant in men's causes than their own. (One reason for the uncertainty is that the records of the female union have not survived.) The explanation probably lies in the fact that family, community and work were all closely connected in the boot trades, especially in Melbourne. It is no doubt significant that all the women involved in forming the female union were single.[147] By defending men's wages and conditions, female boot workers were also defending the livelihood of their fathers, brothers and future husbands. Or to put it another way, the defence of men's earnings was seen as the front line in the battle for the survival of the family economy. Women's wages, by comparison, were of secondary importance. In better times, their earnings 'did something to keep the pot boiling'; in times of depression this contribution became even more important.[148] Nevertheless, for most boot factory workers, earnings of men were the major source of family income. That women did not seek wage increases for themselves may in fact have been seen as one way to preserve male rates: increases in female wages may have provoked employers to cut male rates even further. The Wages Board, on the other hand, promised wage justice for all workers. The year 1896 therefore saw a revival in the female union, women as well as men hoping to share in the benefits of the new regime.[149]

There were signs that the boot industry was also reviving. Export markets, particularly in Western Australia, began to expand after 1895 and the general recovery from this time also aided boot manufacturers. However, this was offset to a large extent by the rising price of leather over the same period, so that the Boot Board faced a still uncertain economic climate when it finally brought down its first determination in 1897.[150]

3

Drawing the Line:
The Printing Industries, 1880–1900

In nineteenth-century Victoria only four girls were apprenticed as compositors, and those who had acquired skill at 'type-snatching' elsewhere were rarely employed in Victoria's composing rooms. The 1891 Census recorded only fourteen women compositors compared to 1514 men, and there was no increase in the number of women by 1901. Girls seeking employment in the printing industries were restricted to a narrow range of occupations associated with bookbinding and stationery manufacture. The sexual division of work in the commercial printing industry is well illustrated by the firm of Sands and McDougall.[1] Visitors to the firm's new factory in Spencer Street in 1889 would have seen workers of both sexes performing their separate tasks in much the same way as workers in other large printing firms throughout the city.[2] On the top floor, they would have entered that male stronghold, the composing room. Although light and well-ventilated compared to most Victorian composing rooms, the general atmosphere would nevertheless have been oppressive, especially in summer, with the air thick with lead and uncomfortably heated by the hundreds of gaslights required to give the comps a clear view of their work. In this room the compositors selected the individual letters, and so on, for the line of type and set them in a hand-held stick. These lines were then locked together in a frame to make a forme, or large sheet of metal type. Once corrected by male readers, a mat made from this forme was carried to the presses, where male stereo-typers fitted it into the cylindrical power-driven drums. The whole of this printing process was handled by men. The first female hands to touch the process were those of the folders, who received great sheets of printed paper from the presses. The sheets had to be folded, either by machine or by hand, so that they ended up in the correct order. Sometimes they also had to be cut with long knives. Machines for folding were introduced in the 1890s and, in this case, the woman fed each sheet into the machine. Once folded, bundles of these sheets were placed on long tables in correct order. Another woman, a gatherer, then walked along beside the table, picking up a sheet from each pile until she had a complete article. This was handed to another woman, a collator, who checked that the pages were all in correct order. Any illustrations were then added, either by the collator or a separate woman. A woman working a machine by hand would then number the pages consecutively. The item was then ready for 'sewing', a process which covered both sewing with thread and metal stapling. In each case the operation was performed by a woman, either by hand or, less frequently, on power-driven machines. In the case of large books, grooves were first sawn in the back by men to receive the sewing.

If the article was a magazine or paperback book, a woman would paste on its cover (a task known as wrappering). If it was a bound book, she would add endpapers and paste down the projecting tapes to the flyleaf. At this point the bulk of the women's work was done, and the book passed into the hands of men who nipped the back (that is, placed it in a machine to press the back); cut the edges smooth in a guillotine; glued muslin on the back and sides; made a groove, by hand or machine, at each side of the back, so that the cover would lie flat; cut the covering boards and cloth and pasted them together. The book then went to the blocking-room where more men stamped on any design and lettering. Covers were then fixed by pasting down the endpapers, and the book was 'built up' in a large press. Any gilding was also done by men, as was marbling and colouring of edges. The completed book was then checked and packed.[3]

In the vellum-binding department, the visitor witnessed the binding of ledgers, account books, day books, diaries, bank books, and so on, whether bound in vellum or not. In this department women would be seen folding and sewing as in the printing department, and men performed the later stages of cutting the fabric and boards for covering and fixing the sewn sections of the book together. In addition, females also numbered pages and cheque books, and did perforating and binding work with cut flush covers such as cheque books and common exercise books. Men were also engaged in ruling pages by machine and working indexing machines. As with the printing department, women were allowed to bind only those articles which were cut flush, that is, not requiring the covers turned in over boards and endpapers.

In the stationery department, workers produced envelopes, blotting pads, exercise books, folios, black bordering, files and stamps. As in the other departments, men would be seen cutting the materials and doing any ruling, while women were occupied folding, 'cementing' (gluing) and packing the finished article. As a general rule, only men handled leather and metal, the former used to cover blotting pads, and the latter to provide a fixture in portfolios.

In addition to the above stationery lines, Sands and McDougall also produced mounted cards and maps. Again, men cut the paper and boards for mounting, and women covered the boards with paper and glued on the print. Work mounted on calico was done by men. Greeting cards were also produced here, and the same divisions applied, with women performing the packing. In the cardboard-box and carton section, almost all the workers were female, the exception being the men engaged to work the guillotine machines.

Folding pages and sewing them together preparatory to binding was work which had traditionally belonged to women, but by the time the Victorian industry started in the 1850s women were also doing the gathering, collating and wrappering and in the 1880s they also moved into the binding of items with covers which were cut flush, such as cheque books and common exercise books.[4]

Should the visitors have returned to Sands and McDougall's ten years later (1899), they would have noticed a similarly rigid sexual division of labour, but the line had been redrawn. In addition to the work already performed by women, they would also be seen making leather-cornered blotting pads, recognised as 'girls' work' in 1891, and in 1898 the binding of 'quarter-bound books, cut-flush with turned in paper sides' was transferred to female workers. In practice this meant higher-quality exercise books and some folio account books.[5]

In the newspaper industry, there was virtually no scope for female workers. The entire staffs of the Melbourne daily newspaper offices were male, the only four female compositors apprenticed in Victoria being employed in Massina and Company's commercial printing works.[6] Victorian employers showed less enthusiasm for female compositors than their Sydney counterparts, and Melbourne had no equivalent of Louisa Lawson's *Dawn*, a feminist-inspired attempt to encourage women to enter typesetting. There were isolated cases of country newspapers employing young women to distribute type (i.e. to sort used type back into the case), but these were exceptions to the general rule.[7] Nevertheless, the proportion of females engaged in registered printing factories doubled between the early 1880s and the end of the century, with 1889–90 and 1896–99 the periods of sharpest increase. (See Appendix, Table A5.) But this was due more to structural changes in the industry as a whole, resulting in an expansion of 'female' jobs, than any major invasion of male occupations by women. At the same time, some male jobs, such as hand composition, contracted in the late 1890s as a result of the installation in daily newspapers of 'iron comps', or linotype machines.

The structural changes which accounted for the greatest increase in the proportion of female workers derived both from changes in the product market and from technological innovation. Before the diversification of printing in the 1880s, the industry was almost entirely based on the production of the Melbourne daily newspapers. Production of books was negligible, and a few big firms such as Sands and McDougall, Massina and Company, Firth and McCutcheon and Detmolds dominated the commercial jobbing and stationery trade, which received its main impetus from the growth of weekly and periodical publications in the 1870s. Their main competitors were the small suburban and country enterprises set up by ex-journeymen, who operated with a starting capital of less than £100 and the cheap labour of boys.[8] As the bigger firms continued to expand and mechanise in the late 1880s, these small businesses multiplied, relying on low wages to remain competitive against the rapid labour-saving methods of the big concerns. Nevertheless, employment in the printing industry in the late nineteenth century was characterised by a high level of seasonality and general instability.[9]

Unlike the infant boot and clothing industries, printing did not attract protective tariffs from governments unwilling to impose a 'tax on knowledge'. This, combined with the continuing prejudice against colonial goods, meant that almost all books were imported, as well as most trade brochures and even state school textbooks.[10] The expansion of the

1880s was based on bigger newspapers, longer runs and multiple editions rather than on new dailies, and on the growth of specialised periodicals, advertising and some stationery lines. The application of web rotary speeded up the operation of the presses and necessitated the employment of large numbers of compositors to feed the frames at one end and increasing numbers of workers, many female, to fold, collate, sew and bind the printed pages at the other end.[11]

The 1890s depression had a particularly devastating effect on the jobbing section of the industry, with a dramatic decline in both the number of firms and volume of work, causing both severe unemployment and short-time amongst the workers. In contrast to those in the newspaper offices, however, workers in the commercial jobbing firms were not severely affected by the introduction of the linotype machines in the late 1890s. By 1906 only three Melbourne firms outside the newspaper offices had Mergenthalers: there were four at Sands and McDougall, two at Massina's and one at Fitchett Brothers. Even in these firms the impact was not as severe as in the newspaper composing rooms, as most of the hand compositors were retained for smaller orders. By comparison, the impact on newspaper offices was severe, with both the *Age* and the *Argus* discharging over two-thirds of their composing staff after installing linotypes in 1896.[12]

In the bookbinding department, however, mechanical innovations were less dramatic. Guillotines and hand-backing machines had been in common use since the 1850s. In the late 1880s and 1890s machines were developed for sewing, collating, folding, cutting, rounding and backing, but these were not in general use in Victoria in this period. Case-making machines were an important invention, but they did not appear in Australia until the turn of the twentieth century.[13] In the absence of technological innovations, employers in bookbinding relied on cheapening human labour to cut costs. The major way in which they sought to do this was by replacing trained adult male workers with cheaper female or boy labour. As we have seen, however, there was no dramatic shift in the sexual division of work in the printing industry in the late nineteenth century. To understand why this was so requires an appreciation of industrial relations in this industry.

The class of work open to females in bookbinding was determined by a 'line of demarcation', 'imported into Australia from the Old World, when the industry was commenced here'. This line was defined by the male Bookbinders Union after negotiation with employers, and was jealously guarded by a 'loyal and vigilant membership' against incursions on 'their' territory. The definition of the 'line' was spelt out in the union rules, and members were fortified in their 'loyalty and vigilance' by the prospect of a ten-shilling fine for failure to report to the union any breaches of the rule.[14]

The employers, for their part, were keen to use female labour wherever possible. They often preferred girls to boys on binding work in any case, as girls were said to be cleaner and more careful in performing the folding and gluing associated with bookbinding. The Chief Inspector of Factories, for instance, reported that 'much of the work in this trade is admirably adapted for women, requiring as it does neatness and quick manipulation with the fingers'.[15] When the change from hand to machine case-making occurred in the late 1890s, employers were keen to have this work classified for females.[16] The men fought successfully to prevent this happening, and this proved to be an important victory

4   By the 1890s, a few Australian binderies had introduced mechanically powered stitchers. This one was installed in the New South Wales Government Printing Office in 1891.
Mitchell Library

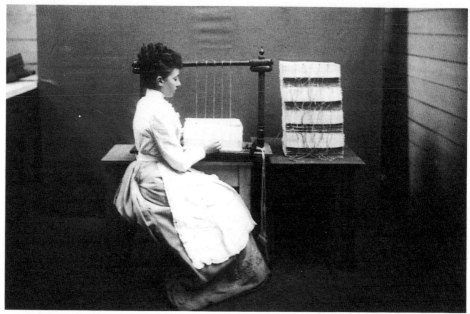

5   Women's bookbinding remained an entirely hand process in the nineteenth century. This picture shows the Government Printing Office, 1891.
Mitchell Library

for the colonial men as twentieth-century trends in bookbinding saw an increasing volume of books bound in this way using the Sheridan case-making machine.[17] But they were forced to make other concessions during the 1890s, including accepting temporary cuts in their wages.[18]

Women were thus still excluded from the bulk of publishers' binding and ledger-making, restricted to the cheaper classes of work which had simple paperback covers cut flush with the pages or covered in paper. Other attempts by James McDougall and his fellow employers to employ girls on 'skilled' work met with stiff opposition from the men. Even threats by McDougall to close up his entire pocket-book department, and by Detmolds to reduce wages by 15 per cent unless the demarcation line was reconsidered, failed to extract further concessions.[19]

Significantly, it was the larger firms like Sands and McDougall's who led the way in using more female labour. Most of the bookbinding and stationery manufacturing was performed by several large, heavily-capitalised firms, usually as an adjunct to printing, so that they faced competition from each other rather than from the smaller cut-price operator who plagued the printing section. Indeed, the rivalry between these firms led them to report each other to the Bookbinders Union for breaches of the union's rules.[20] When even so-called reputable employers like Sands and McDougall's attempted to coerce their female workers into evading the Factories Act, there was little scope for strategic alliances between unionists and groups of employers.[21] In these circumstances, the Bookbinders Union was able to retain its influence only by maintaining 100 per cent unionism amongst male employees in the trade, a task made easier by the concentration of workers in larger factories. Nevertheless, the employers displayed a remarkable persistence in their attempts to move the demarcation line to encompass more females. The fact that this line was so arbitrary in the first place aided the employers. That is, it was a big move to train girls in composing type when they had performed no similar work before. But in bookbinding, the women were used to doing similar work to that performed by the men, sometimes in the same room. Under such circumstances it was relatively easy to move the women to the 'men's work'.

In theory, of course, the division was between 'skilled' and 'unskilled' work rather than between males and females. Work classed as 'skilled' was, according to union rules, to be performed exclusively by journeymen or apprentices at the appropriate rate of pay. Thus, unqualified males were also excluded from skilled work. On several occasions employers did try to use boys instead of men, but the male Bookbinders Union was sufficiently strong to insist on a strict ratio of one juvenile to every three journeymen.[22] In practice, because very few unindentured boys were employed, the rule operated against females, who were not admitted to apprenticeships in bookbinding.[23]

Women's work, by contrast, was not recognised as skilled because they could not control the entry into their craft of unapprenticed 'trainee' labour. This process occurred, however, before the establishment of the Victorian bookbinding industry. Unable to maintain the definition of their traditional work as skilled, they were denied access to 'men's' work, which was preserved as a skilled craft.[24]

It will be clear from the above that the line of demarcation was sharply drawn at any given time. As William Detmold was told by the union when he attempted to stretch a

6   Binding Room, Government Printing Office, 1911.

7   The gender demarcation in bookbinding: women, under male supervision, employ their traditional skills sewing government publications by hand, while men carry out the backing, covering and finishing stages in the exclusively male binding room.

State Library of New South Wales

point: 'Our rules does [sic] very clearly define what skilled and unskilled work is.'[25] It was, nonetheless, flexible in the sense that it could be renegotiated at any point. In many ways, it was like the front line of battle, with employers and male unionists fighting over the disputed territory. The women were caught in the middle, not consulted by either side, silent casualties of the conflict. The weak points in the demarcation line were the simpler tasks performed by the journeymen, and any new operations arising as a result of changed work processes or new products, such as the making of cloth cases by machine.

This case demonstrates only too clearly the social construction of any definition of skill. The definition was determined not so much by the actual characteristics of the work performed as by the relative bargaining power of workers and bosses at any given time. The low status accorded female work reflected women's weak bargaining position in the industry.

Unlike male bookbinders, female print workers had no formal union organisation in the nineteenth century. They did sometimes engage in industrial action to maintain rates and conditions: factory-specific strikes occasionally occurred even in the absence of union officials and funds.[26] But such action was not effective in raising the general level of wages, and women's rates were low by comparison with men's. While adult women were paid between ten and twenty shillings for a full week's work, male bookbinders were paid between fifty and sixty shillings.[27]

Such low rates of pay had consequences for the work process as well as for the women who received them. The cheapness of female labour probably deterred mechanisation in bookbinding and stationery, as it did in the clothing trade. The use of folding machines is an instance. These were not used in Victorian commercial printing firms to any great extent in the nineteenth century. In Britain, however, they were used more extensively, particularly by firms which worked a night shift. The difference was that women were forbidden under the English factory laws from working night shifts, so that folding had to be done at night by more expensive male labour. Folding machines were thus economical if replacing men but not if replacing cheaper women.[28] In Victoria, by contrast, night shifts in commercial printing firms were rare, so employers continued to use their cheap hand labour in preference to the new machines. In newspaper offices, however, where women's employment was dispensed with because of the night-work prohibition, machines were used to fold the papers.[29]

In the male sections of bookbinding, wages remained comparatively high. Employers were anxious to reduce labour costs in this section by extending female labour if possible. This was much cheaper and simpler than mechanisation. When these attempts failed because of the the determined opposition of the male unionists, employers embraced the machines instead. The introduction of the Sheridan case-maker is the most striking example, its introduction following a move by employers to have case-work classified as 'unskilled' (female) labour.[30]

Male compositors were as concerned as bookbinders about the threat of female labour and organised even more effectively than the bookbinders in excluding women from 'their' work. There was no place for women in the intensely masculine world of the composing room, where the Fathers of the Chapels maintained the traditional rituals of initiation and discipline, and the companionship maintained its solidarity in the equally masculine camaraderie of the ale-house. The Victorian typographers had a carefully articulated position on the question of female labour which is well illustrated by an exchange initiated by John Hancock, the editor of the *Australasian Typographical Journal*.

Woman, declared Hancock, is 'a more dangerous foe to labour than John Chinaman himself'.[31] This denunciation was prompted by news of female compositors employed by ' "women's rights" faddists' in Sydney, 'advanced thinkers' who were the sworn foes of trades unionism, or so the editor argued. His comments sparked off a lively exchange in December 1889 and January 1890, but not with anti-unionists as the editor perhaps had expected. Rather, the person who sprang to the defence of women's employment was socialist and loyal trade unionist, William Lane. Writing in the Brisbane *Boomerang*, Lane attacked the misogynist outbursts of Hancock; the debate that ensued exposed the deeper layers of the compositors' objections to female labour. The typographers' response to Lane's argument throws light on their hostility to women as fellow workers, whilst it also illuminates the more subtle issue of sexual identity and its effects on work-place politics and methods of work.

Lane took the *Typographical Journal* to task on its stated intention to 'refuse to recog-nise any office which employs women in the composing room', arguing that because female labour had been used to break down wages was no reason to oppose women as women. He pleaded for a woman's right to enter any occupation on the grounds of jus-tice, deploring the notion that she should always be compelled to seek her livelihood as an 'accommodating housekeeper'. Whilst he agreed that cheap female labour was a problem, he urged united organisation rather than exclusion: 'The printers won't find the girls clamouring for lower wages; if they take them by the hand and teach them the prin-ciples of organisation and the wrongs of labour they will find in women mates, not enemies; staunch allies, not secret foes.'[32] He inferred that the reason they did not adopt his course was because of their 'slavish idea that half the race is born solely to cook for and bear children to the other half'.

The *Typographical Journal* took great exception to these 'extraordinary theories', which seemed to challenge the natural order of gender relations. It found nothing objectionable in the idea that one half of the race was born to cook, etc., for the other half, and was surprised that Lane thought otherwise, especially as his views on labour topics were 'as a rule, thoroughly sound'. It asked rhetorically: 'Surely our Brisbane friend does not want the woman to print and the man to stop at home to make the beds!'[33] Assuming the answer to be 'no', it pointed out that 'the humble position of a maid-of-all-work offers more scope for the proper training of a working-man's wife than can be secured by taking a man's place in a printing office'. By the same token, it made no sense to intro-duce what was essentially casual labour to break down the wages of male breadwinners.

Clearly, the gulf between Lane and Hancock was very wide. Lane's utopian ideals, as Bruce Scates' recent study has shown, prompted him to consider a new gender order.[34] Hancock, at that time more inspired by craft exclusivism than socialism, could see the issue only in the context of the social and cultural status quo. Most women did marry and leave the paid workforce; most men became breadwinners; whenever women had been introduced into male occupations it had been as cheaper labour, which undermined the ability of male breadwinners to provide for their families; therefore, it was to the advantage of both men and women that women should be kept out of men's jobs. All this was entirely consistent with the world view apparently shared by the overwhelming majority of compositors.[35] True, it took no account of single girls supporting themselves and others, nor of mothers left to provide for children. But these were seen as exceptions to an otherwise comfortable rule.

To accept this rationale as the complete explanation of the typographers' hostility to women workers would, however, be to miss a less obvious but nonetheless significant objection. They certainly objected to female labour because it was cheap, but they also objected to it when it was the same price as male labour. When the New South Wales typographers voted on the question of admitting properly qualified female compositors receiving the male rate of pay, only four supported their admission.[36] Melbourne's printers were even more united on the question, and unanimously rejected a qualified journeywoman who applied to join their society on the same terms as men.[37] Female compositors threatened more than the printers' livelihood; they also threatened their sense of manliness. The spectre of the woman printing and the man making the beds was just as haunting, whatever the wages paid to the woman.

Compositors were already vulnerable when it came to the manliness of their occupation. As Cynthia Cockburn has demonstrated, composing, with its strong element of intellectual work, placed its practitioners in an ambiguous position, exposing them to the charge of effeminacy often levelled at such occupations as clerical work.[38] Until the 1880s and 1890s the compositors had managed to retain a manly image by the conditions under which they worked and by the performance of the heavy work of lifting the typeset formes. There was also a sense in which the possession of a skill bestowed on craftsmen both manly pride and independence, as Richard Middleton explained to the 1884 Royal Commission on Shops and Factories:

> An imperfect knowledge of his trade cripples a boy for life . . . [I]t prevents the growth of his manhood. When he becomes a man he cannot assert himself as a man conscious of his artistic strength should do—he has to succumb to unscrupulous employers and take what he can get; but when he is master of the trade he can act in a manly part in engaging with his employer.[39]

This manly independence was further supported by the self-conscious male camaraderie of the Chapel and pub. So when in the late nineteenth century feminists and others singled out their work as being ideally suited to women, male compositors were understandably defensive.[40] Whilst conceding that the quick eyes and fingers and painstaking natures of women might be admirably suited to 'type-snatching', they protested that this did not mean the work was therefore 'light and clean', the accepted criteria of suitable feminine employment. On the contrary, they argued that the women 'cannot make up, neither can they impose and make forms ready for press, or correct forms on the press, as well as men. That is a physical impossibility.'[41] As for the work's alleged cleanliness, the *Typographical Journal* protested that the 'close, malodorous atmosphere of a printing office, with all its grimy surroundings . . . permanently injure a young woman, both in body and soul'. Also believed harmful to the delicate feminine sensibilities was the setting of certain printed matter, such as anatomical textbooks and sensational newspapers, whereas night work in newspaper offices was considered so obviously undesirable for women that no reason needed to be given. Furthermore, not only was the work unsuitable, but 'daily contact with the males must necessarily have a tendency to destroy the timidity and modesty which usually characterise the sex'. Thus, women who 'unsexed themselves' by doing 'man's work' became 'manny' in their habits, and were reported to be found drinking in the front of English bars with other companions who followed the custom of adjourning to a public-house after work.[42] All things considered, nothing short of the 'abolition of girl labour' would satisfy the male compositors.

As we have seen, the Victorian printers were remarkably successful in their aim. The first four girls apprenticed at Massina's in 1884 were also to be the last: Massina's agreed not to repeat the experiment, whilst other firms desiring cheaper labour made do with boys.[43] Whereas Sydney masters obtained trained female compositors from New Zealand, few seem to have made their way to Victoria. The Factories Act of 1885 effectively took care of their chances of obtaining work on the daily newspapers by prohibiting night work for women and boys. It was no coincidence that the typographers' union played a large part in the agitation for this Act, realising the double-edged 'protection' afforded by such protective legislation.

The preservation of composing as a masculine occupation had important repercussions for the way in which the craft was performed. The English experience had shown that where women were employed in composing rooms they were restricted to the lighter tasks of setting and imposing the type, men being employed to carry the finished formes to the presses.[44]

The absence of women in Victoria's composing rooms meant that until the introduction of the linotype, the compositor's work was not subdivided, the compositor performing the full range of tasks. Denied cheaper female labour for the 'type-snatching', employers were doubly anxious to obtain practical models of the new linotype machines to offset the economic pressures of the 1890s. As with girl labour, Massina's were the first to experiment with the machines.[45] And whereas in the 1880s the Typographical Society was powerful enough to insist on the exclusion of women, by the time the linotype machines arrived in the second half of the 1890s the union was so weakened by the effects of the depression that it offered no resistance. Had the linotype not offered such a dramatic saving to newspaper proprietors, they might have been tempted to try cheaper female labour instead, and the typographers would have been hard-pressed to prevent them.[46]

The general course of industrial relations reflected the typographers' change in fortunes. The printing industry was divided between the heavily capitalised large firms and the small suburban and country newspaper and jobbing offices. As in the clothing trade, this division offered opportunities for alliances between workers and employers. In this case, the thirty or so bigger firms belonging to the Master Printers' Association (MPA) co-operated with the union during the prosperous 1880s to enforce uniform standards of pay and conditions upon the smaller firms. Together they tackled the question of boy labour: the employers were anxious to limit undercutting by smaller firms using cheaper labour, and the union was anxious to retain its bargaining position by controlling the number entering the trade. As the episode at Massina's shows, they were equally co-operative when it came to female labour. This alliance was very effective in raising the general level of male wages in the 1880s.[47]

The successes of the Typographical Society in the 1880s, however, made the MPA wary of the union it had fostered, and many members began to fear the power of the 'monster' they had nurtured. When the depression came in the 1890s, they were only too happy to abandon the alliance and take their chances using the new machines against the competition with shops using cheap labour. As mentioned earlier, the compositors for their part offered no resistance to the introduction of the linotype. With funds and membership severely affected by the depression, their chances of resisting successfully were very slim. The *Typographical Journal* argued that resistance would be inappropriate to a society whose motto was 'Defence, not Defiance', and that in any case such defiance would be futile.[48] Rather, the union placed its hopes in defending the privileges of those who remained in work by securing a reasonable rate of payment. As the Board of Management explained, 'Your Board has recognised the fact that it would be futile upon its part to attempt to obstruct the use of labour-saving machinery, but it has claimed for the limited number of future workers a fair share of the profits resulting from the use of such improved appliances.'[49] True to its stated intention, the society's journal regularly carried the advertisement seen in Figure 8, with its graphic message for the superfluous 'hands'.

Other factors may also have influenced the typographers to accept the linotypes without a fight. Ava Baron's study of the USA printing industry found that 'men embraced the linotype because its dirty work made it less respectable for women'. Cynthia Cockburn comments of the British scene that 'to many of the men, the clatter and clunk of the linotype if anything enhanced the manly qualities of the occupation'. Such considerations may also have weighed with Victorian compositors, who kept themselves well-informed about overseas developments in this area. Victorian compositors, indeed, seemed confident that women represented no threat to male employment on the machines, a complacency which was not felt as regards boys.[50]

The society was successful, after considerable negotiation, in obtaining an agreement with the MPA to use only qualified society members on the machines and to pay them an agreed rate whilst learning to operate. Apprentices were allowed on the machines only in their final year, and hours of work were to be restricted to forty-two per week.[51] This agreement, and the fact that several employers either pensioned off their older compositors or offered retrenchment pay, ensured that the linotypes did not 'cause the trouble that was expected'.[52]

That the union was able to secure such favourable terms was largely due to its earlier success in keeping non-society members (including women) out of the trade and the solidarity of members in the new crisis or, to quote the editor of the union journal, 'all that was wanted to secure success was the loyalty of the men'. Of course, the task was made easier by the fact that the economy was beginning to recover when the machines arrived in 1895. And the men's unity and determination was inspired by the threat the machines posed to them collectively as well as individually. The linotype threatened the craftsmen's control on the job. Members were warned that firms 'are preparing to throw their faithful workmen out into the cold and to call in the aid of the inanimate toiler, *who is much more amenable to discipline than the ordinary intelligent compositor* [my emphasis]'.[53]

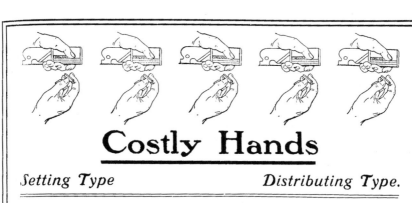

Costly Hands

Setting Type   *Distributing Type.*

Five pairs of hands, may be, working at it earnestly, faithfully, but in a *costly* way for you.

One
Pair of
Hands

Operating an
**American
Mergenthaler
Linotype**

will do as much work and save you Time, Labour, Money.   Easier work for the stone-man.   No pi.   No distribution.   A new dress every time you print.   That's what it means to use an

American Mergenthaler
Quick-Change Linotype

Model 5—Single Magazine.   Model 4—Double Magazine.
180 characters from one keyboard.   360 characters from one keyboard.
5 to 14 point body.   5 to 30 ems measure.   Choice of 300 faces.

A Victorian Printer recently said to us :—
"I am just making my last payments to you for the Mergenthaler Linotype I purchased about two years ago, yet I am better off to-day than ever before. It has more than paid for itself."

American Mergenthalers are Big Money Makers.

Write for Prices and Terms to **Parsons Trading Company,**
Stock Exchange, Pitt Street, SYDNEY.
SOLE AGENTS for the Mergenthaler Linotype Co.

8   As an indication of the union's acceptance of the linotype and its consequences, the union's journal regularly carried this advertisement with its graphic message for hand compositors.
Australasian Typographical Journal, 1 September 1908. (ANU Archives of Business & Labour)

It was vital that unionists regulate access to the machines in order that they have some control over the rates of pay and hours of work, but also over the effect the machines would have on the general balance of power between workers and employers in the composing room. The struggle was thus about exploitation, but it was also about control, or 'bossing', as Cohen puts it.[54] And the two issues were inextricably linked, since the loss of control implied increased exploitation.

The experience of the printing craftsmen in the face of mechanisation contrasts sharply with that of the male boot operatives in the same period. Unable to control entry of non-union labour to the trade, the bootmakers could not regulate the conditions under which the new machines were introduced. They were unable to prevent the use of boys as operators or to insist on piecework rather than weekly wages.

The printers, on the other hand, prevented both. Apprentices, as we have seen, were allowed on the machines only in their final year. As regards time payment, employers reportedly wanted this rather than piecework because 'they considered that the machines would be treated better'. The union's objections to the weekly wage system were similar to the bootmakers': 'it was generally believed', reported the secretary, Hancock, 'that, by the adoption of the stab [established weekly wage] system, they would lose their independence'.[55] Unionists also feared that 'under the wages system they would have a system of tasks' whereby everyone would be speeded up and the slowest discharged.[56] The minority who favoured the time system did so because 'under the piece system the operator had not to depend on his own ability, but on his machine or on the person who kept it in order'.[57] This was a real problem with earlier typesetting machines such as the Hattersley, which were notoriously unreliable. But early experience of the linotype proved that this was not a serious consideration, and, in any case, the union secured the employers' agreement to pay for such lost time.[58] Piece rates also had the advantage, as London compositors found, that any increase in the productivity of the machines and the men would accrue to workers rather than management.[59] Indeed, this is likely to be the real reason employers favoured time rates, since piece operators had as much to lose as employers by abuse of the machines.

The employers, however, were keen to get the machines at almost any price and the Master Printers' Association agreed 'almost unanimously' to the society's terms. Most importantly, the major Melbourne dailies—*Argus*, *Age* and *Herald*—worked their banks of linotypes on the union conditions and 'expressed their satisfaction with its operations'.[60]

Given the success of the linotype in newspaper offices, it is perhaps surprising that more jobbing offices did not install the machines. They were available on lease from the Mergenthaler company, so the cost of acquiring them was reduced. Jenny Williams has tackled this question in her study of the diffusion of new technology in the printing industry at the turn of the century. She concludes that Victoria lacked the necessary economic, political and social framework needed to sustain the new technology's take-off. More specifically, the industry had no tariff protection and the system of technical education at the time was inadequate to meet the demands of the new technology.[61]

But there was more to it than Williams' analysis suggests. Only four commercial printers installed linotypes, and then only a total of seven machines.[62] The newspaper offices, as we have seen, embraced the new machines wholeheartedly, replacing up to two-thirds of their compositors in the process. For them the machines made sense, as they needed to produce large quantities of typeset material as quickly as possible.

The relatively large market for their single product—that is, the daily newspaper—justified heavy capital outlay. By contrast, the commercial printers supplied an enormously varied market, from wedding invitations to the Sands and McDougall *Directory*. Although the latter work was appropriate to the linotype, and indeed this was why Sands and McDougall's installed them, the smaller jobs were more efficiently set by hand. There was no significant book trade in Victoria at the time, partly because of the lack of protection against imported books, partly because of prejudice against the colonial item, and partly because the Australian market for books was, in any case, not very large. The bulk of the commercial printer's work was therefore not suitable to the use of the linotype. However, by the same token, it was not adapted to the use of cheaper female or boy labour, requiring as it did experienced compositors skilled in layout and the use of borders and different typefaces.

The printing industry in the late nineteenth century thus produced similar patterns to those found in clothing and boot manufacture. Where labour was relatively cheap, the tendency was for more extensive use of hand labour; where it was more expensive, employers introduced machinery in an attempt to intensify the productivity of the workers. And in each case, gender proved the deciding factor: men's work, which was more expensive, was mechanised, while cheaper female work remained handicraft or was mechanised to a much lesser extent. Other factors, most notably market demands for varied products in small quantities, placed limits on this mechanisation. Government intervention was of lesser importance. The twentieth century, by contrast, would alter the state's role considerably, beginning with the 1896 Shops and Factories Act which marked the era of special boards for the fixation of wages and conditions.

PART II

Under the Wages Boards

The rooms are often small and with the members tightly packed around the table, most of them smoking, they present a crowded, dingy and uncomfortable appearance.[1]

A description of the proceedings of an underground political group? On the contrary, Professor Hammond's words, written in 1914, describe the meetings of the Victorian Wages Board, a legally constituted wage-fixing body. These deliberations, conducted in the back rooms of the offices of the Chief Inspector of Factories, represented a new departure in Victorian industrial relations: for the first time a state-constituted body attempted to regulate the labour market. Certainly, there had been boards of conciliation in the past, but this time the boards were provided with a chairman whose casting vote could ensure a verdict where collective bargaining failed to reach consensus. The decisions of the Wages Boards were also backed by the authority of the state, which had power to prosecute and fine parties breaching the boards' determinations. In order to understand the history of individual industries under the Wages Boards, it is important to have a more general appreciation of the system and the context in which it operated between 1897 and 1925, the year in which the last of the three industries (printing) made its approach to the federal Arbitration Court.

The new Shops and Factories Act was finally promulgated in 1896 after a stormy passage through the Legislative Council. It provided for the establishment of 'special' boards in five specified 'sweated' trades, and the registration of outworkers. Both these provisions were major parts of the original proposal which hoped to control the 'sweating' of defenceless female workers.[2] On the other hand, amendments which limited the Act's duration to a period of three years placed the boards on an insecure footing from the outset. Not until 1905 were they assured of a permanent existence.[3]

The board system, as it operated for most of its first decades of existence, consisted of five representatives each from the employers and employees, with an 'independent' chairman. With the exception of a period in 1902–03, chairmen had a casting vote in the deliberations.[4] The selection of worker and employer delegates was determined according to regulations framed by the Executive Council. In the first instance, representatives were appointed by the Minister for Labour, who published his nominations in the *Government Gazette*. Employer representatives had to be chosen from amongst the registered factory proprietors, while worker representatives had to be bona fide employees who had worked at their trade for at least six months in the preceding three years. Elections occurred only if objection was made to the Minister's nominations by at least one-fifth of either side. Should an election be called, a roll of electors was compiled from lists of registered occupiers (employers) and employer returns of workers aged eighteen years and over. Outworkers were entitled to separate representation where their numbers constituted more than one-fifth of all employees.[5] Although elections were held in the early years of the boards' existence, they became less common as both sides formed themselves into organisations which made recommendations to the Minister.[6] Only in unusual circumstances were the Minister's nominations challenged, as we shall see in the subsequent chapters on the clothing and boot industries. However, full-time union officials, or 'Trades Hall hangers-on' as one Legislative Councillor dubbed them, were expressly prohibited from taking seats on the board until 1934, as also were company managers.[7]

Chairmen were elected by the board members, the Governor in Council making the appointment only when the delegates failed to agree.[8] Given the emphasis on conciliation, it is ironic that from the outset the boards' most prominent chairmen were police magistrates, men accustomed to making judgements rather than orchestrating compromise. In 1908, for instance, two police magistrates between them chaired ten of the forty-six boards. Former senior civil servants were also a popular choice, four of them accounting for a further nine boards. Four ministers of religion between them chaired six boards, whilst one energetic estate agent sat on eight. The remaining thirteen boards were chaired by an assortment of business and professional men ranging from a shopkeeper to a quantity surveyor.[9] No women were chosen. Only in a few cases did the chairmen have previous personal knowledge of the trade covered by their board.[10]

The success of this method of selecting chairmen depended very much on the personal qualities and experience of the individuals concerned. In some cases, such as that of the Underclothing Board discussed in Chapter Four below, the task proved too much for the man chosen, whereas in others the tact and patience emanating from the chair encouraged a speedy resolution of conflicts.[11] But often the bias of chairmen was all too evident.

In addition to the chairmen and delegates, each board was provided with a secretary, generally one of the staff of the department of the Chief Inspector of Factories. Where boards had female members, one of the 'lady inspectors' acted as secretary.[12]

Boards were usually appointed for a term of three years, but revisions to a determination could be made at any time during that period. Meetings were held in the late afternoon or in the evening.[13] Board members were paid for each session attended. Fees were generous by current wage standards, particularly for female members.[14]

Once constituted, the boards met to discuss the determination. Proceedings were generally informal, conducted around a table with the chairman sitting between the two groups of delegates. Not all were held in the small rooms referred to in Hammond's opening description; some were held in the 'spacious dignity of a conference chamber'.[15] In the early stages of discussion, the opposing parties generally addressed remarks to the chair in order to sway his vote to their side. As Hammond observed, the chairman's power was often more real than apparent. Some chairmen prided themselves on being able to secure a consensus agreement. But in reality they often let the members know what they were prepared to accept (usually a compromise) and one or other side would move the motion to which the other side then agreed.[16]

There was, however, no guarantee that at the end of this often lengthy process workers would receive the wages prescribed in the determinations. There were mechanisms for appeal, and a great deal depended on how effectively the legislation was administered. The main burden of administration fell on the shoulders of the Chief Inspector of Factories and his staff. The personal experience and attitudes of these civil servants were clearly crucial in determining the effectiveness of the whole Wages Board system. As Ernest Aves, an official British reporter on the system, observed, the 'administration would be wrecked not less surely by excessive partisanship than by an attitude of passive resistance'.[17]

In this respect, at least initially, Victoria seems to have been fortunate in its public officials. Harrison Ord, Chief Inspector of Factories for the first thirteen years of the system's existence, had a personal commitment to the scheme. Indeed, he had been closely involved in drawing up the Act of 1896.[18] Although he was by no means always popular with either workers or employers, his enthusiasm and energy were acknowledged by all.[19] From the outset he selected a staff of inspectors who shared his outlook. Miss Margaret Gardiner Cuthbertson held the position of Senior Lady Inspector. Like Ord, she had a clerical background of public service administration.[20] Their administrative experience was supplemented by the practical expertise of a team of sixteen inspectors, three of whom were women. Most of these had previously worked at one or other of the trades covered by the boards.[21] The effectiveness of their surveillance varied greatly with the size of the establishment, the number of factories in the inspector's district, and the energy, astuteness and integrity of individual inspectors.[22]

The problem of systematically and regularly visiting outworkers was clearly the most serious deficiency in the inspectorate system. Although outworkers were registered under the Act, their frequent changes of address and their large numbers, particularly in the earlier period, made comprehensive surveillance practically impossible.[23] In 1897 there were 2382 outworkers registered in Victoria. Although this number declined to 955 in 1903, by 1906 it had increased again to 1431.[24] Unregistered outworkers escaped surveillance altogether.[25]

In the event of apparent breaches of the determination being discovered, the allegations would be taken before either a justice of the peace or a police magistrate. On conviction, the court could fine the offender, but it had no power to order arrears for underpayment of wages until an amendment in 1909.[26]

The Wages Board and inspection system described above operated in each of our three industries for varying periods between 1897 and 1925. The Wages Board scheme was not, however, static during these years. On the contrary, legislative amendments, particularly in the period before 1910, involved important changes to the powers of the boards. In general, these extended the coverage of the board system but curtailed its powers, especially in regard to apprenticeship restrictions.[27] (The power to limit apprentices was restored in 1910.) Apart from minor amendments in 1915, the system's framework remained unchanged throughout this period.[28]

In contrast to the legislative stability existing after 1910, administration of the system fluctuated. The diligence and enthusiasm which Harrison Ord brought to the post of Chief Inspector of Factories were not matched by his successors, and it seems reasonable to assume that the general administration of the Factories Act suffered accordingly.[29] On the other hand, the general state of the economy in the period 1903–25 made breaches of the letter of the law less common than in the preceding decade.

Manufacturing, along with agricultural production and mining, led the slow recovery from the depression of the 1890s. By the time the first Wages Boards sat down to fix wage rates, recovery, although slowed by drought, was well under way.[30]

In the meantime, the previously divided colonial economies merged into a common market with federation in 1901. No longer restricted by colonial tariff barriers, manufacturing in Victoria expanded rapidly. This was particularly true of industries concerned with metals and machinery, food processing, and clothing and textiles.[31]

Manufacturing also benefited from certain structural changes in the Australian economy in the early twentieth century. In particular, although pastoral commodities (meat and wool) still dominated exports, agricultural products were assuming a greater share in the export market.[32] This diversification in the export trade assisted manufacturing, in that wheat and dairy farmers tended to buy local goods rather than the imported ones favoured by graziers. The smaller scale of farms also encouraged a higher demand for locally-produced machinery.[33] More directly, the expansion of agriculture led to the expansion of those industries processing primary products, such as dairy produce and flour-milling.[34] City businessfolk thus continued to be almost as preoccupied with the weather as farmers and graziers, and for the most part the climate was kind.[35]

Despite the 'growth' throughout most of this period, these were not years of dramatic economic expansion comparable to those which preceded the 1890s depression.[36] Australian manufacturing still suffered from a restricted local market and, in contrast to the nineteenth century, population growth did not provide a ready remedy.[37] Australian manufacturers were therefore not in a position to benefit from the economies of scale which resulted from a larger market. Distance was also a problem for Australian exporters.[38] Nor did the influx of capital approach the scale of overseas investment in the 1870s and 1880s, a factor which further limited economic expansion.[39] In any event, until the 1920s banks and stock exchanges continued to show little interest in manufacturing, and retained earnings continued to be a major source of finance.[40] Indeed, as Cochrane suggests, the problems experienced by small-scale manufacturers in obtaining capital might also have provided a check to Australia's industrial development before World War II.[41]

A further limiting factor on the development of manufacturing was the nature of the labour market, or to be more precise, labour markets. Although shortages of unskilled men were almost unknown, this was not the case with either female labour or skilled male labour. Where skilled adult males were concerned, shortages occurred partly because of structural changes in the economy and partly because of deficiencies in the apprenticeship and technical training systems.[42] In the case of structural changes, the shortages were generally brief, involving a period of adjustment to the changed situation.[43] In the latter case, the problem was of longer duration. It was not until the late 1920s that positive steps were taken to ensure more effective industrial training of male workers.[44]

Shortages of female workers were, if the complaints of contemporaries are any indication, even more serious. Seasonal shortages were common throughout this period, but these were more acute in the decade prior to World War I and in the early 1920s.[45] A number of factors were involved in this shortage. Most importantly, there was a decline in the percentage of unmarried women of working age seeking paid work, from 69.5 per cent in 1901 to 50.1 per cent ten years later.[46] It seems that with increased prosperity and the extension of the secondary education system, parents were able to keep their daughters either at home or at school for longer than in the economically depressed 1890s.[47] Business colleges were also beginning to claim significant numbers of girls who otherwise would have been doing paid work.[48] Manufacturing was particularly affected by the lower percentage of girls in paid work, as it coincided with a growing preference for office employment rather than factory work.[49]

At the same time, the expansion of manufacturing, particularly in 'women's industries', meant that the overall demand for female labour had increased.[50] Of lesser importance but no doubt also a contributing factor was the fact that the minimum age at which girls could legally enter factory employment was increased in 1909 from fourteen to fifteen years.[51] While this affected the numbers entering factory work, experienced workers were reportedly lost to neighbouring states which 'poached' Victoria's skilled women.[52]

'Shortages' of women for factory work in the early 1920s had slightly different origins. The paid work participation of single women had recovered to 65.3 per cent by 1921. However, the trend toward white-collar work had gained momentum in the decade following 1911. By 1921 the percentage of employed women engaged in commercial pursuits had jumped to 15 per cent, compared to 11 per cent in 1911. (See Table 3.) Professional employment (mainly teaching and nursing) showed similar increases. Manufacturing showed a slight decline over the same period from 43.6 per cent to 42 per cent, despite the increasing importance of manufacturing within the economy.[53]

The reasons for this shift are less certain. Higher wages were not the main consideration, especially given the extra cost of dressing appropriately for office, shop and school. Probably more important was the perception of office and sales work as more 'ladylike' or feminine than work in a factory.[54] Girls may also have believed that such work would bring them into contact with more eligible bachelors than would be found in factories.[55] It is possible that girls were also affected by the backlash against the increase in women's industrial employment. Fuelled by nationalist and imperialist concerns for the quality of 'the race', these denunciations intensified in the twentieth century.[56]

The fears of national efficiency advocates coincided with those of male (and some female) unionists that women were taking men's jobs. These fears seemed to be supported by statistics of industrial employment which showed a steady increase in the proportion of women compared to men in the workforce.[57] That this increase was largely due to the development of 'women's industries' rather than to female encroachment on traditional male occupations was overlooked.[58] The result was a hardening of union attitudes to female labour. From the turn of the century male unions took steps to exclude women from a whole range of occupations, usually by the devices of protective legislation and equal pay. The unionists' success in securing government endorsement of these strategies in key areas meant that women were increasingly confined to the lower-status, more poorly paid occupations within manufacturing, a fact which can only have made factory work less attractive.[59] The failure of the Clerks' Union to secure equal pay in this period meant that no such barrier existed to female entry into offices.[60]

Table 3 Areas of employment of the female workforce (percentages), Melbourne, 1901–1933

Year	Domestic service	Manufacturing	Commercial	Professional	Other
1901	40.3	34.6	10.2	11.2	3.7
1911	30.0	43.6	11.0	11.7	3.7
1921	23.7	42.0	15.0	15.3	4.0
1933	24.1	39.4	17.9	13.9	4.7

Source: W. A Sinclair, 'Women at Work in Melbourne and Adelaide since 1871', *Economic Record*, vol. 57, 1981, p. 349. Calculated from the *Victorian Census*, 1901, 1911, 1921, 1933.

That industrial unions were able to organise effectively to exclude women reflects the changed situation from the turn of the century. Most importantly, the advent of Wages Boards from 1897 and the Commonwealth Arbitration Court from 1904 raised the possibility of state intervention in the market place on behalf of the male worker. After the turn of the century and the return of prosperity, Victorian unions began to reorganise.[61] The visits of Tom Mann between 1903 and 1910 fuelled this revival.[62] After 1907, increasing disillusionment with the politics of the Australian Labor Party caused further interest amongst the left-wing of labour circles in industrial organisation at both state and federal levels.[63]

The campaign for equal pay received further impetus from the embryonic organisation of women's unions in the few years prior to World War I. The interest in women's unions at this time was partly due to the general interest in industrial unionism after 1907; the THC's Organising Committee, for instance, devoted some of its energies to this end.[64] Interest was also fuelled by the activities of left-wing feminists, who turned their attention to women workers after the granting of the suffrage to Victorian women in 1908.[65] Although operating from concern for economic justice for working women rather than the defence of male jobs, women unionists also organised with equal pay as an objective.[66] That equal pay was not more widespread under the Wages Board system was largely due to the reluctance of chairmen of boards and judges of the Court of Industrial Appeals to decide a matter which, they argued, was the province of the legislature.[67]

Such was the context in which the clothing, boot and printing industries operated in the early twentieth century. The exact periods covered varied with each industry. The boot industry, for instance, was one of the earliest industries to resort to federal arbitration, obtaining an award in 1910. Thereafter the Wages Board system was of little relevance. The clothing and printing trades did not approach the Commonwealth court until after the war, in 1919 and 1925 respectively. For them, the Wages Boards were of more enduring significance. Our focus now shifts to these individual industries, to an examination of their different fates in this period.

4

No more Amazons:
The Clothing Industries, 1897–1919

Work in the clothing trade during the era of the Wages Boards was shaped by the same range of factors which affected the nineteenth-century industry. Product and labour markets, available technologies, gender definitions, worker and employer organisation and state action were all influential. But in the twentieth century the relative impact of these factors changed markedly. Most importantly, developments at government level significantly altered the structures within which employers and workers operated. The federation of the Australian colonies in 1901 opened up more extensive markets for Victorian clothing; this increase in demand for goods affected the demand for labour and, in turn, decisions employers made about the organisation of the labour process. Labour-saving methods (mechanisation and speed-up) were adopted to cope with the need for rapid output.

Employers' decisions were modified by the responses of workers, whose relative power in the workplace increased with greater demand for labour. More importantly, the advent of government wage-fixing bodies at both state and federal level created a more favourable climate for collective worker organisation and gave unions in this industry the opportunity to influence the nature of work in unprecedented ways.

In a less direct way, the federal government's commitment to the European war effort in 1914–18 had repercussions for workers and their work. The war created the opportunity both for more radical and militant responses on the part of workers and for a powerful employer counteraction.

The state affected work in other ways. The granting of votes for women by the Commonwealth in 1901 and the Victorian government in 1908 validated women's role in the public sphere. Whereas the tailoresses in the 1880s and 1890s had sought the protection of male sympathisers, in the twentieth century women unionists showed a new self-confidence and independence. But while this presented a challenge to both male unionists and employers, it was limited in its impact by the strength of entrenched gender ideology and the absence of any shift in the material base of the gender order. Men continued to be the main 'breadwinners' and women continued to marry them and leave the paid workforce for lengthy periods. Thus, while unionists had more opportunity to influence the conditions and wages of work, much of their energy was devoted to defending the position of male breadwinners (and their dependents) rather than to separate economic justice for women. And Wages Boards were not inclined to grant such economic justice as long as the independent woman could be dismissed as atypical.

The 1896 Act had a major impact on the nature of work in the clothing industry. The early Wages Board determinations, which set piece rates in most cases at a slightly higher rate than the weekly wage, encouraged employers to move their production away from outworkers (who had to be paid by the piece) and into factories where they could pay by the week.[1] With the cost of outwork increased, mechanisation, used in conjunction with a weekly wage or task system (or flexible piece rates in the case of the shirt industry) became relatively more profitable. Thus, Ellen Eckersall, a clothing and shirt manufacturer, explained that since the Act outwork was relatively more expensive because inside the factories operations such as buttonholing were done by machine. 'Of course', she added, 'girls have had to work harder for their money than before the Act was introduced.'[2]

The determinations of the various Wages Boards thus represented for employers a new crisis of valorisation. No longer able to cheapen production by cutting outwork rates, they had to devise new strategies to remain competitive. The combination of machinery, subdivision and weekly wages was adopted to varying degrees in all branches of the industry. Whereas piece rates specified a direct relationship between the quantity of work performed and the payment for such labour, weekly wages did not. Providing they paid the specified amount for the time worked, there was no legal limit to the quantity of work (or task) employers could demand of their workers. As one worker put it, the task system was really 'piece work at a reduced rate. It is cheap labour. It is evading the Act.'[3] This intensification of work was facilitated by greater subdivision of garment-making and by the introduction of new machinery and the application of gas and electric power to drive these machines. As a general indication of this trend, the amount of horsepower applied to clothing machinery in Victorian factories tripled in the first decade of the twentieth century. (See Appendix, Table A6.)

The transition to factory production had implications for the age and sex structure of the workforce as well as for the work process. In the tailoring section of the industry, factory production was accompanied by the employment of an increasing proportion of female and juvenile labour. The new methods, requiring less training than the old, made the employment of such relatively inexperienced labour more viable. The increasing employment of juveniles was especially marked in the period between 1903 and 1910 when legal limitations on the employment of young workers were removed. The proportion of female juniors (under twenty-one years of age) in clothing factories rose from 28.7 per cent in 1902 to 38.6 per cent in 1906.[4] The increasing employment of adult women in tailoring is not so dramatically illustrated by the statistics: men were not so much being displaced as relocated into supervisory and managerial positions within the factory system.[5] In the traditionally female sections of the industry (dressmaking, millinery) the process was one of masculinisation rather than feminisation. The advent of the male entrepreneur in these sections contributed to this trend, with the rate of increase of men engaged in dressmaking and millinery increasing at about three times the rate of increase for women during the period before World War I. (See Appendix, Table A6.)

But while the provisions of the various Wages Board determinations prompted employers to adopt different production strategies, they also placed limits on their alternatives. Limitations on the proportions of juveniles which could be employed restricted the use of such labour in the tailoring section, with the exception of the years between 1903 and 1910 when all such restrictions were lifted. Similarly, the 1909 provision for equal pay for the sexes engaged on pressing and cutting effectively checked the gradually increasing trend to employ women in these occupations.

It would be misleading, however, to attribute too much to the provisions of the Wages Boards. The boards certainly initiated the dramatic transitions of the turn of the century, but changes in the product market for clothing at this time fuelled the process. Most importantly, the federation of the Australian colonies in 1901 opened the rest of Australia to Victorian manufactures by removing all tariff barriers between the states. Firms in all sections of the industry installed new machinery in order to keep pace with the increased demand. This was especially important for the underclothing and whitework section, which accounted for most of the large increase in the export of wearing apparel in the five years following federation.[6] And once the trend toward factory production was established, it became self-sustaining. Cheaper production methods led to cheaper goods which in turn increased the demand for factory-made products. Within a decade the purchase of ready-made underwear had been established as the norm in Australian households, and the homemade article increasingly became a Victorian anachronism.[7] Changing fashions also contributed to the adoption of new methods of manufacture. Again, whitework serves as a good illustration. Exquisite underwear became fashionable in the late 1890s, when it was considered refined to have yards of delicate finery concealed beneath the rather severe tailored fashions of that decade. Manufacturers were quick to supply this market, experimenting with special machines for embroidering and adapting ordinary sewers to cope with more complex tasks. The fashion for straw hats likewise created a market for a new product which was well suited to mechanised factory production.[8]

In the dressmaking section, the popularity of the blouse and skirt from the turn of the century eroded the prejudice against ready-made dresses which had retarded factory production in the nineteenth century. One of the biggest problems with ready-made clothing was that it was often ill-fitting. Loose-fitting blouses worn with circular or gored skirts fitted a far greater variety of figure-types than the less flexible all-in-one dress. And as with whitework, the effect on output was self-sustaining, since increased demand enabled greater economies in production, which led to cheaper goods, thus further stimulating the popularity of the ready-made item in comparison to the order or homemade article. The expansion in output also helped overcome the other drawback of factory-made clothes: their lack of individuality.

Ready-made clothing for men had gained much earlier acceptance, largely because it was less varied in style. A relatively standard product also lent itself to greater subdivision. This feature of the product market for men's clothing was exaggerated during World War I, when many tailoring firms became involved in the production of military clothing. A guaranteed market and a standard product encouraged firms to adopt mass production techniques, with factories such as the Commonwealth Clothing Factory installing cutting and pressing machines, new patent sewing machines and in many cases adopting further subdivision of the labour process.

It should be stressed, however, that these changes applied very unevenly across the clothing trades. They applied to men's clothing more than to women's, and to the making of shirts and underclothing more than to outer garments. The order trade, in both men's and women's clothes, was largely untouched by the new methods and machines. Whereas the market for ready-made clothing expanded, with dramatic consequences for methods of production, the market for order goods was at best stagnant. This was especially true of men's order tailoring, so much so that by the end of this period the *Australasian Manufacturer* noted that 'the majority of men no longer wear anything individually manufactured for them'.[9] Handwork and treadle machines were still dominant throughout the order trade. The newfangled finishing machines were of little use in this section because their performance still did not match the hand-stitching of skilled workers. Similarly, powered sewing machines were of little value when precision mattered more than pace. Cutting machines and even knives were inappropriate to the cutting of individual garments. Similarly, the order garment-maker's product was too varied to make much use of subdivision. Nor could employers speed up their workers using tasks and weekly wages, since the order trade was so erratic that they would have found themselves paying workers to sit idle for unknown periods of time in between busy periods.

The supply of labour also limited the extent to which manufacturers could cheapen production by using female and juvenile labour. The labour of women and girls was by no means an unlimited commodity, and clothing manufacturers constantly complained of the difficulty in obtaining suitable labour. This was particularly so in the years 1905–10, and throughout most of the war years.[10]

Wages Board determinations, product markets and the supply of labour thus all affected the nature of work in this period. Other, less impersonal, factors were also important in both generating and limiting change. The agency of employers and workers, acting either individually or collectively, was often decisive in determining whether or not certain practices were adopted or rejected.

Not surprisingly, it was employers in the shirt and underclothing sections who were the most innovative. Edward Price, managing director of E. Lucas and Company of Ballarat, travelled to Europe and America in 1909 in order to study the latest trends in factory organisation: he absorbed the current ideas on assembly lines and mass production which were then applied to the Lucas factory in modified form.[11] James Law, managing director of the Richmond Pelaco factory, obtained his inspiration from books rather than first-hand observation. A self-styled 'New Industrialist', he began his scheme for a 'scientifically managed factory' in 1911. According to his own account, he got 'the germ of his ideas from reading Frederick Winslow Taylor's book on "Shop Management" '.[12] Law hastened to add, however, that it was the inspiration only which came from Taylor: the details of his factory organisation were worked out by a process of interaction between the general principles and Australian conditions. Indeed, although Law was fond of promoting the novelty of his system, it is clear that most of his methods regarding work processes were merely refinements of existing practices in Melbourne's other large shirt and collar factories. Other ideas derived not so much from Taylor's inspiration as from the application of Henry Ford's assembly-line techniques to the manufacture of garments. His methods were certainly 'old-fashioned' compared to what was being done in modern American factories.[13]

Nevertheless, Law was on the road to a more thorough-going system of scientific management, but he was still feeling his way during this period for there are indications that he was experimenting with more dramatic changes. His time-and-motion studies built up a groundwork of information from which more revolutionary strategies could be devised. He experimented with the length of work-periods in order to arrive at the optimum length of the working day. Also in Taylorist vein, his reorganisation of the process of laundering the finished product showed a practical determination to standardise work processes, wherever possible replacing 'rule of thumb' practices. It is clear that this entailed separation between conception and execution. Law also took steps to eliminate as much human labour as possible, replacing it where practicable with machinery. In this, however, he was limited by the existing state of technology. Much of the sewing still had to be finished by hand, as the machines were not available to do the work as well as people. Similarly, although electric cutting machines were available from about 1910, these were not sufficiently accurate to suit the better-quality shirt trade.

Apart from the assembly-line sewing process, there is also other evidence that Law was influenced by Fordist ideas. His early adoption of a limited number of standard products is one example. Where Henry Ford concentrated on the T Model automobile, James Law produced twelve types of collars, in contrast to the 197 styles formerly produced by the Pearson, Law Company (Pelaco's ancestor) and its contemporaries. Like Ford, Law also placed great stress on finding the right person for the job, and by his own report had to wait three years to find two girls capable of performing a certain operation on wing-collars in the same way as one particularly highly productive worker already in his employ. Like Ford, he also advocated the payment of high wages if the worker was efficient and productive. Finally, Law's style of management was in many ways reminiscent of Ford's intrusive, paternalistic methods of industrial relations.

Although employers like Price and Law were keen to acquire new ideas and experiment within their own firms, other employers were more conservative. Many were suspicious of what they regarded merely as an 'American fad'. Nor was this difference simply a matter of individual personality or whim: shirt and whitework manufacturers, who came to their positions as entrepreneurs rather than craftsmen, were more prepared to innovate than employers in the tailoring section who more often had served apprenticeships in the trade.

Workers, acting either individually or collectively, also influenced the timing and direction of changes in the workplace. James Law, for instance, stated that 'one of the reasons there has not been so much new machinery and new ideas is that we have not had the co-operation of labour'. When trying his innovations at Pelaco he 'found a great deal of opposition in many branches of our factory'. That this should have been so was perhaps to be expected, considering that Law stated that he introduced the new methods in response to limitation of output on the part of the cutters. Opposition from workers thus delayed Law's schemes until he eventually sacked his recalcitrant workers and replaced them with more compliant ones.[14]

The Clothing Trades Union also resisted the introduction of the team system into order shops, mainly because it saw the subdivision of labour as a prerequisite for the unlimited entry of female workers into tailors' jobs. The union's decision in 1909 to abandon equal pay for women doing tailoring in 'legitimate' shops if it meant encouraging the team system is a clear example of this perspective: the male unionists saw the team system as an even greater incentive to employ female labour than cheaper rates for women.[15] Few women devoted enough time to the trade to acquire the all-round skills possessed by first-class tailors; subdivided work entailed in the team system, by contrast, offered opportunities to more quickly trained labour.

It seems, however, that there was no consistent worker objection to deskilling as a matter of principle. It was rather the consequences of such subdivision for overall pay rates and employment opportunities that mattered. For example, in 1900 a meeting of shirt and collar workers protested against what was essentially a reintegration of the work process. With the move to factory production in preference to outwork, factory machinists were often required to do the finishing as well as the machining, thus displacing those women who had previously done finishing exclusively. Their protest encouraged firms to install special machines for finishers to operate.[16] The issue in this case was very clearly exploitation rather than job control.

This primary concern with exploitation was also endorsed at an official level within the union. As Carter told the 1919 arbitration hearing, 'the members of the claimant Union care not how the work is subdivided if there [sic] wages are not affected thereby or their employment'.[17] Rather than resisting subdivision within the ready-made factories on the grounds that it deskilled operatives, the union argued that the workers became more skilled on each separate operation and therefore deserved additional monetary reward.[18] Subdivided work, the union argued, should be seen as specialised rather than fragmented.

Unionists' campaigns against 'sweating' also led them to support large factories rather than smaller workrooms. This implied an acceptance of 'modern methods'. The union's success in having outdoor piece rates set at a higher rate than those inside tailoring firms led, as we have seen, to a concentration of work in large factories.

Alf Wallis, Clothing Trades Union organiser, carried this policy even further. He argued that shorter hours for the industry were a good thing because they would encourage greater 'efficiency' on the part of manufacturers. He spoke of the 44-hour week, encouraging employers to adopt 'good methods'. There was no doubt what he meant by 'good methods': he referred to Taylor's works on the subject of the division of labour as a guide for those employers who needed instruction.[19] The union hoped that if it supported new methods, workers would share in the increased productivity by receiving higher wages, shorter hours and better conditions. A similar hope was expressed by the treasurer of the Laundry Workers' Union, Miss Rees, a forewoman at Pelaco. At a Christmas party in 1913 she referred to the increase in wages received during the year and 'hoped that with the introduction of the latest improved machinery which their firm proposed to introduce, that a still further advance would be made by the women workers'.[20] Indeed, Law encouraged the belief that any improvements in the lot of shirt workers were due 'mainly to the change in the method of making'.[21] In one sense Law was right, in that the newer methods were more profitable. However, employers did not automatically pass on the increased profits to workers in the form of higher wages. On the contrary, whatever benefits workers received had been fought for. This is very clearly illustrated by the fact that the Shirt Wages Board (on which Law was an employer delegate) prescribed one of the lowest minimum wages despite the more 'advanced' methods which were general in this industry. The CTU recognised that such was the case and organised to extract 'their share' of the benefits from the employers.

Unionists also hoped that more 'efficient' methods would lead not only to increased productivity and profitability, but would also relieve workers of oppressive manual effort. Carter stated that 'the union will always welcome efficiency on the job, and if they can produce without over-exerting themselves, then I say it is a good thing for the country, and a good thing for the unions, . . . and this union is not likely to obstruct the subdivision of labour'.[22] Apart from official union policy, workers also encouraged changes in manufacturing methods in more informal ways. In the case of power sewing machines, one employer claimed that when they were first introduced 'many factories who could not afford to keep up with the times just dropped out of the trade because workers would go to work for the factories that had the power machines to get away from the treadle'.[23] With workers paid by results, whether by piece rates or the task system, anything which enabled them to work faster and expend less energy was obviously attractive. An advertisement which appeared regularly in the *Tocsin* appealed explicitly to the clothing worker's need to produce at speed, although in this case the machine was a new-model treadle:

> One remedy against sweating lies in the use of up-to-date machines in trades where the mechanical is an essential element. White-workers particularly are subject to this principle, and they will thank J. W. Johnston and Co., of 222 Swanston-street, for his Standard Rotary Shuttle Sewing Machine. Its speed is six-stitches to one revolution of the stand wheel, and thus enables the worker to earn a maximum of wage with a minimum of exertion.[24]

Closer experience of powered appliances made some workers less enthusiastic. Mrs Ellen Eckersall, the proprietor of a large shirt factory, reported that she had had 'girls give up the work because of the noise of the machines'. Workers found that, although the treadles were physically more arduous, they placed less stress on one's nerves.[25] However, as the pressure to produce at speed remained, most stayed with the powered models.

The increasing trend for factories to work the forty-eight hours in five days instead of six was also partly a result of individual workers expressing their preference by 'voting with their feet'. Certainly it suited employers, who found that workers did not settle down to work as well on a Saturday morning, but it also suited many workers, especially women and girls, who found Saturday mornings useful for doing domestic chores. It also gave them two whole days away from the factory.[26]

Workers also resisted new methods when they were found to be inconvenient. May Francis records how her objection as a matter of principle to the use of time machines at Craig Williamson's in 1911 initially received little support from the other workers. It was only when they found that the extra time taken to clock off caused some to miss trams and trains that the majority simply refused to co-operate with the innovation and the clocks were abandoned by management.[27]

As in the nineteenth century, workers could influence methods of production indirectly through their passivity as well as through their protests. The low wages set by the early boards in dressmaking, millinery, shirts and whitework were largely the result of poor worker organisation in these sections. Such relatively low wages made certain kinds of mechanisation less attractive than in tailoring. One large shirt manufacturer reported that she 'never found double-felling machines a success' because 'these machines cost us so much'. With labour still so cheap it was more profitable to keep using the more labour-intensive method associated with the older, cheaper machinery.[28]

As this instance suggests, the relative bargaining power of workers and employers influenced the work process by affecting the price of labour. Industrial relations also affected other crucial factors which influenced the profitability of different production methods: the number of juveniles working in the industry; the types of work open to cheaper female labour; and the hours of work. The 1896 Act changed the framework within which these factors were determined, shifting the decision-making arena away from the shop floor to the Wages Board. And whereas any collective agreements prior to the Act were enforced by the parties to the agreement, in the twentieth century the Factories Office performed this function and intervened in other ways in the relationship between capital and labour.

In general, the Wages Board system tended to magnify divisions between employers and to minimise those which divided workers. The necessity to nominate delegates encouraged union organisation. Where unions controlled the selection of delegates, the employees were assured of united representation. Employers were much less united and the importance of board decisions for the trade as a whole made such divisions more serious than in the days before the boards were established.

As in the nineteenth century, different methods of production and different styles of organisation divided employers as a group and provided the scope for strategic alliances between some employers and the unions. The biggest division on the Clothing Board occurred in 1898 between the delegates representing the 500 or so order tailors and those representing the 30 ready-made factories. The manufacturers were outraged when an order tailor (employer) on the board voted with the workers to raise the wages of female labour by 25 per cent so as to reduce the advantage to the ready-made factories, which relied so heavily on cheaper women workers. As Barnet Sniders, a wholesale clothier, put it, 'the interests of the retail [order] tailors are totally opposed to the wholesale [ready-made] traders'.[29]

There were also divisions within the order trade between those employers who used traditional methods and those who adopted subdivision. Carter explained to the Chief Inspector of Factories, Murphy, that 'it is not the usage or custom of reputable employers' to employ the team system on order work. 'Many employers are in favour of some regulation of the mode of manufacture as a protection to legitimate order trade.'[30] He went on to add that such employers were interested in working with the union to prevent innovations in work processes.

Some employers also worked with male unionists on the question of limiting or excluding female employment. This operated at both the formal level of devising Wages Board determinations and at the informal level of workplace practices and policies. As one employer explained to the Arbitration Court in 1919:

> Certainly one of the witnesses told us of three Amazons, who were employed somewhere and who did the work [of pressing] with equal efficiency to men but the foreman there decided he would not have any more Amazons. We are with the Union there, we do not want them, we do not want to use them, or see them employed . . .[31]

A different sort of division along gender lines occurred on the Underclothing Board in 1917, when the two male delegates were incensed at their colleague, Mrs Edith Oliver, voting with the workers. The reason here seems to have been sympathy on the part of Oliver for her fellow women. Although there is evidence of this sentiment within individual firms, as with other divisions between employers, within the context of the Wages Boards this kind of sex solidarity had more profound ramifications.[32]

The effect of the Wages Board system on workers was quite the reverse, encouraging unity rather than division. In the predominantly female branches of the industry, the creation of Wages Boards between 1897 and 1907 to cover these sections sparked off a number of new unions.[33] These were largely the result of an energetic organising campaign by a handful of committed socialist-feminists. Some of the women involved, such as Mrs Minnie Felstead and Miss Ellen Mulcahy, were middle-class feminists with working-class sympathies. Others—such as Mrs Maria Stellner, Mrs Sarah Muir, Miss Minnie Webber and Mrs M. M. Powell—were working-class women, whose industrial agitation grew out of their own experiences as workers in the sewing trades.[34]

Although the existence of Wages Boards fostered the creation of unions, it could not make up for the inherent problems in organising workers in the women's sections. These unions struggled from the outset. Small memberships could not finance paid organisers, and without paid organisers recruitment was slow. The dressmakers and milliners were the hardest to organise, the majority still working in small establishments with pretensions to 'gentility'. (See Table 4.) As one long-time unionist who started work in 1909 recalled, 'in the early days half the girls used to think that if you belonged to the Union you were lowering yourself'.[35] Wallis singled out millinery workers in particular as displaying 'a surfeit of apathy' about their wages and conditions.[36] Factory Inspector Margaret Cuthbertson agreed with his assessment and thought it applied to dressmakers as well. The reason for this apathy was, she believed, the fact that 'so many girls . . . take it up not with the idea of earning a living but because they do not like housework'. Consequently, they were happy with 'seven or eight shillings a week for pocket money'.[37]

Table 4   Number of shirt and dress factories of various sizes, Melbourne, 1909–1910

	Size of factory (No. of workers)						
	4–10	11–20	21–50	51–100	101–200	201–300	Total
Dresses	239	48	32	20	8	3	359
Shirts	14	5	9	2	4	2	36

Source: Calculated from factory returns, Shirt Board History File VPRS 5466/53, and Dress Board History File, VPRS 5466/52.

The union really only existed in the few ready-made firms, which meant that stock workers dominated workers' delegates on the Wages Boards despite their smaller numbers in comparison with workers from order firms.[38]

The growth of large shirt and whitework factories made organisation in these sections potentially easier, but here the union encountered other problems. The most serious of these was the 'new paternalism' which accompanied the 'new industrialism' of men like Edward Price (Lucas and Co.) and James Law (Pelaco). Law, for instance, believed that 'scientific principles' were just as applicable to industrial relations as they were to the manufacture of shirts. He saw strikes as symptomatic of bad management. He argued that 'we handle this labour problem in a very unscientific manner'.[39] Not only were strikes wasteful, but they indicated the existence of a basic mistrust between capital and labour which was also expressed in worker opposition to new methods of work. He believed it was essential to 'sweep away' the 'bitter hatred and mistrust that exists between employers and their employees' before 'Industrial Efficiency' could be achieved.

According to Law, the first step toward industrial harmony was greater intimacy between bosses and workers. Working on the assumption that it was easier to hate a stranger, he urged employers to take steps to get to know their employees better by meeting them in conference, finding out their grievances and acting on them. At the Pelaco factory, monthly meetings were held on Thursday evenings (outside working hours) and were attended by employees in groups of forty or less. On such occasions Law expounded his industrial philosophy, offering high wages and good conditions in exchange for the workers' co-operation. Lest one mistake this concern with philanthropy, Law was quick to deny the suggestion. As he said, 'the benefit to us has been great. Our production cost has come down, our trade has expanded, and our profits have increased.'[40] He went on to explain the more subtle benefits of his scheme, admittedly with some exaggeration:

> We have at the present moment a very happy and contented staff. Altogether about 500 hands are employed in the business—the majority being girls. We have never had a strike, and we have never had any slowing down of work. Our employees are producing more and more, and they are happy as the day is long.[41]

There was little room for unionism in this cosy scheme.

Organising tailoring workers was less daunting. At the time the first Wages Boards were appointed in 1897, there were already a number of unions covering the tailoring trade. Three unions were exclusively male: the Tailors' Protection Society, the Cutters' and Trimmers' Union and the Pressers' Union. Women were catered for by the old

Victorian Tailoresses' Union, covering stock workers, and the newer union, originating in Ballarat in 1890, which covered the order hands. Although all five unions had disintegrated to varying degrees during the depression, the passing of the 1896 Act was a spur to renewed organisation. The necessity of electing workers' delegates and choosing chairmen for the Wages Board gave the unions a new purpose to which they responded eagerly.[42] By the end of 1899 the Tailors' Society had become so strong that it negotiated a 25 per cent increase on the log rates in the city's major tailoring firms. By the following year the society was organising in country towns.[43]

The creation of Wages Boards also encouraged co-operation between the different sectional unions: the Act specified a total number of five workers' representatives, but it did not differentiate between the various job categories in allocating delegates. If the workers were to avoid elections, it was essential that they co-operate to ensure that no more than five candidates were nominated. Political expediency overrode sectional rivalries, and within a decade all of the unions had amalgamated to form the Victorian branch of the Federated Clothing Trades Union.[44]

But although sectional loyalties were relinquished, gender hostility was not. Herbert Carter, union secretary from 1907 to 1925, recalled the attitude of these early male unionists: 'To my own definite knowledge I know that male representatives on these Tribunals [wages boards] deliberately refrained from using their best endeavours to improve the lot of the women mainly on account of sex jealousy in relation to industry.'[45]

The amalgamation of the sectional unions in tailoring in 1907 institutionalised the divisions between men and women. The executive committee comprised two representatives from each section: tailors, tailoresses, pressers and cutters. As women were eligible to represent only the tailoresses, men were in a clear majority throughout the formative years of the Clothing Trades Union. The union's direction in these early years (1907–15) expressed the masculine preoccupation with excluding women. In 1909 the union made a comprehensive effort to obtain equal pay on all 'male' jobs, that is, cutting, pressing and order coat-making. The trade-off for the employers was to be no rise in the weekly wage of the stock tailoresses, and an increase of only one shilling and sixpence in the rate paid to order tailoresses (other than coat-hands).[46] The employers were co-operative. Equal pay would make little difference to their wages bill for pressing and cutting, as so few women were engaged on these jobs. The proportion of women making men's order coats was also small compared to the numbers engaged on trousers and vests and in the stock trade. The equal pay provision would have been passed in its entirety had it not been for a technical problem arising out of one or two firms adopting different methods of manufacture to the rest of the 'legitimate' order tailors. As it was, the men succeeded in having equal pay awarded for both cutting and pressing, and thus effectively stopped the inroads women had begun to make on these occupations in the early years of the twentieth century. It is extremely unlikely that this would have occurred without the Wages Board system to enforce the agreement reached by representatives of employers and workers.

While the Wages Board system reinforced the power of men relative to women in the industry, it also allowed a disproportionate influence to militant and determined workers. This was especially the case in the under-unionised dressmaking, whitework and shirtmaking sections. Without a Wages Board, the efforts of women such as Mrs Margaret Powell, Miss Lesbia Keogh and Miss May Francis would have probably been ineffective in raising general wage levels because of the problems associated with thoroughly organising these industries. As Wages Board delegates, however, they could win improvements regardless of the commitment of their fellow-workers. On the Underclothing Board, for example, the employees, led by May Francis, succeeded in raising the minimum rate by 50 per cent to thirty shillings per week for female machinists. This was higher than any other clothing board determination at the time. For the first time male cutters were provided for and their minimum rate was also higher than cutters in other sections. (See Appendix, Table A7.) They also succeeded in reversing the permitted proportion of juveniles to adult workers, which had been unchanged since the first determination in 1899. Thus, instead of two juveniles to every journeywoman, the 1917 determination specified a limit of one juvenile to every two adults employed. In an industry which was 'essentially a girls' trade', this was a significant alteration. Even though the employers' approach to the Court of Industrial Appeals succeeded in increasing the ratio to 3:2, the new-style unionists had nonetheless upset the status quo, and shaken the employers' hitherto easy domination of their employees.[47]

But while the Wages Boards gave more opportunities to strong worker delegates, there is a sense in which they reinforced the powerlessness of the weak. Obtaining suitable delegates had always been a problem for the poorly unionised women's sections, especially as the workers' delegates were almost always women sitting down to bargain with, in most cases, a male-dominated group of employers and a male chairperson.[48] As May Francis, workers' representative on the Underclothing Board, recalled: 'My colleagues always seemed tonguetied in the presence of the employers . . . '.[49]

The popularity of police magistrates as board chairmen further intimidated female workers, especially when they were of the same type as Notley Moore, who had a reputation for telling 'smutty stories'.[50] The behaviour of some of these chairmen on the boards did little to put the workers at their ease. Francis Reddin, chairman of the Dressmakers Board in 1911, 'sat back in his chair laughing' at the union's claim for an increase in the minimum wage to thirty shillings, and refused to discuss the wages, saying £1 per week was enough for any woman.[51] It required a particularly confident and determined sort of delegate to cope with such behaviour, and unfortunately many were 'unfit'.[52]

With such pressures on delegates, the early Wages Boards for these sections awarded wages considerably below those in the tailoring trade. (See Appendix, Table A7.) As Ord remarked regarding the first determination of the Shirtmakers Board: 'It seems to me to speak volumes for the reasonableness of the employes when such a minimum [16 shillings] for work requiring a considerable amount of skill is accepted.'[53] Abraham Davis, clothing manufacturer of North Melbourne, also blamed the poor quality of the employees' delegates on the Wages Boards for the low minimums in the women's sections: 'It seems that the better representatives the employes get, they better can fight their battle; for instance, there is skilled work required in white work as there is in clothing, yet the white-workers have fixed the minimum at 15s and the clothing [i.e. tailoring] at 20s.'[54]

Dressmakers, particularly those in the order trade, were the most poorly rewarded for their skill. The women themselves complained of the injustice, and the factory inspectors certainly agreed that the disparity bore no relation to any objective notions of the skill involved.[55] Not until 1911 was the minimum wage for dressmakers raised above 16 shillings per week. On this occasion the rate was set at 21s. 6d. This was still lower than any other clothing board minimum except underclothing (whitework). (See Appendix, Table A7.) However, that the workers were successful in gaining even this advance was a tribute to the intervention of the revived Dressmakers' Union. The union secretary, Mrs Minnie Felstead, took great care to select representatives who would be prepared to fight for a higher rate, but as mentioned the delegates faced derision from the chairman, Reddin.[56]

The strength and unity of the workers' delegates on the 1911 Dress Board was, however, atypical of the dress, shirt, whitework and millinery sections. More commonly, early Wages Board delegates lacked the discipline necessary to carry through their demands. The shirtmakers, for instance, lost their claim for a 35-shilling minimum for laundry workers because one of the workers refused to cast her vote either way.[57]

Even when competent representatives could be found, their intermittent work patterns, especially if engaged in outwork, could render them ineligible to sit. Wages Board delegates also risked being sacked by unsympathetic employers, the unions being powerless to resist such victimisation. This further discouraged workers, many of whom were said to be apathetic to begin with.[58] The amalgamation of the women's unions with the Clothing Trades Union during the war helped overcome some of these problems by bringing more disciplined and outspoken delegates to represent the workers on the boards. Although paid union officials were expressly debarred from sitting, they exercised their influence indirectly. As Francis recalled, 'the Union officials assisted us to understand what was required of us'. The delegates were coached in the best way to put together a case, and witnesses were selected who would support them most effectively.[59] In the case of the Milliners' Board, concerted action by the union thwarted a move by employers to have their own candidates returned.[60]

Thus, while the Wages Board system provided little protection for workers who as a group were industrially passive, it magnified the effect of any kind of militancy or organisation, even though this was by a minority of workers. This has been clearly shown in the case of the poorly unionised women's sections of dressmaking, millinery, and underclothing and whitework. Even in tailoring, where unions were well established, there were groups of workers who remained beyond the union's grasp. But whereas before the establishment of the Wages Boards the existence of non-union outworkers thwarted the efforts of unionists to raise wages, under the board system it was possible to set minimum rates for all workers.

The creation of Wages Boards thus influenced the agreements reached between labour and capital, and in giving more power to assertive workers changed the nature of employer–employee relations. Lewis Cohen, clothing manufacturer, complained that 'We used to be always happy, but now it simply amounts to this, on the one side—"I will get from you all I can" and on the other—"I will give you as little as I can in return".'[61] Certainly, the existence of such a tribunal encouraged workers to protest against conditions to which they might otherwise have acquiesced, although many were still reluctant to complain because of well-grounded fears of victimisation.[62] On the other hand, the boards provided a forum for settling disputes between workers and bosses which might otherwise have erupted into strikes.[63] The increasing disillusionment with the Wages Boards after 1909 fuelled the rising level of militancy within the union, particularly during the war years. As Alf Wallis urged union members in 1915, they must 'realize that they would never get justice from the Wages Board, they must fight the employing class by direct action for any real advantage'. The union was not, however, persuaded to abandon state tribunals altogether, transferring its hopes instead to the federal Arbitration Court.[64]

While the machinery of the Wages Boards structured workplace relations, the activities of the staff of the Factories Office also affected these relationships. Individual officers exercised considerable influence over board proceedings. This was particularly so in the case of the women's sections (dresses, millinery, shirts and whitework) where the inspectors sometimes played a key role in the appointment of workers' representatives. The elections to the Whiteworkers' Board in 1910 and 1911 are a clear instance of factory inspectors intervening in proceedings to ensure that 'milk-and-water people', 'too frightened to say anything to the other side of the table' were returned, rather than the more militant nominees of the Whiteworkers' Union.[65]

The Victorian Factories Office and the Wages Boards which it administered were not the only state influences on industrial relations in this era. The state also played a direct role in the clothing trade in its capacity as employer. The letting of government contracts for post office and military uniforms at cheap rates had always attracted bitter criticism of the Victorian government from trade unionists. As Sarah Muir, Wages Board delegate and tailoress, put it, governments were 'the greatest sweaters in existence—they always have been in the clothing trade'.[66] The example of New South Wales in setting up a state clothing factory in 1904 to handle government contracts was followed by the Fisher federal Labor government in 1910. The new Commonwealth Clothing Factory which opened its doors in South Melbourne in 1911 was intended by its founders to be a model of both efficiency and employer justice.[67] Shortly after its opening, *Labor Call* reported that 'the comfort of the girls [sic] working in this establishment is so well attended to that it reminded one more of a girls' sewing class in school than a factory'.[68] Certainly the regulations issued by the federal Cabinet were models for the time. They provided for two weeks' annual leave plus all federal and state holidays on full pay; sick leave on full pay; and time and a half for all work over forty-eight hours per week. A factory medical officer was provided, as well as dining rooms supplying cheap midday meals. The rooms were cooled in summer by electric fans and heated by steam radiators in winter. Lighting was supplied by electric lights, 'painted a pleasing shade of green', and special emergency buttons cut the power to machines at the first sign of accidents.[69]

From the outset, however, the desire of the factory's founders to provide a model for other clothing factories conflicted with the desire to show that such conditions were possible even for firms competing on the open market. This created friction from the very beginning between the manager, Mr Slade, and the workers over rates of pay and task levels. Ironically, the conflicts which ensued between the Defence Department and the Clothing Trades Union over the Commonwealth Clothing Factory (CCF) were more bitter than any previous dispute between workers and capitalists.[70]

The federal government also affected industrial relations in less direct ways. The existence of the Commonwealth Court of Conciliation and Arbitration after 1904 provided an alternative forum for collective bargaining which had ramifications on worker organisation in the clothing industry. The defeat of the union's claim for equal pay on the making of order frock-coats on the 1909 Wages Board provided the immediate impulse for an organisational drive aimed at taking a case to the federal court. It was not just that the union hoped for a more favourable hearing but that it recognised that one of the major obstacles to equal pay in Victoria had been the fear of interstate competition. The only way around this difficulty, the union reasoned, was to obtain a federal award applicable to manufacturers in every state.[71] So in 1910 the Victorian branch embarked on an energetic effort to organise the other states in order to apply to the Commonwealth Court of Conciliation and Arbitration. Herbert Carter, Victorian secretary, also secretary of the federated union, carried on a relentless campaign to persuade the other states of the virtues of the Victorian scheme.[72] Since it was the tailors who stood to gain most from a federal award, they took a leading part in the union's organisation. As Alf Wallis remarked in 1925, 'the tailors influence was in the past years greater than the pressers or cutters. [The] tailors [were] frightened of [the] females . . . '.[73]

As part of this preparation for the federal case, the union started organising women workers with unprecedented enthusiasm.[74] Drawing on the talents and energies of Melbourne's small band of socialist feminists, the union appointed first Miss Ellen Mulcahy and then a Miss Mantach as paid women's organisers on a temporary basis.[75] It also gave enthusiastic support to the Trades Hall Council's Organising Committee in its efforts to organise women between 1907 and 1914, and, more controversially, to the equal pay campaigns organised in conjunction with Vida Goldstein's Women's Political Association.[76]

Until 1915, however, the Clothing Trades Union had made no attempt to organise non-tailoring garment workers. With the outbreak of war in 1914, the union was forced to reconsider its priorities. A new generation of women unionists, more radical than most of its predecessors, demanded that the union adopt a more industrial style in place of its old craft exclusivism. One of the most prominent was May Francis, the daughter of Irish Fenians, who came to socialism via Vida Goldstein's feminism. As secretary to the Militant Propagandists of the Labor Movement, she took an active part in the anti-conscription campaigns of 1916 and 1917. Her brand of socialism favoured a united working-class stand against capitalist oppression. In particular, she attacked craft and sex exclusivism as incompatible with social justice.[77]

Inspired by her beliefs, she urged the union to extend its organisation to cover the 'female' sections of garment-making: dressmaking, millinery, shirtmaking and her own trade, underclothing.[78] At a time when many traditional assumptions were being thrown into question by the European war, her appeal struck a chord. In 1915 and 1916 the Clothing Trades Union absorbed the small unions covering these women's trades.[79] For a brief period between 1915 and 1919 women and men were equally represented on the executive committee. Amongst the new members were such able women as Lesbia Keogh, 'a fragile but strong-minded woman', representing the dressmakers.[80] Graduate of Melbourne University's law school in 1916, Keogh decided that her talents could be of more service to the working class in a factory than a legal firm. Better known as the poet Lesbia Harford, she was a member of the Industrial Workers of the World (IWW) and closely connected with Melbourne's radical Left until leaving for Sydney in 1919.[81] Her obvious abilities as a public speaker assured her rapid rise to prominence in the union. She became a member of the Dressmakers Wages Board in 1916 and vice-president of the union in 1917, the first woman to occupy any official position within the organisation.[82] Together with Francis, she led the move to radicalise the union, organising lecture series for union members and urging the union to give official support for 'working-class campaigns', such as anti-conscription, the 1917 railway strike and the release of the imprisoned IWW members.[83]

Both Keogh and Francis fought to wean the union from what they saw as its sexism, by no means a secondary consideration. The men were prepared to admit the women's sections to membership because they brought with them valuable funds, but they were reluctant to see this turned into a female ascendancy within the official hierarchy of the union. The first organiser appointed to recruit amongst the new sections was a man, John Cain, who secured the position despite much opposition from the women.[84] In the period immediately following amalgamation in 1915 the increase in membership was spectacular. As Carter, somewhat overwhelmed by the response, wrote to one of his colleagues: 'At the present time we cannot cope with the number of women desirous of joining our Organisation.'[85]

By 1916 women comprised over 85 per cent of the union's membership, but still the 'old guard' resisted the appointment of a female organiser. As Francis herself points out, the appointment of Miss Lillian Whitford in April 1917 was more the result of a 'fluke' than any fundamental change in the union's position.[86]

The issue of the female organiser also illustrates the underlying motive behind the union's official support for equal pay for the sexes. Despite repeated calls for Whitford to be paid the same rate as the male organisers, the request was rejected. Whitford eventually resigned over this issue, complaining that she was the worst-paid official at Trades Hall.[87] The bulk of the funds and energies of the union continued to be devoted to the tailoring section, even though by 1918 its members were in a minority.[88] Such official neglect did little to counter the hostility of employers in the non-tailoring sections, who continued with impunity to victimise and blacklist workers who joined the union.[89]

Gender divisions thus limited the CTU's effectiveness in advancing the position of its female members, especially those in dressmaking, millinery, shirtmaking and whitework. However, the all-women unions which preceded the amalgamations of the war period also had limited success, and merging with the tailoring unionists helped overcome some of their earlier difficulties. It also placed workers in a stronger position to resist the powerful blend of paternalism and patriotism which developed in many clothing firms during the war. The Lucas Company of Ballarat is an outstanding example of the way in which patriotism was mobilised in the cause of industrial peace as well as military effectiveness. Edward Price, who assumed control of the company on his mother's retirement in 1915, was a believer in 'the principles of efficiency' and shared James Law's faith in the personal touch in industrial relations. But Price added a further dimension to this intimacy. As early as 1910 a bonus system was in operation whereby workers were rewarded at Christmas for extra output during the year.[90] The company historian maintains that 'comradeship in work and shared belief in community service' were the formula that ensured sound relations between management and labour. She was referring specifically to the Lucas Company's efforts during the Great War. The 'Lucas Girls' were given every 'encouragement' to raise funds for troop comforts. The famous Ballarat Avenue of Honour is claimed to be the inspiration of Mrs 'Tilly' Thompson, Price's 'lieutenant'; the workers at Lucas' factory raised £10,600 towards the cost of the trees and their plaques. The first instalment of money was the proceeds of a football match waged between the Lucas Girls and the Khaki Girls of Melbourne.[91] Price's eldest daughter was a member of this team. The workers were also allowed to leave their machines to welcome and farewell troop trains, although they then had to make up the lost time before going home at night. The purpose of all this ostentatious patriotic activity was to encourage 'loyalty', both to the firm and its values. Like Law, Price attempted to convince his workers that their interests were identical to his own, and that unions were therefore irrelevant.

The small sectional unions in existence before the amalgamation were ill equipped to deal with such energetic methods on the part of the leading firms in the industry. And these firms were by no means isolated examples of such methods; the other leading shirt and whitework firms also appear to have shared their approach.[92] It was not until these unions amalgamated with the CTU that any serious challenge was mounted to the employer hegemony in these sections. Organising campaigns in 1917 seem to have had some effect in unionising 'a large number of young ladies' from Lucas' factory.[93]

Ironically, the CTU had less success in resisting patriotic fervour at the Commonwealth Clothing Factory during the war. The first serious difficulty arose in 1916, with both the cutters and the machinists complaining that the manager paid the workers disproportionately. Some workers were set higher tasks than others, whilst the senior cutters claimed they were given no additional payment despite their extra responsibilities. Slade, they said, 'is not a fair-minded man'.[94] To complicate matters, there were also problems caused by the introduction of new methods of work. The management sought to balance productivity with justice by adopting the latest technology and methods of manufacture. As a result, Slade attempted to introduce machines to do both pressing and finishing. In both cases the workers resisted the new methods because they displaced workers.[95]

The Defence Department, represented by Senator Pearce, portrayed the dissatisfaction as the work of 'pro-German elements in the factory'.[96] The *Argus* took up the cry, stating that 'the state of the factory walls and the pavements around the factory' were evidence of the existence of anti-conscriptionist elements in the factory.[97] The Defence Department went so far as to employ blacklegs and government inspectors in an attempt to break the strike.[98] It also endorsed Slade's antagonism to the union in a letter to the union secretary: 'Mr. Slade states he is at all times willing to hear any appeals or complaints, provided that they are made direct to himself and not through Mr Carter [CTU Secretary]. The reasonableness of this will of course be readily recognised.'[99]

Despite strong support for the cutters' strike from the 600 workers at the factory, the union was unable to resist the determined fight put up by Slade and the Defence

Department.[100] In the case of the finishers, the union adopted a different approach and called in the Trades Hall Council's Industrial Disputes Committee to settle the strike. The results were again disappointing for the workers. The Minister considered the matter 'trivial' and the IDC appeared to take it only marginally more seriously. They agreed between them that the strikers should return to work on the management's terms and that 'no one would be put off where it possibly could be avoided'.[101]

After these defeats the union's influence at the factory declined rapidly. According to one worker, the union was 'a dead letter as far as the Commonwealth Clothing Factory was concerned'. The 'anti-conscription elements' were overshadowed by the dashing displays of the 'Khaki Girls', a patriotic band of women from the CCF who devoted their spare time to fundraising and recruiting for the war effort.[102] When Wallis attempted to address the workers in the dining room in July 1918 he was forcibly removed by two military officers and forbidden to return.[103] The direct authority of the Minister was by then replaced by the Board of Business Management of the Defence Department, but in practical terms there was little difference between the rule of Labor Senator Pearce and the virulently anti-Labor H. V. McKay who dominated the new board.[104] The workers at the Commonwealth Clothing Factory had learnt, as had the railway workers in New South Wales, that state-run enterprises were just as prepared to attack workers' conditions as any private firm. While the Lucas Girls and the Khaki Girls played football to raise money for the war effort, their employers, capitalist and state socialist, also met on the common ground of 'patriotism'.

While the war in Europe and the activities of the state both had profound effects on industrial relations in the clothing trade, the condition of the labour market continued to have an important effect as well. The general economic recovery from the late 1890s made the climate for unionism more favourable, whilst also encouraging more informal kinds of worker resistance. This was especially so when workers knew they were not easily replaced, such as in the seasonal rush from spring to Christmas. The generally improved state of trade in all the sewing sections from the early twentieth century to the 1914–18 war also favoured worker defiance. This took various forms. Employers complained that with the shortage of female labour workers were becoming too independent. Factory Inspector Collopy reported in 1909 that 'on account of the difficulty in obtaining labour, girls are very often independent and careless at their work, and manufacturers say they are frequently afraid to interfere, because they fear that the girls may leave them'.[105]

Factory-based strikes also occurred, such as the one referred to above over the issue of the installation of new machines for finishing which displaced hand-finishing of shirts.[106] Collective bargaining at the factory level was also directed at raising rates of pay. Mrs Margaret Powell referred to 'all our contentions and fights with Mr Keleher over prices'.[107] (Keleher was the manager of Foy and Gibson's clothing factories.) The women's bargaining no doubt explains in part why even whiteworkers at Foy and Gibson received what unionists considered 'a fair wage'.[108]

There are also hints of other, less easily categorised forms of group protest. As one employer reported, 'the only trouble we have is a little hysteria'.[109] No doubt everyone but the manager appreciated the release such episodes afforded to the tension of working under pressure with hundreds of machines filling the air with their whirr and clatter.

The singing which employers liked to think of as evidence of a happy and contented workforce could also be used to make life uncomfortable for the boss: women vied with each other to think up the most humiliating words to accompany popular tunes.[110] Throwing reels of thread at unpopular supervisors was a more individual expression of workers' exasperation with their conditions.[111] When labour was in short supply, it was also possible for individuals to extract concessions from employers by threatening to leave for 'greener pastures'. As an employer expressed it, girls were 'becoming more alive to their worth'. Another told of workers engaging in informal productivity bargaining, citing 'constant instances' of girls accompanying their requests for pay rises with 'the frank admission that they *could* do more work, and that if the rise were granted they *would*'.[112] And according to Ernest Aves, enquiring into the Wages Board system for the British Government, the return of prosperity after the turn of the century put a natural break on the imposition of tasks. He maintained that by 1906–08 things were 'finding their level' as workers learnt to measure and regulate their output more effectively.[113]

In the final analysis, however, the Wages Board era had been a disappointing one for workers. Initial wage increases were accompanied by more intensive workloads despite the moderating effect of 'pacing'; and rather than the state assisting the most exploited workers it quickly became apparent that the strongest workers extracted the greatest rewards from the system. And as the century entered its second decade, other limitations with the system became apparent. Most importantly, Wages Board decisions had no jurisdiction outside the state of Victoria; the pace of change was thus limited by the need for Victorian industry to remain competitive with neighbouring states.

The rapid inflation of the war period and the government's reluctance to allow cost-of-living increases to flow on to wages caused further dissatisfaction. By 1919–20 inflation had eroded real wages to such an extent that wages and salaries in the clothing trade constituted a mere 52.1 per cent of net value added, compared to 66.5 per cent in 1908.[114] But undeterred by these experiences, workers turned once more to a state body for relief, this time the Commonwealth Court of Conciliation and Arbitration.

5

THE WORKERS BAFFLED: THE BOOT INDUSTRY, 1897–1910

Despite the advent of Wages Boards, the market for footwear continued to play a major role in shaping the work process in the Victorian boot and shoe industry. The economic recovery of the late 1890s was hampered in the boot trade by the rising price of leather. The last few years of the century were particularly uncertain. Exports fell, and many manufacturers stockpiled goods against further increases in the price of leather and expected wage increases as a result of the Wages Boards. Even after federation the industry faltered. The increase in interstate trade as a result of the Commonwealth tariff doubled Victoria's exports of footwear in 1902, but the following years were not ones of steady and uniform growth. Drought caused a downturn towards the end of 1902, and uneven tariffs caused problems for manufacturers of certain lines, particularly children's shoes. The years between 1904 and 1907 were generally better, with manufacturers extending their premises and putting in new equipment. By 1908, however, the post-federation boom was virtually over. Rising leather prices again caused disruption; more serious was the increasing competition from neighbouring states.[1]

The intense competition which characterised the industry in the 1880s and 1890s thus continued into the first decade of the twentieth century. Unlike sections of the clothing trade, where the Wages Board determinations signalled a new direction in manufacturing practices, in the boot industry competitive employers responded to the new conditions by intensifying their depression strategies. Those without machinery either acquired it or closed down, whilst those already mechanised were ever willing to install the latest devices supplied by the British United Shoe Machinery Company (USMC).[2]

The most significant development in boot and shoe machinery during this period was the consolidation of the role of the United Shoe Machinery Company. Arriving in Victoria with its Goodyear welter in 1891, the company initially sold its products as well as

The Methods of Fifty Years Ago.

THE use of Machinery and Modern Methods enable men to make better shoes, and more of them, and have progressed from one triumph to another.

We are constantly endeavouring to produce the best, not only in machines, but in the supplies that are used with them, and are always ready to demonstrate their value by test. We also employ the most expert technical knowledge that it is possible to obtain.

If you have problems, in the solution of which we can assist, a word from you will be sufficient. If there is any information you desire to obtain regarding the best machines, and the most progressive methods, our services are yours to command.

THE UNITED SHOE MACHINERY CO.

83 CLARENCE STREET, SYDNEY.   28 ST. FRANCIS ST., MELBOURNE.

9 A USMC advertisement of the early twentieth century would have had a mixed appeal to Victoria's bootmakers. There were many amongst the ranks of both masters and men who felt a nostalgia for the quieter 'methods of fifty years ago' and the days when the shoemaker's shop served as a centre for political discussion (note the notice of a 'Town Meeting' on the wall).
Australian Leather Journal, 15 December 1905, p. 523. (State Library of Victoria)

leasing them. By 1900 it had perfected its royalty system whereby machines were available only for lease, with payments fixed according to the output of each machine.[3]

At first sight the USMC's terms seemed irresistible. It cost a manufacturer almost nothing to acquire the very latest in bootmaking technology and, as royalties were tied to output, the manufacturer need not fear the burdens of meeting time-payments during slack periods. It soon became obvious, however, that the scheme had its drawbacks. Most important was the condition that the manufacturer agree to use USMC machinery

10   The new Rex pulling-over system, 1905. This picture shows the 'system's' key features: subdivision of the process of pulling-over, with each subdivision tied to a different machine. Although women are shown here as part of the 'team', Victorian boot manufacturers did not exploit this aspect of the system which was promoted by the scheme's developers as a further advantage in cheapening production costs. *Australian Leather Journal*, 15 June 1905, p. 66. (State Library of Victoria)

exclusively. Furthermore, replacement parts could be secured only from the company, allegedly at inflated prices. Despite these drawbacks, the leasing system did enable Victorian factories to keep abreast of the latest developments in boot machinery.[4]

Most of these developments were refinements of former models, with adaptations to improve the quality of work or their ease of operation, as well as adding even further subdivisions. The Goodyear welter and Blake sole-sewer were still the key pieces of equipment in the making room. The development from 1905 of a mechanised and subdivided method of pulling-over, known as the Rex system, completed the mechanisation of making.[5] In 1906 the *Argus* reported of bootmaking that 'there is probably no manufacture in Australia in which specialisation and the perfection of parts have been carried to a higher degree'.[6] The clicking room, formerly the least mechanised section, experienced a dramatic change in methods with use of presses for cutting uppers from 1907. The invention of machines for folding uppers prior to sewing provided the first major innovation in women's work since the introduction of the sewing machine. From the turn of the century these new appliances were increasingly powered by electricity instead of gas or steam.[7]

Although electricity and the latest American appliances imparted a 'modern' air to the early-twentieth-century boot factory, the most significant innovation was in methods rather than machines.[8] Subdivision of the work process was a feature of the mechanised factory from the outset but in this period the most up-to-date factories carried the process further, applying it to management as well as the shop floor. The separation of conception and execution, of mental and manual work, which is implied in the increasing subdivision of tasks was systematised during this period. The boot operative, who in the past had a working knowledge of the general processes involved in constructing a boot, was left with only a small part of this understanding. As a Victorian writer for the *Australian Leather Journal* commented in 1902: 'With the exception of the clicking room and rough stuff rooms, bootmaking is merely an assembling of parts, in the manufacture of which the boot operative takes no part, and by the aid of machinery with the construction of which also he has had nothing to do.'[9] This writer went on to point out that if the operatives need less knowledge, foremen and superintendents 'have nowadays far greater responsibilities than formerly'. Not only were foremen expected to assume the burden of the operatives' displaced knowledge but they were also held responsible for the discipline of the workers in their charge. As 'Boomerang', another Australian writer on modern methods, explained, the foreman 'should also be a strict disciplinarian, and allow no "larking" or unnecessary talking during working hours'.[10] The stricter discipline demanded in the modern factory extended to other forms of 'unnecessary' behaviour: 'Allow no smoking, as it is disgusting, and a positive disgrace to any manager when strangers enter and see men wasting their employer's time puffing or chewing tobacco.'[11]

The concern to make the most economical use of the 'employer's time' was evident in the increased monitoring of the worker's daily activity. At a general meeting of the Bootmakers' Union in 1900 it was reported that 'machine Telltales' had been introduced into the shops and a record of the time starting and leaving was kept by them, 'also the time taken at the W.C.'.[12] Other bureaucratic methods were also recommended. 'Boomerang' advocated the issuing of printed slips to the men so that the foreman could tell 'if any of them are not "earning their salt" '.[13] Naturally, such a system would impose additional demands on foremen so that large factories would find it necessary to appoint a clerk to assist in the extra accounting.[14]

All this monitoring, however, would have been ineffective in saving labour without attention to the basic principles of modern factory management. According to 'Boomerang', the first of these was the careful selection of workers and their specialisation in particular tasks. Believing that 'every man is made to perform some particular duty in the world', he urged managers to 'see that you get the right duty fixed upon the right man'.[15] Some men, it seems, were born to spend their lives on the end of an American loose-nailing machine. This being the case, they should be kept at the one class of work as much as possible so as 'to get through more work and be more efficient than one who is being continually shifted from one thing to another'.[16]

Extending this principle of finding the 'right' person for the job, tasks would be graded according to the skill they demanded of the operative and work allocated accordingly. For example, in the clicking room men would cut the good work; improvers would cut the common work; boys and girls would be employed cutting linings and tending small labour-saving machines.[17]

Speeding-up accompanied this process of fragmentation. With machines placed so as to ensure an uninterrupted flow of work, workers were kept at maximum pace by the operation of the team system on weekly wages. Under this system each worker had to work quickly and constantly to avoid holding up the team's work. The task system ensured that the team as a whole worked hard in order to fulfil its quota. As 'Boomerang' pointed out in his discussion of the putting-up (making) department: 'You will find it to your advantage and profit if you work the whole of this room under the system, especially if you determine to have good, quick workmen who are companiable with each other, and will willingly look into each other's ways.'[18]

The machining and fitting room, being female territory, presented peculiar problems to factory disciplinarians. This was largely because of the perceived 'nature' of the female sex: along with the pig and the hen, woman had a nature which was always in opposition. In order to counter this tendency, 'Boomerang' advocated the employment of 'a good piece of domestic diplomacy'. Foremen were to treat their female workers with the same skills they employed in the home in order 'to get a woman to do what you wish'. Thus, it was no use appointing 'a big, clumsy lout of a man as overseer of machinists and fitters ... or you will have half your girls in tears and the other half as obstinate as mules', which in either case means a great loss of time.[19]

But it seems that women's affinity with pigs, hens and mules was not the end of the problem. 'Boomerang' also advised foremen to keep all materials under lock and key, as 'many girls are like magpies, whose acquisitiveness amounts almost to an act of theft'. In fact, the difficulties in making this female department profitable seemed altogether too daunting. 'Boomerang' claimed that he knew of no factory able to show a profit on its fitting and machining room. This, he believed, was largely the result of the restricted supply of female labour in Australia. 'You cannot "make a silk purse out of a sow's ear",' the columnist concluded.[20]

All this represented a more systematic and 'scientific' approach to management than that applied in the nineteenth century. It still, however, lagged behind methods in America's most up-to-date factories. Here the process of separating conception and execution was carried a step further. Instead of the employer's relying on the personal supervision of the foreman, there was 'a desire completely to anticipate all supervision from the office'. For instance, the subdivision of orders into convenient departmental quantities was made in the office rather than by the departmental foremen, thus placing greater dependence on office routine. The foreman, thus freed from such decision-making, was able 'to confine his attention to the criticism of the work, and, in smaller firms, [it enabled] the abolition of the foreman altogether'.[21]

Victorian factories were also less specialised than American firms, although after federation there was a dramatic change in this respect. Whereas factories in the 1890s produced up to sixty different styles of footwear, by the early twentieth century most had restricted themselves to producing styles within the one grade, such as pumps, bricks or children's.[22]

In general terms, the market for boots and shoes thus continued to play an important part in shaping the work process and the nature of the industry by creating a situation in which manufacturers sought new ways to remain competitive. It would be misleading, however, to suggest that employers were free to choose whichever strategies suited them best. As in the nineteenth century, workers could and did affect the decisions made about the work process. But for both workers and employers, the 1896 Factories Act marked a significant departure in industrial relations. Whilst previously their conflicts had been settled on the shop floor and picket-line, after 1896 they became focused on the meetings of the Wages Board. The issues, however, were unchanged: How was work to be organised? Who was to make this decision? How hard would employees have to work and for what reward? Mutually acceptable answers were to prove elusive.

In November 1897 the Wages Board, in which the bootmakers had placed so much hope, overturned its original 45-shilling minimum wage for adult males and replaced it with a mere 36 shillings. Union Secretary Billson, usually the voice of moderation and compromise, was bitterly disappointed. As he told the Trades Hall Council:

> The law, the Government and the manufacturers all seemed in league to baffle the workers. The workers had been peaceful and keeping clear of strikes in order to secure for themselves a fair minimum wage under the Factories Act, but the very fact of their being peaceable and submissive had been taken advantage of.[23]

Billson certainly had ample grounds for complaint. The union had persuaded its membership to avoid strikes in the hope of a more 'civilised' solution to their grievances. Although the 1896 Factories Act was not all they hoped it would be, it nevertheless did provide for the creation of Wages Boards, offering some prospect of a negotiated peace. But the deficiencies in the Wages Board system were obvious from the very first sitting. Employers and employees viewed each other with uncompromising hostility, unable to agree on any major points. This left the chairman, police magistrate J. Keogh, in the position of arbitrator: his casting vote decided every point at issue. As he was very well aware, his lack of practical experience was a significant deficiency in arriving at an informed decision.[24]

When the first determination was announced towards the end of 1897, more serious flaws in the system, from the workers' point of view, were exposed. The majority of employers immediately protested to the Chief Secretary against what they saw as an impossibly high male minimum wage of 45 shillings per week. The Chief Secretary, Alexander Peacock, responded to their appeal by invoking the provisions of the Act giving him power to suspend the determination for a period of up to six months. In the meantime, he referred the question of the minimum wage back to the board, again placing the onus on the chairman to reach a decision. Keogh, after hearing further evidence, decided to vote with the employers, reducing the minimum to 36 shillings. To unionists, the employers' arguments reeked with hypocrisy. William Greenwood, Bedggood's manager, argued that a minimum of around 35 shillings would be more effective as it was so low 'it would not pay a man to try and get the better of that wage'. Hugh Thomson suggested that 'the result of raising the minimum to such an extreme [45 shillings] would mean that the men would be over-wrought'. John Abrahams complained that Victorian manufacturers could not make goods cheap enough to compete with the protected local product in Western Australia. He added that he 'was positive that 35 shillings was not enough for a man to live on but he must take into consideration the state of the trade'. Evading the question of how he intended to operate his factory with labour unable to live, he also pushed the humanitarian line that the 45-shilling minimum would increase sweating by forcing employers 'to sell the material to the men and buy back the goods'. That such transparently self-interested arguments were the ones which swayed Keogh raised serious doubts in workers' minds about the benefits of the whole system.[25]

For the unionists, this defeat seemed far more serious than any they had suffered during strikes or lockouts. The employers had, in effect, turned the workers' final weapon against them. For some the irony was too much. Chummy Fleming, for instance, left the union to start a 'little repairing shop'. He gave as his reason for leaving the union that he 'had fought and suffered with it' but he 'would not work for a scab's wage of 36 shillings'. He added that 'a number of the old fighters who had been in the [1884] lock-out also left the Union'.[26]

Nor did the task of rallying the newer members prove any easier. Thomas Walker complained at a union meeting that 'there was not a spark of unionism in the whole trade. It had all been crushed out of them.'[27] Committee member Robert Solly agreed with this assessment, saying that 'unless the bootmakers were prepared to fight as their forefathers did . . . they deserved no better treatment than was being meted out to them by Parliament and those entrusted with the administration of the Factories Act'.[28] However, as Billson pointed out, it was more than 'vitality and fighting spirit' that was needed: 'The operatives, instead of combining solidly and fighting vigorously, divided themselves into sections, said nasty things about each other and permitted the Fat-man . . . to sit back in his easy chair, smile and laugh up his sleeve at their weaknesses and disunion.'

There was, indeed, a distinct lack of co-operation between the Bootmakers' Union and the Clickers' Union. This continued after the amalgamation of the two sections in 1897, the clickers distinguishing themselves by their lack of general interest in union affairs. The fact that the makers and finishers, the mainstay of the union, considered the clickers 'were not taking the interest in organisation that they should do' caused considerable resentment. Indeed, one member accused them of being a 'mean lot of Skunks' for accepting higher wages fought for by other sections.[29] On occasions even the makers and finishers failed to present a united front. An attempt by the finishers at Hyams' factory in 1898 to obtain 'better wages and abolition of task system' failed when the makers refused to support them, even though they 'agreed that the Finishers were right'.[30]

The 'female branch' was separate again, with each of the male sections vying with the other for the women's patronage at Wages Board elections.[31] Unlike the tailoresses, the female boot operatives did not elect female delegates, putting their trust in the men to represent their interests. Their trust was sometimes misplaced, as the 'misappropriation' of the branch's funds by the honorary male treasurer and secretary showed.[32]

Nor did the 1896 Act initially encourage co-operation among these sectional unions in the same way as it did in the clothing trades. Rather, it fanned the flames of rivalry . The disappointment accompanying the fate of the first determination promoted apathy and despair rather than the 'strong, united, vigorous and determined fight' for which the union leadership called.[33] The 'mass meetings' organised by the union to consider the factories legislation during 1899 and 1900 were a grim reminder of this apathy, often attracting as few as 20 or 30 out of a total membership of more than 900. The union was so weak that when breaches of the Factories Act were discovered it responded by taking the employees concerned out of the factory and providing them with funds until alternative employment could be found. Victimised unionists were similarly assisted.[34]

The efforts of the 'old fighters' to inspire resistance to the 36-shilling minimum did, however, bear some fruit. Although disappointing by the standards of earlier campaigns, sufficient support was forthcoming to sustain 'constant complaints and representations' to the Chief Secretary until a revised determination was brought in in July 1898.[35] Although not restoring the 45-shilling minimum, it raised it significantly to 42 shillings. Considering the alternative most workers seemed reconciled to this rate. Furthermore, the vexed questions of boy labour and female labour had been settled with a reasonable degree of satisfaction, at least to the adult male workers. Ironically, this apparent victory encouraged complacency rather than militancy amongst boot operatives in general.

The effect of these early determinations on the unionisation of the female workers was particularly important. As long as women presented some threat to the general wage standards in boot factories, the men were anxious to encourage their organisation. This became an even higher priority once the minimum was declared, some employers preferring to employ cheaper female labour rather than pay even the meagre amount of 36 shillings to a man. The workers' delegates had been instructed to raise the matter on the Wages Board in order to 'settle the Question of Defining Females work in the Factories'.[36] The encroachments were on the 'male' departments of making and finishing, the men being determined to 'do Their best to stop it if possible'.[37]

Not surprisingly, the employers were less than enthusiastic about the union's attempt to fix a clear line of demarcation between men's and women's work. After several months' negotiations the union agreed to raise the age at which lads could be considered 'improvers' to twenty-one (instead of eighteen) on condition that the employers would agree 'to restrict the Employment of Females to machining and fitting department'.[38] The new determination, effective from 18 July 1898, thus provided for equal pay on all the major male work. Although in the trade-off 'the age limit[s] for both Males and Females had been so altered as to nullify their effect', the union hoped that the ratios limiting juvenile employment would prevent excessive use of boy labour.[39]

The men were effective in their attempt to restrict female labour to traditional 'female' work. Despite the increase in the percentage of boot workers who were female from 29.2 in 1898 to 36.9 in 1910, there was no significant shift in the sexual division of labour. (See Appendix, Table A8.) Male unionists, ever alert to attempts by employers to break down this division, in 1910 could find only 'one or two instances in Victoria where girls were doing male work'.[40] The increasing proportion of women employed is explained by the continuing advances in 'labour-saving' machinery for men's work compared to the lack of innovation in machinery for sewing uppers.[41]

Having disposed of any threat females presented to male jobs, the union officials and executive, all of whom were males, virtually ignored the female membership. As male rates of pay gradually crept up over the next ten years, first to 45 and then to 48 shillings, females received no advance on their original 20 shillings. There is no evidence of any female involvement in Wages Board cases after the original case in 1897. Little effort was made to organise women, despite several requests by female members for official action. When the THC wrote to the VOBU in 1905 regarding organisation of females, it 'was decided to ask Shop Presidents to endeavour to get two or three and report to next mtg'.[42] None reported back. In view of the fact that the male unionists were supposed to be representing their female workmates on the Wages Board, it is quite alarming to read a 1907 Federal Conference resolution which regretted that the 'absolute lack of organisation prevents us at this juncture drawing up conditions of labour, etc., for [female] departments'.[43] In fact, when the union finally reached the federal Arbitration Court in 1909 it made no claim at all on behalf of its female members, although there was 'plenty of evidence of the necessity of and the desire of the Females to get an alteration of the unsatisfactory conditions'. The reason given was that their small numbers meant 'little hope of success at the present juncture'.[44]

Women members were even denied the roles traditionally accorded to them in labour circles. When the Children's Hospital Bazaar Committee asked the union to nominate two female representatives, Mrs Billson and Mrs Solly, wives of the secretary and president respectively, were chosen.[45] Similarly, on union social occasions the 'Wives of the Members of the Executive' were invited to act as the refreshment committee.[46]

The neglect of women by male unionists was made easier by the high turnover of female workers. In 1901, 53.5 per cent of female boot workers were under twenty-one years of age.[47] By 1906 the figure was approximately 60 per cent.[48] As with the sections of the clothing trade where juveniles predominated, unionisation of such workers was difficult even where the will to organise existed. All the women active in the 'Female Branch' before its amalgamation with the VOBU were single.[49] This fact, and the general youth of the female workers no doubt made it easier for the men to patronise them. Indeed, it was the women themselves who unanimously voted for a male unionist to represent them on the Wages Board rather than a member of their own sex. They also sought men to act as officials.[50] It would probably not have surprised the female unionists that the men took it upon themselves to 'guarantee that no intoxicating Drink should come in the Hall' during a social evening held by the Female Boot Operatives Union in 1896.[51]

Part of the problem in sustaining a union movement for men and women arose from the very novelty of the situation. Boot workers were the first in Victoria to attempt such a thing. Indeed, the male unionists agreed to amalgamate with the women only on condition that the 'Trades Hall will permit of mixed meetings (Male and Female)'.[52] While the rules proved amenable, it was probably more difficult for women to penetrate the intensely masculine milieu of the union meeting.

Left to their own devices, female boot operatives for the most part reverted to the limited, more spontaneous protests of pre-union days. For instance, when one young woman was sacked without explanation in 1899, rather than appeal to the union, she had her mother tackle the proprietor directly. The incident resulted in the mother, Alice Niebert, bringing an assault charge against the manufacturer after he struck her with a heel planer and 'kicked her into the street'. In his defence he argued that the complainant was excited 'and commenced bullying him, and refused to leave the shop'.[53] The 'magpie acquisitiveness' complained of by employers could also be seen as an individualist response to the failure of the official bodies to award reasonable wages to female workers.

The problem of boy labour was not so easily resolved to the satisfaction of the men. From the union's point of view, the employment of boys on 'some monotonous process of machine service, in which the only promotion possible for the human being is to become a machine himself', was not only detrimental to the youths concerned but also in the long run undermined the bootmakers' claim to a skilled rate of pay.[54] Unable to restrict entry to his occupation or to insist on standards of training, the bootmaker was unable to maintain rates of pay which his former monopoly of skills made possible. Indeed, by the early twentieth century the new regime had so devalued his skills that he was paid less than a builder's labourer.[55] The discrepancy between bootmakers and other tradesmen was even greater. Cabinet makers, for instance, who were awarded the same minimum as bootmakers under the Wages Board in 1897 (45 shillings) were by 1909 receiving 64 shillings per week compared to only 48 shillings being paid to bootmakers.[56] The fact that under the Wages Boards employers were obliged to provide grindings, colours, power and equipment was little compensation for this decline in status and remuneration. The 1896 Factory Act had done little to prevent this process of deskilling. The proportional limitation on the apprentices and improvers who could be employed, provided for by the very first determination, offered only a temporary check to the growing practice of using boys instead of men. Even supposedly reputable employers like the Bedggoods made no secret of their preference for cheaper juvenile labour. As John Bedggood reasoned: 'At 20 they are called "improvers" and get 20s a week, and at 21 the law makes them "adults", and forces us to pay them a minimum wage of £2/2/- a week . . . . so we get rid of them.'[57] An influential section of boot employers was thus determined either to overturn the Factories Act altogether or else get rid of the apprenticeship clauses. From the turn of the century these employers joined with others in the Victorian Employers Federation, which was formed from a desire to counter the Wages Board legislation. It is significant that boot manufacturers such as T. Y. Harkness and J. S. M. Thompson were prominent in the affairs of the VEF.[58]

It was this anti-labour offensive on the part of employers which finally aroused the Bootmakers Union from its apathy. The early years of the century saw a Trades Hall industrial organising campaign initiated by Fleming on behalf of the bootmakers.[59] The program of 'shop-by-shop organisation of the trade' included an attempt to reorganise country centres, which met with mixed results. As in the 1890s, attempts to organise Geelong bootmakers were not successful.[60]

The success of the employers in having the apprenticeship restrictions lifted in 1903 was the signal for a renewed effort. In its desire for a 'thorough organisation', the union 'was prepared to take all and sundry into the fold Women Boys and Men . . . '[61] Significantly, special provisions were made to attract boys to union membership.[62] The task was not an easy one, however; the secretary found that some workers required 'a little more Independent Spirit' as they refused to join the union until receiving a guarantee that their employers were not hostile.[63] Nevertheless, the union pressed on, a committee on boy labour and the 'ever-increasing task system' vowing to 'try and force' a remedy should the law fail to do so.[64]

Identifying the legislature as a crucial arena of conflict, the bootmakers determined to get more sound Labor men returned to state parliament. Indeed, two of their own number, J. W. Billson and Robert Solly, were successful candidates. The union was also an enthusiastic supporter of Tom Mann, urging the Trades Hall to engage his organising skills in order to boost the Labor vote. The connection between the appointment of Tom Mann, the return of Labor to state parliament and the control of boy labour was explicitly made in a report by VOBU secretary Long in 1904.[65] Plans for a federal union, until then merely dreams of a few visionaries, were given priority on the union agenda. The setting up of the Commonwealth Court of Conciliation and Arbitration in 1904 held out the prospect of a more sympathetic hearing than that experienced in the Wages Boards.

The campaign for industrial federation was also stimulated by the political federation of the colonies in 1901. Until then, employer arguments against wage increases out of consideration for their intercolonial trade had had relatively little force in protectionist Victoria. The Commonwealth changed all this. Uniform duties on overseas imports and free trade between the states gave employers a much stronger case for keeping Victorian wage rates at least on a par with those in rival states.[66] The fact that New South Wales had no apprenticeship restrictions also created problems for unionists seeking to limit juvenile labour in Victoria. A federal award, providing uniform conditions throughout Australia, would thus overcome objections to improved wages and conditions on the basis that such improvements would disadvantage Victoria's manufacturers in competition with other states with lower standards.

A further reason for the union's enthusiasm for federal arbitration was the failure of the Wages Board to provide any check on the use of the team system and the 'brutal and vicious system of weekly wages' to speed up workers.[67] The method of payment played an important part in intensifying work. The mechanisation of factories was from the outset accompanied by the use of weekly wages. This practice continued into the twentieth century in Melbourne factories, and was invariably accompanied by set tasks designed to force the pace of work.[68] The effectiveness of this system in speeding up workers was all too obvious to employers, who soon extended the practice to handwork.[69] Arthur Whybrow, one of the modern manufacturers, assessed the advantages of weekly wages over piecework: 'Under the log rate method of paying, the workman was careless and irregular, and there was no inducement for the employer to get the most out of his workmen's time by systematic management.'[70]

The Wages Boards, which workers hoped would remedy this grievance, in fact had the opposite effect. The piecework log had been designed to correspond to the original minimum wage of 42 shillings. When this was replaced by the 36-shilling minimum the disparity between the two systems of payment was very great. The effect was similar to that in the clothing trade: manufacturers would not use pieceworkers when they could get the work done so much more cheaply by weekly workers. The 1896 Act therefore dealt the final blow to the already declining piecework system. By 1898 there were only 300 pieceworkers compared to 3329 on weekly wages.[71] Ten years after the first determination, Factory Inspector Shay reported that she had little trouble in enforcing the minimum wage but the task system was still a problem, combined as it was with management which was more disciplinarian, with 'very strict supervision' kept on workers 'so as to get as much work done as possible for the money paid'.[72]

In the light of these developments, the union's earlier agreement to weekly wages in conjunction with machinery was revealed for what it was—a tactical concession made from a position of weakness. As soon as the Wages Board offered the possibility of increased bargaining power for workers, the official policy was reversed. A mass meeting of the trade, held to elect Wages Board delegates, agreed to Fleming's resolution that all delegates sign a pledge to support piecework for makers and finishers whether working by hand or machine. The male clickers and female fitters and machinists, who were less subject to speed-ups and preferred weekly wages for their own work, agreed to 'go along with the rest of the trade re piece work'.[73]

A committee was appointed to draw up a schedule of piece rates but from the outset the project encountered difficulties. In mid-June 1897 it reported that 'it is not practicable to work on a peace [sic] work statement in conjunction with the Machines in Making'.[74] The committee apparently persevered and later that month presented the schedule for machine making to the Wages Board. Despite the employer delegates' threat to resign over the issue, the unionists voted to proceed with their claim.[75]

In the meantime, the board's determination specifying the 36-shilling minimum weekly wage and piece rates for handwork came into operation at the end of 1897. This further strengthened the men's resolve to fight for piece rates on machine work. Any minimum wage, they argued, led employers to select the 'race horses of the trade' and pay them the minimum wage; the old and the slow were discharged to 'walk about and starve'.[76] Their objections were supported by the fact that 300 men were registered with the union as unemployed, 'mostly the old and slow workers the minimum was supposed to protect'.[77]

Attempts by the union's delegates to have the Wages Board reconsider the question during 1898 and 1899 failed to produce a machine scale of piece rates. The employers argued that such a scale was impractical, 'and if practical undesirable'. They stated that 'it would require more time and attention to Book the work in and out to the operatives than to make and Finish the Boots'.[78] The chairman, Keogh, showed his usual indecision and refused to cast his vote either way.[79] Thereafter the workers abandoned the attempt and turned instead to devising ways to abolish the task system.[80]

When the attempt to abolish the task system failed, unionists looked for ways to regulate it.[81] There is no evidence that employees' delegates sought Wages Board determinations which specified tasks or quotas to be achieved before workers received the minimum wage. It is unlikely that such a scheme would have met with the board's approval. Unionists relied on more direct methods of regulating output. The problem, however, was not a simple one. Young men in particular engaged in record-breaking contests amongst themselves. Although these kinds of games were more usually associated with piecework, the rewards for individuals were similar. As Burawoy and others have noted, playing games enabled workers to survive psychologically in an increasingly alienating work environment.[82] But the long-term effects of this 'self-murdering game' on the workers, individually and collectively, were only too apparent to the union leadership.[83] Unionists could also see that a solution to the resulting speeding-up lay with the workers themselves. If they all slowed down, none could be singled out for dismissal and they would still get the same wage. The difficulty was to inspire the 'race horses' with such a collective spirit. The services of Ben Tillett were enlisted in 1898 to speak against racing.[84] A few years later, as noted earlier, the union pressed the THC to engage Tom Mann as an organiser. It is probably no coincidence that Mann was an advocate of output limitation, arguing that if employers would pay only low wages they must expect a smaller effort from their workers.[85] This propaganda against racing seems to have been effective, as little mention is made of such games after 1900. It is probable that with the recovery of the industry in the next decade workers were successful in collectively moderating the effects of the task system. They did not, however, eliminate it and the potential remained for employers to speed up workers in times of recession by choosing only the fastest workers.[86]

Difficulties also occurred in the union's attempts to regulate the use of machinery. The men were not opposed to the machinery as such, realising from past experience in their own co-operative factory that a factory 'could not succeed without modern equipment and therefore large capital investment'.[87] Rather, they believed that it should not be only the employers and the public who benefited from the cheaper production of the 'labour-saving' machines: 'the introduction of machinery in the trade should result in an improvement in the conditions and a reduction in the hours of labour'.[88]

The ideal, at least, was shared by manufacturers. The *Leather Journal*, extolling the virtues of modern bootmaking machinery, waxed lyrical about the romance of the evolution of the cobbler of yesterday into the marvellous 'stitcher' of today—'a practical, sensible romance which builds up capital and incidentally elevates labour'.[89] In reality the tale of mechanisation, from the workers' point of view, bore more resemblance to tragedy than romance. As Higgins pointed out, the so-called 'labour-saving' machines saved no labour to the worker: 'These machines require close attention and great care, in order to avoid the spoiling of the material, or the maiming of the workers. The strain of the work is intense.'[90]

That the workers were not sharing in the benefits of modern technology they believed was due mainly to the use of boys instead of men to operate machines.[91] Not only did the boys displace adult workers but their unrestricted use meant that they were usually taught to operate one machine only, as employers could not hope to provide all-round training for such large numbers of apprentices. This in turn led to the deskilling of boot operatives as a group, reducing both their status and their earnings. As Higgins expressed this problem: 'If competent men resisted low wages, the employer probably could make shift to get on with the "improvers" for a while, until the journeymen saw an empty cupboard and hungry wife and children, and were brought to their senses.'[92] But it should be stressed that it was not the machines themselves which were held responsible by organised labour for this state of affairs: it was the way in which they were regulated. The union's new banner, commissioned in 1907, showing operatives working the new machines, represented a willingness to incorporate the realities of the modern factory into the traditional conception and iconography of the craft.[93] Employers and workers alike agreed that although the machines were quicker it took a good deal of practice before an operator became expert in their use.[94] Some of the more difficult machines were said to require two years' training and this was to master one part only of the process of boot construction.[95] To avoid the monotony and deskilling of such mechanised work and to increase the workers' flexibility and bargaining power, the union suggested that all boys be apprenticed and taught the whole range of machines connected with any particular process. Thus, a lad apprenticed to 'welting' would learn not just the hand process but also the Goodyear welter and rapid stitcher and the other machines associated with making a welted boot.[96] This represented a compromise between the older practice of apprenticing lads to 'making', 'finishing' or 'clicking' and that favoured by employers of making each of the major machines separate subjects for apprenticeship. The employers were anxious to reinforce the subdivision of work by isolating the skills acquired on each individual machine. At the other extreme, by tying apprenticeship so closely to the construction of different types of boots, rather than to separate processes in general bootmaking, the union was attempting a reintegration of the labour process and greater worker flexibility.[97]

Early attempts by unionists to secure a Victorian Apprenticeship Act to implement this scheme were unsuccessful, while such an innovative scheme had little chance of being accepted by the Wages Board. Even the union's claim for substantial increases in juvenile wages was rejected by the chairman as a surreptitious way of limiting boy labour and was thus declared 'contrary to the law as passed by Parliament'.[98] As Billson argued at the first interstate conference of boot unions, a federal union would have prevented the disastrous results from past strikes and also have 'insisted on men instead of boys on machines'.[99] An appeal to the federal court for a new system of apprenticeship thus represented the major reason behind union organisation in the period 1903–09, as the regulation of boy labour was believed to be the key to a satisfactory accommodation with the new machinery and methods.[100] At the same time, the union appealed for shorter hours, as this was seen as a way of avoiding unemployment caused by the spread of machines.[101]

These years also coincided with a change in the leadership of the union. The leaders of the 1880s and 1890s had by 1904 all moved on or died. In 1904 Arthur Long, active in both the Melbourne and Ballarat unions since the late 1890s, was elected secretary. His was not only a fresh face but also a new style. Free of any association with the bitter conflicts of previous decades, Long's conciliatory approach appeased many hostile employers.[102] Convinced that strikes were 'an old-fashioned, barbarous method' of settling disputes, he determined to organise the trade for an early appeal to the federal court.[103] The Commonwealth Court of Conciliation and Arbitration thus became the focus of the workers' hopes for benevolent state intervention, so bitterly disappointed by the Victorian legislature.

For the employers, the union's decision to approach the federal court was most unwelcome. Suddenly the Wages Board system, previously denounced as 'the most disastrous legislation that has ever been perpetrated on an industry', became 'equitable and conciliatory', giving 'fairly general satisfaction'.[104] In fact, the Wages Boards had done little to modify the bitter legacy of the depression years. Any decrease in open conflict was due more to the 'crushed spirits' of the workers than to their greater faith in the generosity and goodwill of employers. Indeed, it could be argued that the employers' behaviour over the first determination increased the level of mistrust by betraying what in the past had been one area of common ground: the mutual fight of employer and worker for high protective tariffs. As the Bootmakers' Union indignantly wrote to the Chief Secretary on the reduction of the minimum wage in 1897:

> We also desire to protest against the Exports of Victorian made Boots and Shoes being brought in evidence as a reason for reducing The Minimum Wage. The Workmen have assisted the Manufacturers and The Government to obtain a duty which would Protect them and prevent low wages being enforced in This Colony and now having got Protection for the Manufacturers The retention of the Intercolonial Trade is given as a reason for the payment of Low Wages . . . [105]

This experience led workers to be far more cautious in future. Although they were still prepared to co-operate with manufacturers to obtain high federal tariffs, protection was no longer the unifying force it had been in the nineteenth century.[106] The manufacturers had come to appreciate more fully that protection was a two-edged sword, high duties on imported footwear being offset by tariffs on imported leather. Boot manufacturers were therefore less enthusiastic about high duties on the former if it also meant high tariffs on the latter.[107] For their part, the workers no longer believed in the good faith of employers to pass on the benefits of protection to their workers. Their appeal to the federal court was therefore a recognition that state intervention was necessary to reinforce the 'mutual trust' so dear to employer polemicists.

Ironically, the employers were also placing their faith in state action to defend themselves against this renewed worker mobilisation. In their case, they hoped that an appeal to the High Court would invalidate the Commonwealth Arbitration Court's decision.[108] The collapse of the Boot Manufacturers' Association after the settlement of the federal tariff should not be seen as an indication of lack of interest on the part of employers. It was in all probability part of their strategy to thwart the machinery of the federal court, forcing the union to cite individual manufacturers as respondents rather than an employers' association.[109] But although this succeeded in causing the union considerable inconvenience, it could not prevent industrial relations in the Victorian boot trade becoming focused at a federal level.

The Wages Board system clearly played an important role in structuring worker–employer relations in the years 1897–1910, while the decisions arrived at by the board had direct effects on the ways in which work was organised at the factory level. Anticipation of the minimum wage encouraged a further frenzy of mechanisation in the late 1890s; sections previously untouched by machines, such as strong work, either mechanised or moved interstate where handwork was not subject to a piecework schedule. The fixing of a minimum wage in itself sounded the final death-knell to the piecework system in factories, as it was cheaper to operate on a system of wages and tasks than on the piece rates prescribed by the board.

The board's determinations also influenced access to different sorts of jobs. Equal pay provisions reinforced the existing sexual division of labour, while limitations on the numbers of juveniles employed initially discouraged their employment. Conversely, when these restrictions were lifted in 1903 there was a significant increase in the number of juniors of both sexes engaged for boot factory work. The proportion of boys increased from 30.8 per cent in 1902 to 37.7 per cent in 1906. The percentage of female workers under twenty-one years increased from 54.1 to 57.2 over the same period.[110]

The market for female factory labour provided some check, however, on the employment of female juniors. There were reports of difficulties in attracting enough girls to boot factories as early as 1899 but these became more frequent in the period 1905–09.[111] In the latter year, Factory Inspector Thear reported that one firm at least was offering a 2s 6d bonus to girls for each of their friends recruited to the work.[112] Nevertheless, the fact that almost 60 per cent of the workers in the upper-closing rooms were not entitled to even the small wage set for adult women must have limited the incentive for technical innovation in this section. And the fact that such workers were difficult to organise and easily ignored by male unionists ensured that their minimum rates of pay remained at the 1897 levels throughout this period.

The Australian market for boots and shoes also played a major role in defining the limits of productive reorganisation. Changing fashions heralded the rise and fall of whole sections of the trade, as the decline of strong work before the advancing light-weight, machine-sewn boot demonstrates.

The size of the Australian market limited the types of labour process which were profitable. The more restricted application of scientific management methods to Victorian factories compared to those in America can largely be explained by the different markets each industry supplied. For instance, the reason that foremen in Victorian factories continued to play a more central role than those in America was not ignorance of American practices. The *Leather Journal* kept manufacturers informed of overseas trends, and many Victorian boot manufacturers travelled abroad, especially to America, where they observed the latest methods.[113] As the *Leather Journal* noted, 'there are men in the trade who are quite alive to the advantages of specialisation and classification'.[114] Nor was it because of a fondness for the 'happy-go-lucky, go-as-you-please system in vogue in some factories'.[115] Rather, it reflected the more restricted nature of the Australian market: 'the population has hitherto been too small, and therefore the demand too limited'.[116] It was much easier to 'anticipate all supervision from the office' when each factory limited its production to a few standard lines. This was also the reason that Australian manufacturers gave for preferring weekly wages to piece rates, as was the American practice. The degree of specialisation in Australian factories made piece rates impractical and would require 'an army of juvenile clerks' to record the output of different sizes and styles.[117]

To some extent, however, Victorian manufacturers imitated the 'efficient' methods of American producers, despite the fact that the American methods were designed for a much larger product market. The short-term expansion of Victoria's interstate trade after federation obscured the real limitations of the Australian market. After the initial expansion and 'modernisation' of methods, Victoria's boot factories were left with excess capacity. As early as 1904 the *Leather Journal* observed that to provide full employment for the plant now erected 'requires not merely a steady demand, but an ever-increasing and ever-booming consumption of boots and shoes'.[118] Part III will show how far the Australian market was able to fulfil this requirement.

6

EDUCATING THE GIRLS: THE PRINTING INDUSTRIES, 1901–1925

The most striking feature of the printing industries in the first few decades of the twentieth century was the application of new technologies. Applied in Victoria from the turn of the century, these processes put colour and illustration into a whole range of previously unadorned products and created a taste for artistic display which transformed the world of advertising and packaging.[1] The economic recovery after the late 1890s meant an expanded market for commodities, providing an ideal environment for the indulgence of these tastes. The expansion of Victorian markets after federation in turn increased the demand for both advertising and packaging.

And whilst consumers were aware of this transformation in the public face of the products they purchased, less visible were the equally radical changes occurring behind the scenes in the printing and packaging factories. Workers of both sexes in a whole range of occupations, from compositor and lithographer through to cardboard-box and paper-bag makers, were all affected by these new techniques. These effects were, however, very uneven. The new technologies in some cases created new skilled work or required enhanced skill from traditional craftworkers. In other cases, workers were both displaced by the new machines and deskilled by the subdivision which accompanied them. In still other instances, new technologies created new categories of 'unskilled' workers.

These changes at the market and technology level were mediated through the determinations of the various printing industry wages boards. Uniform limitations on the number of juveniles who could be employed helped to counter the growth of boy labour which had occurred in suburban and country composing rooms during the depression of the 1890s.[2] Forced to pay journeymen's rates for hand composition, many employers installed linotypes or their cheaper imitations to reduce their wages bills.

In the women's sections of the industry, the slightly increased minimum rates awarded by the boards also encouraged mechanisation. The paper-bag industry, for example, remained a largely hand industry until the first determination of the Wages Board in 1907. Although this increased wages by an average of less than two shillings, competition from imported bags made by unregulated labour led Victorian manufacturers to mechanise as many lines of bags as possible.[3]

A similar trend occurred in the women's sections of bookbinding. In the early 1900s, Victorian firms acquired machines which had been in use in Britain since the 1880s.[4] The rapid expansion of printing in the first decade of the twentieth century would probably have necessitated the use of the machines eventually. However, the Wages Board determination meant that women's sections were already mechanised when shortages of female industrial labour occurred from 1907 which would otherwise have precipitated this change.

At a more general level, the legal sanction which Wages Board determinations gave to the demarcation between men's and women's work, combined with the low rates paid to women, was crucial in deciding the pattern of industrial production in the printing industries in the twentieth century. These determinations were in turn the product of the sexual politics of the industry as a whole.

In April 1912, Walter Gee, bookbinders' delegate on the Printers Wages Board and president of the Women Bookbinders Union, suggested to a meeting of the male bookbinders that 'this society should endeavour to obtain some control in matters with the Women Bookbinders such an affiliation would strengthen our hands and the Girls could be educated as to how far they could do Bookbinding'.[5] The members needed no further persuasion and immediately resolved to seek an amalgamation of the two unions. Enforcing the line of demarcation between men's and women's work thus continued to be a major preoccupation of male bookbinders, despite the legal sanction given to this sexual division of labour by the Wages Board determinations. By 1900 the point at which 'unskilled' work ended was at quarter-bound cut-flush work which had paper sides turned in over the end-boards. This was embodied in the first determination of the Printers Wages Board in 1901, the only subsequent alteration being the 1902 Wages Board decision to allow women to operate the new indexing machines at the female rate of sixteen shillings per week. Any infringements on 'male' territory by females were in this period dealt with by the Factories Office as well as the union.[6] The men were fortunate in the attention given to their complaints by Factory Inspector Alfred Bishop. A compositor by trade and former union activist, he was appointed to the Factories Office in 1902 where he remained to provide a 'sympathetic interpretation of his duties' to the workers until his death in 1932. His background no doubt made him more willing to police demarcation issues than would perhaps otherwise have been the case.[7] The combination of legal sanction and vigilant administration meant that the threat of cheaper female labour was effectively contained.

Nor did the early twentieth century realise earlier male fears that the industry would be swamped by female labour. Mechanisation and subdivision operated on the work of female bookbinders to restrict opportunities for women. Contrary to the claims of

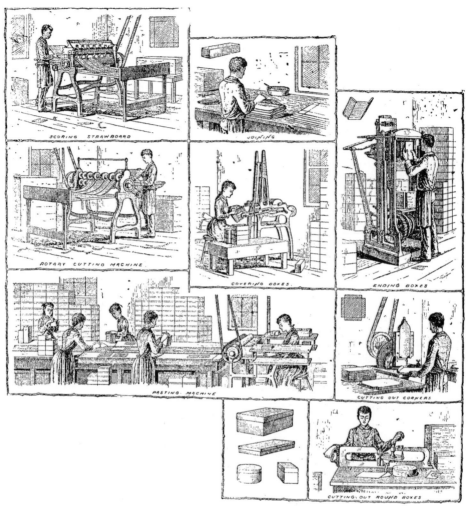

11   Early steam-powered paper-box making machinery which came into general use in Victoria before the Great War. Note the sexual division of labour, with men performing all the 'dangerous' work on the cutting and scoring machines.

Town and Country Journal, 13 April 1895, p. 30.

historians, there was no significant increase in the proportion of women employed in book-binding over the period 1900 to 1925.[8] On the contrary, there was initially a decline in the percentage of women employed as women's work was mechanised in the first decade of the twentieth century. From the turn of the century, increasing numbers of firms installed the new folding machines, such as the ones advertised in Figure 11. Machines were also used for staying, wire-stitching, punching, round cornering, gluing and numbering, together with improved models of sewing machines which could handle the back sewing of ledgers previously done entirely by hand. These machines, combined with 'an intense specialisation' of tasks, initially reduced the numbers of female workers in bookbinding firms. By 1925 the figure had recovered to 20.8 per cent of total employees, but this was still below the 1898 percentage of 24. (See Appendix, Table A9.)[9]

Given that there seems no real reason for male bookbinders to have felt especially threatened by women workers in this period, why were they so anxious to interfere in the affairs of the women's union? Their concern seems to have been based on the potential threat that women represented and in particular on the spectre of an entirely female union over which they would have no control. Their fears were fuelled by the fact that the women's union was being organised by two well-known socialist-feminist activists, Miss Ellen Mulcahy and Mrs Barry.[10] Having no particular sympathy for either socialism or feminism, the male bookbinders saw the rapid growth of the new union as a challenge to their supremacy on more than one front. Feminists, in particular, alarmed the male craftworker as they challenged the basis of his 'skill' and encouraged women to attempt new, more lucrative avenues of employment. The *Woman's Sphere*, for instance, advocated bookbinding, along with boarding-house keeping, as 'other avenues for women':

> The practical part of the work can be learnt in a short time, and is most interesting and pleasant. Artistic designing, gilting, etc., are advanced departments, requiring special talent and skill, but simple binding can be learnt by anyone who has a taste for mechanical work, and should furnish a much more remunerative livelihood than many occupations in which some of our women are eking out such struggling existences . . . [11]

The fact that a 'female' was teaching her own sex the art of bookbinding for a fee of £4 4s per quarter no doubt added to their alarm.[12] And they were no more prepared to acquiesce in this challenge to their masculinity than were the typographers before them.

For their part, the women, under the tutelage of Barry and Mulcahy, sought a relationship of independent co-operation with the men. The blatant self-interest of the male bookbinders must have been only too evident to the women. Without a union of their own until 1910, they were also without a female representative on the Wages Board. Their interests were left in the hands of the men. That 16 shillings was fixed as the general minimum for female bookbinders in 1902 indicates how strongly these men pushed the case of their female shopmates. Male bookbinders received a minimum of 52 shillings, while even the most 'highly skilled' women—the sewers and takers-down of letterpress—received a mere 20 shillings, the same as the most poorly paid adult woman under the Clothing Board.[13] The cardboard-box and carton section, which had three women as well as two men on its Wages Board, was able to secure minimums of 18 shillings and 22s 6d respectively (payable after four years), even though prior to the determination employers were paying up to 6 shillings less than these amounts.[14]

When the minimum male wage in the printing trades was raised from 52 shillings to 56 shillings in 1906, no increase was claimed for the women. As Inspector Bishop reported, this did not go unnoticed by those affected:

> The remark has been made to me that the Board did not show much consideration for the females working under the Determination as affected by the bookbinding provisions, as they have made no attempt to get them an increase in the low minimum of 16 shillings, and comparisons were made between this rate and that paid in the boot and clothing trades, where the minimum is 20s. The females have no representative on the Board.[15]

Women employed making stationery, who from 1911 were covered by the Women Bookbinders' Union, were even worse off, having no determination at all covering their occupation until 1917. They were, consequently, amongst the lowest-paid of all female industrial workers.[16]

With this history of men's efforts on behalf of their female workmates in mind, women unionists were cautious of any alliances with the men's union. They were prepared to ask men's advice on industrial matters and even to have them as honorary presidents, but they were determined not to subordinate their separate identity to the patronage of the male Bookbinders Union.[17] When it came to membership it was 'strictly a women's union', while the important office of secretary was reserved for women.[18] The fact that no separate provision was made for a women's representative on the Printers Board limited their independence, however, forcing them to rely on the male bookbinders to 'fight their case'.[19] This proved a serious problem as the men did not fight their cause with much conviction. Shortly after formation of the women's union the women formulated a claim to raise all wages for women to a flat rate of 30 shillings, rather than the two existing rates of 18 and 20 shillings. The bookbinders' delegate said the men were 'rather dubious' of presenting the claim as the chairman would not accept it. They suggested the claim be for 28 shillings in the case of sewers and takers-down of letterpress and 24 shillings for others.[20] The men succeeded in getting only 21 and 23 shillings respectively, and this was decided without calling evidence.[21] At the same time, the bookbinders were 'proud to say that the men were the second highest paid trade under the Wages Board System'.[22]

Despite this obvious handicap, the women tried to maintain their independent stance even after the formative years when Barry and Mulcahy had moved on. They continued to receive support from older labour women, in particular Mrs Minnie Felstead and Mrs Louisa Cross, both feminists with strong records of organising within the industrial and political labour movements.[23]

By the end of the 1914–18 war, however, the situation was changing. Moves toward the One Big Union affected the printing industry as they did the clothing trades. The women, too, were affected by the logic of 'one industry, one union', although their experience of the fraternity of male unionists made them wary of formal amalgamation. The post-war record of this relationship did little to allay their fears. For instance, in 1920 Secretary Cross received a report that Frank Burke, Wages Board delegate and secretary of the Bookbinders Union, had negotiated with an employer to introduce the 'speeding-up system' to his shop. Louisa Cross regarded this as a 'very serious matter' and reported it to the executive of the male union. The executive, suspicious as ever of women taking initiatives, were unsympathetic to Cross's appeal, their president, Arthur Leovold, implying that the women were pursuing some feminist cause rather than a 'working class issue'. Cross was quick to reply that she saw no necessary distinction between the two, but rather that she had always done her best to further the interests of 'working women'. She contrasted her position to that of Burke who, as Wages Board delegate, 'had never given us any assistance'.[24]

It was in this atmosphere of mutual antipathy that attempts were made by the federal body of the Printing Industry Employees Union of Australia to draw the remaining

Victorian unions into the 'Big Union of Printers'. It took the Melbourne printing strike of 1920, however, to convince the women that alliance with a large industrial union was in their best interests.[25] Concerns about the quality of the race and national security, heightened by the recent war, also played a part. Improving the conditions of working women in order to improve their child-bearing capacities assumed more importance than the concerns of feminists for women's independence. Minnie Felstead, acting president of the Women Bookbinders and Stationery Employees Union at the time of amalgamation, expressed this change of priorities:

> As an advocate for equality this woman's question is no question at all. There are modes of interaction that know no cavilling of great or less, and the erection of a sex barrier in the Trade Union Movement is economically unsound. Men may have the intellectual fathering, but women must have the physical mothering of the Movement; and I think that the amalgamation of the Printing Industry of Australia will be a big step in the improvement of the working conditions of the women employed, and thus help to make them fit daughters of the country's noblest traditions and fit mothers for her future sons.[26]

But, although Felstead hoped for a relationship which knew 'no cavilling of great or less', still the women's suspicions of the men remained. Their reluctance to join the PIEUA was not, as Hagan argues, due to their anxiety to follow the lead of the typographers. It was rather that they hoped to amalgamate on terms which would not render them completely voiceless in the new organisation.[27] The terms accepted by their New South Wales counterparts were certainly not encouraging in this respect.[28] Indeed, they could not have been totally unaware of the contempt with which they were regarded by some of the men in the PIEUA. For instance, one of its officers wrote understandingly to Leovold, secretary of the Victorian Bookbinders Union, at the time of the amalgamation proposals: 'As you know, Women are funny "Cattle" . . . Take them all round they're a damned nuisance.'[29]

Certainly the women faced considerable opposition in their attempts to get equal treatment under the terms of amalgamation. The Provisional Board of Management was itself stacked against the Women Bookbinders, according them 15 delegates to represent their 800 members, the same number allowed the male Bookbinders with a membership of 300.[30] The Typographers Society, with just over twice the membership of the Women Bookbinders, were allowed over five times the number of delegates (77). This weighting was significant in that the Provisional Board decided a number of important matters affecting women, such as the structure of the new branch and the rates of pay for the woman organiser.[31] The executive committee was similarly stacked against the women's sections. The Women Bookbinders and Boxmakers were given the same number of delegates as the male Bookbinders, even though they had twice as many members, while the Typographers were given twice as many delegates as any of the other sections.[32]

The question of a female organiser for the new branch proved the decisive issue. The women were determined that specific provision should be made for a paid organiser of their own sex.[33] The fact that all the paid officers of the other amalgamating unions were to be retained by the PIEUA gave them their way. The Women Bookbinders Union immediately made their honorary secretary, Louisa Cross, a full-time, paid secretary on a salary of four pounds per week.[34] There was thus a certain onus on the PIEUA to provide for her as well as for the male officials. The men were by no means happy about the arrangement, but could hardly object as it appears that the Bookbinders had used exactly the same tactic a few weeks earlier.[35]

In any case the majority conceded the point rather than lose the chance of 'controlling' the women.[36] They consoled themselves with the thought that it was only a temporary concession, which could be reviewed after the amalgamation was sealed. As the New South Wales secretary put it, 'the price must be accepted until time and experience cause changes'.[37] To hasten the lessons of time and experience, the men backed an attractive young woman for the position of female organiser against the solid personality of Cross, hoping that an 'early marriage' of the former would provide an opportunity to appoint a man in her place. As one of the male officers quaintly expressed it: 'Regarding the lady organiser, the most desirable girl from our point of view is certain to be snapped up to be President of a Union of two with prospects of increasing to not more than a dozen.'[38] Alas, Cross was elected by a sizeable majority of the female members.[39]

But although the Women Bookbinders succeeded in having a woman organiser appointed, like the women in the Clothing Trades Union they could not secure her equal pay.[40] Nor could they secure any revision of the PIEUA rules regarding representation of women on the federal council. Most of the men argued that the council was constituted to consider the 'big questions', and could therefore see no possible reason why women should want special representation. Advisory committees, which were allowed for each section, had no power to do other than advise the board of management. The board was under no obligation to accept their recommendations.[41]

The rules were eloquent, however, on the advantages the men expected from amalgamation. Rule 5:8, for instance, stipulated that 'Members of the Women's Advisory Committees shall not accept employment in the section of the industry now covered by male labour, without having obtained the permission of the Board of Management, and shall use every endeavour to discountenance any proposal to this end.'[42] There were thus severe structural constraints on the role women could play in the Big Union. Theoretically they had an equal chance with the men for offices such as president, secretary and delegates to various industrial councils. But in practice their smaller numbers ensured that they were rarely successful. The pessimists were vindicated when even the female delegates to the Trades Hall Council were defeated by three men.[43]

Before the formation of the PIEUA, the only other printing union with women members was the Cardboard Box and Carton Employees Association which also embraced paperbag workers. Approximately 75 per cent of the workers in this section were women and they provided the overwhelming majority of union members.[44] Formed in 1906 by a small group of women anxious to have a Wages Board appointed for their trade, the union was assisted in its efforts by members of the Trades Hall Council Organising Committee.[45] Certain 'fair employers' were also sympathetic to the Wages Board, as they found that 'even with their advanced machinery and allowing for the smallest margin of profit, they cannot retain orders, as, no matter how low the price they quote, some of the manufacturers in the trade will cut lower'.[46] The agitation was successful and the necessity to select delegates for the Wages Board assured the association of an ongoing existence.

It quickly became obvious, however, that men and women would play different roles within the union structure. Although the union had been established by women, within a year the offices of secretary and president were filled by men.[47] Women still formed almost all the positions on the executive committee and were generally far more active members than the men.[48] Indeed, on several occasions the union found it impossible to muster sufficient men to form a committee to draw up a log of claims for men's occupations on the Wages Board.[49] The same half-dozen men in fact carried the burden of representing their colleagues from the time of the first Wages Board until amalgamation with the PIEUA.

It would, therefore, be wrong to assume that the role this handful of men played was not welcomed by the female membership. On the contrary, it was women who nominated men for official positions and women's votes which secured them in office.[50] It was certainly not a case of an active male membership organising to elect their own sex in the face of apathetic female members.

Why then were these women so willing to be governed by male officials when their counterparts in bookbinding held out for so long as a separate women's organisation? The major reason seems to be the inexperience of women unionists compared to men. The high rate of 'wastage' amongst women activists in the Cardboard Box Association meant that any potential officials were not around long enough to build up comparable expertise. The men's attitude to the appointment of an attractive young woman to the position of organiser was based on a firm appreciation of the limitations that women's domestic roles placed on their industrial activity. All too often a promising young female unionist would be lost to the cause as a result of marriage. The arduous and often unpleasant nature of the work, in many cases made worse by the new machinery and methods, possibly also contributed to girls' leaving the trade for more pleasant work.[51] Employers had every incentive to employ juveniles in preference to adults because their labour was so much cheaper. The specified ratio of apprentices or improvers to adults under the Wages Board determination provided little deterrent to their employment, and the increasing subdivision of labour provided ample scope for the use of quickly trained girls.[52] In the 1920s, between one-third and one-half of female workers in the printing and allied trades were under twenty-one years of age, with the figure for cardboard boxmaking approaching 50 per cent. The tendency to employ juveniles was so pronounced that it was felt necessary to include a clause in the 1925 arbitration award stipulating that 'no department shall be manned exclusively by juniors'.[53]

The importance of age as a factor determining women's union involvement was commented on by contemporaries. Jean Daley, herself a labour activist, writing in 1934, observed that

> If there are few women on the executives, or in official positions, it is largely because the industrial life of a woman is largely incidental. The real business of life is to marry and become wife and mother just as it has been in all ages. As a rule, the older woman is an active union worker, the juvenile worker very indifferent both politically and industrially, with shining exceptions.[54]

Her point is well illustrated by the printing unions. Unlike the Women Bookbinders, the boxmakers did not have any members of the ilk of Ellen Mulcahy or Louisa Cross.

Mulcahy seems to have been committed to politics rather than husband-seeking, and devoted many years of her life to this cause.[55] Louisa Cross was representative of the married woman who was relatively free of domestic ties and was therefore in a position to make a long-term contribution to unionism.[56] The women in the box and carton union were, by contrast, almost invariably young and marriageable. They rarely stayed in the workforce long enough to accumulate much industrial experience. This inexperience had several effects on the pattern of industrial relations. Firstly, it meant that the spontaneous, factory-specific protests which normally characterised pre-union militancy persisted for many years after the formation of the Cardboard Box and Carton Employees Association. Unused to industrial action and union procedures, the predominantly young workers sought their own remedies to specific problems.[57]

The demographic composition of the boxmakers' association was also important in determining methods adopted by the men to enforce the sexual division of labour. With such an apathetic male workforce and so young a female membership, male unionists realised that direct action was 'out of the question' for their industry.[58] They were thus particularly anxious to enlist the aid of the state, firstly in the form of a Wages Board determination and later in an appeal to the federal court. The claim was the familiar one of equal pay for the sexes when engaged on 'men's work'.[59] Direct action against women unionists was resorted to only when the state failed to support the union's claims for equal pay. In 1920, for instance, the Wages Board, on the casting vote of the chairman, rejected the union's claim for equal pay on rotary cutting and scoring. In response the union declared any female filling a vacancy on these machines 'to be guilty of disloyal conduct to the Association and will be dealt with accordingly'.[60]

A third factor of importance was the limited revenue which such a membership generated. As contributions were roughly proportional to members' earnings, a predominance of female juniors did not produce a very healthy bank balance. This factor was an important influence on the union's willingness to link up with the PIEUA. Members were assured that the Big Union was interested in 'Men, not Money': 'of course that includes women too'.[61]

The sexual politics of the printing industry clearly played an important part in determining work processes and work practices. These effects are most apparent in relation to decisions of the various Wages Boards. At the most obvious level, the location of the demarcation line sometimes encouraged new methods. The fixing of a woman's rate for machine indexing and a man's rate for hand indexing, for example, encouraged the adoption of new mechanical methods.

At a more complex level, the definition of all women's work as unskilled, and the low rates awarded, encouraged the employment of young workers who saw their work as a stopgap only. Women and girls solely dependent on their wages were unlikely to choose the printing industry when earnings were so low and prospects for advancement negligible. In 1909, for instance, Inspector Cuthbertson found that the eighteen shillings paid to most female print workers was at least two shillings short of what it cost a girl 'wholly dependent on her own resources' to live 'decently'.[62] The Women Bookbinders Union found that 'girls leave the trade to seek other avenues of employment owing to the poor remuneration for the work performed'.[63] The absence of mature single women and married women with dependents in turn reinforced the nature of the work: the young girls who comprised the majority of the workforce made ineffective unionists and failed successfully to challenge the intensification of the work process, its subdivision or its remuneration. The speed, unpleasantness and dead-end nature of the resulting work methods fed into a kind of vicious circle by contributing to the high labour turnover.

The hostility shown by men in the industry to women workers had its effects in other directions. In addition to acquiescing in such low rates for women's work, male book-binders showed a distinct lack of concern for the conditions under which women worked. There is little comment on the printing union's official attitude to scientific man-agement. In August 1911, the *Typographical Journal* published an editorial praising Taylorism, but six years later the *Printing Trades Journal* published an article hostile to the 'pernicious system known as "Taylorism" '.[64] The impression is that the matter was a purely academic one, as most of the craftsmen in the printing trades did not have first-hand experience of the more negative sides of scientific management methods— subdivision of tasks, speed-ups and monotony. The case discussed earlier involving the secretary of the Bookbinders' Union, Burke, and speeding-up of women workers in fact suggests that men may have directly contributed to the deterioration of women's work experience. Even where conditions were supposedly safeguarded by the Factories Office, there are suggestions that this protection was not forthcoming. Inspector Bishop, diligent in his policing of any stepping across the line of demarcation, was less vigilant in the case of the almost all-female boxmaking section. Indeed, the union complained of the failure of the Factories Office to inspect boxmaking factories, and that 'when inspectors do come to the factories which was very seldom they do not enquire whether the girls were receiv-ing the correct piece rates'.[65]

Nor was it possible for women, unassisted, to challenge the definition of their work as unskilled. In the case of women in bookbinding and stationery, they did not even have a representative of their own sex on the Wages Board. The men who supposedly rep-resented them were more interested in maintaining the difference between women's work and 'skilled' work in order to preserve their own margins for skill. Those in the cardboard-box and paper-bag sections, who did have women representatives on the Wages Boards, lacked the industrial strength needed to back up any serious challenge to employers on the board. The apprenticeship system afforded women no protection against definitions of their work as unskilled. The four-year 'apprenticeship' provided for by most determinations was merely a way for employers to avoid paying adult rates to juniors. The employers, who did not recognise these occupations as skilled, were under no obligation to teach the girls anything.[66] And while restrictions on the proportion of apprentices in male trades protected the status of the 'craftsmen', the absence of such effective limitations contributed to the poor bargaining position of women workers.

Unlike the women, both compositors and bookbinders were able to use apprenticeship to preserve their occupations as 'skilled' trades. In the case of the compositors this involved a combination of restrictions on the number of apprentices and the revival of a more thorough training scheme. In both these endeavours they had the co-operation of members of the Master Printers' Association, who wanted to limit boy labour in the offices of their competitors and also benefited from the greater technical expertise on the part of their journeymen.[67] Despite improvements to the linotype which made it more versatile, the 'iron comp' could still not replace the human version when it came to display work. The increasing demand for such work in newspaper advertising and publishing as well as in the jobbing trade created a new role for the twentieth-century compositor. With the straight matter being set on the linotype or monoline, the hand compositor was left with what he claimed was the most 'skilled' part of his old work, that part which called upon his artistic rather than his more mechanical talents.[68] As the union argued in its case before the Commonwealth Court of Conciliation and Arbitration in 1925, 'the skill of the hand compositor doing display work under modern conditions calls for more of the skill of the artist than of the artisan'.[69]

Employers, too, felt that the modern conditions of composing required a generally higher level of expertise than that acquired by most tradesmen who picked up the trade in the 1880s and 1890s. It was agitation by the Master Printers' and Overseers' Associations which led to the setting up of technical classes in printing in the late 1890s to help fill the gap between the knowledge of the old tradesman and that required of the twentieth-century craftsman. In 1911 Mr B. McMahon, instructor in printing at the Working Men's College, reported that 'the necessity of the classes is shown by the number of Master Printers who send their apprentices for tuition, in many instances paying their fees, and others half the fees; as they have neither the time nor the opportunity, and often not the qualification to give the necessary tuition'.[70]

The male bookbinders, unable to make a case for additional training, concentrated their efforts on limiting entry to the craft at the apprenticeship level. Restrictions on proportions of boys, in practice in operation since the 1870s, were embodied in the Wages Board determinations. Like the compositors, their effective union organisation ensured that these proportions generally were not exceeded even during the period 1903–08 when legal restrictions under the Wages Board were inoperative. The bookbinders thus continued to be recognised as skilled workers in spite of employer attempts to challenge parts of their work as 'skilled', while compositors had their craft status reinforced by the active assistance of employers.[71]

Linotype operators, those 'princes and potentates of the printing world', had more in common with bookbinders, using their industrial muscle to ensure their continued acceptance as the elite of the trade.[72] From the outset, compositors had obtained control of the composing machines and were able to have this work defined as skilled because of their strategic position when the machines were introduced. Before the Wages Board was established the Typographers' Society had been able to obtain the employers' agreement to a very favourable scale of piece rates for machine composition and a maximum working week of forty-two hours. Most importantly, only qualified compositors or apprentices in their final year of training were allowed to operate the machines.[73] These conditions were embodied in the first Wages Board determination and maintained throughout the years to 1925. Minimum rates for linotypists were originally set 35 per cent higher than those for hand compositors. Although the margin narrowed to 15 per cent over the ensuing twenty-four years, many continued to earn very high sums on piecework. In 1926, for instance, piecework linotypists on the Melbourne *Herald* averaged £12 to £14 per week, with some men exceeding £14. The male basic wage at the time was only £4 4s.[74]

And although linotype machines had originally displaced compositors, the expansion of the printing industry meant that opportunities for employment in this trade increased significantly in the early twentieth century. Indeed, it is not at all surprising to learn that in 1927 their spokesman declared that 'we do not regret the introduction of these machines, although the position was pretty bad at first'.[75]

The combined effect of these provisions was the continued recognition of linotypists as 'specialists', while in other cases where workers were doing the more straightforward, manipulative aspects of a craft the work might be seen as fragmented or deskilled. The work of sewing machinists, for instance, bears a relationship to the craft of garment-making similar to that which the work of the linotype operator bears to the broader craft of typesetting. Lacking the bargaining power of the latter, sewing machinists were treated as less skilled than tailoresses while linotypists were treated as more skilled than hand compositors.

One might wonder why it was that these craftsmen, who were able to secure their status and pay at such relatively high levels, continued to work in unhealthy and danger-ous environments. Ironically, these two factors were opposing sides of the same coin. Referring to the period before 1925, Hagan and Fisher comment that

> Piece-work compositors showed great interest in the early deaths of their fellows, and attributed most of them to the type of dust that accumulated in the crowded and ill-ventilated offices in which they worked. But despite some quite passionate statements not once did they take industrial action to have owners reduce the dust in the air. Instead they preferred to work at hazard, claiming compensation in higher setting rates for the shortening of their working lives.[75]

There were also other compensations for tolerating unhealthy conditions: such con-ditions helped preserve men's sense of manliness and deterred female employment on their work. The industrial strength which supported this craft status derived, at least in part, from the fact that linotypists were men.[76] At the same time, their willingness to work in such conditions was also a function of their masculinity. The dirt, noise and fumes associated with the composing room did not decrease with the introduction of the linotype machine. Indeed, as Ava Baron points out, these features of the Mergenthaler were ones which commended it to male compositors in preference to other, cleaner com-posing machines.[77] In the nineteenth century the grime of the composing room was used to justify the compositor's craft as a masculine occupation. In the twentieth century the same features were used to define linotyping as 'men's work'. This was particularly important given the resemblance of linotyping to that rapidly expanding feminine occu-pation, typewriting. In the 1920s, with the movement for shorter hours, the health haz-ards of the trade assumed a different tactical significance, but this should not obscure the lingering importance of the association of danger and dirt with masculinity.[78]

The question of danger was one which also affected the bookbinders and boxmakers. The dangers which guillotines posed to their operators were exacerbated by the refusal of many operators to use the safety guards provided because they saw such guards as a reflec-tion on their 'ability as workmen'.[79] Females and boys were not allowed to use these machines, the implication being that tackling such danger required a man.[80] The slur which the guards cast on the operator's ability was also seen as a slur on his manliness.

There is no evidence that the first two decades of the twentieth century saw any significant modification of this definition of masculinity. Men approached the Arbitration Court in 1925 with much the same preconceptions as their predecessors had taken to the Wages Boards. Nor were the women of the 1920s any better placed to mount a challenge to male definitions of their work. We have already seen how amalgamation with the PIEUA did not enhance women's power within the printing unions. Ironically, women were assured of a representative of their own sex on the Printers Wages Board only when it was clear that the Wages Boards were to be superseded by the federal court.[81] The fact that prior to going to the court in 1925 the decisions regarding the relative margins for skill in the industry were decided in conference between male employers and male unionists is a clear expression of women's position within the PIEUA.[82] We shall see in the following section how this arrangement was to affect both men and women under federal arbitration.

The era of the Wages Boards had thus brought mixed benefits to workers in the printing industries. It had bolstered the position of those able to define themselves as craftsmen in all sections by giving legal reinforcement to existing lines of demarcation between skilled and unskilled work. Physical conditions in many factories improved. Some workers also achieved substantial initial wage increases under Wages Boards. Those working in non-union firms had their hours and wages raised to those prevailing in the big unionised city establishments. Suburban and country firms were also forced to employ more journeymen because of the limitations on boy labour which already applied to city businesses.[83] For men employed in the city firms, however, the Wages Board made little direct difference.[84] Women in most branches of printing and bookbinding also gained some initial increase in wages, despite the low minimum of 16 shillings awarded them. As Inspector Cuthbertson reported, 'the rates formerly paid ... were very low'.[85] The 'very small number' engaged on book-sewing, for which 20 shillings was awarded, received little benefit.[86] Women in the cardboard-box and carton trade fared better, receiving 22s 6d and 18s per week respectively under their first determination in 1908, representing an average wage increase of over 5s per week to each employee.[87] The fact that piece rates were set by the board also brought significant benefits to workers, in particular by preventing the arbitrary cutting of rates as soon as workers earned more than the minimum wage.[88] Female workers in the stationery trades were by comparison very badly off. With no determination until 1917, their wages were amongst the lowest of any trade. In 1909, for instance, adult women averaged only 16s 4d per week, while the large number of juniors brought the overall average down to 11s 5d.[89]

But apart from these benefits, the Wages Boards had, by the early 1920s, proved a disappointment. Wages failed to keep pace with the rapid inflation of the war period so that by 1920 all workers were receiving less in real terms than they had been in 1913. This experience led workers to place more emphasis on shorter hours as a more durable gain than wage increases, but again the Wages Boards were a disappointment.[90] In 1920 an eight-week strike, involving women bookbinders as well as compositors and male bookbinders, failed to win a 44-hour week for the Victorian industry. The old strategy of using direct action in conjunction with Wages Boards had finally proved bankrupt.

The workers concluded that 'wages boards as they function in Victoria are a futile institution. They seem to exist merely to make minor adjustments and suggested innovations are looked upon with extreme disfavour.'[91] The federal court seemed to offer more promise, being less constrained by statutory limitations on its powers. It remained to be seen if it would 'be any better as to results'.[92]

PART III

The Era of
Federal Wage-fixing

> The object of the wages boards is primarily to prevent sweating or under-payment; the object of the
> Federal Court is to preserve or restore industrial peace.[1]

Justice Higgins' comments identify the fundamental difference between the federal and Victorian systems of industrial regulation. This difference in purpose was reflected in the powers and functions of each tribunal. Where the Wages Boards sought merely to eliminate sweating by fixing minimum standards in wages and hours, the jurisdiction of the Commonwealth Court of Conciliation and Arbitration covered any matter in dispute between the two parties.[2] The Wages Boards thus had limited powers only to deal with such important issues as the regulation of apprenticeship and equal pay for the sexes.

There were other obvious differences between the two systems as they were originally structured. The court's proceedings resembled practices in civil courts, rather than the conference style of the Wages Boards. The emphasis on the resolution of disputes placed employers and employees in an adversary relationship from the outset, in contrast to the boards where it was assumed that members had at least a common interest in suppressing 'sweaters'. And rather than the practical and practising employers and employees who sat round the boards' tables, the case for each side in the federal court was conducted by professional advocates. These were usually paid officials of employer organisations or unions, although lawyers were also found conducting cases.[3] Lacking the current practical knowledge which board members brought to their discussions, the court relied on the evidence of witnesses supplied by each side.[4] Similarly, where chairmen of the Wages Boards were laymen, the court was presided over by judges who attended to their duties dressed in legal robes and wigs.

A further significant difference, at least from the point of view of employers and workers, was the costs of each system. Board members were paid for the time they spent in conference and as they generally sat in the evening there was little lost work time to be provided for. By contrast, the court sat during the day and witnesses had to be reimbursed for the time lost from work. As proceedings covered more than one state, the parties also had to provide travel and accommodation expenses for witnesses and advocates. Where legal counsel was employed, this too had to be paid for. The court involved further expense to the party initiating the dispute, which was usually a trade union: notices of the union's claims had to be forwarded to each employer named in the case; should the employers reject the claims, as they usually did, further typing and postal charges were incurred in serving notice of the date of the hearing on employers. Where there were numerous individual employers involved, such as the hundreds engaged in the clothing and boot trades, such administration was extremely costly to the petitioner.[5]

The federal system also entailed long delays which were not evident with Wages Boards. The large number of cases compared to the small number of judges and the necessity to call witnesses accounted for the time-consuming nature of court proceedings. By the 1920s, delays of eight months were usual, while many industries waited from one to two years or longer for their cases to be heard.[6]

Decision-making processes in each system revealed other differences. Where the Wages Boards proceeded in a rather ad hoc fashion, with almost no guidance from the legislature, the federal court was more concerned to achieve consistency between its various decisions.[7] This was helped by the fact that only a few judges presided over all the cases. More importantly, judges showed a legal concern for precedent and principle which was not evident in Wages Board rulings. As Higgins himself pointed out, the 'awards must be consistent one with the other, or else comparisons breed unnecessary restlessness, discontent, industrial trouble'.[8]

And while dissatisfied parties could appeal to the Minister for a suspension or review of a Wages Board determination, no such appeal existed in relation to federal awards, except in so far as they were considered unconstitutional.[9] This difference was especially pronounced in the early years of the court under Higgins' presidency. His decisions tended to be more innovative than those reached by state Wages Boards and gained importance because they influenced other judges and because they were not subject to appeal.[10]

There were also differences in jurisdiction. The awards of the federal court applied to at least two states whereas the determinations of the Wages Boards applied only to the state of Victoria. On the other hand, within each state, federal awards applied only to union members in the employ of respondents to the dispute; the court had no power to order a 'common rule' for all workers in an industry. Wages Board determinations applied to all workers within the specified geographical area.[11]

Enforcement of decisions was also very different in the two systems. To police the determinations, the Wages Boards were supported by a department of factory inspectors who had wide powers of entry and inspection.[12] The federal court had no such administrative machinery. There were no inspectors attached to the court. Enforcement became a matter of vigilance on the part of unionists, who were severely hampered in their surveillance by limited access to the workplace and employer records.[13]

By the end of the 1930s some of the differences between the federal and state systems were considerably lessened. Wages Boards extended their jurisdiction beyond the 'sweated trades', and the establishment of the Court of Industrial Appeals in 1903 introduced an element of arbitration to the state system. Meanwhile, the conciliatory role of the Commonwealth court was enhanced with legislative changes in 1928.[14] Important differences, however, remained. The expenses and delays associated with the federal court had increased rather than diminished, making a federal award less attractive than it otherwise would have been.[15] Most importantly, changes to the Arbitration Court's powers in the 1920s considerably strengthened that body's judicial role. In 1926, judges of the court were appointed for life, giving them authority to interpret their own awards and to determine penalties and injunctions in the event of breaches.[16] Further amendments in 1928 considerably strengthened federal powers in the event of strikes and lockouts. Penalties in these cases were much more severe than under state legislation on shops and factories.[17] In the industrial strife which accompanied economic downturn in the late 1920s and 1930s, these 'penal powers' assumed grave significance for workers. The bloody and bitter strike by waterside workers in Melbourne during 1928 resulted in fines of £1000 being awarded against the Waterside Workers' Federation. This conviction was the first secured under the 1928 amendments, and served as a serious warning to other unionists contemplating federal awards or considering direct action whilst under the jurisdiction of the federal court.[18]

A decision by the High Court in 1926 further decreased the attraction to unions of a federal award. Prior to this decision, unions had enjoyed the benefits of the High Court's decision in the 1910 Whybrow case regarding the respective authority of state and federal awards. The effect of the Whybrow decision was that whichever award prescribed the higher wages was the one which prevailed. Unions therefore had nothing to lose and everything to gain from an approach to the court. The 1926 decision meant that federal awards prevailed over state awards, regardless of their terms. With the increasing conservatism of the court this decision removed the attractions offered by the 1910 verdict.[19] On the other hand, federal awards did have the advantage of interstate application, something which could never be hoped for under a state system alone. It was for this reason that industries which faced interstate competition continued to seek a federal settlement of their grievances.

There were, of course, some enduring similarities between the federal and state structures. Most importantly was the common illusion of the 'independent' arbiter, be he chairman or judge. Although supposedly unconcerned in the outcome of the battle between employers and employees, such arbiters did have a vested interest. Wage increases, according to contemporary belief, led to increases in the cost of living. Chairmen and judges were consumers too, and had no more desire than the next person to pay more for the goods and services which cushioned their existence. As well as being consumers, arbiters were also men. As such they shared in the privileges of a patriarchal society, only one of which was relatively cheap female domestic labour. They had, therefore, no desire to disrupt the gender order by innovative decisions on such things as equal pay and female margins for skill. The self-interest of adjudicators therefore acted as a conservative influence in both spheres, modified only by the professionalism and altruism of individuals.[20]

Concern about the cost of living and the stability of sex roles was very real in the 1920s and 1930s, amongst workers as well as judges. This period saw the movement of women workers into non-traditional manufacturing occupations, such as the metal, rubber and electrical industries, while the general trend toward work in white-collar jobs continued.[21] This concern was often expressed at the trade union level as a move to protect the jobs of men.[22] As one unemployed man put it: 'That women should be employed and men unemployed is topsy-turvydom. It is an inversion of the natural order.'[23]

As the manufacturing economy faltered in the late 1920s, so this hostility to the employment of women intensified. In Victoria the employment of girls in the bolt and core making departments at the Sunshine Harvester Works provided a focus for union opposition to cheaper female labour.[24] As depression deepened from 1927, married women in particular became the scapegoats. The employment of women was now seen as a threat to the jobs of single women as well as men.[25] The *Labor Call*, weekly labour newspaper, described the existence of wage-earning wives as 'an anti-social policy of the most pernicious kind'.[26] Some employers responded to these protests by refusing to employ married women, while many wives who continued to work kept their wedding rings a guilty secret.[27]

The campaign against married women was both misdirected and counterproductive. It is doubtful that the exclusion of a small number of working wives would have opened many jobs to single women, whereas many of those who worked contributed vital money to families where, for a variety of reasons, male earnings were inadequate. As some of the better-informed commentators pointed out, even where male 'breadwinners' were receiving a 'family wage', there was no compulsion on men to pass on the portion allotted as the woman's share to the wife. Some simply chose not to.[28] In the long run the stigma attached to married women's paid work affected employers as well as workers of both sexes. The slow recovery of the economy from 1931 was led by manufacturing industries, especially 'women's industries' such as clothing, boots and textiles.[29] By the middle of the decade these industries had absorbed the available female labour and were beginning to experience shortages. The employment of married women would have been one way of overcoming this shortage, but there was no rush of wives anxious to re-enter the factories (see Chapter Eight). Finally, as the case of the boot trade shows, shortages of female labour in sections of an industry could slow down the entire production process. Had there been more women workers, it would have been possible to employ more men in the other sections which worked in conjunction with the women's departments.

The vilification of women's paid work in general (as distinct from that of working wives) was similarly misguided. As feminist investigators have pointed out, the apparent 'feminisation' of industry was due to lower levels of unemployment in 'women's industries'. Rather than women 'taking men's jobs', the labour market remained as rigidly sex-segregated as ever.[30] And while many workers of both sexes railed against those considered less deserving of employment, employers reaped the benefits of labour disunity. Individual women in the late 1920s and 1930s exhorted the workers to take a united stand against attacks on their wages and conditions, but their pleas fell on deaf ears.[31] Divided by sex, ethnicity and marital status, the working class in general was ill equipped to deal with the challenges presented by the depression. The nature of the challenge and the responses of the workers varied, however, from industry to industry, as we shall see in the chapters which follow.

7

DIPLOMACY AND GUERILLA WARFARE: THE CLOTHING INDUSTRIES, 1919–1939

In August 1922, almost 2000 clothing workers from Melbourne's dressmaking, shirt, underclothing and millinery firms gathered in the Trades Hall to discuss reductions in their rates of pay. Not since the agitation against sweating in the 1890s had there been such a large and enthusiastic gathering in the trade.[1] But apart from the scale of the agitation, the situation had little in common with the protest meetings of the 1890s. In the two decades which had elapsed, the world of the clothing worker had changed dramatically. In place of the unregulated workplace of the 1890s was the whole machinery of Wages Boards and Arbitration Court. And while the female clothing worker of the nineteenth century was at the employer's mercy in an overcrowded labour market, the early 1920s saw this situation reversed. Girls leaving school in the 1920s had wider options than their mothers and grandmothers, and many chose 'to go into lolly factories or jam factories or become stenographers' rather than follow the sewing trades.[2] The rapid expansion of textile factories after the war attracted many girls, especially as the starting pay was twice as much as that paid to beginners in the clothing trades.[3] The early 1920s were also prosperous ones for clothing manufacturers, with comparatively steady demand for their products. Their only serious problem was the shortage of skilled female labour.[4]

The combination of these factors meant that the outcome of the 1922 meeting was also very different. The reductions themselves had been introduced in accordance with adjustments in the consumer price index, under the authority of the arbitration award. The unanimous resolution to resist these cuts had a complex result in terms of actual strategy. The union was bound to appeal to the court and in the meantime the workers were unable to strike. But this did not eliminate resistance. On the contrary, workers carried out an informal campaign against employers who reduced pay rates. With clothing manufacturers short of suitable female labour, it was an easy matter for individual workers to find alternative employment. What happened was in effect a boycott of all cut-rate employers. These tactics had in fact been in operation in the tailoring section since February of 1922 and had been very successful. The few cases in which opposition did erupt into actual stoppages were quickly dealt with by the union officials, who advised the strikers to return to work and give in their notices.[5] In this way general reductions were prevented and the workers adhered to the letter, if not the spirit, of the arbitration law.[6] Some employers, at the instigation of the Victorian Chamber of Manufactures, attempted to stop the practice by compiling a black list of employees but the strategy foundered on disunity in their ranks.[7] These employers, in the past so fond of invoking the inviolability of the laws of the market, were forced to submit to the consequences of a labour shortage.

This episode highlights several important aspects of industrial relations in the clothing industry during this period. Firstly, it shows that, given the possibility of success, clothing workers could be both militant and effective in their resistance to employers. Their frequent changes of employment must be seen in this context as a resistance strategy, not as a shirking of conflict as Beverley Kingston has argued.[8] Secondly, the inter-war years saw the consolidation of the power of the officials within the Clothing Trades Union. The officials' analysis of the industrial situation and their assessment of appropriate strategies prevailed. As Carter himself observed: 'The influence that permeates this industry as far as the individuals who are officers of the Union is concerned is such that the employees are guided by their advice.'[9] The existence of what Wallis called the 'foreign element' also predisposed the officials to invoke the authority of the state rather than to attempt thorough shopfloor organisation.[10]

By the 1920s the officials were firmly committed to arbitration rather than direct action as the way to improve wages and conditions.[11] They reasoned that the preponderance of women in the union meant that direct action would not be effective.[12] Arbitration was costly, but there were large numbers employed in the industry; even though just over half were unionists, their contributions ensured a comparatively healthy bank balance.[13] The officials devoted their energies to preparing arbitration cases, recruiting new members and collecting contributions in order to finance their activities. They took pains not to antagonise employers so that they could continue this work on factory premises during working hours. By the mid-1920s members recalled nostalgically the 'old days' when officials used to give stirring speeches at factories.[14] As May Francis complained, 'there was too much diplomacy' on the part of organisers.[15]

This concentration of union effort on arbitration took its toll of both officials and members. In the heady days of 1922–23 the 'guerilla war' against reductions had united all in a spirit of comradeship, mass meetings ending with enthusiastic singing of 'Solidarity Forever'.[16] By contrast, the painstaking work of preparing arbitration cases seemed very dull. Attendance at meetings dropped off and several times did not even provide a quorum. Carter confessed that he 'felt stale for the want of something to do'. He went on to say that the union's efforts had become too stereotyped. 'It was losing its soul and was too straight laced ... The whole thing was being professionalised and it seemed to be all a question of jobs.'[17]

And as the reliance on arbitration reinforced the dominance of the officials within the union, so too did it reinforce the ascendancy of men over women. Female workers especially felt alienated by the whole process of courts, judges and cross-examinations. No doubt many men would also have been overawed by the court's formality and procedures, but women experienced added discomfort because of the maleness of the environment. The experience of being interrogated about one's annual underwear requirements by a group of men was one which few women could face with equanimity.[18] The world of the court was a man's world, better left to the talents of the male officials.

The reliance on arbitration also reinforced this position in more subtle ways. Appeals to the court were very expensive affairs, so that the union's financial position assumed great importance. This affected gender relations in the union in two ways. Firstly, as each male member paid twice as much in dues as the average woman it made more economic sense to concentrate the union's organising efforts on the male sections, that is, men's and boys' order and ready-made clothing. The mass of female workers employed in dressmaking, whitework, underclothing, millinery and shirt factories were given lowest priority.[19] This led to very uneven union coverage. At Myers, for instance, the tailoring workroom was almost 100 per cent union while at the same time most of Myers' other workrooms were almost 100 per cent non-union.[20] Secondly, the emphasis on recruiting members and collecting dues led to a quest for quantity rather than quality in union organisation. Organisers were evaluated on this basis. This in turn led indirectly to the replacement of the only woman organiser with a young man in 1923, on the grounds that Whitford was not as cost-effective as a man.[21]

The decision to give priority to the No. 1 Section, as the men's and boys' section was called, coincided with a decline in female representation on the union executive. After the war the union embraced several allied trades, namely umbrella making, straw hats, fur work, dyeing and cleaning, and examining. All of these sections were represented on the executive by men. The brief balance of the sexes which had been achieved in 1917 was upset, and for the 1920s and 1930s men outnumbered women by at least three to two. After the resignation of May Brodney (formerly May Francis) in 1927 the few women who remained on the executive presented little challenge to the hegemony of the male officials.[22]

By the late 1920s the arbitration system had helped men within the Clothing Trades Union assume a disproportionate amount of power and influence. Indeed, despite the majority of female membership the officials persisted in seeing it as a masculine concern. Strong union shops were said to be 'virile', while Carter claimed that the union's acquiescence in wage reductions 'would be tantamount to denying their own man-hood'.[23] When enthusiasm for the cause waned in the mid-1920s, he lamented the lack of 'young men with an ideal and willing to express it' to revive the fighting spirit.[24] It was as though the women members were invisible. Figures 12 and 13, although from a later period, capture this perception of the movement in the 1920s and 1930s. Note the handsome young organiser in Figure 12 enticing the young woman unionist, watched benevolently by the fatherly figures of the secretaries. Indeed, Wallis liked to describe himself as 'a sort of secular Father Confessor' to the members.[25]

12 This vivid visual representation of women's ideal relationship to the union appeared on the cover of the *Voice* of the Clothing Trades Union, vol. 1, no. 7, Autumn 1948.
ANU Archives of Business & Labour

A third point arising out of the 1922 resistance relates to the attitude of the employers. The attempt to blackball workers leaving their employers without a written certificate of release originated in the Chamber of Manufactures. As the union journal pointed out, the VCM had been captured by 'extremists'.[26] Their policies were not supported by the majority of clothing manufacturers, as the failure of the counter-boycott indicates. The union was quick to exploit these differences within the employers' camp. The choice of allies was not difficult, given the militantly anti-union stance of employers such as James Law. Law's stance had important repercussions in the industry. He was president of the Clothing Trades Section of the Chamber of Manufactures at the time of the reductions. In the mid-1920s he led a determined opposition by some employers to the union, forbidding officials to enter their factories and sacking unionists. Only the intervention of the Arbitration Court guaranteed officials rights of entry. Shirt manufacturers in particular continued their opposition throughout the 1930s.[27]

In addition to this organised opposition was the personal example Law offered. He strenuously opposed union influence within his own factory. His formula for industrial relations was impressively effective. Dining rooms, lunchtime entertainment, recreation rooms and a chatty company newspaper complemented Law's paternalistic style to undermine any attempt by the union to recruit amongst his workers.[28] The union's dismal failure to counter this approach no doubt contributed to the diplomacy shown to other employers: had others been as hostile as Law, the union would have been in a very sorry state. Pelaco was not alone in its provision of such facilities; industrial 'welfare schemes' gained in popularity in the 1920s and were most popular amongst manufacturers of wearing apparel. Nevertheless, such firms remained a small minority.[29]

13   Another graphic illustration of the marginalisation of women within the Clothing Trades Union. Propaganda drawn from a predominantly male union movement was used uncritically in the union's journal where its appeal in a largely women's industry must have been very limited. This appeal appeared on the front page of the *Australian Clothing Trades Journal,* November 1941.

ANU Archives of Business & Labour

In summary, then, relations between workers and employers in the 1920s were focused on the federal Arbitration Court where the union mounted two major cases, one in 1922 and the other in 1927. Outside the court the union concentrated its efforts on recruiting members whilst not antagonising employers. Collective direct action in support of pay and conditions was discouraged. At the same time, individual workers were able to take advantage of their relative scarcity to bargain with employers. Lack of unity amongst employers ensured that such bargaining usually worked to the employees' advantage.

With the downswing in the clothing trade from 1927, the situation began to change. The growth of contracting and outwork presented new problems to both the union officials and those employers being undercut.[30] Despite the existence of both state Wages Boards and federal arbitration awards, controlling cut-rate outwork was by no means an easy matter. The first difficulty was in relation to administration and policing of the two sets of legislation. The Commonwealth Arbitration Court had no officers of its own to police its awards, so that in practice this was left to the union officials. Theirs was a difficult task. They had to negotiate the labyrinth of Melbourne's backyard and fly-by-night factories, and faced legal restrictions on their right to enter factory premises to inspect for breaches of the award. Hostility by some employers and lack of co-operation from employees made their task unpleasant and on occasions dangerous. The union officials found that young girls and recent immigrants were particularly uncooperative in giving evidence about rates of pay. Ignorance and fear made both groups of workers particularly susceptible to exploitation. Officials often encountered abuse from employers, and on one occasion Wallis was punched in the face.[31] Their powers to eliminate sweating were further restricted by the fact that, for much of this period, their jurisdiction extended only to union members in the employ of manufacturers who were respondents to the award. In 1936 almost half of Victoria's 1000 or so registered clothing factories were small and employed non-union labour and, as such, came under the jurisdiction of the state Department of Labour. These small factories together employed over 8000 of the state's 20,613 clothing workers.[32]

The state Department of Labour was even less well equipped to police the Shops and Factories Act. In the 1930s its inspectors had to police the provisions of approximately 180 Wages Board determinations in over 12,000 factories. As a campaign against sweating noted in the 1930s, the Factories Department was 'utterly understaffed and for this reason entirely ineffective'.[33] Low piecework rates, 'stretch-out' of tasks, non-payment of overtime and excessive overtime were matters which remained undetected after the perfunctory questioning of employees (often in the presence of employers) which usually passed for factory inspection.[34] Many employers took advantage of this situation and made it a rule not to employ unionists so that they would continue exclusively under state, rather than federal authority.[35]

The union's response to these difficulties was to intensify its policy of using the arbitration system to defend working standards. In the first instance it sought and won the court's recognition that officers of the union were to be regarded as officers of the court for the purposes of policing arbitration awards.[36] The years of playing the part of the moderate, 'reasonable' union had borne fruit. The next target was to enable the union to sue employers who breached awards and to compel workers to give sworn evidence regarding their wages. This required an award for compulsory unionism. Again, the union was successful, the award for compulsory union membership for female clothing workers being granted in 1931. When contractors still evaded prosecution by challenging the definition of themselves as employers, the union pressed the court to make the principal employer, that is, the one who issued the original contract, responsible for the wages and conditions under which the work was carried out. Judge Drake-Brockman also agreed to this claim after a special hearing on outwork in 1937.[37]

It seemed the union's policy of trusting to the 'generosity of Judge Drake-Brockman' had paid off.[38] But as the 1930s progressed it became increasingly apparent that the policy was only partially successful. Even when breaches of the awards and determinations were discovered, legal loopholes and High Court challenges made successful prosecution of sweaters a most difficult task. Numerous alterations to the outwork provisions in the both federal and state legislation in the period 1928–39 failed to plug these loopholes. Rather, the problems increased throughout the 1930s and in some cases attempted reforms only exacerbated the difficulties. For example, the 1928 award tried to reduce the exploitation of homeworkers by forbidding respondents to employ outworkers directly. The respondent was, however, allowed to enter into a contract with a non-respondent to have work done outside the respondent's factory. This caused a short-term fall in work being given to individual outworkers and an immediate increase in the number of small 'backyard' factories operated by contractors. This provision in fact seems to have exacerbated the problem by involving middlemen and removing the responsibility of the principal employer.[39]

Not only was the policy ineffective in providing the legal protection which officials hoped for, but it also became obvious that relying on arbitration had unforeseen costs for the workers. The emphasis on recruiting members and piling up dues had created a certain amount of cynicism and alienation amongst workers, especially the women. This sense of alienation was observed by an anonymous unionist in 1938. Although she expected some action on a case of underpayment at her workplace, she pointed out that most of her fellow machinists were sceptical: 'The girls at the factory say all the union worries about is that you pay Mr. Wilson your contributions.'[40]

The increasing employment of European migrants, particularly Italians, Poles and Yugoslavs, made the task of achieving close relations between organisers and workers even more difficult, while evidence of anti-Semitism on Wallis' part cannot have improved the union's relationship with Jewish workers.[41] In addition to the generally low priority given to women members, several specific instances of neglect no doubt contributed to women's suspicions of the male officials. The first episode occurred in 1920, when the union was forced to negotiate with the employers for an increase in wages to cover inflation. The compromise reached on this occasion was that 'the women should only get half the increase that the men got', as Carter put it. This represented a relative decline in wages for the women, as they had been awarded 57 per cent of the male rate by Higgins in the previous year.[42]

The other cause of dissatisfaction was the rather half-hearted way in which the men prosecuted the union's claim for equal pay for the sexes. Despite the strenuous efforts of

Muriel Heagney and a number of women in the industry to prepare cases for federal arbitration in 1922 and 1927, their claims were not treated seriously by the court. This is hardly surprising, since the union officials themselves were not convinced of the justice or viability of the proposal. Carter, who was in charge of the union case, doubted the justice of claiming equal pay for workers who remained in the industry 'for only seven years', and also believed that to introduce the scheme would require a prohibitive tariff in order to maintain the competitiveness of Australia's clothing industry.[43] The consistent refusal of the union to grant equal pay to its woman organiser and female clerks must also have created doubts about the sincerity of the union's own equal-pay claims.[44]

By 1935 even the officials were becoming concerned at the level of disillusionment. In December of that year it mounted a campaign to combat sweating in the Brunswick factories. Significantly, it employed the services of a woman, Muriel Heagney, to assist its own male organiser, Ted Smith.[45] Both found that, apart from the hostility of employers, the 'greatest obstacle' in enrolling new members arose in relation to fears about arrears of dues and prosecutions by the union to recover these. 'The intrusion of the policeman into Union affairs', Heagney reported, had had 'a lasting and baneful effect' on the women.[46]

Heagney also pointed out that formal meeting procedures had a 'very stultifying effect on people of all ages and particularly on young women'. She suggested instead that frequent informal meetings and social gatherings be organised amongst Brunswick workers to 'create a medium for greater co-operation between the Union officials and the workers in the various factories'. She also urged the appointment of a woman organiser, as 'there was a general consensus of opinion that it was helpful to have a woman organiser to discuss phases of women's conditions not adequately and freely discussed in the routine of formal Union work'.[47] The latter suggestion was ignored. Indeed, Wallis still espoused the belief that 'most women in industry preferred to work for men and to have men as their industrial organisers'.[48]

Meanwhile, there were signs of serious discontent in Melbourne's largest men's clothing factories. Traditionally the backbone of the union, the women in these factories chose the temporary absence of Secretary Wallis from the state as an occasion for a strike against changes to the process of machining trousers. The strike involved 150 women at Ellinson Brothers', Frieze Brothers' and Sackville's. Previous to the dispute, machinists made trousers almost wholly throughout with the exception of buttonholes, button loops and bands which were made on separate patent machines. An overlocking machine had recently been introduced which did the side seam in the leg, seat seam and crutch. The proprietors of these three firms proposed to use these overlocking machines in conjunction with a team system comprising one journeywoman and two improvers. Instead of machining the trousers throughout, the work was to be subdivided into four or five operations, depending on the style of the bands. A meeting of the machinists unanimously resolved to oppose the new system on the grounds:

1. That it will speed them up and increase their output.
2. That their earnings will be lessened.
3. That the juveniles will not be taught all sections of trousers.
4. That being part of a system each one is bound by the speed set by the team with an inevitable injury to their health.[49]

Clearly, their main concern was that the new method was a form of increased exploitation.

The Militant Minority Movement of the Communist Party was anxious to extend the strike and set up relief and propaganda committees to deal with its management, but the union officials were just as anxious to prevent a communist ascendancy in the factories.[50] Wallis rushed back from Tasmania and set up shop committees of his own, and thus assumed control of the strike.[51] After a protracted dispute lasting several months, he persuaded the women to modify their demands and accept some innovation, providing their earnings did not fall.[52] There was no guarantee against speeding-up, the first objection stated by the strikers.

The outcome of this dispute indicates several significant developments in the union's position since 1922. The official position was still one of active encouragement of more 'efficient' methods of production. The union had always allied itself to the large-scale manufacturer because it equated large-scale production with better pay and conditions. As Carter told the Arbitration Court in 1927, 'it suits us to have the industry in more or less the control of the bigger people'.[53] Big factories were easier to organise and police than the fly-by-night backyard operator. With the re-emergence of outwork in the late 1920s, this alliance became even more important. But support of big industry also implied an acceptance of mass production methods. Indeed, Wallis and Carter were at pains to emphasise the union's support for these more 'rational' methods.[54]

By the 1920s, however, the consequences of this policy were becoming apparent. The early 1920s saw an increasing conviction within the union that the workers were becoming 'the victims of the Juggernaut of industry', to use Higgins' colourful phrase.[55] From its aggressive stance in 1919, demanding a share in the higher profits, the union retreated somewhat in the face of greater experience with the new methods. It had become clear that the employers not only wished to cheapen production by increasing output through subdivision, but that they desired to reduce costs even further by eliminating margins for skill and speeding up the workers. Instead of talking about workers sharing in increased profits, the union's emphasis shifted to insisting that it was not fair that employers reaped greater profits at the expense of the workers.[56]

This disillusionment with the employers' sense of justice was even more evident in the 1927 arbitration hearing. It was also obvious that more workers were dissatisfied with the effects of the new methods. They complained about the bad effects that the noise, speed and monotony had on their health.[57] The union was also less enthusiastic about the new methods, realising that the subdivision of labour deskilled workers and made them more susceptible to unemployment and wage reductions. The claim for compulsory apprenticeship with apprentices being taught all sections of the 'craft' was the union's attempt to accommodate subdivision. Like the bootmakers, they hoped this broad-based training would give workers greater flexibility in the labour market and also support the claim that their work was specialised rather than fragmented.[58]

Wallis' position on shorter hours encouraging 'industrial efficiency' had changed radically between 1919 and 1935 in the light of this experience. By 1935 he admitted that shorter hours usually led to speeding up rather than genuinely 'labour-saving' methods, so that 'the benefit to the workers individually and collectively will be again annulled'.[59]

But the union was still not prepared to change its official stance regarding innovations in production. It still regarded scientific management as the lesser of two evils, the alternative being sweated outwork. What did change was the way in which the officials justified their stance to their members. Wallis, in his appeal to the strikers in 1935, emphasised the futility of their opposition to the team system: 'In every industry, everywhere, no union or strike has been able to prevent new methods and machines . . . and . . . that if employees struck against acceptance of the new method of manufacture and the new machines they would not have one chance in a hundred of preventing new methods.'[60] The only hope, he argued, was to prevent the worst features of the system from being introduced and to keep up the price of labour.

The difference in attitudes on this issue between the officials and the machinists is evidence of the increasing distance between them. Both groups objected to the increased exploitation of the changed methods, but they each had different criteria of what exploitation involved. For the women, decreased earnings were an important factor but secondary to the decreased quality of the work experience and consequent detrimental effects on the workers' health. The officials tended to see the issue purely in terms of earnings. This difference arose out of the two groups' different experiences of work. Neither Carter nor Wallis had worked at the trade since before the war. Their experience of work even in those days did not coincide with that of the female workers. An order tailor and cutter respectively, neither experienced the pressures of working as machinists. As subdivision and mechanisation increased in the late 1920s and 1930s, so too did the disparity between these experiences. This was also true for the majority of male unionists who supported Carter and Wallis. Even those who worked in factories which employed subdivision of labour usually did so as supervisors in charge of female operatives.[61]

This distance between the officials and the female members was also reflected in the policy of the union in regard to outwork. The union's aim was to abolish the practice altogether.[62] The attractions of such a policy were obvious enough. Outworkers were no easier to organise in the 1930s than they had been in the 1890s, and policing their conditions seemed impossible. But whereas such a policy may have succeeded with a male workforce (as indeed it had in the boot trade in 1884) it was doomed to failure in the clothing trade. Too many women, tied to the home by their domestic responsibilities, were prepared to sabotage any such attempt to remove their livelihood.[63]

While the 1935 strike highlighted these aspects of the union's relationship to the workers, it also alerted the officials to significant problems with their policy regarding arbitration. Reviewing the history of the clothing trades awards at a national conference of the union in 1937, one of the organisers observed that the policy of industrial peace they had pursued seemed to have backfired. Referring to the trouser machinists' strike in 1935, organiser Maurice Callard recalled that in that instance 'the girls struck and the bosses rushed around'. He contrasted the effectiveness of militancy with the 'diplomatic' policy pursued by the union, saying that 'if he, as an Organiser, walked into the shop he would be arguing for six months'. And, as he pointed out, the 'position had the same effect upon a Judge or Court: if the industry jumped out they took notice'.[64]

In their defence the officials maintained that they lacked an army to carry on a war against the bosses. They 'had portions of an army, however, and could carry on guerilla warfare'.[65] This reassessment prompted a more militant spirit. 'Comrade' Wallis told a general meeting of the Victorian branch in 1940 that he believed the clothing workers had been 'penalised' because of their 'allegiance to constitutional methods'. They had received no increases in margins for skill since 1928, whereas skilled workers in other, more 'militant', industries had been given quite considerable increases.[66] The late 1930s saw a revival of union organisation directed at building rank-and-file enthusiasm. Social gatherings, sporting competitions and factory addresses once more became a feature of union activity.[67] By 1937 this policy was showing signs of success, and young people began to take an active interest in the union's affairs for the first time since the agitation of 1922. The experience of organising campaigns revived the spirits of organisers like Ted Smith, who had the chance to 'penetrate many aspects of organisation which are not encountered in the ordinary course of work for the Union'. By this he meant that he devoted special attention to examining 'the state of affairs in the factories, the psychology of the employers and employees, their reactions to our Union, sympathetically or otherwise'.[68] The close of the decade thus saw a spirit of defiance in the union not seen since the early 1920s.

How far did this 'peace', punctuated by sporadic outbreaks of rebellion, affect the nature of work in the inter-war period? At the most general level it is clear that the union's support for arbitration and the organising priorities which this entailed reinforced existing trends in relation to the work process. Those sections which were already subject to substantial subdivision, such as shirts, continued to lead the field in relation to innovative work processes. The failure of the union to organise these sections and the unwillingness of the court to flout trade customs regarding apprenticeships combined to give manufacturers a free hand. After the war, James Law continued his innovations, building on his time-and-motion studies to 'rationalise' every aspect of his factory. In general terms, as he put it, this meant adopting the method of 'placing the management in the hands of those who are capable of managing, and putting the work in the hands of those who are capable of doing the work'.[69] Juveniles, it seems, were capable of doing a large part of this executive work where 'every operation has been rendered fool-proof'. Over 60 per cent of female workers were under twenty-one years of age and almost one-third of these were under eighteen.[70] Law made no apologies for his preference for young girls. He maintained that in most cases industrial employment was seen by girls as a stepping stone to matrimony. 'The present-day girl', he argued, 'is looking for work where she can get the most money in the quickest time.' Furthermore, he added, 'the man who is able to put his industry into such a position as will cope with that demand by the girls is the one, I think, who is best able to achieve satisfactory results'.[71] He managed this task by putting juveniles on piece rates almost from the outset, instead of putting them on improvers' wages, which were fixed according to age, until they reached twenty-one. Because the work was so subdivided, workers could become proficient in a matter of months. Thereafter as juniors they usually earned more on piecework than on the relevant wage for their age. Compared to a journeywoman's earnings, however, their earnings were not so impressive, which accounts in part for the high turnover and preponderance of juveniles.[72] This system of putting juniors on piece rates had the added advantage of circumventing the restrictions on the employment of juveniles, since pieceworkers were counted as adults whatever their age. It also may account for the contradictory image Pelaco has maintained of paying good money yet being a sweatshop.

The keys to Law's system remained the separation of conception and execution and the location of the 'right' person to perform each. By the end of the war the sewing of garments was already minutely subdivided so that the 1920s saw only an extension of this principle. The big change occurred in the cutting department, where even the cutter's work was subject to time-and-motion studies and specific instruction from 'the planning department'. At the Pelaco factory in the late 1920s the most economical layout for any pattern was calculated not by the cutter but by the head draughtsman in the planning department. The cloth was then carried on lifting trucks operated by boys and was laid on tables where the pattern was marked by a perforating machine operated by girls. After a boy had chalked the perforations, the cutter simply cut through the layers with an electric cutting machine.[73]

A further innovation in this period was in the 'scientific' approach to personnel selection. As Law explained, finding the right person for the job was no longer simply a matter of trial and error:

> Our employment girl downstairs has been well taught and has read a great deal of psychology, and knows the type of individual who would fit the different jobs ... She knows by looking at a girl's head and hands, the shape of her mouth, eyes, etc., and can tell to a certain extent what any girl is particularly useful for.[74]

Industrial psychology (or should it be industrial phrenology?) had made its appearance on the Victorian scene.

But whereas industrial relations in the shirt industry, and arbitration awards for this section, provided little impediment to productive innovation, the reverse was true of the manufacture of men's and boys' clothing. Indentures which insisted on apprentices being taught all parts of a garment, and limitations on the number of apprentices which could be employed, discouraged innovations which relied on untrained juvenile labour. Perhaps more importantly, concentration of union effort on organising this section made the militant resistance, such as that which occurred in 1935, both more likely to occur and more likely to succeed.

The court's award for equal pay on pressing, cutting and dress coats also discouraged subdivision of these occupations in the tailoring section, particularly in the latter two. Equal pay removed the incentive to subdivide work where manufacturers hoped to use this in conjunction with quickly trained, cheap female labour. In all sections of the trade Law's cutting methods stood out as the only chink in the armour of the craftsman cutter. By 1938 others had joined the assault, seeking to separate the tasks of marking in and cutting out, but before World War II the move had made little impression on the craft as a whole.[75]

On the other hand, the court's failure to award margins commensurate with the skill of many female workers doing 'women's work' may have deterred innovation in sections like dressmaking: the rates being paid were so low that further cheapening of labour by subdivision was of less obvious advantage than if the undivided work had been paid for at male craft rates.

The court affected the shirt industry in a similarly negative fashion. By not restricting the employment of juveniles or providing for craft apprenticeships, it gave free rein to the shirt manufacturers.

Similarly, the failure of arbitration awards to control contracting had led to exploitation of workers in these factories and the lowering of standards for others in respondent factories. Most importantly, the use of arbitration awards to control excessive tasks and cutting of piece rates proved futile. The only effective answer to these practices was shopfloor resistance; the poorly organised dress and shirt sections which had been unable to mount such resistance in the past continued to suffer the greatest exploitation despite the arbitration system.

In general, federal arbitration reinforced existing trends in the clothing trade. Its awards affected the nature of work by defining the options available to employers, but these definitions often amounted to a formalisation of existing customs and practices within the trade. Where radical departures were attempted, such as in the control of outwork, they were not very successful in achieving significant modifications.

More important in determining the nature of work processes was the ongoing limitation of the Australian market for clothing. Employers were alert to the latest methods and developments in use overseas, but the more restricted nature of the local market often made these methods impractical.[76]

Technological developments in this period were also important in both encouraging and limiting innovation in methods of work. The 1920s saw the development of a greater variety of specialist machines and an improvement in existing models. The new machines performed many of the old hand operations quickly and efficiently. Felling, tacking, padding, basting and seaming could all now be done mechanically, and even shank buttons could be sewn on by machine. Embroidery machines replaced hand labour while machines to perform tubular work, such as sleeve and trouser felling, were also developed. Patent machines which made hip pockets and trouser loops, and special attachments to assist with feeding these machines, reduced the time spent adjusting cloth prior to sewing. To some extent these eliminated the most difficult part of the work: guiding material through the machine at a very fast pace.[77] The demand for these special machines was such that one company, the Union Special Machine Company, devoted the whole of its operation prior to the mid-1930s to developing improved models.[78] In some cases, improvements on older models produced dramatic increases in output. For example, buttonhole machines in use in 1920 could do 800 buttonholes per day; fifteen years later a good operator on the Reece trouser buttonhole machine could do 4000 in one day.[79] Even the straight sewer was improved, with speeds increased from 3500 to 5000 stitches per minute. Improved gearing made these speeds instantly available to the operative.[80] The 1930s also saw the limited introduction of sewing machines powered by individual motors.[81] But by the mid-1930s the machinery manufacturers recognised that the sewing machine had reached its maximum practical speed because higher speeds were inclined to break both operators and cotton. As one manufacturer put it, 'speeds above a reasonable limit lose their efficiency, due to the undue strain of concentration by the operator, and the difficulty in obtaining at reasonable cost cottons that will stand passing through the machines at such speeds'.[82]

The relationship between sewing machine technology and methods of work is nicely illustrated by ready-made tailoring. Ready-made tailoring factories had divided the work to some extent since the turn of the century. This was especially so with trouser-making, where pockets, bands and linings were prepared separately, and hemming, buttonholing and button-sewing were performed by different workers. The new patent machines reinforced the subdivision of many preparatory and finishing tasks, but the straight sewing usually remained in the hands of the one machinist who sewed the garment throughout. This situation began to change only in 1935 when new overlocking machines prompted employers to experiment with subdivision of the actual making.[83]

As the case of trouser-making also shows, however, the availability of technology did not determine methods of work in any mechanistic sense: how it was applied depended very much on the decisions of employers and the response of employees. And the relative bargaining power of capital and labour was most immediately determined by the labour market. The Arbitration Court did mediate this relationship to some extent, but only in minor ways. In the final analysis, the court reflected the contours of the labour market. And in the fiercely competitive 1930s, few workers had cause to celebrate the benefits of the system in which their union had put its trust.

8

THE CINDERELLA OF THE SKILLED TRADES: THE BOOT INDUSTRY, 1911–1939

Looking back over the history of the Boot Trade Union Federation in 1939, Jim Maloney, secretary of the New South Wales branch, characterised the dominant strategy of the union before 1936 as one of 'peace at any price'.[1] This chapter will focus on the way in which this peace was achieved and the consequences of this bargain for all concerned.

Both parties to the 1909 federal arbitration award emerged from the case very much the poorer. The cost of financing advocates and witnesses amounted to about £3000 for each side.[2] In addition to the monetary expense was the time and energy expended on preparing the case. And at the end of it all the Arbitration Court could not guarantee uniformity, since the award applied only to the 38 respondents, leaving a further 256 manufacturers outside its jurisdiction.[3] Chastened by the experience, both employers and workers were receptive to any scheme which promised a cheaper and more effective solution to the problem of settling industrial differences.[4]

The Round Table Conference had much to recommend it. Representatives from employers and the union in each state met in interstate conferences and negotiated agreements on wages and conditions. The representatives then returned home and ensured that the agreement was embodied in the award of each state wage-fixing tribunal.[5] In some cases the agreement was also made a consent award of the federal court. This arrangement was cheaper, quicker and more effective than arbitration. Instead of £3000 in costs, each side could expect to pay about £500 per conference.[6] There was no need to worry about the delays attendant on bringing the case to court, nor the time taken with hearing cases and preparing judgements. By embodying the agreement under state legislation, the officers of the particular government labour departments were responsible for its enforcement. Furthermore, the agreement applied to all employers, not only those named as respondents. Finally, each side still had the option of an appeal to the court should conferences prove abortive in settling differences. In theory, at least, Round Table Conferences represented the partnership of capital, labour and the state, working in the interests of peace, prosperity and justice for all.

The reality did not always measure up to this lofty scheme for industrial consensus. The 'spirit of sweet reasonableness' on numerous occasions proved unable to reconcile the diverse interests and tempers of the various parties.[7] Meanwhile, the personalities and policies of the arbitration bench, rather than offering neutral adjudication, at various times seemed to hold out greater hope for one side or the other. Nor did the uniformity of conditions offered by conference lay to rest the 'bitter feeling which . . . existed between different employers'.[8] The possibility of securing a separate state determination in order to gain an advantage over rival interstate manufacturers was sometimes too tantalising for certain employers. Finally, there were always those in both camps who preferred direct action to either conciliation or arbitration. The peace was at best an uneasy one.

The first decade of conferences saw the arrangement working smoothly with apparent satisfaction to all concerned. The federal award came into operation in 1910 and the subsequent years to 1920 were ones of almost general prosperity for the boot trade. Victorian manufacturers in particular did well out of the boot boom which accompanied Australia's involvement in the 1914–18 war, accounting for about 60 per cent of Australia's total production. Between 1913 and 1923 the number of factories doubled and the value of plant and equipment increased threefold, while production of boots and shoes increased by almost 40 per cent.[9]

But the onset of the post-war recession in 1920 exposed the fragility of this consensus.[10] A strong rank-and-file agitation developed in Victorian boot factories to reduce the working week from 48 to 44 hours or less in order to offset the growing unemployment in the trade.[11] At the same time, New South Wales employers were forced to increase their rates above those decreed by the interstate agreement because of an award of the state arbitration court.[12] Victorian manufacturers thus had an advantage over their rivals in Sydney and, even though they conceded the 44-hour week in 1921, the minimum hourly rate in Victoria was still less than that paid in New South Wales. The interstate conference in March 1921 agreed on a formula to restore uniformity to the trade.[13]

An active section of the Victorian manufacturers, however, was reluctant to concede their advantage and rejected the conference's decision, resolving in future to settle their differences in the Victorian Wages Board. This move was designed to preserve their edge over New South Wales for at least another six months, as the Wages Board would not normally be convened without their co-operation before that time had elapsed.[14] The plan backfired. Representatives from the union and the majority of the large employers (including two of their Wages Board delegates) persuaded the Minister for Labour to convene the board immediately, that is, before any change in the delegates was possible.[15] The outcome was not unexpected. T. Y. Harkness and Daniel Hellings, the two employers' delegates who had supported the union's request for the board to be convened, voted with the workers to incorporate the terms of the conference agreement in the new determination.[16]

The crisis was not yet over. A narrow majority of the Manufacturers' Association voted to replace Hellings and Harkness on the reconstituted board and their recommendation was accepted by the Minister despite a petition against this change signed by twenty-five major employers who between them employed about 3000 of the 11,700 Victorian boot workers.[17] The new delegates approached the board with drastic proposals for altering the determination. This move also failed as a large meeting of the Manufacturers' Association narrowly rejected the proposals and ordered the delegates to adjourn the board indefinitely.[18]

Defeated in their own organisation, the more militant manufacturers were forced to accept a return to the Round Table. Between 1923 and 1931 these conferences again functioned more or less smoothly, with decisions generally following precedents set in the federal court.[19] The deepening of the economic depression in 1931, however, saw a revival of agitation by the militant section of manufacturers, who this time carried a majority of their fellows with them in withdrawing from the federal agreement.[20] In returning to the Victorian Wages Board they hoped to secure more favourable terms than those their Sydney competitors could obtain under the aegis of the Lang government.[21] Again their attempt was thwarted, this time by the union's threat to bring the case before the federal court. Employers in all states agreed to a conference with the union and the result was an agreement which was registered as a consent award in the federal court.[22]

For two more years the trade limped through the depression. The cumulative effects of years of short-time and unemployment, combined with speeding-up, began to tell on the passivity of the workers. Approximately 1000 male workers lost their jobs altogether during the depression years from 1928 to 1935, while those at work were lucky to average three-quarter time.[23] Those fortunate enough to find work had to contend with employers' demands that they work faster and faster. As Frank Ponchard, a boot operative, recalled: 'You couldn't lift your head in the Depression or you'd get the sack. Fair dinkum. The employers really took advantage of the workers—they knew you couldn't get a job. They worked you as hard as you could go.'[24] Matters came to a head in late 1934 when the New South Wales branch of the union proposed an approach to the federal court for some relief.

Ever since Judge J. Lukin's removal from the court in 1929, New South Wales had favoured an appeal to what was seen as a slightly more sympathetic bench.[25] The New South Wales action posed a serious threat to the authority of the Victorian officials, particularly Arthur Long, who was federal secretary. In the face of growing rank-and-file dissatisfaction and jibes from the 'Reds' that he was 'a bosses' man', Long was forced to bow before the militant mood of his members.[26] The union approached the employers with a demand for a 30-hour week, a proposal obviously intended as a pretext for filing a case in the federal court since it was clear that the employers would reject it. The outcome was predictably abortive and the Round Table was finally replaced by the court bench.[27]

How far did the era of interstate conferences bring benefits to either employers or employees? In its main objects, the strategy was spectacularly successful. The expense of arbitration hearings was eliminated. Even allowing for the cost of the entertainment of delegates, the savings were considerable. Secondly, the interstate agreement achieved an unprecedented level of industrial peace. This was appreciated by both management and workers, neither of whom relished the prospect of strikes or lockouts. Workers in particular must be seen as the major beneficiaries of the peace as in general they had fewer reserves to fall back on in the event of disputes stopping their wages. Those who recalled the troubled decades before 1910 were acutely aware of this fact. Arthur Long recalled that 'after much experience in my early days of strikes year in and year out the true trade unionist had nothing much left for his work, after paying the [strike] levies'.[28]

Manufacturers, of course, also benefited from uninterrupted production. This was particularly appreciated during the boom-time war years when the commitment of the union officials to the federal agreement was seen as largely responsible for the maintenance of 'discipline' amongst the more volatile rank and file.[29] Union records bear out this impression, with Long working hard to prevent stoppages in the face of a certain amount of worker discontent. In fact, few disputes occurred in regard to the terms of the agreement, most dissatisfaction being confined to specific grievances at individual factories. The exception to this was the threatened strike over the question of reduced hours in 1920–21. In this case a reduction in hours under the agreement averted potential conflict.[30]

What other gains were to be had from this peace? The answer is by no means clear and largely depends on one's perspective at the pay desk. It also depends on how one evaluates the alternatives: that is, what different result could have been expected under arbitration or under the combination of the Wages Board and direct action?

In order to tease out the various strands to this question it is useful to look at the points of view of the groups on either side who most consistently advocated the peaceful policy of the Round Table. On the workers' side, foremost advocate was Arthur Long, initially Victorian Branch secretary and also federal secretary. Thomas Richards, who succeeded Long as Victorian secretary, was also committed to the policy. They were supported by a majority of the executive and a majority of the members.[31] They believed that workers could expect a fair deal from 'reasonable and reputable employers' if they were approached in the right spirit, and that such a deal could be enforced on less reasonable manufacturers.[32] Conferences also had the advantage of being able to arrive at an agreement more to the liking of both sides. As the union's federal committee put it: 'the great advantage of Conference is . . . being able to say no to any objectionable condition but, when in Court, you must take what they give you or do as the Timber Workers did [i.e. strike]'.[33]

On the employers' side, most of the major manufacturers supported the conference system. Arthur Whybrow, Australia's largest boot manufacturer until the mid-1920s, was also the most sympathetic to the needs of his workers and the most conciliatory in his approach to the union.[34] He was usually supported by other 'reputable' employers such as Thomas Young Harkness, Daniel Hellings and the Bedggood family.[35] Veterans of the campaign to mechanise bootmaking, they had no desire for further radical change in the work process or further acrimony in their dealings with their workers. Some also had factories in more than one state and for them uniformity of wages and conditions had obvious advantages.[36] Even that maverick amongst manufacturers, William Marshall, deprived of his cheap boy labour by the Higgins award, supported collective bargaining in preference to the arbitrary arbitration of the state.

On the other hand, most of the smaller manufacturers were prepared to be led by a few of the disaffected 'big men'. W. D. Cookes (of the giant Ezywalkin firm) and

J. H. Sharwood were relative newcomers to the trade and were entranced by 'modern' methods in industry, even if their industrial relations style lacked sophistication. Seduced by scientific management with its logic of subdivision and payment by results, they attempted to break down the status of male bootmakers and hive off their less skilled tasks to cheaper female and boy labour. The smaller manufacturers, caught in the wholesale cost-price war, were carried along in this quest for cheaper labour.[37]

At the heart of the matter was the status of the male boot worker as 'skilled', and the flat-rate margin for skill of 12 shillings which he received under Higgins' original award. Prior to the award in 1909, Wages Board determinations had distinguished between the 'more skilled' operations of clicking, stuff-cutting, making and finishing and the 'less skilled' work of lining assistants, assistant stuff-cutters and men involved in treeing and cleaning up boots. The 'skilled' category under the Wages Board accounted for about 90 per cent of the male workers.[38] For Long and his colleagues, Higgins' judgement represented a considerable victory. By providing a broad-based apprenticeship and a flat-rate margin, his award effectively stopped the wholesale degradation of the bootmakers' craft which had been occurring since the introduction of machinery and subdivision in the 1890s. The benefits to the male worker went beyond monetary rewards. As one bootmaker noted, the more varied work experience which resulted meant that 'a worker can feel that in his particular calling he is realising his manhood rather than functioning as a machine'.[39] The rehabilitation of the bootmaker's masculinity was reinforced by equal pay provisions under the Wages Board determination which repulsed any possibility of invasion from cheap female labour. At the same time, restrictions on the numbers of apprentices and improvers employed checked this source of cheap labour and reduced overcrowding in the adult section of the trade.[40] Given the history of the previous two decades, it is impossible to underestimate the gain which Higgins' award represented to male workers. The interstate conferences were seen by them first and foremost as a way to preserve these gains. Seen from this point of view, the Round Tables cannot be seen as anything but a success. The apprenticeship system continued in its broad form and was in fact reinforced by the Victorian Apprenticeship Commission in 1932.[41] The flat-rate margin, although seriously eroded by inflation in the war years and the 1920s, nevertheless acted as a disincentive to the employment of 'green' labour.[42] In the peak production war years some manufacturers had used men 'off the streets' on the simpler tasks in the making and finishing rooms.[43] Moves to 'classify' such tasks at cheaper rates would have no doubt led to the widespread use of untrained men on this work. From the union's point of view, then, the Round Table preserved bootmaking as a skilled occupation for tradesmen, even though some of these tradesmen were not as well rewarded for their expertise as they might have wished. As Arthur Long explained:

> we fight at all costs for a flat rate minimum by which means we claim we maintain a higher basis for the average man and a better wage for the trade all round. For many years the more skilled operative did not approve of that policy, but to-day they recognise they are better off.[44]

So important was the principle of the flat-rate margin that the union was prepared to concede the possibility of higher wages rather than agree to classification. As J. E. Ager, president of the Manufacturers' Association, pointed out in 1938: 'I think the position

14   Stitching and clicking departments, Edwards' 'Crown' boot factory, Clifton Hill, 1908.
Australian Leather Journal, 16 March 1908, p. 743. (State Library of Victoria)

was largely that for many years we have gone on a flat rate, and as long as the Union's demands for higher wages were kept within reason we didn't worry too much about it, although we recognised it was not really a fair basis of payment.'[45] J. J. Maloney, secretary of the New South Wales branch of the union, put the situation more forcefully when he wrote that throughout the years up to 1935, 'the employers always held over the head of the Union the big stick of Classification . . . So, in order to save the flat rat[e] of 12/-, the wages rates and working conditions were sacrificed.'[46]

The union was also successful in confining women to the upper-machining and packing departments. It suffered an initial setback in 1911 when it had to concede some work on the new Fortuna skiver to women. Under threat of strike action, however, the Wages Board reversed its decision.[47] From 1913 the interstate conferences endorsed the line of demarcation between men's and women's work established by the Victorian Wages Board.[48] The subsequent history of Round Table Conferences was the history of the extension of male labour rather than the reverse. With the growth of slipper making and children's shoe manufacturing, for instance, any disputes about which sex should perform certain new ambiguous classes of work were settled in the men's favour.[49] The increase in female workers relative to men from the early 1920s was partly due to the increase in these latter classes of footwear which were mainly 'female' work as customarily defined.[50] (See Appendix, Table A10.) It was also a reflection of the higher level of male unemployment and the increased demand for machinists to perform the extra work on the fashionable fancy uppers. So, despite an increase in the percentage of workers who were female from 39.9 in 1920 to 50.4 in 1934, there was no shift in the division of work in women's favour.

As a defensive strategy, interstate agreements were thus very effective. Indeed, given the court's record in other cases it is unlikely that the workers would have gained much more during the 1920s and highly likely that they would have had to concede territory to cheaper labour (both male and female) under the changed attitude of the bench in the 1930s. The 1938 award, to which we will return shortly, is indicative of what could have been expected at any time during the 1930s. Not only did this award classify male labour but it also extended the range of tasks which could be performed by women at 'women's rates'. Nor does it seem likely that direct action could have offered any greater security. Plagued by intermittent employment, the union was hardly in a position to engage in a show of strength with manufacturers. In any event, costly strikes seemed a pointless exercise when peaceful negotiations appeared adequate to defend the workers' position.

The continuance of conferences also helped maintain workers' earnings in the face of emergency cuts imposed by the federal court in 1931. In the boot industry such cuts were not imposed by conference until 1932, and even then the amount of the reduction was only half that prescribed by the court and was imposed in two stages at six-monthly intervals, giving the workers further reprieve.[51]

15 Separated into women's 'departments' in the factories, women had a symbolic role only to play in the union's affairs: Executive Committee, Victorian Branch of ABTEF, with union banner, 1915.
ANUA E141/20.

From the manufacturers' point of view, the court's reinforcement of male work as skilled was not as disastrous for the trade as many had feared. The 12-shilling margin was moderate compared to those paid in other skilled trades, and the broad-based apprenticeship produced a more flexible workforce.[52] Victorian boot manufacturers thus discovered what Marx had noted in *Capital*: that there is an inherent contradiction between the increasing specialisation of workers and industry's need for a versatile workforce.[53] This flexibility was of particular advantage during the years of comparative labour shortage between 1915 and 1920. Nor did most manufacturers resent the restrictions on boy labour. Before the award it was only the odd manufacturer, notably William Marshall, who took excessive advantage of the unlimited number of apprentices allowed under Victorian legislation between 1903 and 1911. The interstate agreement following the award brought these manufacturers into line and removed the slur on Victoria's employers which such practices had attracted. Indeed, in 1910 the employers' representatives on the Victorian Wages Board petitioned the Minister for Labour to reintroduce legislation to limit the number of apprentices.[54] When Marshall again attempted to exploit a loophole regarding boy labour in the 1930s, other manufacturers co-operated with the union to have his practices stopped.[55]

Most of the major boot manufacturers, as the *Leather Journal* proclaimed, had no desire to sweat their workers if it was possible not to and still remain competitive. They exerted more influence than the 'number of employers . . . who seem to have no regard for their employees at all'.[56] The journal believed that

> It is safe to assert . . . that the Australian boot manufacturers as a body are possessed of an earnest wish, a most sincere desire, for the betterment of the affairs, both hygienic and financial, of those who are in their service . . . they have repeatedly demonstrated their consciousness of the fact that a workman or a workwoman who is well clad, well fed, well housed and contented, is consequently capable of rendering a much better return to those who employ him or her than can one who is ill clad, under fed, poorly housed, and discontented.[57]

Interstate agreements gave the 'reputable employers' the opportunity to live at peace with their consciences and their workers without fearing the 'sweater' in the next state.

Those manufacturers who at times wished to break away from conference saw in the Wages Board an opportunity to gain an advantage over their interstate rivals. But even had they succeeded, their advantage would have been short-lived. State wage-fixing tribunals were notoriously reluctant to make any award which would disadvantage local manufacturers in interstate competition. It is therefore highly likely that any concessions wrested from the Victorian Wages Board would have eventually been secured from other state tribunals. The result would have been a magnification of that destructive competition to which Higgins referred in his 1909 judgement, which in the long term was to no-one's advantage. Conferences ensured a degree of peace in the 'fight' amongst manufacturers as well as in the struggle between capitalist and worker.

Measured in terms of actual advances for workers, the record of conference agreements is less impressive. Because these agreements followed the general pattern of precedents set in the court, the boot trade tended to lag behind other industries which gained concessions from its awards. For instance, the clothing trade won the 44-hour week in 1919; the boot trade in 1921. Overtime payments, including meal money, were not brought into line with the 1919 clothing trade award until 1932. There was no allowance for a higher rate for casual work in the boot trade. While workers in other industries had secured weekly hiring in the 1920s, the boot trade had to wait until the 1938 federal award. Until then employees were engaged by the hour and could be sacked at a moment's notice. Rest periods, also granted to clothing workers in 1919, were not granted at all under interstate agreements in the boot industry. On the other hand, concessions made by the union in 1916 to allow 'green' adult female workers into the trade at lower rates of pay had serious repercussions for women during the depression.[58] Union officials were prepared to make concessions on these points rather than jeopardise what they saw as their two most important gains—the 44-hour week and the flat rate for men.[59] These agreements were likewise silent regarding factory conditions such as eating and seating accommodation. The concern for the health and welfare of Australia's future mothers, which was at the forefront of discussions on women's working conditions before the court, seems not to have been an issue to the men who decided these matters at the interstate conferences.

The fate of women workers in the boot trade is in fact the most serious blot on the history of the Round Table agreements. As we have seen, women's working conditions were not considered an issue. Their wages were of more importance, but only insofar as they posed a threat to men's jobs. In the women's departments of upper-machining, beading and packing, women were, with one exception, all accorded a minimum wage of less than 52 per cent the male rate. The obvious question is why were all men in the trade deemed skilled when almost all women were paid as unskilled workers?

The explanation does not lie in the different degrees of expertise required. At least two Arbitration Court judges (Beeby and Curlewis) considered machinists' work to be skilled and deserving at least the same remuneration as machinists in the clothing trades.[60] David Johnstone, former secretary of the New South Wales branch of the Bootmakers' Union and subsequently secretary of the Boot, Shoe and Slipper Manufacturers' Association, maintained that 'it is common knowledge in all industries where sewing machines are used, that the boot machinist is ahead of many other machinists in skill and aptitude, and eminently suitable, and much sought after for the many positions offering'.[61] Indeed, an independent commentator believed that the increasing demand for fancy uppers in the 1930s required an even higher degree of skill on the part of machinists.[62] Certainly, their work required accuracy so as not to spoil expensive upper leather. Operatives also had to possess considerable dexterity to be able to do this work at speed.

If we can assume that machinists did possess a degree of 'skill' and, as we have seen, their services were sought after by manufacturers, why were they not rewarded by legal margins in the same way that men were, or women in the clothing industry? The answer is complex. Under the original Boot Wages Board determination, all women in the trade were awarded a flat minimum of 20 shillings per week, regardless of their occupation. This rate, as we saw in Chapter Five, increased by only one shilling over the course of the first decade of the century. Thus in 1911, women received a mere 38.8 per cent of the male rate, which had increased from 42 to 54 shillings. The first federal award did not apply to women, but it indirectly affected their wages. In the wake of considerable dissatisfaction on the part of women workers about their wages, and anxiety by men over female competition, the union made moves on the Wages Board to have women's wages adjusted. The workers' delegates applied for an increase on the same principle as that which had been granted by the federal court: a flat marginal rate set at an average level of skill for the industry. For women, the convention calculating wages at half those paid to men was also employed. The rate for women was thus calculated by halving the male basic wage (42s) and adding half the male margin (12s). The amount arrived at was therefore 27s. It seems the union asked for 27s 6d to allow a slight area for compromise.[63]

The employers, however, sought a classification of rates, ranging from 22s 6d (the existing minimum) to 24s for machinists and fitters and 26s for vampers. Under this scheme the majority of workers would have received 24s. Wax-thread machinists were considered by both sides to be in a completely separate category (the union claimed 32s 6d as their margin). When the matter came before the Board, the question was decided on the casting vote of the chairman who voted for a compromise: a flat rate of 25s 6d and 32s 6d for wax-thread machinists.[64] This formula effectively reduced the flat rate to an unskilled wage, representing only 47.2 per cent of the male rate. From 1913 this proportion was incorporated into interstate agreements at the Round Table Conferences.[65]

The disparity with machinists in other trades became very obvious once the clothing trade received an award of the federal court. The formula Higgins used was to fix a minimum of about 52 per cent the male basic rate and margins at two-thirds those granted to men.[66] This meant that, although the basic wage in the clothing trade was slightly lower than the boot trade's flat rate, in practice most of the women workers, who were machinists, received margins considerably above this amount. The disparity was noted by Judge Curlewis in the New South Wales Arbitration Court in 1920 who announced his intention to give women the same proportion over the living wage as the men were getting, 'or something of that sort'. He proclaimed that he was 'not going to have women with four years' experience on skilled work kept on the living wage. It is ridiculous.'[67]

Curlewis' intentions were, however, thwarted. The union representative explained to him that they could not ask any more than 39 shillings because this was the amount agreed to by the interstate conference. Although a further conference raised the amount to 44 shillings, it was still no proportionate advance in comparison with the men.[68]

These rates were translated into the agreement between manufacturers and the union at the 1921 interstate conference. Judge Curlewis' outburst on the injustice of the amounts fixed for skilled women had no impact: the conference did not reconsider its formula but continued to fix women's rates at less than 50 per cent those of men. The attention devoted to the question is indicated by the following report of conference proceedings: 'At the Friday session of the conference, the pay of females was dealt with, and numerous minor matters, all business being disposed of in time for lunch.'[69]

Nor was any reassessment of women's wages attempted at any subsequent conferences. This was one instance where federal Arbitration Court precedents were not followed. Had they adhered to Higgins' formula, the flat rate would have been more in line with that paid to the few wax-thread machinists, who received between 58 and 61 per cent of the male rate.

It seems, then, that women were awarded so little because no attempt was made by the union delegates to have the amount increased. Given the chronic seasonal shortages of skilled machinists and the over-award payments which were made to attract them, manufacturers would probably have been receptive to an increase in the minimum had it been bargained for.[70] The Arbitration Court precedents would have added weight to such a move. The fact that increases were not sought reflects the almost invisible profile of women within the union. Women made up about one-third of the membership, but they were forbidden under the rules from holding the position of shop president.[71] This effectively debarred them from positions of responsibility within the union structure. The union's ordinary business was conducted by regular meetings of shop presidents—all men. Between meetings an all-male executive attended to outstanding business. Logs of claims for presentation to employers were drawn up by the all-male federal council without formal consultation with female members. On the rare occasions on which someone suggested that female representation was desirable, the suggestions were virtually ignored.[72] Indeed, the only times when the union appeared to notice its female members were on occasions where they could be used to secure some advantage for their male workmates. For example, no attempt was made to organise women for the appeal to the federal court in 1909 because at that time the threat was from boy labour, not females. However, shortly after this award we find officials in both New South Wales and Victoria anxiously organising women. Why? Because in the meantime employers had introduced female labour to operate the new Fortuna skiving machines.[73] As with the bookbinders who were so enthusiastically helping their women's union at the same time, the men's motives were explicit. The secretary of the New South Wales branch explained:

> To the employees, male and female, this was a serious question, for to the male it was the end of a recognised dividing line in the trade. The female, who was unorganised at this period, could see that she was to be used on certain minor machines because she was cheap compared to the apprentice in the stuff-cutting department, and it did not need much argument to convince the females that they should join the union.[74]

After this flurry of activity, women again slipped from view until the classification and longer hours scare of 1922. On this occasion a new tactic emerged: the organisation of special mass meetings of female operatives as a way of demonstrating union power. It seems that manufacturers feared a strike of women more than one of men because of the relative scarcity of competent female labour. The union secretary, Arthur Long, explained to his New Zealand counterpart that 'There is no doubt the employers feared a strike as trade was very busy and female labour in particular very scarce.'[75] Ironically, the otherwise invisible female membership proved the union's major asset in this show of strength. Nine hundred women attended the mass meeting.[76]

It is not hard to explain why women played such a small role in union affairs. Quite clearly, the men felt it was none of their business and, with the exceptions mentioned, made little attempt to encourage women to join.[77] Long's energetic and sustained recruitment of men, involving visits to factories where he addressed the workmen and then set up his folding table and chair in order to sign up members, had no equivalent where women were concerned.[78] And, while male union members refused to work alongside male non-unionists, shop presidents often did not even bother to ask women to join.[79] The rigid sexual segregation of the factory was carried over into union affairs. Women generally met separately.[80] On the rare occasions when mixed meetings were held, the Temperance Hall was secured as the venue and the balcony set aside for 'the females'.[81] From their gallery, women could watch the real deliberations being conducted below. Where separate meetings were held, their major purpose was to endorse the action of officials or to give them *carte blanche* to act on the women's behalf.[82] And while other unions with women members met from time to time to discuss matters of common interest, the Boot Trade Union was conspicuous by its absence. Requests for delegates to such meetings were invariably ignored.[83]

How is the historian to interpret this situation? Are we looking at overwhelming female apathy or insurmountable male hostility? I would suggest that although there were undoubtedly elements of both, the more important reason lies in the relationship between the family and the workplace in the bootmaking suburbs of Collingwood, Richmond and Clifton Hill. Bootmaking dominated these suburbs, especially Collingwood, and as the major employer of labour often drew fathers, brothers, sisters and occasionally mothers and wives into the same industry.[84]

In these circumstances, the upper-closing room served the same function as the home: a separate sphere for women where they need not trespass on 'men's work'. And in the same way as the ideology of separate spheres decreed a division between public and private, domestic and political activity, so this division was replicated in the factory and its politics. Men carried on the important business of union decision-making on behalf of their womenfolk, who were kept at a safe distance in the machine room or the Temperance Hall gallery. A Trades Hall circular from 1921 'requesting all Unionists [presumably male] to see that their daughters and sisters are members of the Union covering the Industry in which they are employed' is evidence of pervasive patriarchal attitudes in the union movement.[85] These attitudes added to the problems of organising seasonal workers with high levels of turnover.

As within the home, women to some extent colluded in this 'protective' invisibility. A mass meeting of women in 1922, for instance, carried a resolution which concluded with an undertaking to 'place ourselves unreservedly in the hands of the Boot Trade Federation'.[86]

One could also speculate that the prevalence of short-time amongst male workers, which posed a threat to their position as the breadwinner within the home, made it even more imperative that women should be kept in their place at work. Indeed, some men may have even considered it in their interests to keep women's wages low as a way of enhancing the value of their own contribution to the family economy.

The women members who put their faith in the male unionists to look after their interests were in retrospect misguided. That women's and men's interests were not identical is most starkly indicated by the plight of women such as Mrs Ellen Don, left a widow

with two children to support. Managing on a machinists' wage of £2 9s proved impossible and she was forced to board out her daughter, seeing her only once a month.[87] Other
women were also the main supports of families, whether of their own children or of
invalid or unemployed parents.[88] For them it must have been little consolation to know
that their situation was not typical of female workers, and that in setting the wages for
women, men had in mind their sisters and daughters whose livelihood was partially sub-
sidised by male earnings.

Nor were attempts to exclude women from certain occupations always seen by the
women as in their interests. In the lean days of winter 1931 a deputation of 'girls', dismissed because of a shift in the line of demarcation on slipper making, certainly perceived their interests as separate to those of the men who replaced them.[89]

It would also be misleading to suggest that women had no separate appreciation of
their rights or, indeed, of the benefits of collective action. Throughout this period there
are instances of effective strikes by women against specific attacks on their working conditions. Such strikes were supported by unionist and non-unionist alike.[90] The response
of women to calls by the union to resist collective attacks by employers on workers' conditions also indicates a sensitivity to class issues as well as a willingness to trust male
unionists.[91] And even this expressed willingness to be guided by men had its limitations
in practice, as there are several cases of female strikers refusing to accept the advice of the
union secretary on the dispute.[92] Women thus tried to negotiate some control in an
industrial relations structure which otherwise neglected them.

'Speeding-up' was a problem which proved beyond the conciliatory powers of the
Round Table Conference. As we saw in the first part of this chapter, workers worked at
full speed in order to retain their jobs. This was especially true of the depression years.
The union seemed powerless to intervene. Its officials complained to the manufacturers'
representatives about this 'driving system', only to be told that it was the workers' own
fault: they should not work so 'terrifically hard'.[93] This response, denying the limits to
individual 'choice' in the matter, was unhelpful. Manufacturers were similarly constrained. Individual employers were clearly unwilling to reduce workloads when their
competitors might continue to drive their workers. The real problem was structural as
well as personal. The boot industry as a whole was over-capitalised. Too many firms
competed for too few orders, allowing retailers to play one manufacturer off against
another in order to get lower wholesale prices.[94]

There were a limited number of solutions to the situation, individual resistance not
being one of them. Firstly, manufacturers could have combined to resist price-cutting by
retailers and rationalise production. Attempts at price regulation were not attempted.
The Manufacturers' Association, as one commentator put it, could not regulate anything.[95] Or, as the Victorian union secretary quipped, the manufacturers 'have an
Association which exists to cut one another's throats'.[96] Similarly, there was no attempt
to limit competition and production costs by reducing the range of styles produced by
each firm. It is unlikely that such an attempt would have succeeded, given the previous
history of divisions within the manufacturers' camp.

Secondly, the workers could have combined to limit their output. This, too, was not
attempted during the worst years of the depression. With so many 'walking about', those

with jobs were not inclined to complain about having too much work. More importantly, there was no structure to accommodate the kind of factory-specific action required. The union's emphasis on monthly meetings of shop presidents was hardly designed to foster rank-and-file militancy.

The third possible solution was the slowest, the most painful, and the one which prevailed. A process of economic attrition occurred during which a number of manufacturers 'went to the wall'. Although they were replaced by new hopefuls, the overall number of manufacturing firms declined.[97] At the same time as this process of rationalisation was occurring, the economy as a whole was making a slow recovery, thus increasing demand for boots and shoes. With this increased demand, retailers were less able to name their price and manufacturers were under less pressure to cheapen production. Similarly, increased employment opportunities made workers less vulnerable to the driving tactics of manufacturers. For their part, bosses and workers waited more or less passively for the return of prosperity.

A further problem with which the Round Table Conference proved unable to deal was the sweating of workers in the basket shoe industry. (Basket shoes were sandal-style shoes made from strips of woven or plaited leather.) Manufacturers in this section were not members of the Boot Manufacturers' Association and were immune to pressure from fellow employers regarding their methods. The union for its part used the state Factories and Shops Act to prosecute breaches of the Wages Board determination, but the more persistent offenders managed to evade the law. By placing workers on contract, or making them shareholders in the company, the principal employer could not be convicted. Some even went to the extent of erecting partitions around each small group of workers for which they charged rent as 'factories'.[98]

The other strategy open to the union was not pursued partly because of intolerance and racism on the part of the Boot Trade Union officials.[99] When basket shoe workers formed themselves into a union in 1935 and went on strike, they received only limited support from the union which would not permit these workers to become members of its organisation.[100]

Apart from the basket shoe industry, the second half of the 1930s saw a radical change to the industrial climate in the boot trade. Militant left-wing pressure forced the more 'moderate' federal union leadership to reassess it tactics. Conferences were abandoned in favour of an appeal to the Commonwealth court. In their quest for better wages and conditions, the militants were prepared to fight the employers on the issue of classification if necessary.[101] At the same time, shop committees were formed in a number of factories with the express purpose of combating speed-ups. These met with moderate success.[102]

The new mood in the union, fuelled by the activities of the Militant Minority of the Communist Party, also encouraged more active female involvement in union affairs.[103] There was now a larger number of married women and older single women in factories, and they tended to be more confident and more aware of the realities of women's economic position. Such women, drawn into factories in the changed economic conditions of the 1930s, also contributed to a slightly higher profile for women in the industry. For the first time the union responded to requests for women delegates to general conferences by issuing shop notices and calling for nominations.[104] Meetings of women, which secured 'good representation', were also held to discuss the new log of wages and conditions.[105] At the same time, however, a circular from Muriel Heagney requesting co-operation on the Equal Status Committee was ignored, and a proposal to appoint a woman organiser rejected by 38 to 24, with the secretary opposing the appointment.[106]

Meanwhile, the union served its new log of claims on employers. These included a 30-hour week and a minimum male wage of £7 10s.[107] In retaliation, the employers submitted a claim for reclassification, arguing that the industry could no longer afford to pay men wheeling raw material on trolleys a skilled wage.[108] It seems that most employers did not want reclassification, because it would only complicate accounting, but having held it up as a threat to the union for so long they were obliged to go through with the claim.[109]

Because of a backlog of cases in the court, however, the bootmakers' claim was not heard until 1937. The sitting of the court was brief and dealt mainly with the more urgent matter of adjusting wages and the question of trainee apprenticeships in New South Wales. The 1937 award was clearly given to keep the peace until a more full investigation of the trade could be made, as parties were given leave to apply for a variation after six months.[110] The workers in particular were dissatisfied with the small increases in wages. Had it not been for the possibility of a rehearing in the near future, strikes would probably have been resorted to. As it happened, the officials persuaded the more militant members to bide their time and application was duly made to the court.[111]

The hearing occurred in May 1938 and involved a thorough reconsideration of the whole trade. The union had modified its claims since 1935, this time asking for a 40-hour week and a male rate of £5 5s. It also sought an increase in the base rate for women to 60 per cent of the male rate. The employers, however, pursued their counter-claim for reclassification.[112]

In arriving at his decision, Beeby was concerned to rescue bootmaking from the 'backwash' into which it had been forced under the original award.[113] As he pointed out, Higgins had not set men's wages in line with those in other skilled trades because of fear that increased wage costs would lead directly to increased importations.[114] The situation had changed since 1910. Although imports were recovering slightly from their almost negligible contribution in 1930–31, they posed no serious threat. As Beeby saw it:

> I do not think that the danger of influx of foreign products is sufficient to deter the Court from prescribing what it deems to be proper wage rates and conditions of employment for the industry, and feel confident that the Tariff Board will recommend such tariff readjustments as may be necessary.[115]

Having decided not to take into account the question of imports, Beeby was confronted with the task of setting a rate which would more fairly reflect the skill of the trade than the existing 12 shillings. He maintained that it was not disputed that bootmaking was a skilled trade—'skilled in the sense that [it requires] knowledge of the qualities of materials used and high manipulative ability acquired by years of experience in most of the processes'.[116] Like Higgins, he recognised that bootmaking had become a machine industry with a high degree of specialisation, but he too saw an important distinction between the operation of these machines and the work of mere machine-feeders in other industries. Few bootmaking machines were automatic; they were, rather, 'tools of the trade' requiring dexterity and concentration in order to produce satisfactory results. And although the work was subdivided, evenness of manipulative ability was crucial to the job:

> Operatives work in teams at great speed. Each on completing his process passes the work on to the next in the team. Before a boot is completed it passes through the hands of from 30 to 40 employees. Some of the processes appear simple, but, on inspection, employers admitted that with odd exceptions one was as important as the other. Defective workmanship in any might spoil the ultimate result.[117]

Beeby also pointed out that although a 'workman may use only one machine or power-driven tool year in and year out', he required years of training on a range of tasks before being put in charge of that machine. Furthermore, interchangeability of labour was essential to keep the team system operating smoothly. For these reasons, he maintained that boot operatives could justifiably claim to be on 'a higher level than the ordinary run of semi-skilled workers'. They could not, however, expect to be placed on the same footing as those trades calling for 'mental effort', such as engineering, electrical trades and carpentry.[118]

Nor was he prepared to give increased margins on processes 'which are admittedly of a simple nature', requiring 'no skill and limited experience'. The problem which confronted him was the 'impossible task of assessing the comparative value of almost every process'. He rejected from the outset any attempt to fix rates for the multitude of classifications proposed by the employers. Such a scheme, he believed, would be 'both unjust and impracticable' because of the interdependent nature of the various separate tasks. The solution he arrived at was to 'narrow the gaps' between the various classifications in order to provide average justice. He thus provided for overall increases in margins for men. At the same time, he marked out a number of 'simpler' tasks for a reduced margin (9s) with the explicit intention that such work would be assigned to unapprenticed male labour or females.[119]

The union was by no means pleased with the award, particularly with the additional boy labour permitted. Nor were the men happy about the clauses which extended the use of female labour at female rates to a range of 'men's work' such as inking edges and preparing shanks.[120] In extending women's work, Beeby hoped to compensate employers for wage increases and also to make the line of demarcation between the sexes consistent with that prevailing in accessory factories.[121]

Beeby's award was of more obvious advantage to women. Inspecting operations at boot factories to assist him in assigning skill margins, both the judge and 'his assistant', a Miss Beeby, visited the women's departments. Miss Beeby in particular was reportedly very impressed with the skill and speed the women displayed in machining uppers.[122] Beeby considered the sewing of uppers was 'harder and more exacting than ordinary machine sewing . . . The craze for fancy uppers involves a great increase in the skiving and machining and decoration of small parts before their final assembling into complete uppers.'[123] He added that: 'On inspection I was impressed with the speed at which the women work, and the intense application to their tasks which is necessary.'

The subsequent award broke new ground in acknowledging a degree of skill on this work and all sewing machinists were awarded a margin of three shillings per week.

As Beeby commented, this amount at least brought them more in line with women doing comparable work in the clothing trades. Other machinists received a margin of half that amount. Had Beeby applied the same principle to the assessment of women's skill as he did to that of men, however, these amounts would have been much greater. Sewing machines were as much 'tools of the trade' as were making and finishing machines, and the dexterity, knowledge of materials and responsibility for evenness of quality were every bit as great as in the men's departments. That he did not grant them more was clearly because of the traditional practice of fixing women's rates in general below those of men. He was also concerned to achieve parity with rates awarded in the clothing trade.

Women also gained from provision in the award for a rest period each morning 'on account of the high speed at which they worked'. What had previously been a privilege granted in a few factories thus became a general condition of the trade. Female boot operatives were at last approaching minimum legal standards in the clothing trade.[124]

In addition to the changes it brought to women, Beeby's award had revolutionary implications for men. Although bootmakers had lost their cherished flat rate, they had on balance gained in status and payment. On the other hand, they faced the prospect of more female and boy labour in their midst. It remained to be seen whether this combination would indeed rescue the trade from its longstanding 'backwash'.[125]

The federal Arbitration Court thus played a decisive role in determining the nature of work in the boot and shoe industry in the period from 1911 to World War II. Even when wages and conditions were negotiated in conference rather than in court, these negotiations were conducted within the framework set by the 1910 award and with reference to prevailing trends in other court awards.

The restrictions which awards and agreements placed on the employment of boys and females meant that manufacturers had little opportunity to experiment with new forms of production based on cheap, quickly trained labour. At the same time, the broad-based apprenticeship and flat rate for men's work encouraged employers to adopt methods which made most effective use of a flexible workforce. In practice, this meant preserving the existing team system, whereby an interchangeable group of men performed moderately subdivided work. Greater subdivision would have complicated apprenticeship training and reduced the flexibility of the team.

The size of the Australian market for boots and shoes continued to have a major influence on the work process in this period. Although heavy tariffs effectively protected local producers from import competition, the market could still not sustain mass-production techniques to any great extent. The great variety in styles and sizes demanded by retailers meant that specialisation by producers was rare. Only those manufacturers who controlled retail outlets were able to rationalise their output in this way. For most factories, product variety precluded systematic use of scientific management techniques which relied on minute subdivision and forward planning. It also made piecework impractical.

The labour market added to the effect of product markets to discourage innovation in the direction of Taylorism. The chronic oversupply of male labour, in particular, solved the fundamental problem which Taylorism would have addressed: how to make sure that workers worked hard for their money. The discipline of the market ensured that individuals performed at maximum speeds; it also discouraged collective resistance by offering a pool of unemployed labour to break strikes.

Finally, the Anglo-Australian gender order continued to exercise an important indirect influence on the nature of work. It ensured that men's and women's work remained rigidly demarcated and that women's work was undervalued. Not only did this affect the women and girls who worked in the women's sections, but it also meant that men were excluded from two of the main areas of expansion in this industry between the wars: slipper production and the preparation and machining of fancy uppers. Thus, in the late 1930s, while employers enticed married women back to the factories, men could not find work and manufacturers could not meet their orders because of a shortage of machinists. The preservation of existing gender arrangements in the factory was achieved at some cost to all concerned.

9

MARGINAL MATTERS:
THE PRINTING INDUSTRIES, 1925–1937

Peter Cochrane, in his overview of the history of work in Australia, has argued that the state played an important part in 'getting the idea [of Taylorism] off the ground'. In the years between the wars, he writes, ' "progressive" arbitrators pressed it upon sluggish manufacturers'.[1] While this assessment is probably true in general terms, the history of the printing industry during this period reveals a rather different record. The state, in its role as federal arbitrator, acted primarily as a conservative force: it retarded any impulses towards the subdivision of labour by generally refusing to award different rates for different aspects of 'craft' work. Nor did its conservative role stop with the work process. Arbitration awards reinforced the existing sexual division of labour in the workplace and differential rates of pay for the sexes and in so doing reinforced the prevailing gender orders in the wider community.

The years from 1925 to 1939 were thus ones of consolidation rather than change in the printing industry. There were few technological innovations, so that any changes which did occur were continuations of existing trends rather than departures. Machines became faster and there were more of them, but they were basically the same as those in operation before 1925. The exception to this was the bookbinding department, where changing fashions in office stationery had important implications for workers in this section. Loose-leaf systems were gaining in popularity in this period in preference to bound account books, while card systems replaced several other classes of bound work. Much of the material used in loose-leaf and card systems was traditionally 'women's work', as defined by the arbitration award in 1925. Women consequently found their services in greater demand. Conversely, male bookbinders experienced a decline in the volume of their work.[2]

The cardboard-box and carton department was also disrupted by changing tastes. From the late 1920s cartons increasingly replaced boxes, leading to the temporary displacement of workers from the box section. Boxmakers were also displaced by automatic machines introduced to make boot boxes in 1928. These machines made the entire box, including cutting, gluing and pressing, the only hand operation being the stacking of the finished boxes. In this case, however, it was women who were more adversely affected.[3]

However, while the court's role was generally a conservative one in this industry, there was one major exception. In 1925 it granted the entire industry a reduction in the working week from 48 to 44 hours. The court's decision on this matter, and its verdicts on issues concerned with definitions of skill, provide revealing insights into the role of the state in shaping work.

In 1923, the newly amalgamated Printing Industries Employees Union of Australia was busy preparing its first case for submission to the federal court.[4] Amongst the claims put forward was that from the Victorian Women and Girls Advisory Committee for a flat rate for all women employed in the industry and the abolition of piecework. The rate they proposed was near the existing 'skilled' rate paid under the Wages Board schedule, which differentiated between the wages of workers according to supposed levels of skill.[5]

Their rejection of 'classification' (or a scale of rates) was a strategic decision aimed at raising the general level of female wages. Under the existing schedule, only a few workers were entitled to the top rate. Most were awarded either the basic wage or one or two shillings above it. The women unionists as a group were therefore prepared to forgo an increase in the top rate in the hope of securing significant increases for the majority. This strategy was in fact similar to the one employed by male bootmakers in 1910 and endorsed by Higgins in his award. The women's attitude to classification, as does that of the bootmakers, illustrates the dangers of generalising about the effects of arbitration awards without paying due attention to specific cases. Bennett, and others, have assumed that there was an intrinsic advantage in workers as a group having detailed job descriptions or classifications rather than a flat rate.[6] As this case shows, whether or not classification was an advantage depended on whether such schedules included different rates for different jobs and if so, what percentage of workers fell into each category.

The women's suggestions were rejected by the federal council of the union. Instead, the official claim sought a classification of wages which differentiated between various levels of 'skill'. Most importantly, it provided for the basic wage to cover a large section of the female workforce. And in the absence of a comprehensive piecework schedule, employers were to have virtually a free hand in fixing piece rates, which were the dominant form of payment in the boxmaking section.[7]

Why did this happen? Why was it that female workers, who comprised between 35 and 55 per cent of union membership, were given such low priority in the quest for improved wages and conditions? Clearly, their low priority reflected the powerlessness of women within the union. As we have already seen, the terms on which the women's unions amalgamated with the PIEUA structured this powerlessness. Women were denied special representation on the federal council, while their smaller numbers made their election by general ballot extremely unlikely. Indeed, it was not until 1939 that any woman succeeded in a ballot for the position of councillor. The constitution of the union did provide for a woman's delegate in a purely advisory capacity at the invitation of the other councillors. After 1931 the councillors consistently voted against issuing such invitations, despite concerted lobbying by the women and E. C. Magrath of New South Wales. Women therefore had no voice at all on the union's most important policy-making body in the crucial years between 1931 and 1939.[8]

Nor were they better placed in the Victorian branch. It is significant that the Victorian delegates led the opposition to a woman sitting on federal council.[9] Their stance was symptomatic of a generally unsympathetic attitude to the female membership. Louisa Cross irritated her male colleagues by showing no signs of retiring from her position as organiser. (She did not retire until 1951.) Cross carried out her duties in an atmosphere of more or less mutual suspicion and antagonism. On one occasion Frank Burke, former secretary of the Bookbinders' Union, accused her of stacking the board of management in order to prevent his election as temporary organiser.[10]

Apart from Cross and the clerical staff, no women held paid positions within the union. We saw in Chapter Six how the executive committee was structured to give predominance to the men. The board of management, although structurally more open to female representation, in practice had less than 20 per cent female membership. This was partly the result of apathy on the part of female members but also reflected the unwillingness of men to have their shops represented by women. In theory, each shop was supposed to elect its own delegates to the board. In practice, it was often difficult to persuade anyone to accept the position. An investigation by the executive committee (into allegations of stacking the Board levelled at Cross) in 1931 revealed that what usually happened was that someone was persuaded to take on the job of delegate and they might or might not ask for their shopmates' approval. Enthusiastic women could probably therefore have secured a place on the board without much difficulty. On the other hand, they may have found their male colleagues less apathetic if the practice became widespread. As one male unionist (a compositor at the Modern Printing Company) commented when asked how he and his male workmates felt about the appointment of Miss Hyndman to the board without their knowledge: 'he thought that possibly they would have tried to get a man to represent them'.[11] In any case, the women who had kept the earlier women's unions alive were by the late 1920s and 1930s approaching middle age and retirement and there were few young women with similar commitment available to replace them.

A change in the union's structure in 1929 provided for an elected annual conference to replace the half-yearly meetings as the major legislative body of the branch. Delegates were chosen on a sectional basis, a system which automatically excluded the possibility of a female majority because of the sex-segregation in the different sections. At the first conference, for example, only nine of the twenty-eight delegates were women, although at that time women comprised approximately half the branch's membership.[12]

At a less quantifiable level, it appears that male printing unionists continued to think of the union as a male affair. In his New Year greeting to members in 1936, the federal president, Gordon Fry, announced that: 'In striving for those things [worthwhile in life] we are not fighting for ourselves only; we are fighting for our wives, our mothers, young brothers and sisters, and our children.'[13] And although there were notable exceptions, hostility and indifference dominated the union's attitudes to the women members. The councillors gave no reason for rejection of women's proposals for a flat rate and the abolition of piecework, but it seems that they recognised that such claims would meet with strong opposition from employers and they felt they had more important battles to fight on their own behalf.

Whatever the men's reasons, the fact remains that the union rejected the women's claims. The union's first claim in effect sought the court's endorsement of the status quo, and the court obliged. The result was a little tinkering here and there with margins, but overall the women workers received no real advance on the old rates. As Deputy President Webb observed: 'The margins for skill [for females] are not nearly as great as the margins for skill granted to male workers and the employees complain bitterly about that.'[14] Not until 1936 was a more comprehensive review of their margins attempted, although this too had disappointing results. Both cases, however, are extremely illuminating as regards the court's approach to the whole issue of defining skill, especially as it affected women's work.

It is clear from the various Arbitration hearings that the judges were guided in their decisions by a set of ad hoc principles as to what constituted 'skill'. But, as the subsequent discussion will show, these principles were often mutually contradictory or not amenable to 'objective' assessment.

One of the most fundamental considerations affecting the Arbitration Court judges in regard to wage fixation was the principle of setting different rates according to different qualities of work performed. The secondary wage, or margin above the basic wage, as it applied to 'skill', was awarded for 'exceptional gifts or qualification' necessary to a particular occupation. Such a margin was intended primarily to encourage workers to acquire the extra 'skill of an artisan'.[15] It was not, however, intended to allow for the range of individual abilities workers brought to the job. Rather, it represented a minimum level of competence, with higher rates for extra ability being accounted for by market forces.[16]

The task of setting this minimum margin was not an easy one. As a starting point in assessing the appropriate rate, the court examined the nature of the work entailed in any particular occupation. This usually involved hearing evidence from witnesses as well as observation on the shop floor.[17] However, as analysis of the history of the court's judgements in general has shown, judges have not adopted any consistent, detailed criteria for assessing the value of work.[18] Bennett has argued that the only consistency has occurred in relation to the insistence that skilled trades embrace a wide range of tasks.[19] In the printing cases examined here, judges were influenced by the discriminatory content and difficulty of the work performed as well as the task range of a particular occupation. To attract a designation as 'skilled', workers had to show that their normal occupation required considerable training and knowledge, as well as some degree of calculation or judgement.[20] Other factors which might influence the level of the margin were responsibility and artistic judgement.[21] Hazardous work could also be considered skilled, but only insofar as it required skill to avoid accident.[22]

In practice, objective assessment on these issues was extremely unlikely. Witnesses disagreed about the difficulty of performing particular tasks and the amount of training required to become proficient. Workers without formal apprenticeships for their occupation were the worst affected in this respect: estimates of training time in some cases varied from a few days to four years.[23]·Even where formal apprenticeships did exist, as with compositors, allowance had to be made for the mutual advantage to employer and employee of artificially extending the apprenticeship period. That is, a lengthy apprenticeship bolstered the worker's claim to a skilled margin while at the same time providing the employer with six years' cheap labour.

The question of artistic judgement was also problematic. For instance, everyone agreed that setting type attractively required some sense of proportion and balance, but that this amounted to 'art' was open to dispute. As the employers' advocate pointed out, milliners and dressmakers also needed to show a sense of proportion and balance in their work, the implication being that one would not therefore consider them to be skilled.[24] The final picture which formed in the judge's mind about the skill of any particular occupation was thus the product of a series of judgements about these imprecise issues, more or less influenced by the persuasiveness of the witnesses and advocates for either side.

Having formed some idea of the nature of the work, the judge still faced the task of assigning it a monetary value. His most important guide in this respect, following the precedents set by Higgins, was usually the existing rate.[25] Problems arose, however, where rates varied significantly, a not infrequent occurrence since awards covered many different states. When such a situation arose, the court's response seems to have been aimed at compromise. In the first compositors' case, for instance, Victorian compositors had their margin reduced by two shillings while those in Sydney, Hobart and Adelaide had theirs increased under the terms of the award.

A further major consideration was what might be called the principle of relativity. This operated in two ways. In the first instance, it meant that judges tried to set the margin for any given occupation so as to maintain the existing hierarchy of margins within the industry. Indeed, in the first printing case before the court, Deputy President Webb hoped that after fixing the rates for compositors the parties would easily agree to the rates for other occupations by adopting the same proportionate increase.[26]

In the second instance, some judges were concerned to fix rates so that they corresponded roughly with comparable occupations in other industries. The extent to which these comparisons influenced the court varied from judge to judge. Webb, for example, declared that he could not 'properly and fairly compare one trade with another, although it is very natural that one should try to do so'.[27] Nevertheless, he did mention opinions which considered the skill of compositors to be equal to that of tradesmen in the metal industries, and such comparisons were also made by the union.[28] The attainment of parity with engineers seems to have carried more weight with Dethridge, influencing him to increase the hand compositor's margin to the same level as that awarded by Beeby in the metalworkers' case.[29]

Both these applications of the principle acted against any fundamental reassessment of the value of certain jobs, particularly those performed by women. For example, Webb admitted in his 1925 judgement that female workers had done relatively badly out of his award. He thought their work deserved a higher rate, but he refused to increase his award because it would put printing industry workers on a higher scale than other female workers within the court's jurisdiction.[30] As he explained, 'Under the award as I drew it I prescribed a base wage for female workers which I had prescribed in several other awards, and I also prescribed margins for skill which have relation to margins for skill prescribed for female workers in other awards of the Court.'[31] This meant that even when women's work was recognised as requiring considerable skill, as was the case with embossers, the margins awarded were only one-third those awarded to men in comparable occupations.[32] This is the most glaring example of the guiding principles being in conflict. In order to maintain parity with women working in other industries, relativities within the industry had to be sacrificed. And in maintaining parity of the full wage (basic wage plus margins) between industries, the equality in relative proportions had to be sacrificed. Thus, women in the clothing trade generally received margins two-thirds of those paid to males in that industry, while women in printing received only one-third the margins paid to their male co-workers.

It is important to consider why Webb (and his successors) decided to resolve the conflict of principles in this way. Why did they decide it was more important to maintain comparability with female occupations in other trades than with male occupations in the same industry? Although neither judge felt it necessary to give a detailed explanation, we can nevertheless make a few inferences. In their role as Arbitration Court judges, neither Dethridge nor Webb saw wage justice for women as a very high priority. More important were other economic, social and political considerations. For instance, if women's wages in the printing industry were significantly increased, it would have been extremely likely that women in other industries would have pressed for comparable increases. Refusal of these claims, which presumably could not be justified by reference to 'objective' criteria of work value, would have exposed the court to accusations of injustice. Conceding the demands would have resulted in widespread wage increases for women. According to the logic of the day, apparently shared by judges, such wage increases would inevitably lead to price increases, the cost of which would be borne by consumers.[33] More importantly, according to this logic, the price of female wage increases would be borne by men on fixed incomes. As Dethridge and others pointed out, judges were also men on fixed incomes.[34] Greater economic equality for women would also have upset the prevailing gender order whereby men gained power from women's economic dependence. The sex of the judges was therefore of double significance. As well, they often employed female domestic labour. For all these reasons, judges had a vested interest in keeping the general level of female wages down.

Endorsing wide differences between male and female rates in the same industry, on the other hand, had the virtue of not upsetting the status quo. The political consequences would be slight. As Judge Webb commented in a related case, 'it is not a matter of great importance, except to the girls'.[35] Given the powerlessness of women within the printing union, there was hardly likely to be any concerted move by the union as a whole to redress the injustice.

The age of workers also determined whether or not they were awarded skilled rates. Judges assumed that workers under twenty-one years required less to live on than adults, so they refused to award them the full margin even though it might be conceded by both sides that the worker was as efficient as an adult. This further discriminated against women, a large proportion of whom were juniors.[36]

Theoretically, at least, the 'needs doctrine' dominated court assessments of *base rates* throughout this period, with an increasing influence of the capacity of industry to pay towards the end of the 1930s. However, the capacity of industry to pay *margins for skill* always influenced judges in defining work as skilled. As was the case with the Commonwealth Arbitration Court in general, the weight of this consideration varied with time. Webb declared in 1925 that it carried little weight with him, that it would not justify him 'in depriving employees of the margin to which they are justly entitled'.[37] Ten years and a depression later, attitudes had changed. The union felt it necessary to demonstrate the prosperity of the industry in order to justify its claim for higher margins, while the employers argued against increased margins because of the 'convalescent' state of the industry after the depression.[38] Dethridge clearly took such market considerations into account. In the bookbinders' case, for example, he reluctantly reclassified a section of the bookbinders' traditional work as unskilled in order to cheapen labour costs. By allowing females at female rates to do work such as making blotting pads and files, he bowed to employer pressure to try to make Australia's stationers more competitive in relation to imported products, especially from Japan.[39] In this case, the desire to facilitate 'the proper expansion of work in the industry' led the judge to depart from Higgins' formula in the fruitpickers' case (1912) whereby 'men's work' was awarded a man's rate, even when performed by women.[40]

Dethridge's reluctance to move the traditional line of demarcation in bookbinding points to another major influence on the definition of work as skilled or unskilled: the desire of the court to protect the livelihood and status of male craft workers. As Webb pointed out in his 1925 judgement, the issue was not simply a matter of whether the work was skilled or not. As he explained: 'The matter cannot be decided on the mere fact that women can do this work. What I have to decide is the amount of work in this industry which should be fairly reserved for men who devote their lives to become expert in this work and for the apprentices whom they undertake to teach.'[41]

The changes in the 1937 award provide a striking instance of the operation of this principle. Like most 'skilled' crafts, some aspects of the work were simpler than others and could be performed by relatively untrained workers. By dividing these tasks from the core of 'craft' work and prescribing for them a lower rate of pay, the court was inviting the subdivision of craftwork and the use of cheaper labour. Under the 1925 award, for example, the making of blotting pads with paper bound edges was classed as skilled male work and attracted a margin of twenty-four shillings. Under the 1937 award, this same work was demoted to the status of semi-skilled female work and given an eight-shilling margin.[42]

In general, however, the court's judgements in the printing cases reflect its reluctance to break down the craftsman's traditional skills by endorsing increased 'classification', and hence further subdivision of labour. The case of letterpress machinists is one example. Letterpress machining traditionally attracted a skilled margin comparable to bookbinding and hand composition. In the case of letterpress machining, semi-skilled workers being paid lower rates had, under the New South Wales state award, been doing the more routine work on small platen machines. The employers sought a reclassification under the federal award to separate out this work and provide it with a lower margin. This Webb refused to do, explaining that he did not wish to encourage the use of unskilled labour.[43]

A further factor which Dethridge claimed influenced his assessment of the level of skill was the pace of work. In justifying an increase of three shillings per week in the compositor's margin in 1937, he explained that he did not believe there had been any appreciable change in the amount of skill required in hand composition since 1925, but that the compositor 'has to use those qualifications under rather greater stress and with quicker decision than formerly'.[44] This is a rather surprising verdict, given that in no other case was the speed of work taken into consideration. Nor was there any particular stress placed on speeding-up in the union's case.[45] It seems probable that Dethridge used this as an excuse to bring the compositor's margin into line with the twenty-seven shillings awarded to tradesmen in the metal industry by Judge Beeby.[46]

Finally, decisions of the Arbitration Court in respect to skill margins were always influenced by the outcome of collective bargaining between employers and the union. This was a formal part of court procedure: conferences between the two parties, presided over by a judge, attempted to reach agreement on as many rates as possible. Only when such conciliation failed to produce consensus was the matter put to the court for arbitration. We have already seen how women's lack of power within the union disadvantaged them from the outset in this process: their claims were not even endorsed by the union, let alone the employers or the court. However, their cause was not entirely without champions. The union's industrial advocate throughout the period was E. C. Magrath, a man who advocated the cause of the less powerful with almost as much enthusiasm as he did that of the craftsmen. A less determined advocate might have been prepared to compromise more readily so as to avoid the expense and labour of a hearing. The temptation to sacrifice some rates, particularly those of the less powerful members (females and unskilled) must have been very strong. That Magrath did not do so is clear: female as well as male margins were brought before the court both in 1925 and 1936. Magrath's influence was such that he was able to secure more favourable awards for women than had a less able or committed person presented their case. The employers' advocate, George Anderson, on the other hand, was competent enough but was no match for his New South Wales adversary.

The printing cases of the 1920s and 1930s suggest, however, a limitation to the usefulness of using the formal record of court proceedings as a guide to the real power dynamics of an industry. They conceal as much as they reveal about the collusion and compromises which must have been arrived at between the two parties to any case.

There was also a less obvious way in which the collective power of workers and employers affected awards. The PIEUA was a very strong union, with its funds and membership relatively unscathed by the depression. There was always the possibility that should the court disappoint the members they might choose to do without it altogether. The Victorian branch threatened as much at the time of its application to the court in 1934.[47] Indeed, the PIEUA as a whole launched a campaign against arbitration in the wake of the 1937 award. That the union did not choose to flex its industrial muscles on behalf of its female members is significant.

Laura Bennett has argued that skilled male workers perform work that is characteristically different to unskilled women's work. Indeed, it is the characteristic of this work (in particular encompassing a broad range of tasks) which gave workers the strategic base for their industrial muscle. These characteristics of male skilled work came to be adopted by the Arbitration Court as its indicia of skilled work. The court adopted the ideology of skill which prevailed in the Australian marketplace at the time of its inception. The converse of this argument is that women were typically unskilled workers because the technological and market structure of their work was not conducive to craft organisation. That is, their work was typically fragmented and repetitive. In awarding low skill margins for women, she argues, the court was simply reflecting the different nature of women's work which lacked the features of craft organisation and therefore gave them little power in the labour market.[48]

The printers' case is of particular interest in relation to this argument because it was not typical of the industries in which women were employed—those characterised as labour-intensive, technologically stagnant, poorly unionised and subject to high levels of seasonal unemployment and outwork. The printing industries in general had more in common with 'men's' industries such as engineering than with other industries employing women. However, as we have seen, women in printing occupations fared little better in the industrial arena than their contemporaries doing more typically female work in more typically female industries. The majority of women print workers, who performed monotonous, repetitive tasks, received rates comparable to similar female workers in other industries, despite the fact that the printing industry in general did not conform to the usual model of a woman's industry and despite the fact that the union that represented them was one of the country's strongest. The minority of women who performed work which on the court's own criteria conformed to the craft or semi-craft model were unsuccessful in having their margins reflect these skills. That women's work was not better paid in the printing industry was partly the result of their lack of power within the union and consequently within the arbitration system. It also reflected the weakness of their industrial position before the court entered the wage-fixing arena. This was especially crucial for female bookbinders, whose occupation had been recognised as a skilled, apprenticeship trade in the eighteenth century. The subsequent decline of their craft was the result of the failure to limit entry to apprenticeships, more than of deskilling as a result of mechanisation and fragmentation. This failure was itself the consequence of factors exogenous to the work process, principally the high turnover of female labour due to women's domestic roles.[49] The court's reluctance to revalue women's work in accordance with the criteria which it applied to male crafts reflected the conservative nature of the Commonwealth Arbitration Court in general, and especially in the 1920s when the whole system was under attack from non-Labor politicians. It also reflected the masculinist and white supremacist political economy of the court judges, who gave low priority to wage justice for women.

Given that women's work was so poorly paid, why did they not move into the better-paid men's areas? Here the answer is also complex. The union's rules forbade the transfer of female workers to male occupations without the approval of the board of management. Other structural constraints limited the kinds of work they could do. At the most obvious level, so called 'protective' clauses in the 1925 award limited the work which females could do in printing firms. They were prohibited from working night shifts and from working alone after six o'clock at night. This effectively kept them out of newspaper offices almost entirely. Females were forbidden to wash-up, clean or adjust printing machines, and to lift heavy weights; they were allowed to perform only the smallest class of bronzing work and then for not more than two hours per day.[50]

Customs and practices evolved over the history of the industry also excluded women. These included the practice of apprenticing only boys to men's trades, thus preventing women from acquiring the skills necessary to perform the better-paid work. Equal pay was the other major device used to exclude women from certain jobs. Male and female schedules were listed separately in the awards of the court; where the female list contained no equivalent to work listed for men they were to be paid the male rate.[51] The authority of the court was thus given to long-standing practices in the industry which before the awards were enforced by a combination of union regulation of members and agreements with employers.

As we have seen, the role of the state in relation to the printing industry was generally a conservative one, reinforcing the status quo. However, on the question of hours its role was more radical, granting a general reduction of the working week by four hours in 1925. It is somewhat ironic that the female workers, whose interests were in many respects neglected by the union, became the key element in the union's strategy to secure a reduction in hours. Union officials were acutely aware of the court's record on this question. Most pertinently, Judge Higgins had awarded a 44-hour week to the clothing trades on the grounds that shorter hours would improve the health of female workers, the future mothers of the race. Male workers also had their hours reduced so as to avoid the disruption which would occur in factories if the two sexes worked different hours.[52] Interpretations of the court's authority to set 'standard hours' for any industry also favoured an appeal based on female hours.[53] The union obviously had these precedents in mind when it commissioned an enquiry into the health of female workers in the printing industry preparatory to going to court.[54] It even went so far as to secure the services of Dr Ethel Osborne, the same expert witness who had convinced Higgins of the necessity for shorter hours in the clothing case. The strategy paid off, the entire industry being awarded forty-four hours. It is clear from their judgements that the health of the female workers was the key to the decision. Dethridge and his fellow judges all accepted Osborne's conclusions as being 'substantially correct' regarding the harmful effects of employment in this industry on the health of women workers. And protecting women's health was seen as being in the national interest.[55]

The state, represented by the Arbitration Court, thus brought to the workplace an agenda wider than the interests of either employers or employees. On balance, however, their decisions in the printing cases were more favourable to workers than employers. And while male workers may not have made great advances under arbitration, they certainly gained more than they would have under the Wages Board system.[56] The possible exception to this is the male bookbinders, who were forced to concede jealously guarded territory to female labour in 1937. In general, though, the Arbitration Court protected men's jobs from female competition by use of both protective clauses and equal pay.[57]

The court also protected the work of craftsmen in another way. By refusing to 'classify' certain aspects of a trade as less skilled, the court directly retarded the subdivision of the labour process. Webb's refusal to classify further aspects of bookbinder's work as unskilled delayed subdivision in this craft for a decade. Similarly, letterpress machinists in New South Wales had their work subdivided when some of the platen machining was given to non-tradesmen by the New South Wales court. The craft of the Victorian letter-press machinist, by contrast, remained intact, protected by the award of the Common-wealth court. The employers' failure to have this work classified by the court in 1925 possibly discouraged further applications to have the work of other tradesmen subdivided, particularly as Webb had stated it as a matter of principle that it was 'wrong' for the court to classify occupations or 'to do anything else' calculated to break down skilled trades.[58]

It is perhaps ironic that the more reluctant the signatories to the PIEUA amalgamation, the more their sections gained from arbitration. The typographers and women bookbinders, who were unenthusiastic, were better off under federal wage fixation. The male bookbinders, who led the move for amalgamation, were also initially pleased with the outcome of the arbitration case, believing that the court's endorsement of the existing demarcation line had 'settled for all time' the right of male binders to turned-in work.[59] The ensuing ten years saw them use the authority of the court with enthusiasm in their campaign of 'unceasing vigilance' against female encroachments.[60] They were, however, much less enthusiastic about the court after the 1937 decision to concede significant areas of stationery to female labour.

The cardboard-box makers, who also welcomed the prospect of federal arbitration, had to wait until 1937 before experiencing significant benefits from the move. In that year the long-awaited piecework schedule was ratified by the court, bringing uniformity and accountability where in the past employers had had a virtual free hand in setting domestic rates.[61]

It is not surprising that the compositors profited by the arrangement. The structure of the federated union ensured that their interests received priority. What is surprising is that the women bookbinders also did fairly well. The federal awards were more generous than they could have expected under the Wages Boards. But in contrast to the composi-tors, this owed nothing to their position within the union. On the contrary, it occurred in spite of their relatively powerless status. What gains they made must be largely attributed to Magrath's advocacy and the strength of the female witnesses before the court. As the board of management observed, 'the whole strength of a case depends on the evidence [of the witnesses], and in this regard there was nothing left to be desired'.[62] That they did not make even greater progress was due to the essentially conservative nature of the court and the fact that the union as a whole was not prepared to make a stand on wage justice for women.

Conclusion

In a discussion of methods of factory organisation, Stephen Wood and John Kelly have argued that we cannot 'assign priority to a single factor in management strategy, whether it be labour, technology or markets, but must determine such problems empirically'.[1] Their conclusion parallels my own. Labour and product markets, technology, the supply of capital, racial and gender orders and the activities of the state all affected the development of the labour process. These external factors shaped the options which faced management in its decisions about the organisation of work. They likewise affected the way in which workers responded, defining the parameters of a dynamic of work. As the subsequent discussion will argue, the interaction of all these factors, differently weighted, produced a specific dynamic of work in each of the three industries studied.

Before returning to the operation of this dynamic, we need to review the major ways in which work changed in these industries over the period from 1880 to World War II. Firstly, can deskilling be identified as 'the major tendential presence within the development of the capitalist labour process'?[2] If by deskilling we mean the breaking down of complex tasks into a series of simpler operations, then the answer must be an unqualified 'yes'. In each branch of the clothing trade the major trend was for the making of garments to be subdivided, firstly into cutting, sewing and pressing; secondly, into the making of a narrower range of garments; and thirdly, into work on increasingly smaller parts of each garment. This process of fragmentation operated unevenly, affecting women's work more than men's, shirtmaking more than tailoring, sewing more than pressing and pressing more than cutting. In bootmaking a similar process occurred. Workers were initially divided into clickers, upper sewers, makers and finishers; then, according to the type of shoes they made; and, finally, according to the kind of specialised machine they operated. As with clothing, the process was uneven. The work of male clickers and female machinists was less fragmented than that of men making and finishing. Male printers were divided into linotype operators and hand compositors, each performing different aspects of the original compositor's work; stationery, cardboard-box and paper-bag workers of both sexes had their work transformed from a relatively complex hand process to the more simple act of machine feeding. Mechanisation also affected the work of male and female bookbinders, although subdivision affected women's work more than men's.

However, as we have seen, it is not possible to formulate a simple equation between fragmentation and deskilling. In objective terms, fragmentation usually involved a degree of 'reskilling' because it was generally associated with mechanisation. Workers needed retraining in order to perform under the new conditions. Thus, operating a sewing machine is a different skill from wielding a needle and thread. Manipulating a hide of leather on a stuff-cutting machine is a very different operation from cutting out soles with a knife. And dealing with the noise and vibration of a pedal-operated stapling machine was a far cry from the quiet, sedentary occupation of the hand book-sewer. The skills employed were as different as those of the hand compositor and the linotypist. And these examples are in addition to the more obvious cases of reskilling which arose out of new processes, rather than new ways of doing old jobs. Print workers engaged on the various forms of photo and colour reproduction are one instance of the former; boot workers operating the new cement process introduced in the 1930s are another.

It might be argued, however, that although these skills associated with more mechanised production were different, they were intrinsically 'easier' and required less training to acquire. To some extent this is true. A person who has had no prior experience of either a needle and thread or a sewing machine would probably become useful on the machine more quickly than with the needle. But an intrinsic part of the operation of manufacturing machinery was speed, and this speed constitutes a separate element in the assessment of skill. Intensification of work, or speeding-up, was a feature of each of these industries in this period. Workers were required not just to produce accurate work, but to produce this work more and more quickly. It was no use, for instance, being able to guide pieces of cloth accurately through a machine: the worker had to be able to do this quickly. To deny the crucial role of speed would be to argue that a two-finger typist, who could produce accurate work given unlimited time, was 'skilled' in the same way as a professional typist. Any deskilling, then, arising from the simplification (or narrowing range) of tasks was offset by the increased speeds at which these tasks had to be executed.

The situation is further complicated by the question of whether work was becoming fragmented rather than specialised, the difference being that fragmented work requires less skill whereas specialised work involves the concentration of skill on a narrower range of tasks. Thus, the linotypist could be seen as a specialist compositor, one who has the same training as a hand compositor but in addition has the ability to operate a typesetting machine. By contrast, the maker of chocolate boxes at MacRobertson's factory may have developed considerable expertise on one particular type of box, but was unable to get work anywhere else because her skills were too specific. Since she lacked a general training in making cardboard boxes, her work was fragmented rather than specialised.

This distinction seems straightforward enough, but in practice it is not so clear. The process whereby skills are socially constructed and given a value independent of any objective features of work content operates also in the definition of work as fragmented or specialised. The same processes which define certain work as skilled and unskilled define work as specialised and fragmented. To return to the linotyping case: it could be argued that the work the linotypist performed was, in fact, fragmented rather than specialised. The work set on the machines was the 'straight matter', such as newspaper articles. This was the simpler part of the general compositor's work. The more complex part was the display work, which required judgement, and this was reserved for the hand compositor. The pattern is a familiar one wherever machinery has been introduced to craftwork: machines have been devised to perform the simpler tasks while the more complex tasks have remained the province of the craftworker. Thus, in tailoring, the machinist sews the seams while the tailor does the 'fitting', that part of the work requiring judgement. Objectively, then, the position of the linotypist is analogous to that of the sewing machinist: they are both doing fragmented work. But, as we have seen, linotypists became the elite of the printing trade, having both the highest rates of pay and the highest status. Sewing machinists, on the other hand, had lower status than tailors (and craft tailoresses) and were paid considerably less. Both kinds of work were fragmented, but one was socially constructed as 'specialised' while the other was not. In making generalisations about the general trend to fragmentation, then, it is important to bear in mind that this has occurred even when status indicators might suggest otherwise.

In addition to the trend toward fragmentation and mechanisation, all three industries showed an increased ratio of female to male workers. This process was also very uneven. Tailoring experienced an influx of women in the late nineteenth century, but the trend was halted in the early years of the twentieth century. In the other branches of the clothing industry there was no increase in the proportion of women employed. On the contrary, there were slightly more men engaged in the industry from the early twentieth century. The proportion of women employed in boot and shoe making did not increase significantly until the late 1890s. Thereafter, they rose slowly so that as a proportion of total boot workers their numbers increased from about one-quarter in the 1890s to almost a half in the 1930s. Printing also showed a general trend toward feminisation, the most dramatic increases in women employed occurring in the period 1900–14.

With the exception of tailoring, though, feminisation did not mean that women were moving into 'male' occupations. In both printing and bootmaking the increasing proportion of women employed reflected expansion in established women's occupations. Thus, the growth of the cardboard-box industry provided more jobs for women in this traditional women's industry. Faster methods of printing and the expansion of stationery production similarly drew more women into 'women's' sections of these industries. Women were likewise required in increasing numbers to fit and machine uppers in boot factories. The mechanisation of men's bootmaking had no equivalent in the women's sections: the only way for the uppers department to keep pace with the rest of a factory was to employ more workers, and traditionally these were women. Where men were moving into 'women's' industries (dressmaking, millinery, shirts, whitework), it was largely in the capacity of supervisors and managers in an expanded factory system. Only in the case of cutting and design work were men clearly performing work which had formerly been a female preserve.

A third aspect of work relates to the question of control. Did fragmentation mean diminished worker control over the labour process? Did the ways in which capitalists exercised control in the workplace change significantly? The earlier discussion on the association between fragmentation, mechanisation and speed implies that workers experienced diminished control over the way in which they performed their work. Certainly, the breaking down of work into smaller parts inevitably left less room for discretion. Likewise, machines limited the scope for individual variation in performing tasks. The question of speed is more complex. In some circumstances increased pace did reflect less control. The bootmaker who was too afraid to go out at night for fear of losing speed the next day, and consequently his job, clearly had little control over the work process. On the other hand were compositors and linotypists who worked quickly in order to achieve high earnings on piece rates. They were not in danger of having their piece rates cut because of these earnings, nor of losing their jobs or living wage if they chose not to work so hard. Thus, speed can be considered an indication of loss of job control only where workers faced dismissal or unacceptable loss of earnings for being too slow. Unfortunately for the workers, very few were in the position of the elite printers. The overwhelming majority of workers had little choice but to work as fast as they could.

Was this loss of control a reflection of widespread adoption of scientific management methods? In a few cases there is evidence of self-conscious and systematic application of Taylorite ideas. The Pelaco factory is the most important example, although other shirt factories also followed its lead. More common was ad hoc adaptation of American methods to Australian conditions. Information gleaned from trade journals and from management visits abroad was incorporated into factory organisation in Australia, especially in the years immediately preceding and following World War I. The general trend of these changes was towards scientific management principles: the separation of conception and execution; the tying of fragmented work processes to particular machines; and the selection of different types of workers to perform different types of work. However, the transformation was a very uneven one and, in general, lagged behind developments in the United States of America. Printing firms showed less interest in such schemes than clothing and boot factories. And when it came to implementation, shirt factories were noticeably more successful than other kinds of clothing manufacturers and boot producers. And throughout this period the clothing industry included an alternative method of production to the factory system: domestic outwork. The fact that outwork increased during the 1930s significantly qualifies any generalisation about the trend toward scientific management practices in these industries.

The existence of outwork also raises the question as to how far scientific management was important as a method of labour control, as distinct from a system to maximise productivity by most effective use of resources. What role did scientific management play in ensuring that workers worked hard, were careful with materials and did not engage in collective opposition to their employers? The answer in the case of outwork is obvious. It was irrelevant. Competition amongst outworkers and low piecework rates ensured that workers worked at a pace to satisfy contractors. Their isolation minimised the possibilities of collective resistance.

Inside factories the situation was more complex. Scientific management techniques, particularly payment by results and close supervision, encouraged workers to work hard. These methods were, however, not the only ones employed, nor were they the most important. Those firms most interested in Taylorism also adopted welfarist and paternalist styles of management. In the context of the war, this was overlain with overt patriotism. Managements thus hoped to subvert unionism amongst their workers by encouraging employees to identify with the aims and methods of their employers. The evidence suggests that this strategy was very effective.

The existence of rigid sexual divisions of labour, both in the home and the workplace, also reduced the likelihood of collective opposition to management. Women's roles in the home limited their participation in union affairs. In young single women the expectation of marriage undermined militancy, adding to the problems inherent in organising young and temporary workers. Older women with dependents, having experience of the limitations of marriage as a secure option to paid work, were generally more militant. However, their dual role as homemakers and breadwinners left them little time for regular union organisation. Mature single women, who formed the backbone of women's union involvement in the twentieth century, were in a minority. Only in the tailoring section of the clothing trade were they found in sufficient numbers to have any real impact.

Sexual divisions in the workplace undermined the tendency of factory production to produce a more homogenised workforce. Men and women experienced work differently because they did different jobs and were paid at different rates. These differences divided workers, producing suspicion and hostility between the sexes. As the clothing and printing industries demonstrate, different experiences of work prevented a common strategy to combat the intensification and fragmentation of work.

The interaction between the domestic gender order and the sexual segregation of paid work also prevented any general movement amongst workers to raise the level of female wages. Such general increases were seen as a threat to the earnings of male breadwinners, and were opposed by most men and some women. The clothing and boot industries demonstrated this logic most overtly.

Authority patterns within the patriarchal family were also used to reinforce the control of employers over employees. Younger workers were placed under the supervision of older workers, and women under the supervision of men. A common practice in the nineteenth century, it continued with the move to more 'modern' methods of factory management. Male tailors, for instance, were placed in charge of teams of females doing subdivided work. And implicit in the paternalist style of companies such as Pelaco and Lucas was the rhetoric of 'the family firm', with its appeal to patriarchal patterns of authority as well as familial loyalties. 'The family', however, could also act against management control. An injustice to one worker could invoke the wrath of other family members. However, the fact that firms continued to employ family imagery in their dealings with workers suggests that, on balance, it reinforced the authority of management.

At another level, the transference of domestic patterns of gender relations to the workplace acted against an independent movement of female workers. This was most noticeable in the boot industry, where the proximity of factories to workers' homes meant a higher incidence of members of the same family working together than was the case for either the clothing or printing industries. This retarded female involvement in union affairs because men assumed this responsibility on their behalf. Similar situations occurred, although in less extreme form, in the other two industries. Men occupied positions of authority even when in a minority in a union. Unions thus pursued policies which suited the male membership, and these were not necessarily in the best interests of female workers. Different work experiences created different interests, while sexual politics helped ensure that men's interests received precedence.

A further way in which control of the workforce was maintained is in the area described by Burawoy as 'games'. There is evidence that such practices did occur and that they helped workers accept the new system of working. Thus, linotype operators prided themselves on their speeds and their earnings. They clearly had no interest in challenging a system which they were able to turn to their own advantage. Where working at high speed might otherwise be considered a hardship, in the linotypists' case it was used to bolster the status of men whose work could potentially have been classed as deskilled. In the clothing trade, competitions organised by supervisors encouraged workers to work hard, but in this case the rewards were more modest: sixpence or a box of lollies was considered sufficient incentive. In the boot trade, races also took place between workers, the only reward being the status attached to the accolade of 'race-horse'. With the exception of the linotypists, however, it is doubtful that such methods were an important and enduring form of 'manufacturing consent'. Unions were alert to their significance and officially opposed such practices.

There is one other way in which employers maintained control over their workers: via the discipline of the market. Thompson has argued that the relation of ownership itself is insufficient to secure management control over the labour process.[3] This is not always true. In the boot and clothing industries during the depression of the late 1920s and 1930s, for example, the most powerful control over workers was the fear of unemployment. Scientific management may have been needed to make more efficient use of resources, but it was not needed to discipline the workforce. The market did that.

Finally, there is the question of payment and conditions. Were the years between 1880 and 1939 marked by continuous improvement in these respects, from the workers' point of view? The two severe depressions of the 1890s and 1930s make nonsense of such a suggestion. The continuing realities of underemployment in industries like bootmaking, even in relatively prosperous times, also make generalisations about earnings very difficult. Official rates of pay were one thing; actual earnings were quite another. Some general trends are, however, evident. Inside factories there was a marked decline in legal hours of work. Factory legislation of the 1870s and 1880s had limited the hours which women and juveniles could work to forty-eight per week. This was extended to men under the first Wages Board determinations around the turn of the century. Linotypists were the most favoured, working only forty-two hours under the 1901 printers' determination. The next reduction in hours occurred under the auspices of the Commonwealth Arbitration Court. Clothing workers secured a 44-hour week in 1919, followed by boot workers in 1921 and the printing industry in 1927.

Payment for public holidays was also an innovation in these years. This was provided for under the Wages Boards during the first decades of the twentieth century, and was incorporated in the federal awards for each industry. Paid annual leave was not legally provided for, with the exception of the printing industry which secured this concession in 1937. In a few cases, however, employers did provide paid holidays of their own accord.

The five-day working week also became more common in the period beginning with World War I. This became standard practice in the clothing and boot trades in the inter-war period, although the printing industry was more resistant to the change. Some employers converted to five days in the early 1920s, only to revert to Saturday morning work as well later in the decade.

Physical conditions in factories showed general improvement. The sewering of Melbourne from the 1890s and the provincial cities in the 1920s made factories healthier and more pleasant places to work. New factories, especially those built in the expansionary years following federation and the war, provided better lighting and ventilation. Some firms also provided dining-rooms in the pre-war period, and this became more general in the 1920s. In isolated cases, facilities for workers even ran to pianos, radios and sporting equipment. However, alongside these 'model' factories, there were still many of the 'backyard' variety. Operating in unlined tin sheds, workers endured seasonal extremes of temperature and the company of vermin. Such establishments were particularly common in the boot and clothing industries, with conditions deteriorating in the 1930s depression. And no matter whether the factory was a shed or a brick edifice, few employers appreciated the importance of providing their workers with comfortable seating in this period.

The question of workers' health and safety is a separate study in itself and has been touched on here only as it relates to workers' experience of their work. However, the evidence suggests that better ventilation and safety procedures in factories were offset by problems arising out of changed work processes. Thus, women working in printing factories may have been exposed to less fumes, but they had to operate machines at high speed which caused considerable jarring to the body. The increased pace of work in all industries seems to have caused physical stress to workers.

On the question of wage rates and earnings, it is also possible to draw some tentative conclusions. Real wages (both rates and earnings) declined from the late 1880s to the late 1890s. They recovered in the first three decades of the twentieth century, exceeding the early 1880s level by the end of the war. These levels were eroded by inflation in the post-war period, although they recovered again in the 1920s before falling in the depression. They rose in the late 1930s, but not to their mid-1920s levels. Within this general pattern, however, there were important variations. Male bootmakers suffered a general decline in earnings from the 1890s. Although this decline was arrested by the 1910 arbitration award, bootmakers' real wages did not improve significantly in the period to World War II. Indeed, they fell in relation to the wages of other skilled tradesmen. The earnings of outworkers in the clothing trade declined in the early twentieth century when those of inside workers were increasing. They were also slower to share in the post-depression recovery in the 1930s. And the fact that more juveniles were employed during the depression contributed to the general decline in workers' earnings in this decade. How-ever, it must be stressed that these are tentative conclusions only. More definitive state-ments would need to be based on extensive analysis of the cost of living in comparison to actual rather than nominal pay rates, making appropriate allowance for short-time and seasonal unemployment.

How were all these changes to work determined? At the most fundamental level they were precipitated by changes in product markets. Thus, the stagnation of markets for boots in the late 1870s and early 1880s precipitated the valorisation crisis which led to employer attempts to cheapen production by cutting labour rates. However, as this same case illustrates, the market precipitates change but it does not determine the direction which that change will take. The employers' response to the crisis of valorisation was to cut piece rates, which in turn led to a 'crisis of exploitation' from the point of view of the workers. Their strategy to relieve this crisis included the elimination of outwork. The suc-cess of this strategy depended on the sexual division of labour within the homes of the workers, whereby it was women rather than men who took responsibility for the daily and generational reproduction of the workforce. With the move to factory production, workers had greater ability to resist rate-cutting. This led to a new valorisation crisis for the employers. The drawing in of all workers under the factory roof had provided them with the circumstances in which to implement a new strategy to cut production costs: mechanisation and subdivision. This move, accompanied as it was by severe economic depression, led to another 'crisis of exploitation' for workers. But this time they had exhausted their industrial bargaining power. The strategy instead became political: they turned to the legislature for relief. The Wages Board, however, proved a disappointment. It failed to regulate boy labour which, combined with subdivision, steadily eroded the bootmaker's claim to skilled status. The federal Arbitration Court was more co-operative. It prescribed a broad-based form of apprenticeship and restricted the number of boys entering the trade, thus reinstating men's bootmaking occupations amongst the skilled trades. The price they paid for this arrangement was acceptance of a margin for skill below that generally paid to other tradesmen. Women's wages, not being within the court's jurisdiction, were also kept below rates in comparable occupations. This system was accepted by a majority of employers and employees for the next two decades. Acceptance was based on a general expansion of the industry, as manufacturers took advantage of leased machinery and easy credit to try for a share of the booming wartime market. However, contraction in the market for boots in the 1920s precipitated another valorisation crisis. As this crisis deepened with the onset of general depression late in the decade, employers took the initiative. Where possible, they employed new technology (such as the cement process) to cheapen production. More generally, they successfully intensified, or speeded up, work. This again led to a crisis of exploitation as workers reacted against these moves to cheapen further what was already comparatively cheap male labour. Again their solution was an appeal to the adjudication of the state in the form of the Commonwealth Arbitration Court. The court's decision in 1938 fore-shadowed radical change to existing practices in the industry.

A similar pattern emerged in the clothing industry, although this was more complex because of the three distinct branches involved. All three branches, however, were

influenced to varying degrees by the major shift in the product market from order garments to those sold ready-made. Without this shift there would have been no substantial
development in the factory system of production. All three branches also shared a labour
market with common features: a largely female workforce, a significant number of
whom were willing or needed to carry out work in their own homes. This meant that
when product markets contracted and manufacturers looked for ways to cut costs, more
extensive use of outdoor labour was usually the simplest option. Intensifying the work of
indoor workers occurred at the same time, but was generally not as effective in cutting
costs as outwork. Most concerted attempts at intensifying inside work, however,
occurred in times of market expansion. The years immediately following federation, the
war years and the 1920s were thus the periods of most dramatic innovation in clothing
production. In this case experimentation was a strategy to expand production with a
female labour force which was not expanding at the same rate.

In contrast to the situation in the boot trade, there was no strong dialectic between
employer initiatives and workers' responses in the clothing trades. The sexual division of
labour in the home, which made outwork an attractive source of income for women with
domestic duties, prevented this kind of dynamic. Workers in factories had little room to
manoeuvre as long as employers had the option of sending work outside.

The only branch where workers did have an active input in the shaping of work processes was the tailoring section. In this case, state legislation in the form of prescribed
piece rates (under both Wages Boards and federal Arbitration Court) limited the role of
outwork. Before this occurred, however, men in the industry were fighting a losing battle
against the use of cheaper female labour to reduce the cost of tailoring. The stagnation of
clothing markets in the late 1870s and 1880s caused a crisis of valorisation for clothing
manufacturers in the same way as it had for boot employers. Men's labour was the most
expensive engaged in tailoring, and the strategy adopted by employers to cheapen it was
to adopt simpler, more subdivided work processes and to use women instead of men on
this work. This occurred both inside and outside factories. They also sought to cut rates
paid to these female workers. The result was an 'exploitation crisis' for workers. In the
1880s this erupted in the tailoresses' strike, which checked piece-rate cutting in the short
term, but eventually failed to maintain earnings as employers turned increasingly to outwork in the late 1880s and 1890s. For male tailoring workers, the crisis produced a determination to exclude women from the trade. This was expressed in union organisation in
the 1890s. It was also a major motive behind their support for Wages Boards. Their strategy was to limit outwork so as to curtail the extension of female labour outside the factories and 'legitimate' workrooms, whilst campaigning for equal pay to prevent further
incursions on the work of inside male workers. As we have seen, this strategy effectively
stopped the trend toward female labour in the making of tailored garments.

In the twentieth century, official representatives of the clothing union (all of whom
were men) accepted scientific management as the only alternative to sweated outwork
and the feminisation of tailoring. Indeed, they encouraged employers to experiment with
such methods so as to forestall these developments. The expanded factory system offered
plenty of employment at both craft and supervisory levels for men. But this solution also
had an inbuilt contradiction: there was a gap between the official's perceptions and the

actual work experience of the female members. Thus, female clothing workers experienced a further 'crisis of exploitation' which led to a challenge to methods of manufacture such as the 1935 strike of Melbourne trouser machinists.

Employers in the printing industry were at times also anxious to reduce the cost of their male workforce, most of whom received skilled rates of pay. In the 1880s, for instance, the recovery of the printing trade had encouraged many craftsmen to go into business on their own accord, as the capital required was not great. In the early 1880s there was therefore an expanding market but also an increasing number of competing firms. Reducing costs became important if firms were to get a share of the orders. However, the industry was not generally suitable for domestic production. This meant that any attempts to introduce women to do 'men's' work usually met with successful resistance from tightly organised male workers. Boy labour was also tried, and although this was generally more widespread, especially in small jobbing offices and country newspapers, it was checked by the opposition of unions and large employers. The pressures of competition in the early and mid-1880s were not sufficiently strong, however, for employers to pursue drastic changes in methods of production. Only with the economic downturn from 1889 did they look more seriously at ways of reducing costs. Thus, in 1891, male bookbinders were forced to concede a small area of work to female labour. It was also in the 1890s that linotype machines were brought in to cheapen the costs of composition, and mechanised production of cloth-casing cheapened bookbinding.

Other major changes to work processes in printing also occurred because of limitations on the use of female labour. The rapid expansion of the bookbinding, stationery and cardboard-box industries in the early years of the twentieth century, fuelled by new printing technologies, occurred at a time when the supply of female workers was inadequate to meet the expanding demands of industry. The installation of folding, sewing and gluing machinery in this period enabled machines to keep pace with the output of men's sections of factories without employers having to extend the use of more expensive male workers to traditionally female areas. When the stationery trade experienced market pressure in the 1930s as a result of import competition, further technological innovation was not a solution: manufacturers were already using the most modern equipment available. The extension of female labour was again seen as a solution. The union was predictably resistant to this suggestion. Male bookbinders were already feeling threatened by the shifting market demand for loose-leaf filing systems (women's work) in preference to bound account books (men's work). The state, however, intervened: the Commonweath Arbitration Court declared a movement in the 'line of demarcation' in bookbinding which expanded the range of work which could be performed by cheaper female labour.

The same factors which account for change in work processes and conditions also account for continuities. Where the market was the key factor in precipitating change, it was also the most important limiting factor on innovation. Specifically, the small size of the Australian consumer market, and the limited extent of export trade, placed practical constraints on product specialisation and mass production. This was the major reason that the boot and clothing industries lagged behind developments in countries with mass markets, such as the United States. The extreme seasonality of markets for boots and clothing also discouraged the installation of expensive equipment which might lie idle for months of the year. This consideration was, however, offset to some extent in the boot trade with the use of leased machinery.

Labour markets could also constrain innovation, both directly and indirectly. In the boot trade, for instance, shortages of women for factory work discouraged employers from using female labour in place of men on subdivided work. Shortages of skilled female machinists in the early 1920s also deterred manufacturers from introducing a system of classification aimed at breaking down male skills. On this occasion, it was not that they intended to use women on men's work, but rather that employers feared a strike of female machinists in defence of their fellow workers and relatives.

Developments in technology and technical expertise also placed limits on productive innovation. In the printing trade, for instance, the use of linotype machines in jobbing offices was restricted by the unsuitability of the machines for display work. The clothing trade was similarly limited in its use of motive power before the widespread use of electricity from the early twentieth century. Alternative nineteenth-century sources of power were either more expensive and less reliable (gas) or not suited to fast, light sewing machines (steam). The delay in developing sophisticated cutting machines for both clothing and boots similarly retarded mechanisation of these processes until well into the twentieth century.

In the Australian context, the state also played an important role in limiting productive innovation which was aimed at deskilling and/or feminisation of the workforce. Tariffs which protected local industries such as clothing and boots against import competition reduced the incentive to become more 'efficient'. Taxes on imported machinery also discouraged local manufacturers from employing the latest technology. Protective legislation which excluded women and juveniles from certain types of work, together with Wages Board and arbitration awards for equal pay on 'men's' work, removed one of the major incentives to subdivide work: the opportunity to employ cheaper, untrained workers on the separate parts.

Limitations on the proportion of juveniles which could be employed had a similar effect. These were especially effective when combined with apprenticeship provisions. Provided under both the state Apprenticeship Act and the federal arbitration awards, these ensured that some workers received a broad-based training even when subsequently employed on subdivided work. This reinforced their status as skilled workers, and their claims to higher rates of pay. Thus, linotypists underwent a six- or seven-year apprenticeship although only one year of this was actually devoted to learning to use the typesetting machine. Male bootmakers and workers of both sexes engaged in tailoring also had provision for such general training. The state's reinforcement of these workers' claims to craft status removed the incentive to fragment the labour process even further where the major benefit was the employment of cheaper labour. The Arbitration Court's reluctance to classify work, with different rates of pay for the 'less skilled' sections, had a similar effect.

At a more general level, the gender order (divisions of labour in the home and workplace; ideologies of men's and women's place and constructions of masculinity and femininity) also narrowed the options of manufacturers who contemplated productive reorganisation. Protective legislation which limited the types and hours of women's work was a product of this gender order (and also reinforced it). The low wages paid to women also arose out of their association with reproduction and domestic labour. In an industry such as clothing, where the overwhelming majority of workers was female, moves to cheapen labour were of less value than in men's industries because labour was already so cheap. The only significant savings occurred where juveniles could be employed in place of adults.

Constructions of femininity deterred some employers from employing women on work which was considered masculine. The case of the 'Amazons' in the pressing room is the major instance of this. However, employers in all three trades were influenced by ideas about respectability, the definition of which had clear gender dimensions. Work perceived as 'unrespectable' or 'unfeminine' would be less likely to attract female labour. This affected manufacturing employers in the twentieth century because office and sales work offered more 'feminine' employment to young women. There were thus fewer women available for employers to use in any moves to replace men. The need to appear respectable in order to attract female labour also constrained employers in the types of work on which they could employ women. In the boot factories, for instance, employers were very reluctant to engage in the 'disgusting' American practice of employing the sexes side by side. This effectively meant women's confinement to the machining and packing rooms. Similarly, the breadwinner–dependent model of most working-class families provided the material base for a determined effort on the part of men (and some women) to exclude women from 'men's' jobs and so preserve the income of the male breadwinner. Again, this economic motivation was reinforced by less tangible desires to maintain the existing gender division of labour and hence men's masculine self-definitions.

The limitations imposed by the availability of capital are obvious. In the nineteenth century, when most firms relied on reinvested profits and family finance, large-scale expenditure on expensive plant and machinery was not an option for many. Likewise, when economic recessions encouraged employers to innovate, the same pressures generally restricted the availability of credit and investment capital from banks and shareholders.

These factors acted together to construct the site for management and worker struggles over the shape of work. Employers do not generally have an inbuilt propensity to change the manufacturing process. If profits are steady they are unlikely to seek drastic changes. It is only when profits are threatened—when a valorisation crisis occurs—that they look for ways to increase productivity. But although the recognition of a valorisation crisis might be a simple matter, the solution to the crisis was never obvious. Many manufacturers were deterred from innovation by realistic assessments of the obstacles before them.

The few cases where manufacturers did adopt thoroughgoing Taylorist systems involved employers who were unusually determined and able to overcome these limitations. Thus, the Pelaco shirt company was able to adopt mass-production techniques by specialising in one fairly standard product. Energetic marketing and strict quality control ensured that Pelaco received a large share of the otherwise limited Australian market. Unlike tailors, workers in the shirt industry (almost all of whom were women) had not been able to secure either a broad-based apprenticeship or effective restrictions on juniors. The restrictions which did exist were easily avoided by Law's strategy of putting all his workers on piecework. The adoption of a paternalistic style of management ensured that his small staff of permanent workers acquiesced in his production methods. Clearly, these were not tactics which could be adopted by more than a minority of firms: neither the product market nor the labour market could sustain such methods.

The same is true for workers. All other things being equal, inactivity is the easiest course. It is only when exploitation arising out of changed work processes reaches unacceptably high levels, or threatens to reach these levels, that they respond. However, the assessment of what is acceptable or unacceptable is a subjective matter. This is especially important since workers' input to the shaping of work needs to be collective to be effective. In what circumstances does a group of workers arrive at a common decision that something needs to be done? It is clearly not simply a matter of the degree of exploitation. If that were so, female outworkers would be among the most militant instead of the least militant. Obviously, there needs to be a certain level of association between workers so that they can appreciate their common lot. The isolation of outworkers in the clothing trade, and their resulting passivity, was thus a powerful factor ensuring the continuity of the outwork system.

Another important ingredient in workers' perceptions of exploitation and their proposed strategies to overcome it was the influence of radical political ideologies. Anarchists such as Chummy Fleming and communists active in both the clothing and boot industries in the 1930s helped to channel workers' experiences into active protest against the existing system.

In a slightly different vein, the popularity of Taylorism amongst sections of the post-war international socialist movement[4] may have influenced socialist union officials such as Alf Wallis to advocate scientific management for the clothing industry. At the same time, workers espousing ideologies which questioned the acceptance of Taylorism and related versions of 'efficient' management were sometimes not in a position to influence the direction of organised labour's response. Thus, Lesbia Harford, a member of the Industrial Workers of the World, and May Brodney, an unorthodox socialist, drew on ideologies which did question the efficiency of scientific management from the worker's point of view.[5] Their feminism and shopfloor experience also made them more sensitive to the implications of management decisions for female workers. But, although they were aware of the potential of scientific management to increase exploitation of workers, their influence was less than that of men such as Wallis because of the structured powerlessness of women within the union hierarchy. It took a further two decades for the experience of women workers to generate conclusions similar to those arrived at theoretically by Harford and Brodney. Only then did shopfloor militancy pose a challenge to management initiatives to fragment work.

As each of these cases illustrates, work was shaped by a progressive dynamic between the capitalist imperative to extract surplus value, the workers' desire to resist exploitation, the intervention of the state, advancements in technology, and the availability of capital. And this dynamic operated within the shifting parameters of product and labour markets, and the less flexible dictates of the gender order.

APPENDIX:
SELECTED EMPLOYMENT STATISTICS, VICTORIA, 1880–1939

Table A1 Employment in factories in selected major industries, 1868–1900

Year	Bricks, pottery, glass, etc.	Metals, engineering and products	Textiles	Clothing	Boots	Food, drink and tobacco	Sawmillers and joinery	Furniture, cabinets, etc.	Paper, printing, etc.	Total Manufacturing Employment
1868	980	3,377	210	3,732	615	3,474	2,122	368	1,123	17,953
1878–79	1,152	6,723	1,307	5,901	3,212	5,153	2,456	1,023	2,860	34,629
1881–82	1,599	8,643	1,348	8,543	4,013	6,325	3,731	1,589	3,519	45,316
1885–86	2,388	10,998	1,171	8,243	4,100	6,897	5,235	1,685	4,603	51,459
1889–90	3,629	14,152	1,193	8,215	3,819	7,668	6,612	2,345	5,530	59,431
1893–94	1,181	7,764	932	7,890	3,307	7,161	2,758	935	4,793	41,882
1896	1,452	9,089	1,233	10,324	4,088	9,024	2,984	1,482	4,913	50,439
1900	1,907	11,908	1,531	14,501	4,764	11,723	4,053	1,561	5,595	64,263

Source: Linge, *Industrial Awakening*, Appendix 1, pp. 744–5.
Note: The figures for clothing employment seriously under-represent actual employment as they do not include outwork or small workrooms. According to the Census, for instance, there were over 20,000 employed in the clothing/textiles industries in 1881; in 1891 the figure was 28,539.

Table A2   Females employed in selected manufacturing industries, 1881–1901

Year	Food and drink		Clothing and textiles		Print		Total female manufacturing employment
	n	%	n	%	n	%	
1881	1,775	7.4	20,977	89.5	718	3.1	23,440
1891	1,415	4.9	26,440	92.2	507	1.7	28,662
1901	1,367	4.4	28,338	91.0	714	2.3	31,121

Source: Victorian Census, 1881, 1891, 1901.

Table A3   Males employed in selected manufacturing industries, 1881–1901

Year	Art and mechanical production	Textiles and dress	Food and drink	Metals and minerals	Building and construction
1881	27,347	10,664	10,251	14,315	N/A
1891	27,880	10,928	7,178	14,330	33,144
1901	20,676	13,571	13,522	48,455	27,392

Source: Victorian Census, 1881, 1891, 1901.

Table A4   Employment in Victorian boot and shoe factories, 1886–1901, by sex

Year	Males	Females	Total	Females as % of total
1886	2,691	953	3,644	26.2
1887	2,683	970	3,653	26.5
1888	2,892	1,023	3,915	26.1
1889	2,855	999	3,854	25.9
1890	2,789	1,086	3,875	28.0
1891	2,781	1,057	3,838	27.5
1892	2,635	1,022	3,657	27.9
1893	2,525	947	3,472	27.3
1894	2,769	1,026	3,795	27.0
1895	3,148	1,079	4,227	25.5
1896	3,122	1,148	4,270	26.9
1897	3,325	1,265	4,590	27.5
1898	2,998	1,237	4,235	29.2
1899	3,033	1,233	4,266	28.8
1900	3,020	1,284	4,304	29.8
1901	2,870	1,381	4,251	32.5

Source: CIF Reports, 1886–1901.
Note: The numbers of men engaged in bootmaking are slightly under-represented because of the persistence of outwork for certain lines (e.g. strong work). The Census gives the following figures.

	Males	Females
1881	6,469	447
1891	6,838	816
1901	6,361	1,157

However, these are overestimates of male employment, as repairers are included. Females, on the other hand, are under-represented, especially in 1881, because of the inclusion of many probable employees in the category 'shoemaker's wife' (there were 770 so designated in 1881) and 'sewing machinist'.

Table A5 Employment in printing and bookbinding factories, 1881–1901, by sex

Year	Males	Females	Total	Females as % of total
1881*	2,557	143	2,700	5.3
1886†	2,960	456	3,416	13.3
1887	3,063	457	3,520	13.0
1888	3,125	502	3,627	13.8
1889	3,538	565	4,103	13.8
1890	3,613	847	4,460	19.0
1891	3,411	745	4,156	17.9
1892	3,359	817	4,176	19.6
1893	3,037	689	3,726	18.3
1894	2,912	629	3,541	17.8
1895	2,831	641	3,472	18.5
1896	2,822	788	3,610	21.8
1897	2,860	867	3,727	23.3
1898	2,769	873	3,642	24.0
1899	2,977	988	3,965	24.9
1900	2,930	823	3,753	22.0
1901	2,902	613	3,515	17.4

*From *Victorian Census*, 1881.
†The figures for 1886–1901 are derived from CIF Reports. There were no reports before 1886. The percentage of females employed in 1881 was probably higher than the 5.3 indicated by the Census because of the inclusion of working proprietors, almost all of whom were males.

Table A6 Employment, factories, horsepower and fixed capital in clothing factories, 1901–1921

Year	Industry	No. of factories	Persons employed Males	Persons employed Females	Females per 100 males	Juveniles Males	Juveniles Females	Horsepower of machinery	Land and buildings £	Plant and machinery £
1901						*(under 15)*				
	Clothing and tailoring	221	1,376	4,462	324	16	83	118	312,200	25,780
	Dressmaking and millinery	205	93	4,845	5,208	1	108	48	221,450	12,760
	Underclothing and shirts	53	102	2,322	2,277	2	85	117	46,530	17,250
1911						*(under 16)*				
	Clothing and tailoring	427	2,404	8,236	343	92	368	306	491,159	52,371
	Dressmaking and millinery	530	243	9,652	3,972	8	509	214	365,660	40,863
	Underclothing and shirts	152	266	5,750	2,162	6	302	454	181,321	55,485
1921										
	Clothing and tailoring	485	2,106	7,089	337	63	259	472	718,575	82,845
	Dressmaking and millinery	475	333	8,780	2,637	7	585	384	650,750	76,525
	Underclothing and shirts	171	338	5,300	1,568	7	335	717	296,665	102,810

Source: 'Factory Statistics' supplied by Office of Government Statist, Melbourne, to 1935 Select Committee on Working Week Appendix A, ANUA E138/18/64.

Table A7 Minimum factory wage rates (shillings per week of 48 hours) as prescribed by Wages Boards in clothing industries, 1898–1917

	Tailoring (Slop)		Dresses (Slop)		Millinery		Shirts		Underclothes	
	M*	F†	M*	F†	M*	F†	M*	F†	M*	F†
1898	49	20	—	—	—	—	—	16	—	16
1902	49	21	—	—	—	—	—	16	—	16
1905	49	21	—	16	—	—	—	16	—	16
1910	55	21	—	16	—	22s6d	—	20	—	20
1912	60	24	52s6d	21s6d	—	22s6d	60	22s6d	—	20
1917	65	29s6d	65	29	—	25	65	27s6d	70	30

*Male rates refer to minimums for cutters, because this is the only occupation for men which occurs in all other sections. Note that none of the boards, with the exception of men's tailoring, initially provided rates for males. That they did so after 1910 reflects the movement of men into cutting positions within the factory system.
†Female rates are for machinists.

Table A8 Employment in boot and shoe factories, 1898–1910, by sex

Year	Males	Females	Total	Females as % of total
1898	2,998	1,237	4,235	29.2
1899	3,033	1,233	4,266	28.9
1900	3,020	1,284	4,304	29.8
1901	2,870	1,381	4,251	32.5
1902	3,087	1,425	4,512	31.6
1903	2,964	1,530	4,494	34.0
1904	3,400	1,796	5,196	34.6
1905	3,548	1,824	5,372	34.0
1906	3,511	1,933	5,444	35.5
1907	3,539	1,954	5,493	35.6
1908	3,805	2,171	5,976	36.3
1909	3,628	2,148	5,776	37.2
1910	4,093	2,392	6,485	36.9

Source: CIF Reports, 1898–1910.

Table A9 Employment in printing and bookbinding, 1898–1925, by sex

Year	Males	Females	Total	Females as % of total
1898	2,769	873	3,642	24.0
1899	2,977	988	3,965	24.9
1900	2,930	823	3,753	21.9
1901	2,902	613	3,515	17.4
1902	2,858	627	3,485	17.9
1903	2,763	656	3,419	19.2
1904	2,783	670	3,453	15.0
1905	2,886	718	3,604	19.4
1906	2,929	656	3,585	18.3
1907	2,975	694	3,669	18.9
1908	3,245	742	3,987	18.6
1909	3,179	747	3,926	19.0
1910	3,300	707	4,007	17.6
1911	3,349	812	4,161	19.5
1912	3,837	913	4,750	19.2
1913	3,814	1,022	4,836	22.1
1914	4,041	922	4,963	18.6
1915	3,164	892	4,056	22.0
1916	2,978	865	3,843	22.5
1917	2,983	884	3,867	22.8
1918	3,164	910	4,074	22.3
1919	N/A	N/A	N/A	N/A
1920	3,376	975	4,351	22.4
1921	3,470	916	4,386	20.9
1922	3,808	903	4,711	19.2
1923	4,194	1,035	5,229	19.8
1924	4,308	1,119	5,427	20.6
1925	3,956	1,040	4,996	20.8

Source: CIF Reports, 1898–1925.

Table A10 Employment in footwear factories, 1911–1939, by sex

Year	Males	Females	Total	Females as % of total
1911	3,812	2,392	6,204	38.6
1914	4,103	2,468	6,571	37.6
1917	4,120	3,067	7,187	42.7
1920	4,021	2,671	6,692	39.9
1923	5,810	4,809	10,619	45.6
1925	5,350	4,842	10,192	47.5
1929	5,258	4,958	10,216	48.5
1932	4,570	4,495	9,065	49.6
1934	4,310	4,382	8,692	50.4
1937	4,155	4,405	8,560	51.5
1939	4,868	5,223	10,091	51.8

Source: CIF Reports.

Figure A1   *Females as a percentage of total employment in tailoring factories, 1881–1900*

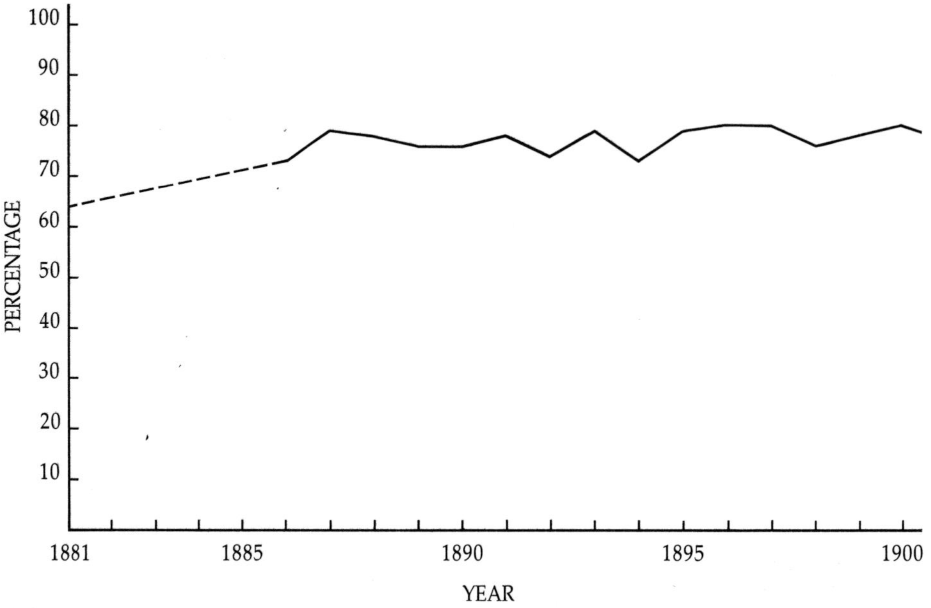

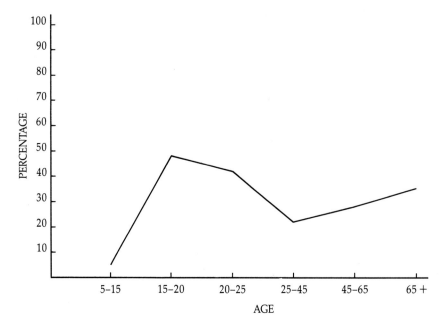

Source: Reports Chief Inspector of Factories, 1886–1900. The figure for 1881 is from the *Victorian Census*, 1881 (There were no CIF Reports prior to 1886.) The figures for 1882–1885 are extrapolations, as there are no definite statistics for these years. *Note:* All the CIF statistics under-represent female employment to some extent, as they do not include outworkers, most of whom were women.

Figure A2   *Female workforce participation rates by age, all females, 1891*

Source: M. French, 'Women in the Workforce, Victoria, 1881–1907', B.A. (Hons) thesis, History Department, University of Melbourne, 1984, p. 25. Compiled from data from *Victorian Census*, 1891.

Figure A3   *Percentage of female workers in each age group, 1891*

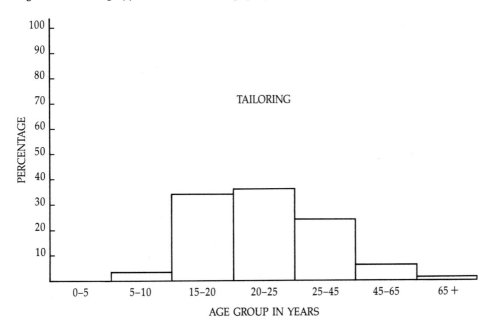

TAILORING

AGE GROUP IN YEARS

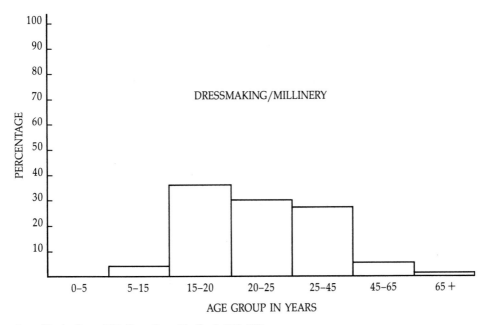

DRESSMAKING/MILLINERY

AGE GROUP IN YEARS

Source: Victorian Census, 1891, Occupations of the People, Table VIIB.

Figure A4   *Value of exports and imports of boots and shoes, 1881–1890*

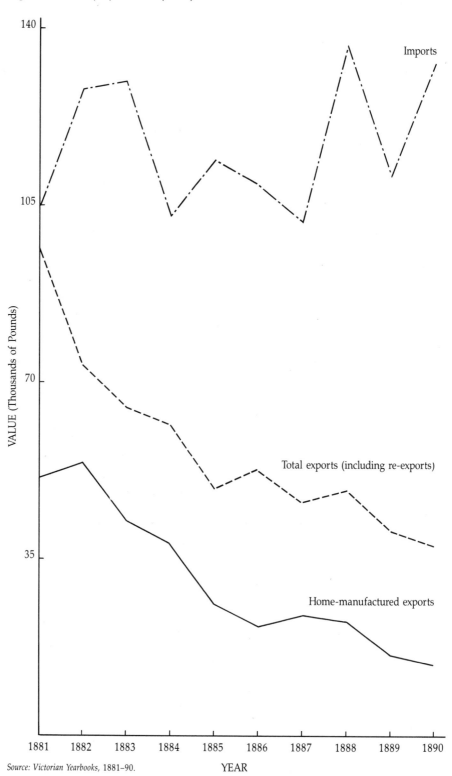

Figure A5 *Value of fixed assets in boot and shoe factories, 1903–1910*

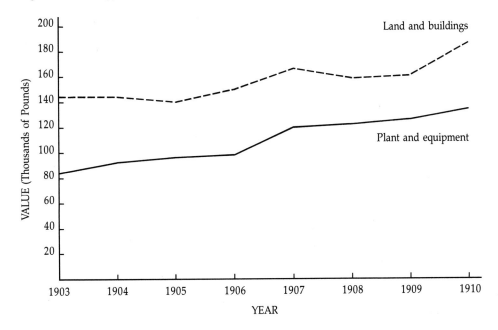

Figure A6 *Horsepower of machinery used in boot and shoe factories, 1903–1910*

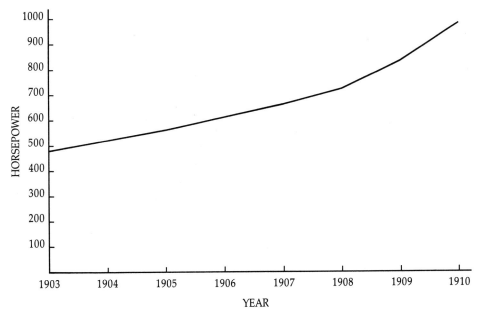

Source: Victorian Statistical Register, 1903–10.

Figure A7 *Employees and factories producing stationery, cardboard boxes, cartons, and paper bags, 1900–1925*

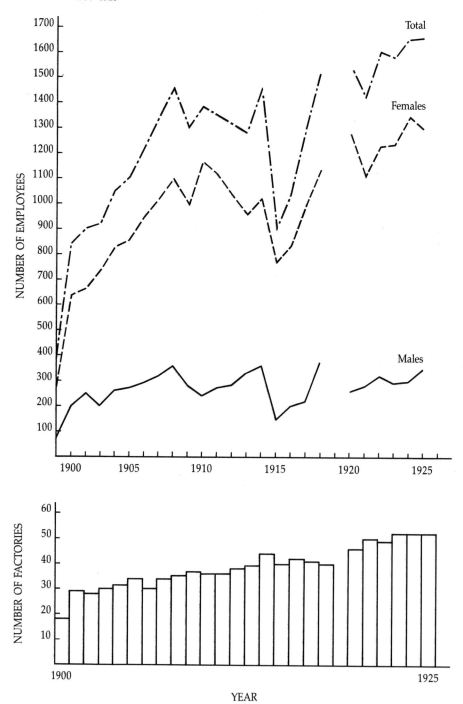

Source: Chief Inspector of Factories Reports, 1900–25.
Note: Figures for 1919 not available.

Figure A8 *Leather footwear imports (to Australia*) and overseas exports (from Victoria), 1909–1928*

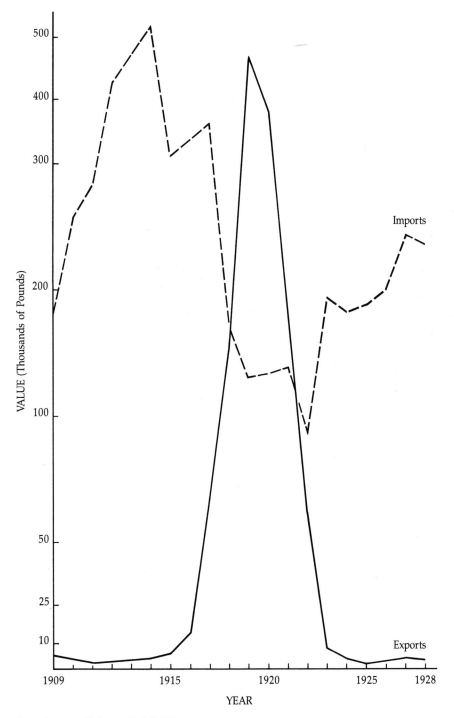

Source: Commonwealth Overseas Trade Bulletins.
*The figures for Australia as a whole, rather than Victoria alone, have been used because these affected Victoria's interstate trade.

Figure A9 *Output of boots, shoes and slippers, 1917–1934*

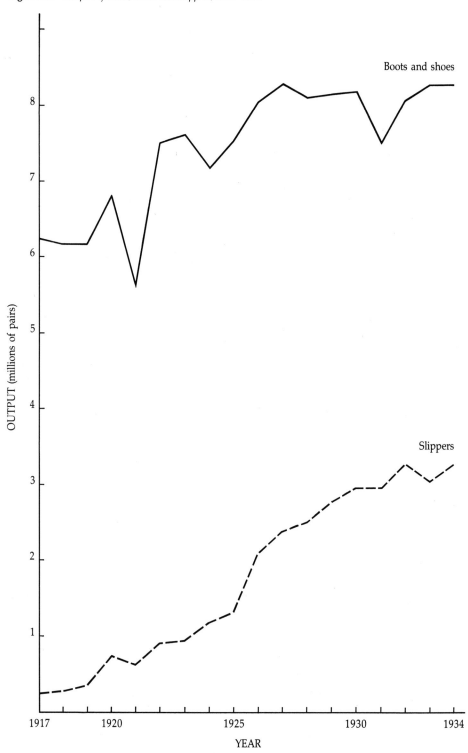

Source: Commonwealth Production Bulletins, 1917–34.

Notes

Introduction

1 John Mathews, *Technology, Trade Unions and the Labour Process*, Deakin University, 1985, Summary.

2 For example, see the article by James Law in *Pelacograms*, 1922; also 'The Song of the Shirt', *Clothing Trades Gazette*, December 1945, pp. 8–9.

3 See J. Storey, 'The means of management control', *Sociology*, May 1985, p. 193. For a critique of these arguments see Sheila Cohen, 'A labour process to nowhere?', *New Left Review*, no. 165, September–October 1987, pp. 34–51.

4 R. Price, 'Theories of labour process formation', *Journal of Social History*, vol. 18, no. 1, Fall 1984, p. 106. Braverman, *Labor and Monopoly Capital*, New York, 1974. This debate began independently in Western Europe. See especially S. Mallet, *The New Working Class*, Nottingham, 1975 (French original 1963); A. Gorz, *Strategy for Labour*, Boston, 1967; R. Panzieri, 'Surplus value and planning: notes on the reading of *Capital*', in Conference of Socialist Economics (eds), *The Labour Process and Class Strategies*, London, 1976.

5 Tony Elger, 'Braverman, capital accumulation and deskilling', in Stephen Wood (ed.), *The Degradation of Work?*, London, 1982, pp. 35–40; R. Edwards, 'Social relations of production at the point of production', *Insurgent Sociologist*, vol. 8, nos. 2–3, 1978, p. 109.

6 Felicity Hunt, 'Opportunities lost and gained: mechanisation and women's work in the London bookbinding and printing trades', in Angela V. John (ed.), *Unequal Opportunities: Women's Employment in England 1800–1918*, Oxford, 1986, p. 74. For a useful discussion of varying definitions of skill, see Craig Littler, *The Development of the Labour Process in Capitalist Societies*, London, 1982, pp. 7–19. See also Charles More, 'Skill and the survival of apprenticeship', in Wood (ed.), *Degradation of Work?*, pp. 109–21; Paul Thompson, *The Nature of Work*, London, 1983, pp. 92–108.

7 Veronica Beechey, 'The sexual division of labour and the labour process: a critical assessment of Braverman', in Wood (ed.), *Degradation of Work?*, p. 64.

8 For a discussion of this distinction, see Littler, *Labour Process in Capitalist Societies*, pp. 7–14.

9 'Technological Change and Skills of Women', Paper presented at Second International Interdisciplinary Congress on Women, Groningen, April 1984, p. 8.

10 *Ibid.*; A. Phillips and B. Taylor, 'Sex and skill: notes towards a feminist economics', *Feminist Review*, no. 6, 1980–1, pp. 79–89; Beechey, 'The sexual division of labour'; A. Game and R. Pringle, *Gender at Work*, Sydney, 1982, pp. 16–17.

11 Littler, *Labour Process in Capitalist Societies*, pp. 7–9.

12 Jim Hagan also acknowledges the importance of manual dexterity in his discussion of the compositor's skill: see J. Hagan and C. Fisher, 'Piecework and some of its consequences in the printing and coal mining industries in Australia 1850–1930', *Labour History*, no. 25, November 1973, p. 22.

13 'Manning the machines: women in the furniture industry 1920–1960', *Labour History*, no. 51, November 1986, p. 25.

14 For further discussion of definitions of skill, see R. Frances, 'The Politics of Work: Case Studies of Three Victorian Industries, 1880–1939', Ph.D. thesis, Monash University, 1989, p. 10, fn. 17.

15 Quoted in Elger, 'Braverman, capital accumulation and deskilling', in Wood (ed.), *Degradation of Work?*, p. 40.

16 A. Friedman, 'Responsible autonomy versus direct control over the labour process', *Capital and Class*, no. 1, Spring 1977, p. 48. See also *Industry and Labour: Class Struggle at Work and Monopoly Capitalism*, London, 1977.

17 'Class, conception and conflict: the thrust for efficiency, managerial views of labor, and the working-class rebellion, 1903–1922', *Review of Political Economics*, vol. 7, no. 2, pp. 31–49. He argues that the defeat of Taylorism by working-class opposition led to the employment of these more subtle forms of control in addition to scientific management.

18 *Labour Process in Capitalist Societies.*

19 'Sexual division of labour and the labour process', p. 55.

20 Diane Kirkby, 'Arbitration and the fight for economic justice', in S. Macintyre and R. Mitchell (eds), *Foundations of Arbitration*, Melbourne, 1989, pp. 334–53, provides an excellent account of this literature.

21 'Doing Time', in V. Burgmann and J. Lee (eds), *Making a Life: A People's History of Australia since 1788*, vol. 2, Fitzroy, 1988, p. 181.

22 *Contested Terrain: the Transformation of the Workplace in the Twentieth Century*, London, 1979.

23 *Segmented Work, Divided Workers: the Historical Transformation of Labor in the United States*, Cambridge, 1982, p. xii. See also Jill Rubery, 'Structured labour markets, workers organisation and low pay', in Alice Amsden (ed.), *The Economics of Women and Work*, Harmondsworth, 1980, pp. 242–70.

24 'Piecework and some of its consequences', p. 39.

25 This connection between piecework and identification with industry prosperity is made by Hagan and Fisher, *ibid.*

26 'Custom, wages and workload', in *Labouring Men: Studies in the History of Labour*, London, 1964, p. 357.

27 *Ibid.*, pp. 359–62.

28 G. D. H. Cole, *The Payment of Wages*, London, 1928, p. 77.

29 'Terrains of contest: factory and state under capitalism and socialism', *Socialist Review* (USA), vol. 11, no. 4, 1981, p. 92. See also *Manufacturing Consent: Changes in the Labour Process under Monopoly Capitalism*, Chicago, 1979.

30 *Learning to Labour: How Working-Class Kids Get Working-Class Jobs*, Farnborough, 1977.

31 Anna Pollert, *Girls, Wives, Factory Lives*, London, 1981, p. 141. For a study which reaches similar conclusions, see Sallie Westwood, *All Day Every Day: Factory and Family in the Making of Women's Lives*, London and Sydney, 1984.

32 e.g. M. J. Nadworny, *Scientific Management and the Unions*, Cambridge, Mass., 1955; D. Montgomery, 'The past and future of workers' control', *Radical America*, vol. 13, no. 6, 1979, pp. 7–24; M. Davis, 'The stop watch and the wooden shoe: scientific management and the IWW', *Radical America*, vol. 8, no. 6, 1975, pp. 69–94; Littler, *Labour Process in Capitalist Societies*; J. Melling, ' "Non-commissioned officers": British employers and their supervisory workers, 1880–1920', *Social History*, vol. V, no. 1, 1980, pp. 193–221.

33 Cohen, 'A labour process to nowhere?', reviews this debate.

34 Storey, 'The means of management control', p. 196.

35 'A labour process to nowhere?', p. 45.

36 Phillips and Taylor, 'Sex and skill', p. 6. Bennett in 'The construction of skill' also argues along these lines, maintaining that fragmented work is not intrinsically less skilled than non-fragmented work but that because women tend to be employed in fragmented work to a greater extent than men, such work is considered less skilled.

37 Beechey, 'Sexual division of labour and the labour process', p. 67.

38 Brown, 'Beyond control', p. 17.

39 Beechey, 'Sexual division of labour and the labour process', pp. 54–62.

40 *Labor and Monopoly Capital*, pp. 271–83.

41 For a discussion of this in the Australian context, see Ann Curthoys, 'The sexual division of labour: theoretical arguments' in Norma Grieve and Ailsa Burns (eds), *Australian Women: New Feminist Perspectives*, Melbourne, 1986.

42 *Ibid.*, p. 144.

43 See especially, Heidi Hartmann, 'Capitalism, patriarchy and job segregation by sex', in Martha Blaxall and Barbara Reagan (eds), *Women and the Workplace: the Implications of Occupational Segregation*, Chicago, 1976; Jane Humphries, 'The working-class family, women's liberation and class struggle: the case of nineteenth-century British history', *Review of Radical Political Economics*, no. 9, vol. 3, Autumn 1977, pp. 25–41; Michelle Barrett and Mary McIntosh, 'The family wage: some problems for socialists and feminists', *Capital and Class*, no. 11, 1980, pp. 51–73; Johanna Brenner and Maria Ramas, 'Rethinking women's oppression', *New Left Review*, no. 144, March/April 1984, pp. 33–71. For Australian contributions to the debate, see Theresa Brennan, 'Women and work', *Journal of Australian Political Economy*, no. 1, October 1977, pp. 34–52; Ann Curthoys, 'The sexual division of labour under capitalism', in Norma Grieve and Patricia Grimshaw (eds), *Australian Women: Feminist Perspectives*, Melbourne, 1981, pp. 39–43; Claire Williams, *Opencut: the Working Class in an Australian Mining Town*, Sydney, 1981; Curthoys, 'The sexual division of labour'.

44 Cynthia Cockburn, *Brothers: Male Dominance and Technological Change*, London, 1983.

45 Braverman, *Labor and Monopoly Capital*, pp. 385–6.

46 Beechey, 'Sexual division of labour and the labour process', pp. 67–71; T. Baudouin, M. Collin and D. Guillerm, 'Women and immigrants: marginal workers?', in C. Crouch and A. Pizzorno (eds), *The Resurgence of Class Conflict in Western Europe*, vol. 2: *Comparative Analysis*, London, 1978, pp. 71–99; L. Bland, et. al., 'Women "inside and outside" the relations of production', in Women's Studies Group (eds), *Women Take Issue: Aspects of Women's Subordination*, London, 1978, pp. 35–78; Marilyn Power, 'From home production to wage labor: women as a reserve army of labor', *Review of Radical Political Economics*, vol. XV, no. 1, Spring 1983, pp. 71–91; Margaret Simeral, 'Women and the reserve army of labour', *Insurgent Sociologist*, vol. VIII, nos. 2 and 3, 1978, pp. 164–180; F. Anthias, 'Women and the reserve army of labour: a critique of Veronica Beechey', *Capital and Class*, no. 10, 1980; J. Siltanen, 'A commentary on theories of female wage labour', in Cambridge Women's Studies Group (eds), *Women in Society*, London, 1981. For analyses of the Australian context, see Ann Curthoys, 'Women—a "reserve army of labour"?', *Refractory Girl*, no. 13, 1977–78; Margaret Power, 'Women and economic crisis: the Great Depression and the present crisis', in E. Windschuttle (ed.), *Women, Class and History: Feminist Perspectives on Australia 1788–1978*, Melbourne, 1980, pp. 412–593.

47   Anthias, 'Women and the reserve army'.

48   R. E. Pahl, *Divisions of Labour*, Oxford, 1984, elaborates on the use of this concept.

Part 1:
Before the Wages Boards

1   For example: G. Davison, *The Rise and Fall of Marvellous Melbourne*, Melbourne, 1978; G. Serle, *The Rush to Be Rich*, Melbourne, 1971; T. A. Coghlan, *Labour and Industry in Australia*, 4 vols, Oxford, 1918 (reissued Melbourne, 1969); A. Briggs, *Victorian Cities*, London, 1964, ch. 7.

2   G. J. R. Linge, 'The Forging of an Industrial Nation: Manufacturing in Australia 1788–1913', in J. M. Powell and M. Williams (eds), *Australian Space Australian Time: Geographical Perspectives*, Melbourne, 1975, pp. 158–62, provides a useful summary of these developments. See also the book by the same author, *Industrial Awakening: A Geography of Australian Manufacturing 1788–1890*, Canberra, 1979, ch. 8.

3   Linge, 'Manufacturing in Australia', p. 159. See also T. G. Parsons, 'Some Aspects of the Development of Manufacturing in Melbourne 1870–1890', Ph.D., Monash University, 1970, esp. Part 1.

4   A. R. Hall, *The Stock Exchange of Melbourne and the Victorian Economy, 1852–1900*, Canberra, 1968, pp. 48–9.

5   Linge, 'Manufacturing in Australia', p. 161.

6   Linge, *Industrial Awakening*, pp. 253, 255, 250, 252; Linge, 'Manufacturing in Australia', pp. 176, 161; Davison, *Marvellous Melbourne*, pp. 45, 64; Parsons, 'Manufacturing in Melbourne', ch. 4; see also G. D. Patterson, *The Tariff in the Australian Colonies 1856–1900*, Melbourne, 1968, ch. 10; N. G. Butlin, *Investment in Australian Economic Development 1861–1900*, Cambridge, 1964, Part B, ch. 3.

7   Davison, *Marvellous Melbourne*, p. 64.

8   *Ibid.* Also J. Hagan, *Printers and Politics*, Canberra, 1966, p. 100; R. T. Fitzgerald, *The Printers of Melbourne: the History of a Union*, Melbourne, 1967, pp. 74–5; W. A. Sinclair, *Economic Recovery in Victoria, 1894–1899*, Canberra, 1956; Hall, *Stock Exchange of Melbourne*, p. 204.

9   Sinclair, *Economic Recovery*, pp. 17, 86; Hall, *Stock Exchange of Melbourne*, p. 204.

10   Linge, *Industrial Awakening*, p. 256; Davison, *Marvellous Melbourne*, pp. 43–4.

11   J. Lee and C. Fahey, 'A Boom for Whom? Some Developments in the Australian Labour Market, 1870–1891', *Labour History*, no. 50, May 1986, p. 18.

12   Davison, *Marvellous Melbourne*, p. 59.

13   Jeff Rich, 'Engineers and Work in Victoria c.1860–1890', B.A. Hons History, Melbourne University, 1986, p. 11.

14   E. Fry, 'Outwork in the Eighties', *University Studies in History and Politics*, vol. 2, no. 4, July 1956, pp. 88–9, provides a good discussion of the relationship between outwork and factory production in the garment industries. See also Raphael Samuel's more extended treatment of the survival of hand-methods of manufacture alongside technologically advanced factories in Britain in 'The Workshop of the World: Steam Power and Hand Power in mid-Victorian Britain', *History Workshop Journal*, no. 3, Spring 1977, pp. 6–72.

15   Davison, *Marvellous Melbourne*, pp. 48–52; Serle, *Rush to be Rich*, pp. 71–4.

16   *Victorian Census*, 1881. The exact figure is uncertain due to the inclusion of dealers in the same category with workers. The Census shows 11,517 women engaged in dressmaking and millinery compared to 3274 in tailoring.

17   Lee, 'A Redivision of Labour', p. 557.

18   This will be discussed in more detail in Chapters 2 and 3 below.

19   See Chapters 1 and 2 below.

20   Davison, *Marvellous Melbourne*, pp. 58–9.

21   Lee and Fahey, 'A Boom for Whom?', p. 18; Lee, 'A Redivision of Labour', p. 556. For an excellent

study of the attack on craft skills in the Victorian engineering industry in the 1880s see Rich, 'Engineers and Work in Victoria', pp. 23–9.

22 Hall, *Stock Exchange of Melbourne*, pp. 48–9; Butlin, *Australian Economic Development*, p. 208.

23 B. Kingston, *My Wife, My Daughter and Poor Mary-Ann*, Sydney, 1975; Davison, *Marvellous Melbourne*, pp. 45, 60–1; W. A. Sinclair, 'Women at Work in Melbourne and Adelaide since 1871', *Economic Record*, vol. 57, 1981, pp. 344–53; 'Women and Economic Change in Melbourne 1871–1921', *Historical Studies*, vol. 20, no. 79, October 1982, pp. 277–91.

24 A. R. Hall, 'Some Long Period Effects of the Kinked Age Distribution of the Population of Australia 1861–1961', *Economic Record*, vol. 39, 1963, pp. 43–52, discusses some of these effects. Unfortunately, Hall does not give a sex-breakdown of his statistics.

25 Davison, *Marvellous Melbourne*, pp. 193–4, discusses the effect of the goldrush children on rates of marriage. The point he makes about the time lag in the arrival of boys of marriageable age compared to girls (because of the difference in age at marriage) is pertinent here. The continuing effect of this would, however, have been offset somewhat by the high level of immigration amongst adult males in the 1880s. See Hall, *Stock Exchange of Melbourne*, p. 52.

26 CIFR 1889, pp. 10–11. See also 1893 Factory Inquiry, p. 57; W. A. Sinclair, 'The Tariff and Economic Growth in Pre-Federation Victoria', *Economic Record*, vol. 47, pp. 77–92.

27 1893 Factory Inquiry, pp. 57, 88, 110.

28 Sinclair, 'Women and Economic Change in Melbourne', pp. 278–91. Sinclair does not consider married women as he finds this causes confusion. On the contrary, the fact that the proportion of married to unmarried women 'changes markedly because of the unstable age composition of the Australian population' (p. 279) is illuminating in its own right.

29 See P. R. Davey, 'Wages Boards in Victoria 1896–1920', Ph.D. thesis, University of Melbourne, 1976, pp. 22–3.

30 'Women and Economic Change', p. 279.

31 'Royal Commission on the Tariff', *VPP*, 1883, vol. 4, Report, pp. xi, xviii, li, lxxx.

32 CIFR 1889, p. 5; also CIFR 1887, p. 4. See also Davison, *Marvellous Melbourne*, p. 60; Coghlan, *Labour and Industry*, vol. 3, pp. 1568–1603 and vol. 4, pp. 2047–58. Also, Parsons, 'Manufacturing in Melbourne', p. 586.

33 The most recent revision of the long-boom thesis is the article by Jenny Lee and Charles Fahey, 'A Boom for Whom? Some Developments in the Australian Labour Market, 1870–1891', *Labour History*, no. 50, May 1986.

34 Evidence James Wyeth, 1895 Tariff Inquiry, p. 159.

35 Lee and Fahey, 'Boom for Whom?', pp. 13–14.

36 Coghlan, *Labour and Industry*, vol. 3, pp. 142–7; Serle, *Rush to be Rich*, p. 100; Linge, *Industrial Awakening*, p. 289; Parsons, 'Manufacturing in Melbourne', p. 570.

37 CIFR 1886, pp. 3, 5; 1887, p. 3; Linge, *Industrial Awakening*, p. 289; Parsons, 'Manufacturing in Melbourne', p. 581; Coghlan, *Labour and Industry*, vol. 3, pp. 1485–6; Serle, *Rush to be Rich*, pp. 105–6; Davey, 'Wages Boards', pp. 14, 26.

38 CIFR 1892, p. 3.

Chapter 1:
The advent of machines and women

1 Evidence Charles Harrison, 1901 Factory RC, p. 694.

2 Female order coat-hands, for instance, did the same work as tailors in the 1890s (tailors rarely made vests and trousers) but were paid an average of 27 shillings per week compared to 50 shillings paid to the men.

3 *The Sweated Trades: Outwork in Nineteenth Century Britain*, New York, 1978, p. 142.

 4 CIFR, 1895, p. 21.

 5 'Women and labour 1880–1900', in Windschuttle (ed.), *Women, Class and History*, p. 92.

 6 First Report, 1893 Factory Inquiry, p. 13.

 7 Kate Purcell, 'Militancy and Acquiescence amongst women workers', in S. Burman (ed.), *Fit Work for Women*, Canberra, 1979, p. 130, disputes the foregoing argument, maintaining instead that it is the conditions of women's labour market which make them non-militant, and that men similarly situated in the labour market behave in the same way. My evidence obviously does not support these conclusions.

 8 Beverley Kingston, *My Wife, My Daughter and Poor Mary-Ann*, Melbourne, 1975, p. 62.

 9 Evidence SA Sweating Inquiry, p. 147, Q. 5620. See also 1901 Factory RC, pp. 123–5.

10 CIFR 1895, p. 21.

11 *Ibid.*

12 Interview with Olga Anderson (née Meyer), March 1982. Olga was born in 1890.

13 *Internationalist*, 11 May 1872.

14 RC on Shops and Factories, *VPP*, 1884, vol. 3, pp. 127–8; 1901 Factory RC, p. 125; 1893 Factory Inquiry, p. 91. See also Sheryl Yelland, 'Adeline Lloyd: a Biography of an Unmarried Woman', *Lilith*, no. 2, Winter 1985, p. 54, for comments on this attitude at a slightly later date.

15 1901 Factory RC, p. 125, Evidence Mrs Sarah Thompson, milliner.

16 CIFR 1888, p. 9.

17 Evidence SA Sweating Inquiry, p. 146, Q. 5585.

18 ' "The Men are as Bad as their Masters . . .": Socialism, feminism and sexual antagonism in the London tailoring trade in the 1830s', in J. Newton, M. Ryan and J. Walkowitz (eds), *Sex and Class in Women's History*, London, 1983, p. 200. See also Bruce Scates, 'Gender, Household and Community Politics . . .', *Labour History*, no. 61, Nov. 1991, pp. 80–7.

19 *Age*, 22, 27 February 1883, p. 5. Evidence Jane McLeod, 1893 Factory Inquiry, p. 104 (McLeod sat on the International Trade Union Congress, Ballarat, 1891, see *Report*, MUA). W. E. Murphy, 'Victoria', in J. Norton (ed.), *A History of Capital and Labour . . .*, Melbourne, 1888, p. 169. For Robertson, See Jean Daley, 'The Trade Union Woman', in Frances Fraser and Nettie Palmer (eds), *Centenary Gift Book*, Melbourne, 1934, p. 131.

20 Lee, 'A Redivision of Labour'.

21 'Rethinking Women's Oppression', *New Left Review*, no. 144, March–April 1984, p. 56.

22 The figures for 1891 were 27 men and 17,316 women. *Census of Victoria*, 1881 and 1891.

23 CIFR 1886, p. 7.

24 Evidence M. Cuthbertson, 1901 Factory RC, p. 644. See also Muriel Heagney, *Are Women Taking Men's Jobs?*, Melbourne, 1935, p. 43.

25 Report W. Kingsbury, 6 November 1896, on Jane McKenzie, Factory Registration Papers, VPRS 1399/2; CIFR 1896, p. 8; 1895, p. 7; 1893 Factory Inquiry, p. 81. Evidence Margaret Cuthbertson, 'Select Committee of the Legislative Council Inquiring into the Alleged Sweating Evil', *SAPP*, 1904, vol. 2, no. 71, p. 147 (SA Sweating Inquiry).

26 *ACTJ*, December 1945, p. 8; evidence Richard Pryor, SA Sweating Inquiry, p. 139.

27 J. T. Day, 'The Boot and Shoe Trade', in H. Cox, *British Industries Under Free Trade*, London, 1903, quoted in Samuel, 'The Workshop of the World', p. 45.

28 Taylor, ' "The Men are as bad as their Masters . . ." ' pp. 187–220, provides an excellent account of the reorganisation of the tailoring industry in the early part of the 19th century in England.

29 Charles Babbage, *On the Economy of Machinery and Manufacturers*, Fairfield, New Jersey, 1971 (first published 1835), pp. 175–6. See also discussion in M. Berg (ed.), *Technology and Toil in Nineteenth Century Britain*, London, 1979, p. 50.

30 Evidence to 1893 Factory Inquiry, p. 28.

31 The precise figure is uncertain due to the number of women who described themselves simply as

'sewing machinists', without specifying a branch of the trade. Presumably some of these would have been doing tailoring, increasing the percentage of 63.5 per cent of those clearly identified as such. *Census of Victoria*, 1881.

32 Evidence Harry Meadows, 1893 Factory Inquiry, p. 105.

33 Evidence J. R. Blencowe, 1893 Factory Inquiry, p. 29.

34 F. H. Cutler, 'A History of the Anti-Sweating Movement in Victoria 1873–1896', M.A. thesis, University of Melbourne, 1957, p. 3; Minutes Tailors' Society, 11 August 1890, MUA.

35 Evidence Harry Meadows, 1893 Factory Inquiry, p. 105.

36 For a description of the modern 'wave' band knife, see *Argus*, 18 April 1885, p. 13.

37 1901 Factory RC, Mr 'F', presser, p. 683.

38 1901 Factory RC, p. 419.

39 1883–84 Factory RC, Q. 4177–8.

40 See C. Burton, *The Promise and the Price: the Struggle for Equal Opportunity in Women's Employment*, Sydney, 1991.

41 See CIFR 1889, p. 11; 1893 Factory Inquiry, p. 39; 1890 Sweating Report, p. 6.

42 1893 Factory Inquiry, p. 28. Also 1890 Sweating Report, p. 4; 1893 Factory Inquiry, p. 69.

43 *Age*, 20 December 1882, p. 6, 31 March 1883; 1893 Factory Inquiry, Evidence Walter McCabe, p. 97; Henry Blomfield, p. 108.

44 Evidence J. H. Blencowe, 1893 Factory Inquiry, p. 28. See also First Determination, Clothing Board, 1897, Ready-made Log of Piece Rates, Females—trousers.

45 'Workshop of the World', passim.

46 1895 Tariff Inquiry, p. 159. For the rest of the year he employed between 30 and 130 hands, p. 158.

47 1895 Tariff Inquiry, pp. 318–19, p. 551; *Cyclopedia of Victoria*, Melbourne, 1903, p. 556.

48 1895 Tariff Inquiry, evidence Charles McIntyre (manager Braeside), i.e. 70 out of 120 hands.

49 Evidence John Keleher, 1893 Factory Inquiry, p. 138.

50 Evidence Walter McCabe, *ibid.*, p. 96.

51 *Australian Town and Country Journal*, 15 September 1888, p. 548.

52 1893 Factory Inquiry, p. 110.

53 'A Boom for Whom?', p. 17.

54 1893 Factory Inquiry, pp. 47, 110; Fry, 'Outwork in the Eighties', p. 80; Linge, *Industrial Awakening*, p. 256.

55 1893 Factory Inquiry, Evidence J. R. Blencowe, p. 28.

56 *Ibid.*, Evidence Abraham Loel, pp. 70–1; see also pp. 110, 125, 138. 1890 Sweating Report, p. 6.

57 J. Hagan, 'Employers, trade unions and the first Victorian Factory Acts', *Labour History*, no. 7, May 1964, pp. 3–4.

58 The campaign to limit male apprentices in the early 1880s was only partially successful, as some employers, such as the Phoenix Clothing Company, avoided the union demands by replacing their society hands with 'free' labour. Evidence of Albion Walkeley (manager, Phoenix Clothing Company), 1893 Factory Inquiry, pp. 60–1; see also p. 28.

59 Evidence 1901 Factory RC, p. 644.

60 The Tailors' Society log, the first of its kind in the clothing trade, was first approved in 1873. This fixed piece rates by calculating a time for each garment and an hourly rate, and also forbade the taking home of work: 1890 Sweating Report, p. 4. The Pressers' Union log was adopted in 1883 during the tailoresses' strike: *Age*, 11 January 1883; 22 February 1883.

61 Evidence to 1884 Factory RC, p. 52, Q. 4302. See also Daley, 'The Trade Union Woman', p. 131.

62 *Investment in Australian Economic Development*, p. 207

63 1883–84 Factory RC, p. 52, especially Qs 4304; 4334; 4355.

64 *Age*, Editorial, 15 December 1882.

65 Brief accounts of the strike appear in Coghlan, *Labour and Industry*, vol. 3, pp. 183–4; Serle, *Rush to Be Rich*, p. 101; Sutcliffe, *Trade Unionism in Australia*, pp. 55–6; Gollan, *Radical and Working Class Politics*, pp. 89; W. Murphy, 'Victoria', in Norton (ed.), *Capital and Labour*, pp. 168–70; McMurty, et. al., *For Love or Money*, pp. 46–7; Ryan and Conlon, *Gentle Invaders*, p. 33. All of these accounts draw to a`large extent on Murphy's original description in Norton, published in 1888, and therefore repeat the factual errors he made. Raymond Brooks' more detailed account, 'The Melbourne Tailoresses' Strike 1882–3: An Assessment', *Labour History*, no. 44, May 1983, pp. 27–8, offers some important new insights.

66 Brooks, 'Tailoresses' Strike', pp. 36–7.

67 A. Summers, *Damned Whores and God's Police*, Sydney, 1975, pp. 347–78.

68 *Age*, 13 December 1882.

69 *Age*, 16 December 1882. The comment was made by a Mr Towart, secrètary of the Salesmen and Assistants' Union.

70 E. Ryan and A. Conlon, *Gentle Invaders*, Melbourne, 1975, p. 33; R. Gollan, *Radical and Working Class Politics*, Melbourne, 1960, p. 89.

71 Evidence to 1893 Factory Inquiry, p. 58. See also evidence G. Barthold, 1884 Factory RC, Q. 3421.

72 Parsons, 'Victorian Manufacturing', p. 580; J. Hagan, 'Employers, trade unions and the first Victorian Factory Acts', *Labour History*, no. 7, May 1964, pp. 3–10.

73 Beath and Schiess donated ten guineas to the strike fund: *Age*, 24 February 1883, p. 58. See also Brooks, 'Tailoresses' Strike', pp. 29–30.

74 *Age*, 20 December 1882, p. 6.

75 *Age*, 9 January 1883.

76 *Age*, 27 February 1883, p. 5: 1883–84 Factory RC, Miss 'E', Q. 4494.

77 G. Barthold, 1883–84 Factory RC, Q. 3419.

78 Letter to Editor from H. Farrar, *Argus*, 17 February 1883, p. 13.

79 1883–4 Factory RC, Mrs 'A', Q. 4353; Blencowe, p. 15; *Age*, 28 March 1883: see advertisements for Beath, Schiess and Co.

80 1883–4 Factory RC, Q. 4388; 4402; p. 60; Q. 4353, 3771; *Age*, 6 March 1883, p. 5.

81 e.g., at the time of the 1883–84 RC (August 1883), there was a strike in progress at Blomfield's factory. Evidence Miss 'C', Q. 4442; 4447; Miss 'D', p. 61.

82 *Argus*, 18 April 1885, p. 13; 1883–84 Factory RC, Miss 'D', Q. 4475; Miss 'E', Q. 4489, 4494; Barthold, Q. 3407. See also Sutherland, *Victoria and Metropolis*, p. 592.

83 1893 Factory Inquiry, Evidence Blencowe, pp. 29, 150; W. McCabe, p. 98.

84 1883–84 Factory RC, Blencowe, p. 14; J. Munro, Q. 4276. See also Cresswell's comments (Mrs 'A'), Q. 4356; 1893 Factory Inquiry, E. J. Bartlett, p. 91.

85 *Argus*, 17 February 1883, p. 13. See also 1893 Factory Inquiry, p. 109.

86 1883–84 Factory RC, Blencowe, p. 15, Q. 3450.

87 CIFR 1889, p. 12.

88 Brooks', 'Tailoresses' Strike', p. 36. For long-term effects, see *Argus*, 18 April 1885, p. 13; 1893 Factory Inquiry, Blencowe, pp. 29, 50; McCabe, p. 98: Sutherland, *Victoria and Metropolis*, p. 592.

89 1883–84 Factory RC, Q. 3408.

90 *Ibid.*, Q. 3407. See also evidence Miss 'D', Q. 4475 and Miss 'E', Q. 4489, 4494.

91 See Thompson, 'Time and Work Discipline', p. 93, n. 125.

92 Fry, 'Outwork in the Eighties', p. 81. Also 1883–84 Factory RC, Q. 3778.

93 *Internationalist*, 11 May 1872, p. 2.

94 CIFR 1889, p. 9. See also CIFR 1886, p. 7; Linge, *Industrial Awakening*, pp. 161, 252; Cutler, p. 29; 1895 Factory Inquiry, Blencowe, p. 28.

95 1893 Factory Inquiry, pp. 47, 57, 85, 86, 123. Also 1901 Factory RC, p. 422; Davison, *Marvellous Melbourne*, p. 67; Sutherland, *Victoria and Metropolis*, p. 592.

96 Frances, 'Politics of Work', Appendix 3, p. 6. See also *Age*, 6 March 1883, p. 5.

97 1883–84 Factory RC, p. 60.

98 1893 Factory Inquiry, p. 116; see also evidence George Denton, pp. 147–9.

99 Evidence to 1893 Factory Inquiry, p. 105. See also evidence J. Wing, p. 116.

100 Tailors' Society Minutes, 29 November 1897. *Age*, 30 May 1890.

101 Pressers' Minutes, 3 June 1891, 1 July 1891, ANUA E138/7.

102 Quoted by H. Carter, evidence to 1922 Arbitration Hearing, ACATU v. Alley, et. al., ANUA E138/18/86, p. 22.

103 Tailors' Minutes, 3 December 1890, MUA.

104 The case of women working the felt hat industry is similar in many respects: *Age*, 20 May 1890. See also circular from the Felt Hat Trimmers' Union, c.1895, MUA.

105 15 July 1899, p. 499.

106 Sutherland, *Victoria and Metropolis*, pp. 597, 598, 616; *Australian Town and Country Journal*, 15 September 1888, p. 548; 1893 Factory Inquiry, pp. 28, 70–1, 110, 125, 138; 1890 Sweating Report, p. 6; Factory Registration Papers, VPRS 1399; 1895 Tariff Inquiry, Richard Pryor (Acme Shirt Factory), pp. 318–19; *Cyclopedia of Victoria*, Melbourne, 1903, p. 556; 1895 Tariff Inquiry, Phillip Mardell, p. 551.

107 Evidence to 1893 Factory Inquiry, p. 110.

108 *Ibid.*

109 Evidence Wing, 1893 Factory Inquiry, p. 117.

110 *Ibid.*, p. 108.

111 See Frances, 'Politics of Work', Ph.D. thesis, Appendix 3, pp. 6–7.

112 1901 Factory RC, p. 436.

113 1893 Factory Inquiry, pp. 116–17.

114 'Custom, wages and work-load', p. 353.

115 1893 Factory Inquiry, p. 97.

116 ' "A time to every purpose": an essay on time and work', in Patrick Joyce (ed.), *The Historical Meanings of Work*, Cambridge University Press, Cambridge, 1987, p. 211.

117 Pressers' Minutes, 1 May 1889; 15 June 1892, ANUA E138/7; 1893 Factory Inquiry, pp. 96, 137.

118 1893 Factory Inquiry, p. 96.

119 Lee and Fahey, 'A Boom for Whom?', p. 17.

120 e.g. 1890 Sweating Report, p. 6.

121 1893 Factory Inquiry, p. 96.

122 White, *Golden Thread*, p. 11.

123 1892 Factory Inquiry, p. 149.

124 1893 Factory Inquiry, p. 98, evidence McCabe.

125 Report W. Kingsbury re Miss Jane McKenzie, 6 November 1896, Factory Registration Papers, VPRS 1399/2.

126 Hagan, 'The First Victorian Factory Acts', pp. 3–10; Bruce Scates, 'A Struggle for Survival: Unemployment and the Unemployed: Agitation in Late Nineteenth-Century Melbourne,' *Australian Historical Studies*, no. 94, April 1990, pp. 42–53.

127 Rickard, *Class and Politics*, pp. 44–5; J. E. Parnaby, 'The Economic and Political Development of Victoria, 1877–1881', Ph.D. thesis, University of Melbourne, 1951.

128 Linge, *Industrial Awakening*, pp. 252–6.

129 Hagan, 'First Victorian Factory Acts', pp. 3–4.

130 CIFR 1895, p. 16.

Chapter 2:
An age of grim adversity

1 *ALJ*, 15 February 1900, p. 836; 'Welcome to Bedggoods', Bedggood Collection, ANUA 57/20.
2 *ALJ*, 16 January 1911, p. 924.
3 *People and Collectivist*, 16 April 1898.
4 *ALJ*, 15 December 1899, p. 753.
5 *Unity*, 14 March 1938, p. 11.
6 1893 Factory Inquiry, p. 53.
7 *Age*, 28 November 1884. See also evidence Arthur Whybrow, SA Sweating Inquiry, p. 142.
8 BM, 3, 4 October 1895, ANUA T5/2/2; 7 October 1895, ANUA T5/1/4.
9 BM, 18 November 1895, ANUA T5/1/4.
10 *ALJ*, 15 September 1898, p. 129; P. J. Rimmer, 'The Boot and Shoe Industry in Melbourne', in J. M. Powell (ed.), *Urban and Industrial Australia*, Melbourne, 1974, p. 115; R. Cameron, 'The Victorian Boot and Shoe Industry', *Economic Record*, vol. 13, 1937, p. 34.
11 Rimmer, 'Boot and Shoe Industry', p. 115.
12 Cameron, 'Boot and Shoe Industry', p. 31.
13 *ALJ*, 16 October 1899, p. 627. 'Rough-stuff' referred to the material used for soles.
14 *ALJ*, 15 May 1922, p. 8. For similar developments in Britain over the same period, see Samuel, 'Workshop of the World', p. 36.
15 *ALJ*, 15 May 1922, p. 8. For an account of how women came to be involved in this way in the American antebellum shoe industry, see Mary H. Blewett, 'Work, gender and the artisan tradition in New England shoemaking, 1780–1860', *Journal of Social History*, vol. 17, no. 2, Winter 1983, pp. 223–4.
16 Blewett, 'New England Shoemaking', states that machines cost between $75 and $125 in the USA in the mid-1850s. For the introduction of sewing machines and their use in factories in Victoria, see *Unity*, 15 March 1960, p. 16; Rimmer, 'Boot and Shoe Industry', p. 115; Coghlan, *Labour and Industry*, vol. III, pp. 1202–3; *ALJ*, 15 May 1922, p. 8.
17 *Unity*, 15 March 1960, p. 17; Davison, *Marvellous Melbourne*, pp. 46–7.
18 Linge, *Industrial Awakening*, p. 253.
19 *Bendigo Advertiser*, 28 June 1879, Supplement, p. 1. I am indebted to Mimi Colligan for this reference.
20 It is not clear how far women were involved in this outwork. See Frances, 'Politics of Work', Ph.D. thesis, p. 129.
21 *ALJ*, 16 October 1899, p. 627; Rimmer, 'Boot and Shoe Industry', p. 115 notes the increasing concentration of footwear factories in Collingwood and Fitzroy over the period 1861–91. See also Davison, *Marvellous Melbourne*, pp. 46–7.
22 1890 Sweating Report, p. 8.
23 The average value of plant and equipment for a boot factory in 1880 was £380, or £10 per worker. Linge, *Industrial Awakening*, p. 253; Parsons, 'Manufacturing in Melbourne', p. 535; *ALJ*, 16 October 1899, p. 627, estimated that before power-driven machinery about £200 was enough to start a factory. See also 1901 Factory RC, James Bennett, p. 319.
24 Linge, *Industrial Awakening*, pp. 253–5.
25 Davison, *Marvellous Melbourne*, pp. 47–8.
26 *Unity*, 15 November 1941, pp. 12–14. The term 'mushroom capitalist' was coined by Benjamin Douglass, president of the THC, during the lockout, *Age*, 21 November 1884, p. 5.
27 *Unity*, 15 November 1941, p. 13.
28 Letter to Editor, *Age*, 22 November 1884.
29 John Hyman, 1901 Factory RC, p. 328; *ALJ*, 15 July 1898, p. 55.
30 *Age*, 6 December 1884, p. 10.

31 *Unity,* 15 November 1941, p. 13.

32 The Victorian Operative Bootmakers' Union was formed 12 May 1879. An association of clickers was not formed until February 1889; *Age,* 18 February 1889. An earlier Shoemakers' Society met between 1864 and 1870 but then faded away.

33 *Unity,* 15 November 1941, p. 13; *Age,* 22 November 1884, p. 10. The log provided for one man in six to be employed on weekly wages and one apprentice to every five men employed on journeymen's pay.

34 *Age,* 24 November 1884, p. 6. The three employers were R. White, G. White and J. Creaney. See also *Unity,* 15 November 1941, p. 13.

35 *Unity,* 15 November 1941, p. 13.

36 *Age,* 20 November 1884.

37 *Age,* 22 November 1884, p. 10; 24 November 1884, p. 6.

38 *Age,* 24 November 1884, p. 6.

39 Letter to Editor from W. E. Trenwith, *ibid.*

40 *Age,* 22 November 1884, p. 10; 24 November 1884, p. 6.

41 *Ibid.*

42 *Age,* 24 November 1884, p. 6.

43 *Age,* 18 November 1884, p. 6.

44 *Ibid.*

45 *Age,* 20 November 1884.

46 *Age,* 22 November 1884; *Unity,* 15 November 1941, p. 14.

47 *Age,* 20 January 1884, p. 5.

48 *Unity,* 15 November 1941, p. 14; Bootmakers' Minutes, January-February 1885, ANUA T5/1/2 and T5/2/2; BM, 4 December 1884.

49 *Age,* 3 December 1884, Supplement; 25 November 1884, p. 6; 15 December 1884, p. 5.

50 *Age,* 22 January 1885, p. 5.

51 Serle, *Rush to be Rich,* p. 108.

52 *Age,* 5 February 1885, p. 5; 11 February 1885, p. 5.

53 Murphy, 'Victoria', pp. 166-7.

54 *Ibid.;* Davey, 'Wages Boards', p. 15; Cutler, 'Anti-sweating', pp. 38-42; Sutcliffe, *Trade Unionism,* pp. 56-7. Coghlan, *Labour and Industry,* pp. 1486-7 and Serle, *Rush to be Rich,* p. 101, do include the 700 women in the total number out of work, but do not mention that they were women.

55 *Age,* 24 January 1885, p. 10; 27 January 1885, p. 6.

56 *ALJ,* 15 June 1898, p. 30.

57 Frances, 'Politics of Work', Ph.D. thesis, pp. 151-6.

58 Matzelinger's lasting machine was patented in 1883. The Goodyear welter was another innovation which manufacturers were slow to adopt. It was patented as early as 1875.

59 1901 Factory RC, T. J. Deslandes, p. 341; 1890 Sweating Report, p. 8.

60 *ALJ,* 15 June 1898, p. 30; Davison, *Marvellous Melbourne,* p. 67; 1894 Tariff Inquiry, T. Y. Harkness, p. 295; BM, 18 January 1892, ANUA T5/1/3.

61 RC on High Prices, 1919, No. 2 Report, p. 13; *ALJ,* 15 September 1899, p. 599; Rimmer, 'Boot and Shoe Industry', p. 115.

62 BM, 27 June 1892, 7, 13 February 1894, ANUA T5/1/3; 25 January 1894, ANUA T5/2/2; 3 July 1895, 13 July 1896, ANUA T5/1/4; *ALJ,* 15 June 1898, p. 26; 16 May 1898, p. 12; *ATR,* 2 February 1894, p. 117; 1894 Tariff Inquiry, pp. 216, 299.

63 *ATR,* 4 March 1895, p. 71; *ALJ,* 15 September 1899, p. 598; CIFR 1893, p. 5; 1894 Tariff Inquiry, Wm Greenwood, p. 288.

64 RC on Technical Education, T. Y. Harkness, pp. 576-7; 1894 Tariff Inquiry, T. Y. Harkness, p. 292.

65 1901 Factory RC, Thos Delves, p. 659; 1895 Tariff Inquiry, Wm Porter, p. 266; *ALJ*, 15 February 1900, p. 836; 17 April 1900, p. 971.

66 CIFR 1895, p. 6; 1894, pp. 3–4; 1893, p. 5; *ALJ*, 15 July 1899, p. 499.

67 *ALJ*, 15 September 1898, p. 129.

68 1901 Factory RC, p. 440.

69 1894 Tariff Inquiry, J. W. Billson, p. 300; BM, 14 February 1895, ANUA T5/2/2.

70 *ALJ*, 15 June 1898; 1901 Factory RC, James Bennett; 1894 Tariff Inquiry, Wm Greenwood, p. 290; BM, January–November 1895, ANUA T5/1/3; 12 June 1893, ANUA T5/2/1; 23 March 1896, ANUA T5/1/4; 2 August 1896, ANUA T5/2/2.

71 CIFR 1895, p. 5; *ALJ*, 15 February 1900, p. 863; 1901 Factory RC, John Bedggood, p. 300; Bennett, p. 320; *ALJ*, 15 August 1898, p. 94; CIFR 1895, p. 6; 1894, pp. 3–4.

72 CIFR 1895, p. 6; 1901 Factory RC, Richards, p. 696.

73 CIFR 1895, p. 5.

74 *ALJ*, 16 October 1899, p. 627; the comment comes from 'Rishi, A Practical Manager'.

75 *ALJ*, 15 January 1900, p. 807.

76 *Unity*, 14 April 1937, p. 10. International Labor Office publication, *Occupation and Health*, Geneva, 1928, no. 137; 1893 Factory Inquiry, John Bedggood, p. 55.

77 1901 Factory RC, Whybrow, p. 440; Alfred Johnson, p. 711. See also Robert Solly, p. 325; BM, 9 April 1894, ANUA T5/1/3.

78 1901 Factory RC, Wm Cabena, p. 346; Angus McLachlan, p. 347; Whybrow, p. 440.

79 *Unity*, 14 April 1937, p. 11.

80 *ALJ*, 15 January 1900, p. 807.

81 BM, 4 October 1895, ANUA T5/1/4; 1893 Factory Inquiry, John Bedggood, p. 55.

82 1901 Factory RC, p. 696.

83 RC on Tech. Ed., Wm Kernot, p. 578; T. Y. Harkness, p. 576; CIFR 1893, p. 5; 1901 Factory RC, Bennett, p. 319; 1893 Factory Inquiry, Bedggood, p. 54.

84 RC on Tech. Ed., Solly, p. 458.

85 *ALJ*, 15 January 1900, p. 789.

86 Chummy Fleming, 'More Memories of the Boot Trade', *Unity*, 15 April 1941, p. 11.

87 BM, March–September 1890; 16 March 1891, ANUA T5/1/3.

88 BM, 18 August 1890, ANUA T5/1/3. The Clickers' Union, begun only in 1889, was virtually destroyed by the maritime strike: BM, 26 February 1894, ANUA T5/1/3. See also *Age*, 24 July 1890, p. 7.

89 BM, 7 July 1890, ANUA T5/1/3.

90 This distinction is used in an article on the boot industry in *Victorian Yearbook*, 1906, p. 761. It is taken up by Graeme Davison in his discussion in *Marvellous Melbourne*, p. 67.

91 E. P. Thompson, *The Making of the English Working Class*, Harmondsworth, 1979, p. 260, comments on this traditional method of wage-fixing in early-nineteenth-century England.

92 Letter to Editor from 'Factory Hand', *Age*, 3 December 1884, Supplement.

93 Hobsbawm, 'Custom, wages and workload' (especially pp. 344–51), comments on the growth of awareness amongst both workers and employers in Europe between 1880 and 1914 of actual labour costs. Attention to cost accounting often preceded reorganisation of the labour process, highlighting areas of inefficiency and heavy expense. See C. Bertrand Thompson, 'Scientific management in practice', *Quarterly Journal of Economics*, November 1914, pp. 262–307.

94 *ALJ*, 15 June 1898, p. 26; *Age*, 3 September 1894; 1901 Factory RC, p. 329. For strikes against reductions, see BM, January–December 1892, ANUA T5/2/1; 7 December 1891; 5 January, 14 March 1892, ANUA T5/1/3.

95 1894 Tariff Inquiry, p. 296. See also *Age*, 27 September 1894, p. 5.

96 CIFR 1894, p. 4; J. W. Billson, 1894 Tariff Inquiry, p. 300.

97   *ALJ*, 15 June 1898, p. 26; 1894 Tariff Inquiry, Greenwood, p. 290; Harkness, p. 292.

98   One of the largest campaigns took place against Marshall's of Port Melbourne, who had a history of 'rigidly excluding' union men: *ALJ*, 2 April 1898, p. 117; *Age*, 27 September 1894, p. 5. See also BM, January–October 1893, ANUA T5/2/1; also Hyman, 1901 Factory RC, p. 329.

99   BM, 3 July, 8 July, 21 September 1893, ANUA T5/2/1.

100 *Age*, 27 September 1894, p. 5.

101 BM, February–June 1894, ANUA T5/1/3; February–April 1894, ANUA T5/2/1. It will be obvious that my interpretation conflicts with that offered by Graeme Davison, *Marvellous Melbourne*, pp. 69–70, who characterises the period 1892–94 as years in which the union continued as a social club only.

102 BM, September–October 1894, ANUA T5/1/3; 26 August, 10 September 1894, ANUA T5/2/2; T. J. Deslandes, 1901 Factory RC, p. 341; *Age*, 3, 27 September 1894, p. 5.

103 *Age*, 3 September 1894. Despite the grim prospects, 10:1 voted in favour of the strike: *Age*, 27 September 1894, p. 5.

104 *Age*, 27 September 1894, p. 6; 19 November 1894, p. 6.

105 BM, 20 July 1895, ANUA T5/2/2. Coghlan, *Labour and Industry*, vol. IV, p. 2051, gives a rather misleading account of the cause of the strike.

106 BM, February–April 1895, ANUA T5/1/3; October–December 1894; January–May 1895, ANUA T5/2/2; 1901 Factory RC, T. J. Deslandes, p. 341.

107 BM, 24 January 1895; 7 February 1895, ANUA T5/2/2; *Tocsin*, 21 April 1898, p. 8.

108 *Age*, 2 October 1890, p. 6, reported membership at 1150. BM, 10 February 1896, ANUA T5/1/4.

109 BM, 18 February 1896, ANUA T5/1/4.

110 Evidence to SA Sweating Inquiry, p. 142.

111 *Ibid*. On the general question of the relationship between management and control and piecework, see W. Brown, *Piecework Abandoned: the effect of wage incentive schemes on managerial authority*, especially pp. 69–70.

112 *Age*, 4 October 1894, p. 5.

113 BM, 12 March, 19 June 1891, ANUA T5/2/1; 10 February 1896, ANUA T5/1/4.

114 CIFR 1895, pp. 5–6.

115 BM, 13 February 1894, ANUA T5/1/3.

116 *Ibid*., 22 February.

117 *ALJ*, 15 September 1899, p. 583, referring to evidence given to Legislative Council Select Committee on Factories Bill, 16 January 1896.

118 1901 Factory RC, p. 325. Solly's account is supported by Arthur Whybrow's evidence to the SA Sweating Inquiry, p. 142.

119 BM, 29 January 1894, ANUA T5/1/3.

120 *ATR*, 2 April 1894, p. 117; 1901 Factory RC, evidence Angus McLachlan, p. 351.

121 BM, July–October 1895, ANUA T5/1/4; July–November 1895, ANUA T5/2/2.

122 *Ibid*., 3 July, 7, 21 October 1895, ANUA T5/1/4; July–October 1895, ANUA T5/2/2.

123 William Greenwood, 1894 Tariff Inquiry, p. 290; Solly, 1901 Factory RC, p. 323; 'Welcome to Bedggoods', Bedggood Papers, ANUA 57/20. Bedggoods in particular brought out 30 men from Leicester and Northampton.

124 Hyman, 1901 Factory RC, p. 329; *ALJ*, 15 June 1898, p. 26; 15 September 1899, p. 583; *Age*, 24 September 1897, p. 6; CIFR 1895, p. 6; BM, March–August 1896, ANUA T5/1/4; January–November 1896, ANUA T5/2/2.

125 Evidence to SA Sweating Inquiry, p. 142.

126 *Ibid*.

127 See Hobsbawm, 'Custom, wages and workload', pp. 348–9.

128 *Tocsin*, 4 November 1897, p. 1, report of Billson's statement to THC; BM, 7 September 1896, ANUA T5/1/4.

129 See Samuel, 'Workshop of the World', p. 58.

130 Evidence J. W. Billson, 1894 Tariff Inquiry, p. 299.

131 RC on Tech. Ed., T. Y. Harkness, p. 577; 1894 Tariff Inquiry, Greenwood, p. 287. See also evidence John Bedggood, 1893 Factory Inquiry.

132 1901 Factory RC, Angus McLachlan, p. 348.

133 *ALJ*, 15 February 1900, p. 837

134 *ALJ*, 15 September 1899, p. 598; 15 November 1899, p. 706; 15 December 1899, p. 753.

135 Evidence T. Y. Harkness, SA Sweating Inquiry, p. 126.

136 *Ibid.*

137 Evidence Harriet Longdill, 1893 Factory RC, p. 103.

138 Evidence to 1883–84 Factory RC, Q. 4091; see also evidence J. Bedggood, 1893 Factory RC, p. 55.

139 *Bendigo Advertiser*, 28 June 1879, Supplement. My thanks to Mimi Colligan for this reference.

140 For examples of females striking in support of males, see BM, May–September 1890; 9 April, 4 June 1894, ANUA T5/1/3. Also 12 November 1896, ANUA T5/2/2.

141 BM, 13 February, 1893, ANUA T5/1/3.

142 *Ibid.*, 18 June, 2 July 1894; 20 August, 17 September 1896, ANUA T5/2/2.

143 BM, 18 June, 2 July 1894, ANUA T5/1/3.

144 Evidence T. Y. Harkness, SA Sweating Inquiry, p. 126.

145 1883–84 Factory RC, Q. 4085; CIFR 1886, p. 6. Flowerists, the most skilled female operatives, could earn 30–40 shillings: CIFR 1889, pp. 10–11.

146 Evidence T. Y. Harkness, SA Sweating Inquiry, p. 126.

147 *Age*, 11 June 1890, p. 6.

148 Phrase used by 'An Oldster', *ALJ*, 15 September 1898, p. 129.

149 BM, 17 September 1896, ANUA T5/2/2.

150 *ALJ*, 16 May 1898, p. 12. See also CIFR 1895, p. 5.

Chapter 3:
Drawing the line

1 For a history of the firm, see H. P. Down, *A Century in Printing: The Story of Sands and McDougall Pty Ltd During Its First Hundred Years 1853-1953*, Melbourne 1956, p. 30.

2 Descriptions of work in the following pages are drawn from various sources, particularly J. Ramsay McDonald, *Women in the Printing Trades*, New York and London, 1980 (first published 1904), pp. 1–16. Although the work process was much the same in Australia as in the UK, the sexual division of labour was slightly different and mechanisation was less advanced. The Bookbinders Union Rules and Minutes and the Report of CIF have been used to identify which workers performed which processes in Australia.

3 The division of labour at Sands and McDougall's was characteristic of large city firms. Small country binderies, however, employed one man who did the work throughout: 1901 Factory RC, Robert Myers Mercer, p. 771.

4 McDonald, *Women in Printing Trades*, p. 7; BBM, 26 February, 26 November 1889.

5 BBM Special Meeting, 12, 19 May 1891; 17 October 1898.

6 Hagan, *Printers and Politics*, p. 62; Factory Registration Papers, VPRS 1399/4, see papers for *Age*, *Argus*, and *Herald*.

7 e.g. *Ararat Advertiser*, factory returns, MUA. My thanks to Michael Biggs for this reference.

8 Hagan, *Printers and Politics*, pp. 26–8, 40–1, 58–9.

9   The seasons in the printing industry were slightly different to those in boots and clothing, which had their downturns in the first and third quarters of the year. Printers were usually busy in the third and fourth quarters but slack from Christmas until mid-year.

10 Williams, 'Victorian Printing Industry', pp. 34–48.

11 Hagan, *Printers and Politics*, p. 58; Fitzgerald, *Printers of Melbourne*, p. 76.

12 Hagan, *Printers and Politics*, p. 100, 104; Fitzgerald, *Printers of Melbourne*, pp. 74–5; Williams, 'Victorian Printing', pp. 26–33.

13 *PTJ*, 11 February 1936, p. 25. See also Hunt, 'Women in London Bookbinding and Printing Trades', p. 84.

14 'Bookbinders Line of Demarcation', *PTJ*, May 1941.

15 CIFR 1886, p. 6.

16 BBM, 17 October 1898. See also John Child, *Industrial Relations*, p. 217.

17 This contrasts with the English situation, where women were employed on the casing machines introduced there in the 1880s: Hunt, 'Women in the London bookbinding and printing trades', p. 84.

18 BBM, 17 June 1892; 14, 15, 17 May 1894. For concessions re the demarcation see Bookbinders Special Meeting, 19 May 1891.

19 BBM, 1886–98.

20 BBM, 13 November 1888.

21 Parsons, 'Manufacturing in Melbourne', p. 570.

22 BBM, 7 August 1884; 5 March 1885; 7 April 1886.

23 CIFR 1886, p. 6; BBM, 5 November 1885.

24 Hunt ,'Women in London Bookbinding and Printing Trades', pp. 73–4; Sally Alexander, 'Women's work in nineteenth century London', in A. Oakley and J. Mitchell (eds), *The Rights and Wrongs of Women*, Harmondsworth, 1983, pp. 89–91.

25 BBM, 12 August 1890.

26 e.g. BBM, 11 June 1895.

27 *Victorian Yearbooks*, 1887–93; CIFR 1886, p. 6.

28 McDonald, *Women in Printing Trades*, pp. 48, 98.

29 e.g. *Typo. Jn.*, January 1889, p. 970.

30 BBM, 17 October 1898; *PTJ*, 11 February 1936, p. 25.

31 *Typo. Jn.*, December 1889, p. 1090.

32 *Ibid.*, January 1890, p. 2000.

33 *Ibid.*, January 1890, p. 1098.

34 ' "Faddists and Extremists": Radicalism in the Labour Movement, South-Eastern Australia, 1886–1898', Ph.D. thesis, Monash University, 1987. See also the exchange between Scates and Marilyn Lake in *Labour History*, nos. 50, 59 and 60.

35 *Typo. Jn.*, January 1891, Editorial.

36 *Ibid.*, August 1890; September 1890, p. 1065. See also J. Hagan, 'An incident at the *Dawn*', *Labour History*, vol. 1, no. 8, May 1965, p. 19.

37 *Typo. Jn.*, November 1892, p. 2307.

38 *Brothers: Male Dominance and Technological Change*, London, 1983, ch. 1 and pp. 132–40.

39 Report on Factory Act, VPP, 1881, p. 30.

40 Hagan, 'An incident at the *Dawn*', p. 19. See also Angela John's introduction to *Unequal Opportunities: Women's Employment in England 1800–1918*, Oxford 1986, p. 9.

41 *Typo. Jn.*, October 1887, p. 809, quoting Chicago *Specimen*; also 1 June 1906, p. 11.

42 *Typo. Jn.*, January 1890, p. 1098; October 1887, p. 809; 1 June 1906, p. 11. On medical and scientific texts, *Typo. Jn.*, December 1871, quoted in *PTJ*, June 1952, p. 57. See also Hunt, 'Women in London Bookbinding and Printing Trades', p. 78.

43 *Typo. Jn.*, May 1890, p. 2033.
44 McDonald, *Women in Printing Trades*, pp. 2–3.
45 *Typo. Jn.*, December 1894, p. 2516.
46 Report CIF 1899, p. 5; *Typo. Jn.*, October 1896, p. 2692, Editorial. Cf. Britain, McDonald, *Women in Printing Trades*, p. 98.
47 Hagan, 'First Factory Acts', esp. pp. 5–9.
48 *Typo. Jn.*, October 1895, Editorial.
49 *Ibid.*, August 1895, p. 2581; see also January 1895, p. 2522; October 1896, p. 2692.
50 'Technology and the crisis of masculinity', p. 25; *Brothers*, p. 31; *Typo. Jn.*, January 1895 and November 1898, especially pp. 9, 12.
51 This agreement was based on the London rules drawn up in 1894: *Typo. Jn.*, December 1894, November 1896. See also Hagan, *Printers and Politics*, pp. 109–10; Fitzgerald, *Printers of Melbourne*, p. 83.
52 CIFR, 1889, p. 5; *Typo. Jn.*, 1894–1906; *Tocsin*, 6 January 1898, p. 5.
53 *Typo. Jn.*, October 1895. An attempt by the Linotype Company to divide the workers and set up a machine operators' union failed: *ibid.* For a similar attempt in London, see Cockburn, *Brothers*, p. 29.
54 See discussion in Introduction.
55 *Typo. Jn.*, November 1898, p. 8. Hancock's argument that weekly wages made for more 'brotherliness' (see Hagan and Fisher, 'Piecework in Printing and Coal Mining', p. 35), was not voiced at this time, as Hagan and Fisher imply, but was made in 1911—long after the issue was settled.
56 *Typo. Jn.*, November 1898, p. 9. This argument was also used, however, by opponents of piece rates who feared that those on the 'better papers' would 'go for each one making the biggest pile and [drag] others down in the process': *ibid*, p. 8. It was this argument, in fact, which persuaded Canadian compositors to insist on time rates. See G. S. Kealey, 'Work control, the labour process and nineteenth century Canadian printers', in Heron and Storey (eds), *On the Job*, p. 89.
57 *Typo. Jn.*, November 1898, p. 9. Country printers favoured time rates presumably because work was less regular: *ibid.*, p. 12.
58 *Typo. Jn.*, November 1896; February 1898, p. 7.
59 Cockburn, *Brothers*, p. 29.
60 *Typo. Jn.*, February 1898, p. 7.
61 Williams, 'Victorian Printing', especially p. 66.
62 *Typo. Jn.*, August 1895, p. 2581.

Part II:
Under the Wages Board

1 M. B. Hammond, 'Wages Boards in Australia', *Quarterly Journal of Economics*, vol. 29, November 1914, p. 347.
2 Davey, 'Wages Boards', pp. 43–61.
3 Ernest Aves, *Report to the Secretary of State for the Home Department on the Wages Boards and Industrial Conciliation and Arbitration Acts of Australia and New Zealand*, London, 1908, pp. 13–14.
4 *Ibid.*, pp. 13–14.
5 *Ibid.*, p. 17. The exception to this was the Furniture Board.
6 See Wages Board History Files, VPRS 5466.
7 Statement by R. B. Rees, member of the Legislative Council, 1903–19, quoted in Davey, 'Wages Boards', p. 89; see also p. 90 for removal of the restriction.
8 Aves, *Wages Board Report*, pp. 18–19.

9 *Ibid.*, p. 18. See also Hammond, 'Wages Boards in Australia', p. 350; CIFR, 1907, pp. 13–59; Davey, 'Wages Boards', p. 109.

10 Aves, *Wages Board Report*, p. 19.

11 *Ibid.*, pp. 18–19.

12 WBHF, VPRS 5466. Also Aves, *Wages Board Report*, p. 19.

13 Aves, *Wages Board Report*, p. 19.

14 *Ibid.*, p. 20.

15 *Ibid.*

16 Hammond, 'Wages Boards in Australia', p. 359. See also Aves, *Wages Board Report*, p. 20.

17 Aves, *Wages Board Report*, p. 22.

18 *Ibid.*, p. 22.

19 R. Frances, 'Harrison Ord: Public Servant', *ADB*, vol. 11.

20 Sidney and Beatrice Webb Biography File, LTL.

21 Aves, *Wages Board Report*, p. 22.

22 e.g. *Labor Call*, 14 July 1910, p. 8; *Woman's Sphere*, April 1901, p. 68.

23 Aves, *Wages Board Report*, p. 23.

24 *Commonwealth Yearbook*, no. 1, 1901–07, p. 438.

25 It is impossible to know exactly how many women took work from factories; see Frances, 'Politics of Work', Ph.D. thesis, p. 213.

26 CIFR 1909, p. 4. See also Davey, 'Wages Boards', pp. 86–7.

27 See Frances, 'Politics of Work', pp. 214–15.

28 The above summary is based on CIF Reports, 1896–1925.

29 This is apparent in both the Wages Board History Files (VPRS 5466) and in the annual CIF Reports. See also *ALJ*, 15 August 1910, p. 199; 15 February 1917, p. 509.

30 W. A. Sinclair, 'Aspects of Economic Growth, 1900–1930', in A. H. Boxer (ed.), *Aspects of the Australian Economy*, 2nd edn, Melbourne, 1969, p. 102; E. A. Boehm, *Twentieth-century Economic Development in Australia*, Melbourne, 2nd edn, 1979, p. 26.

31 Boehm, *Twentieth-century Economic Development*, pp. 163–4; C. Forster, 'Economies of Scale and Australian Manufacturing', in C. Forster (ed.), *Australian Economic Development in the Twentieth Century*, Sydney, 1970, pp. 144–5. See also P. Cochrane, *Industrialization and Dependence: Australia's Road to Economic Development*, St Lucia, 1980, pp. 2, 11; Michael Dunn, 'The Britannic Question: The Empire and the Colonies 1870–1910', *Bowyang: Work on Changing Australia*, Vol. 1, no. 1, March 1979. For a more general account of economic developments in the early twentieth century, see A. G. L. Shaw, *The Economic Development of Australia*, 5th edn, Croydon, 1966, pp. 109–21. For contemporary comment on the boom in manufacturing, see *Journal of Commerce*, 13 October 1903, p. 5; 8 December 1903, p. 5; 18 July 1905, p. 17; 20 June 1905, p. 9; 14 August 1906, p. 5; 4 December 1906, p. 7. There were, however, slight recessions in 1908 and 1913 which marred the general picture of prosperity; see CIFR 1908, pp. 4–12; 1912, p. 3; 1913. See also, Sinclair, 'Economic Growth', pp. 102–3.

32 L. P. Donnelly, 'International Capital Movements, the terms of trade and Australian Economic Growth, 1861–1929', Ph.D. thesis, Brown University, 1970, pp. 87–8.

33 Sinclair, 'Economic Growth', p. 106.

34 Donnelly, 'International Capital Movements', pp. 85–7, 90; Cochrane, *Industrialization and Dependence*, p. 10.

35 Boehm, *Twentieth-century Economic Development*, p. 21.

36 N. G. Butlin, 'Some Perspectives on Australian Economic Development, 1890–1965', in Forster (ed.), *Australian Economic Development*, pp. 282, 302.

37 Boehm, *Twentieth-century Economic Development*, p. 37; Butlin, 'Perspectives of Economic Development', p. 302.

38 Forster, 'Economies of Scale', p. 134.

39 Boehm, *Twentieth-century Economic Development*, p. 37; Sinclair, 'Economic Growth', pp. 102–8; Sinclair, 'Capital Formation', in Forster (ed.), *Australian Economic Development*, p. 34; see also Donnelly, 'International Capital Movements', p. 90.

40 Forster, 'Economies of Scale', p. 155; Cochrane, *Industrialization and Dependence*, pp. 56–9. C. Forster, *Industrial Development in Australia 1920–1930*, Canberra, 1964, pp. 195–208.

41 Cochrane, *Industrialization and Dependence*, p. 61.

42 See Forster, 'Economies of Scale', pp. 155–6; also Butlin, 'Perspectives on Economic Development', pp. 312–14.

43 Forster, 'Economies of Scale', pp. 155–6.

44 See Frances, 'Politics of Work', p. 222, fn. 51.

45 CIFR, 1907–13; *Journal of Commerce*, 6 September 1911, p. 151.

46 A. W. Sinclair, 'Women at Work in Melbourne and Adelaide Since 1871', *Economic Record*, vol. 57, 1981, p. 346. Sinclair's figures only apply to Melbourne where most industries were located.

47 *Ibid.*, pp. 348–50.

48 CIFR 1907, p. 5.

49 CIFR 1907, p. 8. See also 1909, p. 6, and M. Nolan, 'Uniformity and Diversity: A Case Study of Female Shop and Office Workers in Victoria 1880–1939', Ph.D. thesis, ANU, 1989.

50 See CIFR 1906, p. 52.

51 CIFR 1909, p. 6; 1910, pp. 81–2.

52 CIFR 1910, p. 82.

53 Sinclair, 'Working Women Since 1871', p. 349.

54 See Gail Reekie ' "Humanising Industry": Paternalism, Welfarism and Labour Control in Sydney's Big Stores, 1890–1930', *Labour History*, no. 53, November 1987, p. 8.

55 For a discussion of women's move into business and professions, see Kingston, *My Wife . . .*, ch. 5.

56 For the general movements aimed at improving the quality of the race, or 'national efficiency', see A. Hyslop, 'Agents and objects. Women and social reform in Melbourne 1900 to 1914', in Bevege, et. al., *Worth Her Salt*, pp. 230–42; N. Hicks, 'This Sin and Scandal'. *Australia's Population Debate 1891–1911*, Canberra, 1978; C. Bacchi, 'Evolution, eugenics and women. The impact of scientific theories on attitudes towards women 1870–1920', in Windschuttle (ed.), *Women, Class and History*, pp. 132–56; C. Bacchi, 'The nature-nurture debate in Australia 1900–1914', *Historical Studies*, vol. 19, no. 75, pp. 199–212.

57 The *Age* article quoted actually links the two concerns. See also Ryan and Conlon, *Gentle Invaders*, Melbourne, 1975, pp. 64–5.

58 See *Woman's Sphere*, May 1901, p. 74.

59 Lee, 'A Redivision of Labour', pp. 352–72.

60 Davey, 'Wages Boards', pp. 115–16. See also Ryan and Conlon, *Gentle Invaders*, pp. 67–8; M. Nolan, 'Sex or Class? The Politics of the Earliest Equal Pay Campaign in Victoria', in R. Frances and B. Scates (eds), *Women, Work and the Labour Movement in Australia and Aotearoa/New Zealand*, Special Issue of *Labour History*, no. 61, November 1991.

61 *Tocsin*, 17 May 1900, p. 8; 28 February 1901, pp. 5–6.

62 R. Gollan, *Radical and Working Class Politics: A Study of Eastern Australia, 1880–1910*, Melbourne, 1960, pp. 210–11; also *Labor Call*, 16 May 1907, p. 7.

63 *Ibid.* This proved a receptive atmosphere for IWW ideas which gained in popularity up to the Russian Revolution in 1918.

64 *Labor Call*, 22 December 1910, p. 10.

65 For a record of women's industrial and political involvement in this period, see Melanie Raymond, 'Labour Pains: Working-Class Women in Employment, Unions and the Labor Party in Victoria 1888–1914', M.A. thesis, University of Melbourne, 1987, chs 2–3.

66 Minutes Women's Industrial Convention, 23–25 September 1913, MUA.
67 See report of a deputation to the Minister on this issue, *Labor Call*, 31 July 1919, p. 9.

Chapter 4:
No more Amazons

1   For fuller references and a more detailed discussion of the impact of the Act on each section of the industry, see Frances, 'The Nature of Work', pp. 232–82.
2   Evidence to SA Sweating Inquiry, pp. 150–2.
3   Mrs 'D', 1901 Factory RC, p. 680.
4   Davey, 'Wages Boards', p. 180; CIFR 1902, 1906.
5   Frances, 'Politics of Work', Ph.D. thesis, pp. 263–4.
6   CIFR 1901, p. 39; 1902, p. 30; 1907, p. 7.
7   Marion Fletcher, *Costume in Australia 1788–1901*, Melbourne, 1984, p. 175; CIFR 1909, p. 15.
8   Fletcher, *Costume in Australia*, p. 175; White, *Golden Thread*, pp. 13, 20; CIFR 1899, p. 6; 1901, p. 8.
9   15 December 1923, pp. 18–19. See also 1935 Select Committee on the Working Week, pp. 700–1, ANUA E138/18/84.
10 CIFR 1899–1918; Memo McClellan and Co. to Sec. Contract and Supply Board, Department of Defence, 29 September 1916; Letter H. Crossle to.London Office, 10 December 1914, Foy and Gibson Letterbooks, MUA.
11 White, *Golden Thread*, pp. 18–19.
12 *AM*, 24 March 1917, p. 19. The following account of Law's methods is based on an analysis of his writings in *AM*, 28 October 1916, pp. 21–3; 24 March 1917, pp. 19–20; 2 June 1917, pp. 18–19.
13 e.g. Henry Minich, 'Planning the Cutting of Cloth', *AM*, 8 September 1917, pp. 12–13.
14 *AM*, 24 March 1917, p. 19; 28 October 1916, pp. 21–3.
15 *Age*, 28 September 1910; Evidence H. Carter, 1919 Arbitration Hearing, p. 196, ANUA E138/18/4; Letter H. Carter to J. Harper 25, 28 October 1913, ANUA E138/14/3; Minutes CTU, 27 October 1913, MUA.
16 CIFR 1909; Letter J. Cook to Chief Secretary, 19 July 1900, Shirt WBHF, VPRS 5466/52.
17 Arbitration Hearing, No. 89 of 1922, p. 5, ANUA E138/18/86; See also *Labor Call*, 15 June 1911, p. 9.
18 1919 Arbitration Hearing, ANUA E138/18/5.
19 *Ibid.*, pp. 295, 303.
20 *Labor Call*, 2 January 1913, p. 1.
21 *ACTJ*, December 1945, p. 9.
22 1921 Arbitration Hearing, p. 207, ANUA E138/18/6.
23 Evidence J. W. Clarke, 1919 Arbitration Hearing, ANUA E138/18/5.
24 *Tocsin*, e.g. 3 February 1897, p. 1.
25 Evidence to SA Sweating Inquiry, Eckersall, p. 152; M. G. Cuthbertson, p. 145.
26 *AM*, 24 March 1917, p. 20; Evidence Joseph Clark, 1919 Arbitration Hearing, pp. 307–8, ANUA E138/18/5.
27 May Brodney, 'Autobiographical Notes', p. 10, Brodney Papers, Ms. 10882, LTL.
28 Evidence Ellen Eckersall, SA Sweating Inquiry, p. 151.
29 1901 Factory RC, p. 360. See also Evidence J. R. Blencowe, p. 352, John Barnett, p. 365, Alfred Bowley, p. 364, and Report on Clothing Board, p. xxxviii.
30 Letter H. Carter to Murphy (CIF), 3 August 1911, Clothing WBHF, VPRS 5466/40.
31 Evidence W. Read, Arbitration Hearing, p. 302, ANUA E138/18/5.
32 Letter H. M. Murphy to Edward Price and Philip Warland, 25 September 1917, Underclothing WBHF, VPRS 5466/196. See also *ACTJ*, June 1945, p. 8.

33 Minutes Anti-Sweating League, 5, 19 October 1896; 6 December 1897; Mauger Papers, Ms. 403/14, NL.

34 See Raymond, 'Labour Pains', chs 2–3.

35 CIFR 1906, p. 33; *ACTJ*, April 1944, p. 16 (comments of Miss Julia Northausen).

36 CTU Minutes, 18 November 1918, MUA.

37 Evidence to SA Sweating Inquiry, p. 147.

38 The dressmakers were later covered by the Garment Makers' Union (from 1910), but this was also factory based. Dressmakers WBHF, especially File Note, M. G. Cuthbertson, 16 May 1914, VPRS 5466/52.

39 *AM*, 24 March 1917, p. 19.

40 *AM*, 24 March 1917, pp. 19–20. Christmas parties earlier filled a similar function: see *Labor Call*, 4 January 1912, p. 1; 2 January 1913, p. 1.

41 *AM*, 24 March 1917, p. 19.

42 *Tocsin*, 25 November 1897, p. 5; 16 March 1899, p. 6; Tailors' Minutes, 11 January, 20 September, 10 August 1897. The two tailoresses' unions amalgamated in 1899: see Tailors' Minutes, 13 July 1899; *Tocsin*, 9 March 1899, p. 5. For the Pressers' Union, see Pressers' Minutes, 19 August 1896, ANUA E138/7. See also, Davey, 'Wages Boards', p. 227.

43 *Tocsin*, 2 November 1899, p. 7; 20 September 1900, p. 7.

44 For the sake of convenience, this union, and its successor, the Amalgamated Clothing Trades Union, will be referred to as the Clothing Trades Union. The pressers joined with the cutters and trimmers in 1902 to form the Victorian Clothing Operatives Union, comprising 70 members. In 1907 this union joined with the Tailors and Tailoresses to form the Federated Clothing Trades Union. For a general history of the clothing unions, see B. Ellen, *In Women's Hands? A History of Clothing Trades Unionism in Australia*, Sydney, 1989.

45 Evidence H. Carter, 1922 Arbitration Hearing, p. 22, ANUA E138/18/86.

46 Clothing WBHF, VPRS 5466/40. Also *Age*, 28 September 1910.

47 Underclothing WBHF, VPRS 5466/196; For 'girls' trade' see evidence G. T. Felstead to Industrial Appeals Court Hearing re Underclothing Board Determination, p. 27, Brodney Papers, Ms. 10882/19, LTL. The delegates also secured an increase in the minimum wage and claimed equal pay for female pressers for the first time: Minutes No. 2 Group CTU, 24 April 1917, ANUA E138/8.

48 *Labor Call*, 8 September 1910, p. 5; Underclothing WBHF, VPRS 5466/196; Shirt WB HF, VPRS 5466/52. The one exception to the female workers' representative was the cutter, Mr J. H. Leydon, who served 1911 to 1917: Shirt WBHF.

49 'Notes on May Brodney's Membership of Wages Board', Brodney Papers, Ms. 10882/19, LTL.

50 *Ibid*. See also file note, 18 June 1918, Clothing WBHF, VPRS 5466/39.

51 Report THC Meeting, *Labor Call*, 13 April 1911, p. 3; *Age*, 7 April 1911; *Argus*, 7 April 1911.

52 A meeting of whiteworkers in 1897 declared their three delegates 'unfit to represent them': *Argus*, 28 August 1897.

53 CIFR 1898, p. 15.

54 1901 Factory RC, p. 402.

55 CIFR 1906, pp. 24–5; 1910, p. 37; *Labor Call*, 13 April 1911, p. 3; 1922 Arbitration Hearing, Evidence Kitty Ryan, ANUA E138/18/2; CIFR 1905, p. 19.

56 Dress WBHF, VPRS 5466/52; *Age*, 7 April 1911; *Argus*, 7 April 1911; *Labor Call*, 13 April 1911, p. 3.

57 Shirt WBHF, VPRS 5466/52.

58 *ACTJ*, June 1945, p. 8.

59 'Notes on May Brodney's membership of Wages Board', Brodney Papers. Also CTU Minutes, 25 October, 8 November 1915.

60 Press clipping, n.d. (c.1917), CTU Press Clipping File, MUA.

61 1901 Factory RC, p. 369.

62 Evidence E. Pearson, 1901 RC, p. 360; CIFR 1897, p. 8. For examples of victimisation, Report Inspector George Hall, 11 October 1899, Clothing WBHF, VPRS 5466/38; Papers re Mrs Mary Barton, dressmaker, Factory Registration Papers, VPRS 1399/5.

63 Davey, 'Wages Boards', p. 273.

64 Minutes CTU, 22 November 1915; 11 August, 22 September 1919, MUA.

65 This comment was made by the union delegate to the THC, Mrs M. M. Powell. See Underclothing WBHF, VPRS 5466/196; also *Labor Call*, 18 August 1910, p. 3; Letter to Editor from Minnie Felstead, *Argus*, 30 August 1910. For a more detailed account of this episode see Frances, 'Politics of Work', Ph.D. thesis, pp. 322–6.

66 1901 Factory RC, p. 437. See also CIFR 1899, p. 8.

67 *Typo. Jn.*, January 1912, p. 8.

68 25 January 1912, p. 1.

69 *Typo. Jn.*, January 1912, p. 8.

70 'Strike of Cutters at Federal Clothing Factory', p. 6, CTU File, ANUA E138/18/13.

71 *Age*, 28 September 1910; Evidence H. Carter, 1919 Arbitration Hearing, p. 196, ANUA E138/18/4; Minutes 1913 Women's Industrial Convention, pp. 6, 9. See also CTU Minutes, 8 August 1910, MUA.

72 See particularly Carter's letters to the various state unions, Letterbook, ANUA E138/18/13.

73 Rough Minutes Federal Council, February 1925, CTU records, MUA. With the exception of Wallis, who was a cutter, all the secretaries of the CTU in its first 40 years of existence were tailors: *Voice*, Autumn 1948, p. 20.

74 *Labor Call*, 15 June, 27 July 1911; Minutes CTU, 1910–13, MUA; Minutes CTU Federal Council, 8 February 1911, ANUA E138/12/1.

75 *Labor Call*, December 1910–May 1912.

76 CTU Minutes, 6 March 1911; 7 August 1914, MUA; *Labor Call*, 28 August 1913, p. 8. See also Report ALP Annual Conference, 1918, *Labor Call*, 16 May 1918, p. 5.

77 R. Frances, 'Maria May Brodney', *ADB*, forthcoming.

78 'Notes on Alf Wallis . . . '; 'Autobiography', p. 11.

79 CTU Minutes, 14 February 1916, MUA.

80 'Autobiography', p. 15, Bertha Walker Papers. She suffered from a congenital heart weakness which contributed to her early death at the age of 36.

81 'Notes on Alf Wallis . . . ', Brodney Papers; Drusilla Modjeska's introduction to *The Poems of Lesbia Harford*, North Ryde, 1985, provides the best account of Harford's life.

82 Dress WBHF, VPRS 5466/52; Minutes CTU 30 January 1917, MUA; Minutes No. 2 Group, CTU, 19 September 1916, ANUA E138/8.

83 Minutes No. 2 Group CTU, 3 July; 23 October; 20 November 1917; 9 April 1918. See also interview with May Brodney, 1965, Merrifield Collection; CTU Minutes, 1916–18; *Labor Call*, 4 October 1917, p. 11; 28 February 1918, p. 10.

84 CTU Minutes, 13 March 1916; 11 April 1916, MUA. Cain was, like Wallis, a member of the Victorian Socialist Party and probably owed his appointment to Wallis' support. K. White, *John Cain and Victorian Labor, 1917–1957*, Sydney, 1982, pp. 16–17.

85 H. Carter to J. Reddy (Sec. NSW Pressers' Union), 29 September 1915, ANUA E138/18/13. Also CTU Minutes, 5 July 1915, MUA.

86 'Notes on Alf Wallis . . .', Brodney Papers; see also Minutes CTU, 16 April 1917, MUA.

87 Minutes Half-Yearly Meeting CTU, 25 June 1923, MUA.

88 Minutes No. 2 Group CTU, 18 June 1918, ANUA E138/8.

89 See interview with Whitford, *Voice*, Autumn 1950, p. 15.

90 *Ballarat Star*, 18 July 1917; CIFR 1910, p. 68.

91   White, *Golden Thread*, pp. 22–3; J. Bassett, 'Lyla Barnard: Khaki Girl', in Lake and Kelly, *Double Time*, pp. 268–75.
92   e.g. J. Stedman Ltd and Henderson Ltd, *AM*, 24 March 1927, p. 20; Acme Shirt Factory, *Cyclopedia of Victoria*, p. 554.
93   File of Press Clippings, CTU, MUA; CTU Minutes, 30 July 1917.
94   Special Meeting of Cap Workers, 5 August 1915, CTU File on CCF, ANUA E138/18/13.
95   Minutes CTU, 1 March, 3 July 1915, MUA; 'Strike at CCF', CTU File, ANUA E138/18/13.
96   *Age*, 13 June 1916; Minutes CTU, 19 June 1916, MUA.
97   *Argus*, 17 June 1916.
98   *Age*, 25 April 1916.
99   Letter Trumble (Acting Secretary Defence Department), 17 June 1916, CTU file on CCF, ANUA E138/18/13.
100 Minutes CTU, 28 August 1916, MUA; *Age*, 22 April 1916.
101 'Strike at CCF', pp. 4–5, ANUA E138/18/13; Minutes CTU, 2 August 1915, MUA.
102 Minutes CTU, 28 August 1916, MUA; Bassett, 'Lyla Barnard: Khaki Girl', pp. 268–75.
103 Minutes CTU, 29 July 1918, MUA; also *ACTJ*, November 1941, p. 13.
104 See McKay's reported remarks, Minutes CTU, 29 July 1918, MUA.
105 CIFR 1909, p. 34; see also 1910, p. 32.
106 Letter James Cook to Hon. H. McLean, Chief Secretary, 19 July 1900, Shirt WBHF, VPRS 5466/52.
107 'Complaints by Whiteworkers against Thear', p. 2, Underclothing WB HF, VPRS 5466/52.
108 Letter M. M. Powell to Miss Tate, 12 September 1904, Shirt WB HF, VPRS 5466/52.
109 Evidence George Denton, 1893 Factory Inquiry, p. 150.
110 Interview with May Hansford, machinist, August 1985. See also *Cyclopedia of Victoria*, p. 554; *AM*, 2 June 1917, p. 19.
111 Edna Ryan also comments on this form of protest in Sydney clothing factories: *Two-thirds of a Man*, Sydney 1984, p. 38.
112 Aves, *Wages Board Report*, p. 50. Original emphasis.
113 *Ibid.*, p. 52.
114 Davey, 'Wages Boards', p. 311.

Chapter 5:
The workers baffled

1   CIFR 1898–1908; 1901 Factory RC, p. xxxvii (statistics compiled by Comptroller-General of Customs). See also BM, 1898–1902, ANUA T5/2/3; *ALJ*, 1900–08; Rimmer, 'Boot Industry', p. 116; see also Appendix, Figures A5, A6.
2   CIFR 1898, p. 14. See also Report 1897, p. 9; 1899, p. 10. For lists of machines in use in particular factories see regular features in *ALJ*, 'Among the Boot Manufacturers', 1899–1900. See also Appendix, Figures A5, A6.
3   *ALJ*, 1901–3.
4   *ALJ*, 1902–10; 1919 RC on High Prices, No. 2 Report, p. 14.
5   *Labor Call*, 28 February 1907, p. 7; ALJ, 15 June 1905, pp. 66–7; 16 October 1905, pp. 361, 377; 15 May 1922, p. 8.
6   *Argus*, 15 September 1906
7   *ALJ*, 1901–08; Factory Registration Papers, VPRS 1399.
8   1901 Factory RC, John Hyman, pp. 332–3.
9   'Rishi', 'Technical Education in Boot Manufacturing', *ALJ*, 15 November 1902, p. 437.
10 *Ibid.*, 15 September 1902, p. 297.

11 *Ibid.*, 15 November 1902, p. 438.

12 BM, 12 April 1900, ANUA T5/1/4. See also BM, 6 April 1908, ANUA T5/1/6.

13 *ALJ*, 15 November 1902, p. 438.

14 *Ibid.*, 15 September 1902, p. 297.

15 *Ibid.*, 15 November 1902, p. 438.

16 *Ibid.*, 15 September 1902, p. 297.

17 *Ibid.*

18 *Ibid.*, 15 December 1902, p. 52; 15 October 1902, p. 371.

19 *Ibid.*, 15 October 1902, p. 370.

20 *Ibid.*, p. 371.

21 *Ibid.*, 15 August 1906, p. 248.

22 *Ibid.*, 15 December 1902, p. 485.

23 *Tocsin*, 4 November 1897, p. 1.

24 Letter J. Keogh to Chief Secretary, 15 December 1897, BBHF, VPRS 5466/11; 1901 Factory RC, Report on Boot Board, p. xxxv; BM, 16 October 1899, ANUA T5/1/4.;

25 BBHF, VPRS 5466/11.

26 *Unity*, 14 March 1938, p. 11.

27 *Argus*, 8 February 1898.

28 *Tocsin*, 31 March 1898, p. 5.

29 Mass Meeting of Clickers, 24 January 1902, BM, ANUA T5/1/4.

30 BM, 27 July 1898, ANUA T5/2/3.

31 BM, 10, 18 December 1896, ANUA T5/2/2; 7, 12 August 1896, ANUA T5/1/4.

32 BM, 1896–97.

33 *Tocsin*, 31 March 1898, p. 5.

34 BM, 1898–99.

35 CIFR 1898, p. 11.

36 BM, 17 May 1897, ANUA T5/1/4. See also Special Meeting Female Operatives, 12, 24 August, 7 September 1896; *Tocsin*, 18 November 1897, p. 4.

37 BM, 31 May 1897, ANUA T5/1/4.

38 BM, 22 July 1897, ANUA T5/2/3.

39 BM, 5 August 1897.

40 BM, (Federal Council), 22 April 1910, ANUA T6/1/11.

41 *ALJ*, 15 August 1904, pp. 263–4.

42 *Ibid.*, 23 October 1905.

43 Report of Federal Conference Bootmakers Federation, 14 January 1907, ANUA T5/1/6.

44 Minutes Federal Council Australian Boot Trade Federation, 14 April 1909, ANUA T6/1/1. Also *ibid.*, 19 April 1910.

45 BM, 28 May 1900, ANUA T5/1/4; 4 June 1900, T5/2/3.

46 BM, 3 July 1900, ANUA T5/2/3.

47 *Census of Victoria*, 1901, Occupations of the People, p. 71.

48 CIFR 1906.

49 See, for example, the committee appointed to draw up wages, etc., for the first Wages Board, BM, 12 August 1896, ANUA T5/1/4.

50 BM, 20 September 1897, ANUA T5/1/4.

51 BM, 15 October 1896, ANUA T5/2/2.

52 BM, 22 February 1897, ANUA T5/1/4.

53 *ALJ*, 15 April 1899, p. 410.

54 Higgins, 'Judgement 1909', p. 15.

55 In 1909 a bricklayer's labourer was paid 9s per day; bootmakers received 8s. Higgins, 'Judgement 1909', pp. 3–4.

56 *Ibid.*

57 *ALJ*, 15 December 1899, p. 735.

58 Frances, 'Politics of Work', p. 377, notes 55–7.

59 *ALJ*, 15 July 1901, p. 139; *Tocsin*, 15 March 1900, p. 4; BM, 16 September 1901, ANUA T5/1/5. For the 'shop-by-shop' scheme, see BM, 14 July 1902, ANUA T5/2/3.

60 BM, 6 March, 21 August 1899; 11 June 1900, ANUA T5/1/4.

61 BM, 7 July 1903, ANUA T5/1/5.

62 BM, 14 September 1903.

63 BM, 8 June 1903.

64 BM, 9 April 1906.

65 BM, 2 February 1904, ANUA T5/1/5. See also 2 March 1903, 18 January 1904.

66 *ALJ*, 15 July 1902, p. 133. Also Evidence T. Y. Harkness, 1909 Boot Case, *ALJ*, 15 December 1909, p. 434.

67 Quote from Fleming, VOBU meeting, *ALJ*, 15 October 1898, p. 205. See also BM, 3 December 1900, ANUA T5/1/4; 8 March 1909, T5/1/6.

68 CIFR 1898, p. 13; 1901, p. 13; 1901 Factory RC, pp. 392, 493, 491; *ALJ*, 15 August 1897, p. 567; 16 May 1898, p. 12.

69 Higgins, 'Judgement, Boot Case, 1909', p. 24; BM, 8 March 1909, ANUA T5/1/6.

70 *ALJ*, 15 July 1901, p. 131.

71 CIFR 1898, pp. 11–12; also ALJ, 15 June 1898, p. 26.

72 CIFR 1908, p. 19.

73 BM, 12, 14 August 1896, ANUA T5/1/4.

74 BM, 14 June 1897.

75 BM, 28 June, 26 July 1897.

76 BM, 6 January 1898.

77 BM, 24 January 1898.

78 BM, 16 October 1899.

79 *ALJ*, 16 October 1899, p. 649.

80 BM, 10 December 1900, ANUA T5/1/4. See also Evidence J. Hyman, Boot Board Review, BBHF, VPRS 5466/11; 1901 Factory RC, p. 332.

81 BM, 10 December 1900, ANUA T5/1/4.

82 Burawoy, *Manufacturing Consent*, p. 85; T. Nichols and P. Armstrong, *Workers Divided*, Glasgow, 1976, p. 73.

83 Ben Tillett's phrase, *Tocsin*, 31 March 1898, p. 5.

84 *Ibid.*

85 Tom Mann, *What is Ca'Canny?*, leaflet issued by International Federation of Ship, Dock and River Workers, 20 October 1896, cited in Hobsbawm, 'Custom, wages and workload', p. 365, fn. 19.

86 Higgins, 'Judgement 1909', p. 16.

87 BM, Half-Yearly Meeting, 7 August 1908, ANUA T5/1/6.

88 Resolution passed at interstate conference of boot unions, 1902, reported in *ALJ*, 15 May 1902, p. 25.

89 *ALJ*, 15 October 1906, p. 399.

90 'Judgement 1909', p. 10.

91 *ALJ*, 15 May 1902, p. 25.

92 'Judgement 1909', p. 15.

93 BM, 16 July 1906; 9 September 1907, ANUA T5/1/6.

94 See report of evidence to the 1909 Federal Boot Case in *ALJ*, October 1909 – December 1910. Also, Higgins, 'Judgement 1909', pp. 9–10.

95 See evidence of Arthur Williams, *ALJ*, 15 January 1910, p. 513.

96 Higgins, 'Judgement 1909', pp. 15, 21.

97 See Hyman's comments as President of the VOBU to Boot Wages Board in 1897, BBHF, VPRS 5466/11.

98 BM, 21 October 1907, ANUA T5/1/6; *ALJ*, 15 October 1898, p. 205.

99 *ALJ*, 15 May 1902, p. 25.

100 *Ibid*. See also 15 January 1907, p. 620.

101 CIFR 1910, p. 5. See also CIFR 1909, p. 9; 1906, p. 15; 1907, p. 16.

102 e.g. BM, 8 October 1906, ANUA T5/1/6; 2 November 1908, T5/1/5. See also 1932 Interstate Conference, p. 262, ANUA T5/3/1.

103 Minutes Federal Council Meeting, 18 April 1910, ANUA T6/1/1.

104 1901 Factory RC, evidence J. Bedggood, p. 296. *ALJ*, 15 May 1908, p. 1, Editorial.

105 Letter 8 November 1897, BBHF, VPRS 5466/11.

106 *ALJ*, 15 March 1902, pp. 693, 726; 15 September 1902, p. 317; 15 August 1904, pp. 2189.

107 *Ibid.*, 14 December 1907, p. 514.

108 This course was suggested by the *ALJ* as early as 1907: see issue 14 December 1907, p. 514.

109 *Ibid.*, 15 October 1898, p. 278. See also 16 November 1908, p. 349; 15 March 1909, p. 609.

110 CIFR 1920, 1906.

111 CIFR 1899–1909.

112 CIFR 1909, p. 24.

113 The *ALJ*'s personal column lists the overseas trips undertaken by Melbourne manufacturers. See especially reports of H. Perry's visit, 15 January 1909, pp. 503–4; Arthur Whybrow's visit, 15 March 1909, p. 625.

114 15 June 1901, p. 64.

115 *ALJ*, 15 October 1902, p. 371.

116 *Ibid.*, 15 June 1901, p. 64.

117 *Ibid.*, 15 August 1899, p. 554.

118 *Ibid.*, 15 September 1901, p. 301; see also 15 December 1908, p. 399.

Chapter 6:
Educating the girls

1 Ann Stephen, 'Agents of consumerism: the organisation of the Australian advertising industry, 1918–1938', *Media Interventions*, Sydney, 1981, pp. 78–86.

2 *Typo. Jn.*, March 1902, p. 4.

3 CIFR 1908, p. 45.

4 Hunt, 'Women in London Bookbinding and Printing Trades', p. 84.

5 BBM, 23 April 1912.

6 PM (Provisional Board), November–December 1921; (Board), 3 March 1923; 8 September 1924; 13 July 1925; (Exec.) 24 October 1921; 27 February 1922; BBM, 9 February 1904; 28 February 1911; 24 February 1912; 21 February 1918; 22 February 1921.

7 *Typo. Jn.*, January 1902, pp. 2, 8; 8 March 1932, p. 49.

8 Davey, 'Wages Boards', pp. 192, 194, 195, 204; Hagan, *Printers and Politics*, p. 144.

9 Dr Ethel Osborne, *Report of an Inquiry into the Conditions of Employment as Regards the Health of Female Workers in the Printing and Allied Trades*, Melbourne, 1925, pp. 6–9.

10 *Labor Call*, 1 December 1910, p. 2; 18 May 1911, p. 5, re strength of newly formed union. For the activities of Mulcahy and Barry see Raymond, 'Labour Pains', chs 2–3.

11 *Woman's Sphere*, February 1901, p. 50.

12 BBM, 23 August 1904.

13 'Determination of the Printers Board, 9 December 1901', *VGG*, September–December 1901, p. 4565.

14 CIFR 1908, p. 26.

15 CIFR 1906, p. 36.

16 CIFR 1909, p. 62.

17 BBM, 24 October 1911; 8 November 1911; 20 December 1910. See also *Typo. Jn.*, May 1915, p. 8.

18 Women BBM, 26 January 1911.

19 *Ibid.*, 27 October 1910.

20 *Ibid.*, 22 December 1910.

21 *Ibid.*, 2 March 1911.

22 *Ibid.*, 8 December 1910.

23 For Felstead, see Raymond, 'Labour Pains', chs 2–3; for Cross, see especially *PTJ*, 12 June 1923, p. 114.

24 Letters between Cross and Leovold, September–October 1920, Printers' Correspondence.

25 Letter, Cross to Leovold, 28 February 1921, Printers' Correspondence.

26 *PTJ*, 21 December 1920, p. 294.

27 See especially Letter E. C. Magrath to Leovold, 17 May 1921. See also *PTJ*, 21 March 1921, p. 58.

28 See Hagan, *Printers and Politics*, p. 205.

29 Letter B. Eagle to A. Leovold, 30 November 1920, Printers' Correspondence.

30 Box and Carton Minutes (Special), 14 October 1920.

31 PM (Provisional Board), 3 September 1921.

32 PM (Special General Meeting), 16 October 1921.

33 PM (Exec.), 12 December 1921; (Half-yearly meeting), 11 February 1922; see also *PTJ*, 17 January 1922, pp. 17–18; 21 March 1922, pp. 70–1.

34 Letter Imelda Cashman to Leovold, 17 May 1921, Printers' Correspondence.

35 BBM, 30 April 1921.

36 The Bookbinders led the opposition to the appointment: PM (Half-yearly meeting), 11 February 1922.

37 Letter E. C. Magrath to Leovold, 17 May 1921, Printers' Correspondence.

38 Letter, R. York to A. Leovold, 30 March 1922.

39 PM (Board), 20 May 1922.

40 PM (Provisional Board), 3 September 1921.

41 PM (Special), 30 October 1921, Rule 24.

42 This restriction was also directed at 'unskilled' male labour, see Rule 5:7, PM (Special), 9 October 1921.

43 *PTJ*, 13 March 1923, p. 58.

44 The exact proportion fluctuated between 60 and 80 per cent: CIFR, 1902–25. For union membership see e.g. Report Board of Management, PIEUA, Vic. branch, December 1924.

45 Box and Carton Minutes, especially 8, 20 February 1906; 4 January 1907.

46 CIFR 1903, p. 31.

47 Box and Carton Minutes, 20 February 1906; *Labor Call*, 10 January 1907, p. 8.

48 Box and Carton Minutes, 1908–21.

49 Box and Carton Minutes (General), 8 April 1907, also 7 May 1917.

50 See Box and Carton Minutes for this whole period, especially 4 December 1916, 8 September 1919.

51 Osborne, *Female Print Workers*, provides detailed descriptions of the conditions of work in modern printing firms and their effects on workers.

52 Between 1902 and 1911 the ratio was two apprentices or improvers to every adult. In 1911 this was increased to two improvers for every adult plus one apprentice for every three adults.

53 Printing Industry Award, 1925, *PTJ*, 8 September 1925, p. 197; Osborne, *Female Print Workers*, p. 4.

54 'The Trade Union Woman', in F. Fraser and N. Palmer (eds), *Centenary Gift Book*, Melbourne, 1934, p. 132.

55 Kelly, ' "The Woman Question" in Melbourne, 1880–1914', Ph.D. thesis, Monash University, 1982, p. 373; Raymond, 'Labour Pains', chs 2–3.

56 Cross remained as organiser for the PIEUA until her retirement in 1951: *PTJ*, September 1951, p. 99.

57 See for example, CIFR 1908, p. 26; PM (Board), 9 November 1925. See also PM (Executive), 29 September 1924.

58 Box and Carton Minutes (General), 7 July 1919.

59 e.g. Box and Carton Minutes, 24 January 1918; (Special), 9 February 1920, 18 March 1920.

60 *Ibid*. (Special), 18 March 1920.

61 *PTJ*, 21 September 1920, p. 204.

62 CIFR 1909, p. 62.

63 Women BBM, 23 May 1911.

64 18 September 1917, pp. 6–8.

65 Box and Carton Minutes, 27 July 1912. See also 30 August 1909; 12 April 1910.

66 See evidence to 1925 Arbitration Hearing, *PTJ*, 14 July 1925, pp. 145, 152.

67 Davey, 'Wages Boards', p. 195.

68 Judgement Deputy President Webb, 1925 Arbitration Hearing, *PTJ*, 12 May 1925, pp. 83–4.

69 *PTJ*, 12 May 1925, p. 84.

70 Board of Inquiry into Working Men's College, Evidence, *VPP*, 1911, vol. 2, no. 14, p. 231.

71 CIFR 1907, p. 49; *Typo. Jn.*, 1 June 1908, p. 10.

72 Hungerford, *Stories From Suburban Road*, p. 155.

73 The agreement to prevent apprentices using the machines, except in their last year, was achieved by providing a set rate of 60s per week to be paid to apprentices using machines before their seventh year, with the normal 28s for the seventh year.

74 Royal Commission on National Insurance, 1927, evidence, Q. 19761; also Q. 19759. For earnings, see Hagan and Fisher, 'Piecework in Printing and Coal Mining', p. 26.

75 'Piecework in Printing and Coal Mining', pp. 33–4.

76 According to the Victorian *Census* of 1933, there were no women doing this work.

77 'Technology and the Crisis of Masculinity', pp. 23–5.

78 See evidence to 1925 Arbitration Hearing, *PTJ*, 8 September 1925, p. 190.

79 CIFR 1909, p. 74. The observation was made by Inspector Bishop, former compositor, whose conclusions were probably based on personal experience as well as official inspection.

80 Box and Carton Minutes (General), 1 July, 5 August 1918.

81 PM (Board), 9 December 1922.

82 PM (General), 22 August 1925, folio 3.

83 *Typo. Jn.*, March 1902, p. 4.

84 CIFR 1902, p. 27.

85 *Ibid.*

86 CIFR 1906, p. 37; also 1902, p. 27.

87 CIFR 1908, p. 26.

88 See, e.g., Box and Carton Minutes (General), 9 January 1911.

89 CIFR 1909, p. 62.

90 PIEUA, Vic. Branch Half-Yearly Report, 30 June 1922; PM (Half-Yearly Meeting), 23 February 1924, folio 3; (Executive) 2 September 1923 (re WB being partial to employers); *PTJ*, 10 March 1925, p. 50. Re shorter hours, see *PTJ*, 17 June, 15 July 1919; 12 August 1919; 20 April 1920. Also *Labor Call*, 29 February 1920. See also Davey, 'Wages Boards', pp. 119, 121.

91 *PTJ*, 10 March 1925, p. 50.

92 PM (Half-Yearly Meeting), 23 February 1924, folio 3.

Part III:
Federal wage-fixing

1   H. B. Higgins, *A New Province for Law and Order*, London, 1922; republished, London, 1968, p. 31.

2   G. Anderson, *Fixation of Wages*, Melbourne, 1929, p. 31.

3   Before 1928, the Act stipulated that no party could be represented by counsel or solicitor or paid agent without the permission of all parties: Anderson, *Fixation of Wages*, pp. 35–6. After 1928 it was possible for such people to appear at the discretion of the court.

4   It should be noted, however, that the normal rules of evidence applying in courts of law did not operate in the Arbitration Court: see J. H. Portus, *Australian Compulsory Arbitration 1900–1970*, Sydney, 1971, pp. 76–8.

5   Portus, *Australian Compulsory Arbitration*, p. 20.

6   Anderson, *Fixation of Wages*, pp. 41–2, 155.

7   *Ibid.*, p. 156.

8   Higgins, *New Province*, p. 41.

9   Anderson, *Fixation of Wages*, pp. 46, 110.

10 *Ibid.*, pp. 44–5.

11 *Ibid.*, p. 73. This restriction of Commonwealth powers was clearly decided in the Whybrow Case in 1910, 11 *Commonwealth Law Reports*, p. 311.

12 Anderson, *Fixation of Wages*, p. 114.

13 *Ibid.*, p. 63.

14 For more detail, see Frances, 'Politics of Work', Ph.D. thesis, pp. 452–6.

15 *Ibid.*, pp. 35–6; Portus, *Compulsory Arbitration*, pp. 71–2.

16 Anderson, *Fixation of Wages*, pp. 32, 45, 63.

17 *Ibid.*, pp. 63–7, 110.

18 *Ibid.*, pp. 63–7. The penal clauses were, however, rarely used before the war: Portus, *Compulsory Arbitration*, pp. 89–90.

19 Anderson, *Fixation of Wages*, pp. 130–4.

20 *Ibid.*, pp. 311–12, 397–9.

21 This reflected the increasing diversification of Australian manufacturing in the 1920s and 1930s: Sinclair, 'Aspects of Economic Growth', p. 109; Forster, *Industrial Development in Australia, 1920–1930*; Forster, 'Australian Manufacturing and the War', pp. 211–30; Sinclair, 'Capital Formation', p. 35.

22 M. Power, 'Women and Economic Crises: the Great Depression and the Present Crisis', in Windschuttle (ed.), *Women, Class and History*, pp. 492–513; M. Heagney, *Are Women Taking Men's Jobs?*, Melbourne, 1935; Andree Wright, 'The Australian Women's Weekly in Depression and War', *Refractory Girl*, vol. 3, Winter, 1973; *Labor Call*, 12 June 1930, p. 8; 12 April 1934, p. 6.

23 *Labor Call*, 8 January 1931, p. 8.

24 *Ibid.*, 10 March 1927, p. 9; 17 March 1927, p. 10. Jennie Bremner, 'In the cause of equality: Muriel Heagney and the position of women in the Depression', in Bevege, et. al., *Worth Her Salt*, pp. 286–98.

25 *Labor Call*, 25 July 1929, p. 4; 11 December 1930, p. 5. See also earlier debate on this topic in September–October 1926.

26 *Labor Call*, 7 February 1929, p. 1.

27 *Ibid.*, 25 July 1929, p. 4; *Working Woman*, January 1932, p. 1.

28 *Labor Call*, September–October 1926.

29 Boehm, *Twentieth-century Economic Development*, p. 164; see also C. Schedvin, *Australia and the Great Depression*, Sydney, 1970; Butlin, 'Some Perspectives of Australian Economic Development, 1890–1965', in Forster (ed.), *Australian Economic Development*, p. 313.

30 Muriel Heagney's 1935 study, *Are Women Taking Men's Jobs?*, demonstrates this point. In more recent times her argument has been elaborated by Margaret Power, 'Women and Economic Crises'.

31 As early as 1926, May Francis was urging unionists to abandon such destructive attacks and unite in working class action: *Labor Call*, 30 September 1926, p. 4. See also Bremner, 'In the cause of equality', pp. 286–98.

Chapter 7:
Diplomacy and guerilla warfare

1 *CTG*, 15 August 1922, p. 4.

2 Herbert Carter reported that this was the explanation employers gave for the shortage of female labour, 1927 Arbitration Hearing, p. 4213, ANUA E138/18/84.

3 Evidence Wallis, 1935 Select Committee on Working Week, p. 732; CIFR 1921, p. 4.

4 For female labour market, see CIFR 1921–39. Also Victorian secretary's report to Federal Council, 31 December 1921; 31 December 1926, MUA.

5 CTU Minutes, February–August 1922. Also Melbourne *Herald*, 8 February 1922, p. 1 (cutting in CTU file, 'Newspaper Clippings', MUA).

6 *CTG*, 15 August 1922, p. 5; CTU Minutes, 20 February 1922, MUA.

7 CTU Minutes, 20 February 1922, MUA.

8 Kingston, *My Wife . . .* , p. 62.

9 Evidence to 1927 Arbitration Hearing, p. 4728, ANUA E138/18/29.

10 'Notes on interview between representatives of the Clothing and Allied Trades Union and the Minister of Labour (The Hon. J. Lemmon), on 18th November 1928, relating to alleged sweating in the clothing trade.' Papers of Anti-Sweating League of Victoria, Ms. 9338, Box 1062/1(f). Also CTU Minutes, 21 March 1938 (Exec.).

11 CTU Minutes, 26 May 1924 (Adjourned Special) and 7 July 1924 (Half-yearly), MUA.

12 Rough Minutes Federal Council, 1925, MUA; Carter's evidence to 1931 Arbitration Hearing, p. 821, ANUA E138/18/86; Minutes Federal Council Meeting, May 1937, p. 271; Wallis' evidence to 1937 and 1940 Arbitration Hearings, ANUA E138/18/69.

13 CTU file, 'Sweating', MUA; Secretary's Report to Federal Council, 30 November 1938, MUA.

14 CTU Minutes (Exec.), 11 June 1928, MUA.

15 *Ibid.* (Exec.), 5 October 1925, MUA.

16 e.g. CTU Minutes, 19 February 1923 (Special), MUA.

17 CTU Minutes, 26 June 1924 (Adjourned Special).

18 This was standard practice in cost-of-living cases: see especially 1919 Arbitration Hearing, p. 106, ANUA E138/18/5.

19 CTU Minutes, 11 February 1924 (Exec.); 12 May 1924 (General), MUA.

20 *Ibid.*, 27 July 1936 (Exec.).

21 *Ibid.*, 25 June 1923.

22 *Ibid.*, 1919–39.

23 *Ibid.* (Exec.), 11 February 1924; 13 February 1922.

24 *Ibid.*, 23 June 1924 (Adjourned Special).

25 *Voice*, April 1940, p. 2.

26 *CTG*, 15 August 1922.

27 Secretary's Report to Federal Council, 30 June 1924, CTU, MUA; CTU Minutes, 1923–39. Also Report Heagney, 1935 Organising Campaign; Evidence James Law, 1927 Arbitration Hearing, ANUA E138/18/28.

28 CTU Minutes, 27 January 1925; 27 June 1938, MUA; *CTG*, 15 September 1922, p. 8. For Law's opinions on the union see evidence to 1927 Arbitration Hearing, ANUA E138/18/28.

29 F. R. E. Mauldon, 'Co-operation and welfare in industry', in D. A. Copland (ed.), *An Economic Survey of Australia*, Philadelphia, 1931, pp. 183–92.

30 Frances, 'Politics of Work', pp. 466–8.

31 See especially 1935 Organising Campaign, reports of Heagney and Smith, ANUA E138/18/93; CTU Minutes, 1920–39.

32 *Labor Call*, 8 October 1931, p. 8; Evidence Wallis, 1937 Outwork Hearing, p. 3, ANUA E138/18/69.

33 *The State of Workers' Protective Legislation in Australia*, pamphlet, n.d. (c.1935), Papers of Victorian Anti-Sweating League, Ms. 9338, Box 1062/1(b), LTL.

34 Heagney, '1935 Organising Campaign', p. 5, ANUA E138/18/93.

35 Even before the High Court appeal in 1928 it was advantageous to employ non-unionists. Wages Board determinations were consistently lower than federal awards as most boards had not met since 1917. See WBHF, VPRS 5466. For cases of victimisation of union members, see CTU Minutes, 1920–38; CTU file, 'Strikes and Disputes, 1916–1935'; Evidence to 1927 Arbitration Hearing, pp. 1733, 1734, 2133, ANUA E138/18/26.

36 *CAR*, vol. 26, 1928, p. 91.

37 1937 Outwork Hearing, ANUA E138/18/69.

38 *Working Woman*, 15 October 1930, p. 1.

39 CIFR 1928, 1929, p. 6; Evidence Wallis, 1937 Outwork Hearing, p. 15; 1940 Arbitration Hearing, pp. 6–7, ANUA E138/18/69. See also Frances, 'Politics of Work', Appendix 1.

40 Letter to A. Wallis, 9 November 1938, Correspondence CTU, MUA. See also May Brodney, 'Notes on Alf Wallis and the Clothing Trades Union'.

41 'Notes on Interview between representatives of CTU and Minister of Labour . . . , Papers of Anti-Sweating League of Victoria, Ms. 9338, Box 1062/1(f), LTL.

42 1922 Arbitration Hearing, p. 11, ANUA E138/18/86.

43 Rough Minutes General Council CTU, 9 March 1925, MUA.

44 Rough Minutes Federal Council CTU, 9 March 1925; CTU Minutes 23 January 1922; 12 July 1920.

45 See Heagney's report on the campaign, p. 6, ANUA E138/18/93.

46 *Ibid.*, p. 3. See also E. Smith's report, p. 2.

47 Heagney, 'Report Re Special Organising Campaign', p. 6.

48 *Herald*, 6 October 1936, cutting in CTU file, 'Newspaper Clippings', MUA.

49 'Strike of Trouser Machinists', CTU file, 'Strikes and Disputes, 1916–35', MUA; see also CTU Minutes, 18 March, 27 May 1935, MUA. Also *Labor Call*, 21 March 1935, p. 12.

50 'A Call to Action', leaflet in CTU file, 'Strikes and Disputes'. Also *Workers' Voice*, 22 March 1935, p. 1.

51 The shop committees were a blind, according to the MMM, so that Wallis could not be prosecuted under the Arbitration Act or Crimes Act for inciting a strike: 'To All Clothing Workers', leaflet, CTU file, 'Strikes and Disputes, 1916–35'.

52 See terms of settlement in CTU file, 'Strikes and Disputes'.

53 1927 Arbitration Hearing, p. 1565; see also evidence A. Wallis, p. 1734, ANUA E138/18/26.

54 Evidence to Arbitration Hearing, 1 June 1921, p. 207, ANUA E138/18/6.

55 Higgins' Judgment, Archer Case, 1919, p. 3, ANUA E138/18/8; 1922 Arbitration Hearing, p. 5, ANUA E138/18/86; evidence Joseph Morris, 1922 Arbitration Hearing, ANUA E138/18/2.

56 Clause 82 of union's claim, 1922 Arbitration Case, ANUA E138/18/86; also 1921 Arbitration Hearing, p. 207, ANUA E138/18/6.

57 1927 Arbitration Hearing, pp. 1949–2730, ANUA E138/18/26.

58 Evidence H. Carter, *ibid.*, p. 1941.

59 Evidence to 1935 Select Committee on the Working Week, pp. 728–9.

60 'Opinion A. R. Wallis on 1935 Strike', CTU file on 'Strikes and Disputes', MUA.

61 Frances, 'Politics of Work', pp. 481–97.

62 Evidence A. R. Wallis, 1937 Outwork Hearing, p. 1, ANUA E138/18/69. See also *CAR*, vol. 26, 1928, p. 90.

63 CIFR, 1928, 1929.

64 Minutes Federal Council, May 1937, p. 271, MUA.

65 *Ibid.*

66 CTU Minutes, 19 October 1940, MUA.

67 *Ibid.*, 1934–38; CTU Circular re meeting, 21 January 1936, CTU file, 'Circulars and Special Meetings', MUA; *Star*, 17 December 1935 (clipping in CTU file, 'Newspaper Cuttings', MUA).

68 Report E. Smith on 1935 Organising Campaign, p. 5, ANUA E138/18/93.

69 Evidence Law, 1927 Arbitration Hearing, p. 4125, ANUA E138/18/28.

70 *Ibid.*, p. 4143.

71 *Ibid.*, p. 4125.

72 *Ibid.*, passim.

73 *Ibid.*, pp. 4126–9.

74 *Ibid.*, p. 4134.

75 CTU Minutes (Special Meeting of Cutters), 21 July 1937, MUA.

76 Evidence Samuel Frieze, 1927 Arbitration Hearing, p. 2929, ANUA E138/18/26.

77 Heagney, *Are Women . . .* , p. 43; also 1935 Select Committee on Working Week, ANUA E138/18/84; *AM*, 15 December 1923, p. 20. See also L. Lampere, 'Fighting the piece-rate system: new dimensions of an old struggle in the apparel industry', in A. Zimbalist (ed.), *Case Studies in the Labor Process*, New York, 1979, p. 263, for a discussion of the importance of feeding attachments in sewing innovation.

78 Report by Union Special Machine Company to 1935 Select Committee on Working Week, 1 October 1935, ANUA E138/18/84.

79 Evidence J. D. Sutcliffe to 1946 ACTU 40 Hour Week Federal Arbitration Hearing, *PTJ*, June 1946, p. 63.

80 1935 Select Committee on Working Week, *ibid.*

81 White, *Golden Thread*, p. 27, claims that Lucas' factory was the first to introduce these machines from Europe in 1929.

82 Report of Union Special Machine Company to 1935 Select Committee on Working Week.

83 See CTU file, 'Strikes and Disputes, 1916–35', MUA; also testimony of Mrs Ruth Haynes, Collingwood History Committee, *In Those Days: Collingwood Remembered*, Richmond, 1979, p. 31.

Chapter 8:
The Cinderella of the skilled trades

1 *Unity*, 14 October 1939, p. 2; 14 March 1939, p. 3; also 14 July 1937, p. 5.

2 *ALJ*, 15 August 1910, p. 203.

3 *Ibid.*

4 *Ibid.*, pp. 198–200.

5   *Ibid.*, p. 203.

6   *Ibid.*, 16 March 1931, p. 907.

7   Phrase used by the editor of *ALJ*, 20 April 1910, p. 687; see also 15 January 1920, p. 608.

8   Higgins expressed the hope that this would be the result of the award: see *ALJ*, 15 August 1910, p. 202.

9   *ALJ*, 15 June 1925, p. 98; Cameron, 'Inquiry', p. 43. For conferences, see *ALJ*, 15 July 1914, p. 152; BM, 20 May 1918, p. 706, ANUA T5/1/11.

10 For details of the industry in the 1920s, see Frances, 'Politics of Work', Ph.D. thesis, pp. 526–7.

11 BM, 8 March 1920, pp. 954–6; 24 March 1920 (Special), ANUA T5/1/12. Also *ALJ*, 15 October 1920, p. 523.

12 *ALJ*, 15 December 1921, p. 682.

13 *Ibid.*, 15 April 1921, p. 1110.

14 *Ibid.*

15 *ALJ*, 16 May 1921, pp. 79-84.

16 Boot Board Minutes, 22 April 1921, VPRS 5467/2; *ALJ*, 16 May 1921, p. 84; 15 June 1921, p. 163.

17 See petition dated 8 July 1921, BBHF, VPRS 5466/11.

18 *ALJ*, 15 July 1922, p. 264.

19 Report on Conference, *ALJ*, 15 March 1923, p. 1048. See also April 1923 – August 1931.

20 For details of the boot industry in the 1930s, see Frances, 'Politics of Work', pp. 527–38.

21 *ALJ*, March 1931 – March 1932; BM (Federal Council), 2 February 1932, p. 64, ANUA T6/1/2; (Special), 8 February 1932, pp. 10–11, T5/1/19. Also Boot Board Minutes, 20 January to 12 May 1932, VPRS 5467/2.

22 BM (Special), 8 February 1932, p. 10, ANUA T5/1/19; Federal Council delegates' report, BM, p. 72, *ibid.*; Federal Council Meeting 2 February 1932, p. 65, T6/1/2; Boot Board Minutes, 10 August, 6 December 1932, VPRS 5467/2. For transcript of proceedings at 1932 Interstate Conference see ANUA T5/3/1. For final agreement, *ALJ*, June–July 1932.

23 Cameron, 'Inquiry', p. 107.

24 Transcript of interview at Carringbush Library. See also Frances, 'Politics of Work', pp. 559–66.

25 BM (Federal Council), 5 December 1929, p. 151, ANUA T6/4/1.

26 Transcript 1932 Interstate Conference, p. 262, ANUA T5/3/1,

27 *ALJ*, 15 November 1935, p. 59; 16 December 1935, p. 28; BM, Verbatim report of Interstate Conference with Employers, October 1935, ANUA T5/3/2.

28 BM (Special Federal Council), May 1935, p. 70, ANUA T5/4.

29 *ALJ*, 15 April 1921, p. 1110. See also Circular Letter, A. Long to Vic. Boot Manufacturers, 7 June 1922, in *ALJ*, 15 July 1922, p. 266.

30 BM, 19 April 1920, pp. 978–80, ANUA T5/1/12; Boot Board Minutes, 24 November 1920, VPRS 5467/2.

31 Proposals for direct action instead of conferences or arbitration received little support, e.g., BM (Special), 8 February 1932, pp. 10–11; 15 July 1932, p. 227, ANUA T5/1/9.

32 See for example Arthur Long's circular letter to every Victorian boot firm, in *ALJ*, 15 July 1922, p. 266. See also Long's remarks at 1932 Interstate Conference, Transcript, p. 263, ANUA T5/3/1.

33 BM (Federal Council), 5 December 1929, p. 153, ANUA T6/4/1.

34 Letter A. Long to C. A. Watts, 15 August 1923, ANUA N41/191. See also circular issued to the trade by Whybrow, *ALJ*, 15 July 1910, pp. 140–2; also BM, 22 August 1910, ANUA T5/1/7.

35 See petition to Sec. for Labour, 8 July 1921, BBHF, VPRS 5466/11.

36 A. Whybrow, 1918 Interstate Tariff Commission, *ALJ*, 15 March 1918, p. 563.

37 Minutes 1932 Interstate Conference, p. 238, ANUA T5/3/1.

38 *ALJ*, 15 October 1910, p. 326

39 *Ibid.*, 15 June 1925, p. 114.

40 BM (Federal Council), 5 December 1929, p. 153, ANUA T6/4/1.

41 *ALJ*, 15 June 1932, p. 98.

42 For details, see Frances, 'Politics of Work', p. 558.

43 *ALJ*, 16 May 1921, p. 83.

44 Letter A. Long to C. A. Watts, 22 May 1923, ANUA N41/191.

45 1938 Arbitration Hearing, *ALJ*, 15 July 1938, p. 15. See also G. Salfinger, *ibid.*, p. 16.

46 *Unity*, 14 October 1938, p. 2.

47 *ALJ*, April–July 1911, December 1921; BM, 15 February, 3 March 1911, ANUA T5/2/4; 16 May 1910, 20 February, 7 August 1911, T5/1/7.

48 Boot Board Determination, November 1911, *VGG*, 11 November 1911, p. 5490; *ALJ*, 15 September 1914, p. 260.

49 e.g. BM, April–July 1931, ANUA T5/2/18; 27 April 1926, T5/1/14; 8 November 1922, T5/2/9; 12 April 1926 (Federal Management Committee), T6/4/1. See also 6 February 1929, T5/2/16; 22 August 1932, T5/1/19; 1932 Interstate Conference, esp. p. 241, T5/3/1. See also BBHF, 'Slipper Manufacturing', VPRS 5466/11; Boot Board Minutes, 15, 29 April 1926, VPRS 5467/2; *ALJ*, 15 June 1931, pp. 174–5.

50 Appendix, Figure A9 shows the steady increase in slipper production from 212,582 pairs in 1917 to 3,430,800 pairs in 1934.

51 *ALJ*, 15 June 1932, p. 98.

52 J. Maloney, 1938 Arbitration Hearing, *ALJ*, 15 June 1938, p. 18; *Unity*, 14 June 1938, p. 7, pointed out that advertisements for male bootworkers called for expertise in several different operations. See also *ALJ*, 15 May 1925, p. 32.

53 *Capital*, vol. 1, Harmondsworth, 1976, pp. 614–19.

54 For the Victorian manufacturers' views, see *ALJ* interview with T. Y. Harkness, 15 August 1910, p. 203.

55 *ALJ*, 15 February 1937, p. 16.

56 *Ibid.*, 15 September 1919, p. 342.

57 20 April 1911, p. 687.

58 This clause was repealed under the 1932 agreement, *ALJ*, 15 July 1932, p. 227.

59 Letter A. Long to C. A. Watts, 22 May 1923, ANUA N41/191.

60 *ALJ*, 15 May 1920, p. 69; 16 August 1920, p. 339 (Curlewis); for Beeby, see *Unity*, 14 October 1938, p. 10.

61 *ALJ*, 15 June 1926, p. 118.

62 Cameron, 'Inquiry', p. 108.

63 This is my own deduction. Neither the Wages Board nor union records state how the amount of 27s 6d was arrived at as the union's claim.

64 The above account is based on proceedings of the Wages Board, Boot Board Minutes, 24 October 1912 to 25 November 1912, VPRS 5467/2.

65 *ALJ*, 15 September 1914, p. 257.

66 Heagney, *Are Women . . .* , pp. 30–9.

67 *ALJ*, 16 August 1920, p. 339.

68 *Ibid.*, also 15 May 1920, p. 69.

69 *Ibid.*, 15 January 1921, p. 838.

70 See Frances, 'Politics of Work', pp. 544–5.

71 Rules of Victorian Branch of ABTEF, 1912–1939, ANUA N41/211.

72 e.g. BM, 19 April 1920, p. 978, ANUA T5/1/12.

73 BM, 1910–11.

74 *ALJ*, 15 December 1921, p. 680. See also BM, 2 August 1911, ANUA T5/2/4; 7 August 1911, T5/1/7.

75 Letter A. Long to C. A. Watts, 22 May 1923, ANUA N41/191. See also report of women's meeting, 3 July 1922, T5/1/12.

76 BM, 26 June 1922, pp. 1381–2, ANUA T5/1/2.

77 Proposals to appoint a paid female organiser were rejected: BM, 29 September 1913, ANUA T5/1/8; 10 October 1913, T5/2/6; (Federal Council), 1 May 1916, T6/1/1; 9 August 1918, T6/5; 1 March 1934, T6/1/2.

78 He told the Interstate Conference in 1932 that because of his efforts 'the organisation is 100 per cent'. The 'organisation' obviously did not include women workers, about half of whom were not members: Transcript, 1932 Conference, T5/3/1. For description of his early organising methods, see BM, (Special Council), May 1935, p. 119, T5/4; 10 June 1935, T5/1/22; Unity, 14 March 1939, p. 3.

79 Unity, 14 April 1937, p. 6.

80 See Labor Call, 1 June 1911, p. 1, report of Long's intention to hold monthly meetings for females. There is no record of these meetings if they in fact eventuated.

81 e.g. BM (Special General), 25 January 1932, ANUA T5/1/19.

82 Ibid., 25 June 1922, ANUA T5/1/12.

83 BM, 1921–34.

84 ALJ, 16 February 1920, p. 750; Rimmer, 'Boots and Shoes'. Re concentration of boot industry, see T. Richards, 1935 Select Committee on Working Week.

85 BM, 8 August 1921, ANUA T5/1/12.

86 BM, 26 June 1922, ANUA T5/1/12, pp. 1381–2. See also Special Meeting of Females, 19 October 1927, T5/2/14.

87 Transcript of interview, Carringbush Library.

88 e.g. BM, 1913–39, ANUA T5.

89 ALJ, 15 June 1931, pp. 174–5.

90 BM, 1910–36, ANUA T5. Also letter A. Long to C. A. Wickens, 16 September 1929, ANUA N41/197; ALJ, 15 June 1910, p. 73.

91 BM, 26 June 1922, ANUA T5/1/2. See also Johnstone's comments, ALJ, 15 December 1921, p. 680.

92 BM, 14 July 1916, ANUA T5/2/7; 17 July 1916, T5/1/10.

93 J. E. Ager, 1935 Interstate Conference, p. 61, ANUA T5/3/2. See also Salfinger's remarks, ibid., p. 76.

94 Sheehan, closing address, 1938 Arbitration Hearing, ALJ, 15 July 1938, p. 22.

95 Cameron, 'Inquiry', pp. 131–40, esp. p. 138.

96 Richards, 1935 Select Committee on Working Week, Australasian Footwear, 31 October 1935.

97 ALJ, 16 December 1935, p. 28; Transcript 1935 Interstate Conference, p. 18, ANUA T5/3/2.

98 ALJ, 1933–39; BM, 23 August 1939, ANUA T5/2/23; 25 January 1933, T5/2/20; Unity, 14 August 1938, p. 13.

99 ALJ, 15 October 1935, p. 69. BM, 1935 Interstate Conference, p. 7, ANUA T5/3/2.

100 ALJ, 15 October 1935, p. 69.

101 See Unity, 14 October 1938, p. 2.

102 Unity, 14 May 1937, p. 2.

103 BM, 6 October 1935, p. 130, ANUA T6/1/2. See also Frances, 'The Politics of Work', p. 608, fn. 121.

104 e.g. Women's ALP Conference, BM, 13 February 1935, T5/2/22;

105 Ibid., 15 July 1935, T5/1/22; Also 23 March 1936, T5/1/23; Unity, 15 June 1950, p. 16.

106 BM, 31 July 1935, T5/2/22; 8 June 1936, 20 July 1936, T5/1/23.

107 ALJ, 15 April 1936, p. 61.

108 Ibid.; also employers' advocate's address to 1938 Arbitration Hearing, ibid.

109 *ALJ*, 15 July 1938, p. 16.
110 *Unity*, 14 October 1938, p. 3; *ALJ*, 15 February 1937, p. 15.
111 BM, February–March 1937, ANUA T5/1/24. See also *ALJ*, 15 February 1937, p. 65; *Unity*, 14 July 1937, p. 5.
112 *ALJ*, 15 June 1938, p. 12; *Unity*, 14 April 1937, p. 6.
113 Judgment, 1938 Boot Case; *Unity*, 14 October 1938, p. 6.
114 Judgment, 1909 Boot Case, pp. 9–11.
115 *Unity*, 14 October 1938, p. 6.
116 *Ibid.*
117 *Ibid.*
118 *Ibid.*; Judgment, 1938 Boot Case.
119 *Unity*, 14 October 1938, pp. 8–9, 14–16.
120 BM, 10 October 1938, ANUA T5/1/25.
121 See Clauses 5(v) and (w), 1938 Award, *Unity*, 14 October 1938, p. 15.
122 *Unity*, 14 July 1938, p. 11.
123 Judgment, *Unity*, 14 October 1938, p. 10.
124 *Ibid.*
125 *Ibid.*

Chapter 9:
Marginal matters

1 'Doing Time', p. 182.
2 *PTJ*, 10 November 1936, p. 200; 'Bookbinding Process and Line of Demarcation', Printers' File.
3 *ALJ*, 15 September 1928, p. 406; *PTJ*, 12 October 1927, p. 225.
4 See Hagan, *Printers and Politics*, pp. 231–5, for the background to this approach.
5 Minutes of the Victorian branch of the PIEUA, Special Board Meeting, 26 November 1923; Women and Girls' Advisory Committee Meeting, n.d. (late 1923).
6 Bennett, 'Job Classification'; also Carol O'Donnell, *The Basis of the Bargain*, Sydney, 1984.
7 Printing and Allied Trades Employers Federation versus Printing Industries Employees Union of Australia, Commonwealth Court of Conciliation and Arbitration, December 1937, transcript, p. 2, PKIU Archives, Melbourne; also *PTJ*, January 1937, pp. 6–7.
8 *PTJ*, September 1939, p. 206. For discussion of the issue, see *PTJ*, December 1938, pp. 209–10; PM (Board), 13 November 1933; 8 April 1935; 10 March 1937.
9 Report of Federal Council Meeting, Sydney, 5–9 December 1938, *PTJ*, December 1938, p. 209.
10 PM (Board), 14 September, 12 October, 9 November 1931; (Executive), 19, 26 October, 2 November 1931.
11 Testimony of Mr Smith, PM (Executive), 26 October 1931.
12 Report first Annual Conference of Victorian Branch of the PIEUA, *PTJ*, April 1929, p. 75.
13 *PTJ*, 14 January 1936, p. 1.
14 *PTJ*, 13 October 1925, p. 220a.
15 Higgins, *New Province*, p. 6.
16 See Judge C. J. Dethridge's comments, *PTJ*, 12 May 1936, p. 83.
17 In some cases the two were combined, with evidence given on the job, e.g. *PTJ*, 14 July 1925, p. 145.
18 J. Hutson, *Six Wage Concepts*, AEU, 1971, pp. 213–31.
19 'Constructions of Skill', pp. 120–1.
20 e.g. Webb's comments in 1925 Judgment, *PTJ*, 12 May 1925, p. 84. Re training period, *PTJ*, 10 November 1936, p. 199.
21 *PTJ*, 12 May 1925, p. 84.

22   See Dethridge's comments re carton cutting, *PTJ*, 14 July 1925, p. 151. For general analysis of the secondary wage in the Arbitration Court, see Anderson, *Fixation of Wages*; R. O'Dea, *Principles of Wage Determination in Commonwealth Arbitration*, Sydney, 1969, ch. 9.

23   See, for example, 1936 Arbitration Hearing, *PTJ*, 10 November 1936, p. 195; also 14 July 1925, p. 145.

24   *PTJ*, 12 May 1936, p. 81–2.

25   *New Province*, pp. 97–8.

26   Half-Yearly Report of Board of Management, 30 June 1925, p. 1; PM (General), 22 August 1925, folio 2. See also PTJ, 12 May 1925, p. 83.

27   *PTJ*, 12 May 1925, p. 84.

28   *Ibid.*; also 12 May 1936, p. 84.

29   *Ibid.*, 14 July 1936, p. 116.

30   Final Judgment on the Metropolitan Commercial Jobbing Award, *PTJ*, 13 October 1925, p. 220a.

31   *Ibid.*

32   *PTJ*, January 1937, pp. 10, 13.

33   Anderson, *Fixation of Wages*, pp. 311–12, 397–9.

34   *Ibid.*

35   *PTJ*, 12 January 1926, p. 45.

36   *Ibid.*, 14 July 1925, pp. 84–5.

37   *Ibid.*, 12 May 1925, pp. 84–5.

38   See Magrath's comments, 1936 Arbitration Hearing, *PTJ*, 12 May 1936, pp. 72, 83. For employers, see p. 83.

39   Final Judgement, Dethridge, *PTJ*, January 1937, p. 3.

40   *PTJ*, 10 November 1936, p. 200.

41   *Ibid.*, 8 September 1925, p. 195.

42   *Ibid.*, 12 May 1936, pp. 72, 83–4.

43   *Ibid.*, p. 194.

44   Quoted in *Ibid.*, 14 July 1936, p. 116.

45   *Ibid.*, 12 May 1936, p. 87.

46   *Ibid.*, 14 July 1936, p. 116.

47   Half-Yearly Report of Board of Management, June 1934, *ibid.*, 14 August 1934, p. 8.

48   'The Construction of Skill', pp. 118–32.

49   Hunt, 'Opportunities lost and gained', pp. 71–93, and chs 3–6 above.

50   *PTJ*, 8 September 1925, p. 197.

51   *Ibid.*, January 1937, pp. 6, 15; also 13 January 1926, p. 118.

52   Higgins' Judgment, 1919 Archer Case, ANUA E138/18/5.

53   For discussion on this point before the Full Bench, see *PTJ*, 8 November 1927, pp. 257–9.

54   See Magrath's comments, *PTJ*, 8 November 1927, p. 261, where he quotes Higgins' judgement in the Clothing Trades Case.

55   *PTJ*, 6 January 1928, pp. 6–14.

56   PM (Board), 14 May 1934.

57   *PTJ*, January 1937, pp. 6, 15; 12 January 1926, p. 45; 8 September 1925, p. 197.

58   *Ibid.*, 8 September 1925, p. 194.

59   Half-Yearly Report Board of Management, 31 December 1925, p. 1; PM (General), 20 February 1926, Folio 2.

60   Half-Yearly Report Board of Management, 30 June 1934, *PTJ*, 14 August 1934, p. 8; PM (Board), 1927–35; *PTJ*, 1927–34.

61   *PTJ*, January 1937, pp. 6–7.

62   Half-Yearly Report Board of Management, June 1925, p. 2; PM (General), 22 August 1925, folio 3.

Conclusion

1 'Taylorism, responsible autonomy and management strategy', in Wood (ed.), *The Degradation of Work?*, p. 89.
2 Thompson, *The Nature of Work*, p. 118.
3 *The Nature of Work*, p. 124.
4 P. Corrigan, H. Ramsay and D. Sayer, *Socialist Construction and Marxist Theory: Bolshevism and its Critique*, London, 1978, pp. 42, 44, 55, 62, 75, for the use of Taylorism by the Bolsheviks in the USSR between the wars.
5 M. Davis, 'The Stop Watch and the Wooden Shoe: Scientific Management and the Industrial Workers of the World', *Radical America*, vol. 8, no. 6, 1975, pp. 69–94, discusses the IWW's position on this point. Brodney's politics were rather idiosyncratic. However, she consistently opposed scientific management from her first encounter with a 'machine telltale' before World War I to the 1950s when she gave a radio talk on the subject. See Brodney Papers, LTL.

Bibliography of works cited

Primary Sources

Newspapers

Advance Australia; Age; Argus; Australasian; Australasian Footwear; Australasian Manufacturer (known as *Australian Manufacturer* prior to August 1917); *Australasian Printer; Australia Today; Australian Store-keepers' Journal; Australian Town and Country Journal; Australasian Trade Review and Manufacturers Journal; Australasian Typographical Journal; Australian Leather Journal; Bendigo Advertiser; Clothing Trades Gazette; Australian Clothing Trades Journal; Common Cause; Illustrated Australian News; Internationalist; Journal of Commerce of Victoria and Melbourne; Labor Call; Leader; Liberty and Progress; New Idea; Printing Trades Journal; Punch; Socialist; Tocsin; Unity* (official organ of Australian Boot Trade Employees Federation); *Voice* of the Australian Clothing Trades Union; *Weekly Times; Woman Today; Woman Voter; Australian Woman's Sphere; Workers Voice; Working Woman; Woman's Clarion; Woman's World.*

Official publications

Commonwealth Government

Commonwealth Yearbooks, 1901–39.
Census of Commonwealth of Australia, 1911, 1921, 1933.

Victorian Government

Annual Reports of Chief Inspector of Factories, *VPP*, 1886–1940.
Marzorin, F. A., *The Law Relating to Factories and Shops and Other Industrial Matters in Victoria*, Department of Labour, 1939.
Murphy, H. M., *The Law Relating to Factories, Workrooms and Shops in Victoria*, 1911.

Murphy, H. M., *Wages and Prices in Australia*, 1917.

'Report on Conference between Legislative Council and Legislative Assembly regarding Shops and Factories Bill', *VPP*, 1899–1900, vol. 1, p. 362.

Summary of Wages and Conditions fixed by Wages Boards or by Courts of Industrial Appeals to 1st October 1925.

Victorian Government Gazette, 1896–1939.

Victorian Parliamentary Debates, 1880–1940.

Victorian Statistical Registers, Production, 1880–1939.

Victorian Yearbooks, 1880–1940.

Official inquiries

Dalton, R. W., *Report on Economic and Commercial Conditions in Australia to October 1936*, London 1937 (for British Department of Overseas Trade).

Report on Victorian Apprenticeship Conference, 1907.

Aves, Ernest, *Report to the Secretary for the Home Department on the Wages Boards and Conciliation and Arbitration Acts of Australia and New Zealand*, London, 1908.

Board of Inquiry into Working Men's College: Report and Evidence, *VPP*, 1910, no. 60, vol. 3, and 1911, no. 14, vol. 2.

Inquiry into Sweating, *VPP*, 1890, vol. 3, no. 138.

Board of Inquiry into the Effect of the Fiscal System of Victoria upon industry and production, *VPP*, 1894, no. 37; 1895–6, vol. 2, no. 3.

Minutes of Evidence and Reports of Board of Inquiry into the working of the 'Factories and Shops Act 1890' . . ., *VPP*, 1893, vol. 2, no. 47; 1894, vol. 1, no. 12 (Reports); 1895–6, vol. 3, no. 44 (Evidence).

Report of the Public Service Board of New South Wales on the General Working of the State Clothing Factory, with Minutes of Evidence, *New South Wales Parliamentary Papers*, 1905, vol. 2, no. 3.

Royal Commission on Factories Act, Minutes of Evidence, *VPP*, vol. 2, no. 18, 1884.

Royal Commission on the Tariff, Minutes of Evidence, *VPP*, vol. 4, no. 50, 1883.

Royal Commission on Technical Education, *VPP*, 1899–1900, vol. 4, no. 34 (Progress Report); no. 51 (Second Progress Report and Digest of Evidence).

Select Committee of the Legislative Assembly into the Working Week, Unemployment Insurance and other Industrial Matters, Clothing Trades Union Deposit, ANUA E138/18/84; also *VPP*, 1935, vol. 1.

Select Committee of the Legislative Council Inquiring into the Alleged Sweating Evil, *South Australian Parliamentary Papers*, 1904, vol. 2, no. 71, p. 147.

Royal Commission on the High Cost of Living: Report with Appendices, *VPP*, 1923–24, no. 38, vol. 2; 1924, nos. 3, 4 and 6, vol. 1.

Royal Commission on the operation of the Factories and Shops Law of Victoria: Reports with minutes of evidence and appendices, *VPP*, 1901, no. 35, vol. 3; 1902–03, no. 30 and no. 31, vol. 2.

Royal Commission on National Insurance 1926–27. Minutes of Evidence: Unemployment, Distribution Allowances, 1928 (held at PKIU archives, Melbourne).

Ireland, M. B., *Survey of Women in Industry*, Victoria, 1928, Canberra, 1928.

Commonwealth Arbitration records

Application for Revision of the Basic Wage, Commonwealth Court of Conciliation and Arbitration, 10 May 1937, prepared by Muriel Heagney, Riley Papers, Ms. A3222, Mitchell Library.

Commonwealth Arbitration Reports, 1910–40.

Transcripts of evidence of cases brought before the CCCA by Clothing Trades Union, 1919–40, Clothing Trades Union Deposit, ANUA E138/18, ANU Archives of Business and Labour.

Sheehan, P. J, *Bulletin of Proceedings of Commonwealth Arbitration Court*, vol. 1–13, 1927–39.

Printing and Allied Trades Employers Federation v. Printing Industry Employees Union of Australia, CCCA, December 1937, Award and Transcript of evidence, Printing and Kindred Industries Union Archives, Melbourne.

Wages Board records

Papers relating to the operation of the Shops and Factories Acts, VPRS 1373; 5998; 5999; 5466; 5467; 1399.

Non-official enquiries

Cameron, Roy, 'An Economic Investigation and Tariff Study of the Australian Boot and Shoe Manufacturing Industry with Special Reference to Victoria', M.A. Thesis, University of Western Australia, 1936.

Cuthbertson, M., and McGowan, H., *Woman's Work*, Melbourne, 1913.

Heagney, Muriel, *Are Women Taking Men's Jobs? A Survey of Women's Work in Victoria with Special Regard to Equal Status, Equal Pay and Equality of Opportunity*, Melbourne, 1935.

Osborne, Ethel E., 'Report on Enquiry into the Conditions of Employment of Women Workers in the Clothing Trade', Melbourne, 1919.

——, *Report on an Enquiry into the Conditions of Employment as Regards the Health of Female Workers in the Printing and Allied Trades*, Melbourne, 1924.

Employer records

ANU Archives of Business and Labour: Bedggood and Company Pty Ltd; Paddle Brothers Pty Ltd; Paterson, Laing and Bruce Ltd; The Leviathan Ltd.

Melbourne University Archives: Foy and Gibson Pty Ltd, Melbourne.

Trade union records

The bulk of the records of the various clothing and boot trades unions are held at the ANU Archives of Business and Labour. The University of Melbourne Archives also has a large deposit of records of the Victorian branch of the Clothing Trades Union. Printing industry union records are held at Printing and Kindred Industries Union Archives, Melbourne. In all cases the holdings include minutes, letterbooks, financial records, printed journals and circulars and papers relating to arbitration and Wages Board hearings.

General union records include: Minutes of 1913 Women's Industrial Convention, Melbourne, held at MUA.

Melbourne Trades Hall Council, Minutes, 1880–1940, Ms. 7825, LTL.

Private papers

La Trobe Library, Melbourne

Anti-Sweating League of Victoria, Industry reports and correspondence, 1932–47; Brodney (May and Bob) Papers: photographs, autobiographical notes, ephemera, correspondence; Heagney (Muriel) Papers: Correspondence and miscellaneous papers relating to Muriel Heagney's involvement with the Clothing Trades Union; Merrifield (Sam) Collection: subject files and tapes relating to Victorian labour movement; Walker (Bertha) Collection: autobiographical manuscript and correspondence; Sidney and Beatrice Webb Biography File.

Australian National Library

Mauger (Samuel) Collection: Minutes of the first Victorian Anti-Sweating League.

Oral sources

Brodney, May, interviewed by Sam Merrifield, November 1962; Tape in Merrifield Collection, LTL.

Interviewed by Raelene Frances: May Hansford; Olga Anderson, 1982–85; transcripts in possession of author.

Collingwood History Committee, *In Those Days: Collingwood Remembered*, Melbourne, 1979 (a collection of edited interviews).

Koops, Daisy, interviewed by her daughter; transcript at Carringbush Library, Richmond.

Interviewed by Kay Hopwood, 1984: Alice Barker; Louisa O'Neil; Phyllis Tucker; Dorothy White; tapes in Melbourne University Archives.

Contemporary books

Anderson, George, *Fixation of Wages in Australia*, Melbourne, 1929.

Babbage, C., *On the Economy of Machinery and Manufactures*, Fairfield, 1971 (first published 1835).

Central Committee, Women's Department, Communist Party of Australia, *Women in Australia from Factory, Farm and Kitchen*, Sydney, 1933.

Coghlan, T. A., *Labour and Industry in Australia*, 4 vols, Oxford 1918 (reissued Melbourne, 1969).

Copland, D. A., *Australia in the World Crisis*, Cambridge, 1934.

Cuthbertson, M. G., and McGowan, H., *Woman's Work*, Melbourne, 1913.

Harford, Lesbia, *The Poems of Lesbia Harford* (edited by Nettie Palmer), Melbourne, 1971.

Higgins, H. B., *A New Province for Law and Order*, Sydney, 1922.

McDonald, J. R. (ed.), *Women in the Printing Trades: a Sociological Study*, London, 1904.

Marx, Karl, *Capital*, vol. I, with appendix, 'Results of the immediate process of production', Harmondsworth, 1976; vol. III, London, 1972.

Marshall, Alan, *How Beautiful Are Thy Feet*, Melbourne 1972 (first published 1949).

Militant Women's Group, *Woman's Road to Freedom*, Sydney, 1927.

Pratt, A., *The National Handbook of Australia's Industries*, Melbourne, 1934.

Reeves, W. Pember, *State Experiments in Australia and New Zealand*, reissued Australia 1969 (first published 1911).

Schloss, D. F. (ed.), *Methods of Industrial Remuneration*, London, 1898.

Smith, J. (ed.), *The Cyclopedia of Victoria*, 3 vols, Melbourne, 1904.

Sutherland, A., *Victoria and Its Metropolis*, Melbourne, 1888.

Taylor, F. W., *Principles of Scientific Management*, New York, 1947.

——, *Two Papers on Scientific Management: A Piece-Rate System; Notes on Belting*, London, 1919.

Ure, Andrew, *The Philosophy of Manufactures*, London, 1835 (reprinted New York, 1963).

Contemporary articles

Anon., 'The Economic Woman', *Australian National Review*, July 1938.

Cameron, R. F., The Victorian boot and shoe industry', *Economic Record*, vol. 13, 1937, pp. 31–46.

Daley, Jean, 'The trade union woman', in Frances Fraser and Nettie Palmer (eds), *Centenary Gift Book*, Melbourne, 1934, pp. 131–2.

Davis, Helen, 'Our Australian factory worker', *New Idea*, 1 March 1903.

Beeby, G. S. 'The artificial regulation of wages in Australia', *Economic Journal*, XXV, 1949, pp. 321–8.

Collett, C. E. 'Wages Boards in Victoria', *Economic Journal*, XI, 1901, pp. 557–65.

Collier, P. S., 'Minimum wage legislation in Australia', *Monthly Labor Review*, September 1916, pp. 353–9.

Gough, G. W., 'The Wages Boards of Victoria', *Economic Journal*, XV, 1905, pp. 361–73.

Hammond, M. B., 'Wages Boards in Australia', *Quarterly Journal of Economics*, no. 29, 1914, pp. 98–148, 338–61.

Marshall, Alan, 'Boot Factory', in *The Complete Stories of Alan Marshall*, West Melbourne, 1977, pp. 164–7.

Mauldon, F. R. E., 'Cooperation and welfare in industry', in D. A. Copland (ed.), *An Economic Survey of Australia*, Philadelphia, 1931, pp. 183–92.

Murphy, W. E. 'Victoria', in J. Norton (ed.), *The History of Capital and Labour in All Lands and All Ages . . .*, Sydney and Melbourne, 1888.

Thompson, C. B., 'Scientific Management in Practice', *Quarterly Journal of Economics*, November 1914, pp. 262–307.

Trescowthick, C., 'Victoria's shoe trade history', *Australian Leather Journal*, 15 September 1933.

Whitlam, A. G., 'Marketing organisation', in D. A. Copland (ed.), *An Economic Survey of Australia*, Philadelphia, 1931, pp. 111–18.

Wood, G. L., 'Growth of population and immigration policy', in D. A. Copland (ed.), *An Economic Survey of Australia*, Philadelphia, 1931, pp. 9–17.

Young, A., 'Increasing returns and economic progress', *Economic Journal*, XXXVIII, 1928, pp. 527–42.

Secondary sources

Books

The literature relating to work process is too voluminous to cite in its entirety here. I have restricted this bibliography to works actually cited in the text. For a fuller listing see Frances, 'The Politics of Work', Ph.D. thesis, Monash University, 1989.

Amsden, Alice (ed.), *The Economics of Women and Work*, New York, 1979.

Barrett, Bernard, *The Inner Suburbs: The Evolution of an Industrial Area*, Melbourne, 1971.

Beechey, Veronica, *Unequal Work*, London, 1987.

Berg, M. (ed.), *Technology and Toil in Nineteenth-century Britain*, London, 1979.

Bevege, M., James, M., and Shute, C. (eds), *Worth Her Salt: Women at Work in Australia*, Sydney, 1982.

Beynon, H., *Working for Ford*, Harmondsworth, 1973

——, *Born to Work*, London, 1982.

Blake, L. J. (ed.), *Vision and Realisation: Centenary History of State Education in Victoria*, Melbourne, 1971.

Blythell, Duncan, *The Sweated Trades*, New York, 1978.

Boehm, E. A., *Prosperity and Depression in Australia*, Oxford, 1971.

——, *Twentieth-century Economic Development in Australia*, 2nd edn, Melbourne, 1979.

Briggs, A., *Victorian Cities*, London, 1964, ch. 7.

Braverman, Harry, *Labor and Monopoly Capital: The Degradation of Work in the Twentieth Century*, New York, 1974.

Burawoy, M., *Manufacturing Consent*, Chicago, 1979.

Burman, S. (ed.), *Fit Work for Women*, London, 1979.

Burton, Clare, *The Promise and the Price*, Sydney, 1991.

Butlin, N. G., *Australian Domestic Product Investment and Foreign Borrowing 1861-1938/9*, Cambridge, 1962.

———, *Investment in Australian Economic Development 1861-1938/9*, Cambridge, 1964.

Cantor, Milton, and Laurie, Bruce (eds), *Class, Sex and the Woman Worker*, Westport, 1977.

Cavendish, R., *Women on the Line*, London, 1982.

Child, J., *Industrial Relations in the British Printing Industry*, London, 1967.

Cochrane, Peter, *Industrialisation and Dependence: Australia's Road to Economic Development 1870-1939*, Brisbane, 1980.

Cockburn, Cynthia, *Brothers: Male Dominance and Technological Change*, London, 1983.

Cole, G. D. H., *The Payment of Wages*, London, 1928.

Conference of Socialist Economists (eds), *The Labour Process and Class Strategies*, London, 1976.

Connell, R.W. and Irving, T., *Class Structure in Australian History: Documents, Narrative and Argument*, Melbourne, 1980.

Corrigan, P., Ramsay, H., and Sayer, D., *Socialist Construction and Marxist Theory: Bolshevism and its Critique*, London, 1978.

Curthoys, A., Spearritt, P., and Eade, S. (eds), *Women and Work*, Canberra, 1975.

Davison, Graeme, *The Rise and Fall of Marvellous Melbourne*, Melbourne, 1978.

Doeringer, P. and Piore, M., *Internal Labor Markets and Manpower Analysis*, Lexington, Mass., 1971.

Edwards, Richard, *Contested Terrain: the Transformation of the Workplace in the Twentieth Century*, New York, 1979.

Edwards, R., Reich, M., and Gordon, D. (eds), *Labor Market Segmentation*, Lexington, Mass., 1975.

———, *Segmented Work, Divided Workers: The Historical Transformation of Labor in the United States*, Cambridge, 1982.

Ellem, B. *In Women's Hands? A History of Clothing Trade Unionism in Australia*, Sydney, 1989.

Fitzgerald, R. T., *The Printers of Melbourne: The History of a Union*, Melbourne, 1967.

Fitzpatrick, B., *The British Empire in Australia 1887-1897*, Melbourne, 1949.

Fletcher, Marion, *Costume in Australia 1788-1901*, Melbourne, 1984.

Foenander, O. de R., *Studies in Australian Labour Laws and Relations*, Melbourne, 1952.

Forster, C., *Industrial Development in Australia 1920-1930*, Canberra, 1964.

Forster, C. (ed.), *Australian Economic Development in the Twentieth Century*, London, 1970.

Fox, A., *A History of the National Union of Boot and Shoe Operatives*, Oxford, 1958.

Frances, R. and Scates, B. (eds), *Women, Work and the Labour Movement in Australia and Aotearoa/New Zealand*, Sydney, 1991.

Friedman, A., *Industry and Labour*, London, 1977.

Friedmann, G., *The Anatomy of Work*, London, 1961.

Habakkuk, H. J., *American and British Technology in the Nineteenth Century*, Cambridge, 1967.

Hicks, N., *'This Sin and Scandal': Australia's Population Debate 1891-1911*, Canberra, 1978.

Game, Anne, and Pringle, Rosemary, *Gender at Work*, Sydney, 1983.

Giddens, A., *The Class Structure of the Advanced Societies*, London, 1973.

Gmarnikow, *et. al.* (eds), *Gender, Class and Work*, London, 1983.

Gollan, Robin, *Radical and Working-class Politics*, Melbourne, 1960.

Gorz, A. (ed.), *Strategy for Labour*, Brighton, 1967.

———, *The Division of Labour*, Brighton, 1976.

Hagan, J., *Printers and Politics: A History of the Australian Printing Unions 1850-1950*, Canberra, 1966.

Hall, A. R., *The Stock Exchange of Melbourne and the Victorian Economy 1852-1900*, Canberra, 1968.

———, *The London Capital Market and Australia 1870-1914*, Canberra, 1963.

Hungerford, T. A. G., *Stories from Suburban Road: An Autobiographical Collection*, Fremantle, 1983.

Hobsbawm, Eric, *Labouring Men: Studies in the History of Labour*, London 1964.

John, Angela (ed.), *Unequal Opportunities: Women's Employment in England 1800-1918*, Oxford, 1986.

Joyce, Patrick, *Work, Society and Politics: The Culture of the Factory in Late Victorian England*, Brighton, 1980.

Joyce, Patrick (ed.), *The Historical Meanings of Work*, Cambridge, 1987.

Kingston, Beverley, *My Wife, My Daughter and Poor Mary Ann: Women and Work in Australia*, West Melbourne, 1975.

Knights, D., Willmott, H., and Collinson, D. (eds), *Job Redesign: critical perspectives on the labour process*, Aldershot, 1985.

Kriegler, Roy J., *Working for the Company: Work and control in the Whyalla Shipyard*, Melbourne, 1980.

Kuhn, Annette, and Wolpe Ann-Marie (eds), *Feminism and Materialism: Women and Modes of Production*, London, 1978.

Lewenhak, Sheila, *Women and Trade Unions*, London, 1977.

Linge, G. J. R., *Industrial Awakening: A Geography of Australian Manufacturing 1788–1890*, Canberra, 1979.

Littler, Craig, *The Development of the Labour Process in Capitalist Societies: A Comparative Analysis of Work and Organisation in Britain, the USA and Japan*, London, 1982.

Lockwood, D., *The Blackcoated Worker*, London, 1958.

McCalman, Janet, *Struggletown: Private and Public Life in Richmond*, Melbourne, 1982.

Macintyre, S., and Mitchell, R. (eds), *Foundations of Arbitration: The Establishment of the Compulsory Arbitration System 1890–1914*, Melbourne, 1989.

McMurchy, Megan, Oliver, Margot, and Thornlay, Jeni, *For Love or Money: A Pictorial History of Women and Work in Australia*, Ringwood, 1983.

Mallet, S., *The New Working Class*, Nottingham, 1974.

Mathews, Jill Julius, *Good and Mad Women: the historical construction of femininity in twentieth century Australia*, Sydney, 1984.

Mathews, John, *Technology, trade unions and the labour process: Deakin University Working Papers in the Social Studies of Science*, no. 1, March 1985.

Mauldon, F. R. E., *Mechanisation in Australian Industries: A Research Monograph*, University of Tasmania, 1968.

Modjeska, Drusilla, and Pizer, Marjorie (eds), *The Poems of Lesbia Harford*, North Ryde, 1985.

More, C., *Skill and the English Working Class 1870–1914*, London, 1980.

Morris, Jenny, *Women Workers and the Sweated Trades*, London, 1985.

Nadworny, M., *Scientific Management and the Unions*, Cambridge, Mass., 1955.

Nevins, A., *Ford: The Times, The Man, The Company*, New York, 1954.

Nichols, T., and Armstrong, P., *Workers Divided*, Glasgow, 1976.

Niland, John, *Collective Bargaining and Compulsory Arbitration in Australia*, Sydney, 1978.

Norton, J. (ed.), *The History of Capital and Labour*, Melbourne, 1988.

Oakley, Ann, *Sex, Gender and Society*, London, 1972.

O'Dea, Raymond, *Principles of Wage Determination in Commonwealth Arbitration*, Sydney, 1969.

O'Donnell, Carol, *The Basis of the Bargain*, Sydney, 1984.

Pahl, R. E., *Divisions of Labour*, Oxford, 1984.

Pahl, R. E. (ed.), *On Work: Historical, Comparative and Theoretical Approaches*, Oxford, 1988.

Patterson, G. D., *The Tariff in the Australian Colonies 1856–1900*, Melbourne, 1968.

Perlman, Mark, *Judges in Industry: A Study of Labour Arbitration in Australia*, Melbourne, 1954.

Phillips, Ann, *Hidden Hands*, London, 1983.

Pinchbeck, Ivy, *Women Workers and the Industrial Revolution 1750–1850*, London, 1936, 1981.

Pollert, Anna, *Girls, Wives, Factory Lives*, London, 1981.

Portus, J. H., *Australian Compulsory Arbitration 1900–1970*, Sydney, 1971.

Price, Richard, *Masters, Unions and Men. Work Control in Building and the Rise of Labour 1830–1914*, Cambridge, 1980.

Probert, Belinda, *Working Life*, Melbourne, 1989.

Reiger, Kerreen, *The Disenchantment of the Home: Modernising the Australian Family 1880–1940*, Melbourne, 1985.

Rickard, John, *Class and Politics: New South Wales, Victoria and the Early Commonwealth, 1890–1910*, Canberra, 1976.

Ryan, Edna, and Conlon, Ann, *Gentle Invaders: Australian Women at Work 1788–1974*, West Melbourne, 1975.

Ryan, Edna, *Two-thirds of a Man: Women and Arbitration in New South Wales, 1902–1908*, Sydney, 1984.

Sabel, Charles F., *Work and Politics: The Division of Labour in Industry*, Cambridge, 1982.

Salaman, G., *Class and the Corporation*, Glasgow, 1981.

Schmiechan, James, *Sweated Industries and Sweated Labour*, London, 1984.

Serle, G., *The Rush to be Rich: A History of the Colony of Victoria 1883–1889*, Melbourne, 1971.

———, *The Golden Age: A History of the Colony of Victoria 1851–1861*, Melbourne, 1971.

Shann, E., *An Economic History of Australia*, Cambridge, 1930.

Shaw, A. G. L., *The Economic Development of Australia*, 5th edn, Croydon, 1986, pp. 109–21.

Sinclair, W. A., *Economic Recovery in Victoria 1894–1899*, Canberra, 1956.

Sohn-Rethel, A., *Intellectual and Manual Labour*, London, 1978.

Storey, J., *The Challenge to Management Control*, London, 1982.

Summers, A., *Damned Whores and God's Police*, Sydney, 1975.

Sutcliffe, J. T., *A History of Trade Unionism in Australia*, Melbourne, 1967.

Thompson, E. P., *The Making of the English Working Class*, Harmondsworth, 1968.

———, *The Poverty of Theory and Other Essays*, London, 1979.

Thompson, Paul, *The Nature of Work: An Introduction to Debates on the Labour Process*, Houndmills and London, 1983.

Turner, I., *Industrial Labour and Politics: The Dynamics of the Labour Movement in Eastern Australia 1900–1921*, Canberra, 1965.

Walker, Bertha, *Solidarity Forever: a part story of the life and times of Percy Laidler—the first quarter of a century*, Melbourne, 1972.

West, Jackie (ed.), *Work, Women and the Labour Market*, London, 1982.

Westwood, Sallie, *All Day Every Day: Factory and Family in the Making of Women's Lives*, London, Sydney, 1984.

White, K., *John Cain and Victorian Labor 1917–1957*, Sydney, 1982.

White, Mollie, *The Golden Thread: the Story of a Fashion House—E. Lucas & Co. Pty. Ltd. 1888–1963*, Melbourne, 1964.

Willis, Evan (ed.), *Technology and the Labour Process: Australian Case Studies*, Sydney, 1988.

Willis, P., *Learning to Labour: How Working-class Kids get Working-class Jobs*, Farnborough, 1977.

Wilkinson, Frank (ed.), *The Dynamics of Labour Market Segmentation*, London, 1981.

Williams, Claire, *Open Cut: The Working Class in an Australian Mining Town*, Sydney, 1981.

Windschuttle, E. (ed.), *Women, Class and History: Feminist Perspectives on Australia, 1788–1978*, Sydney, 1980.

Wood, Stephen (ed.), *The Degradation of Work: Skill, deskilling and the labour process*, London, 1982.

Zimbalist, A. (ed.), *Case Studies in the Labour Process*, New York, 1979.

Articles

Alexander, Sally, 'Women's work in nineteenth-century London: a study of the years 1820–1850', in J. Mitchell and A. Oakley (eds), *The Rights and Wrongs of Women*, Harmondsworth, 1976, pp. 59–111.

———, 'Women, class and sexual differences in the 1830s and 1840s: some reflections on the writing of a feminist history', *History Workshop Journal*, no. 17, Spring 1984, pp. 125–49.

Anthias, Floya, 'Women and the Reserve Army of labour: a critique of Veronica Beechey', *Capital and Class*, no. 10, Spring, 1980, pp. 50–63.

Arndt, H. W., 'External economies in economic growth', *Economic Record*, XXXI, 1955, pp. 166–97.

——, 'The nature-nurture debate in Australia 1900–1914', *Historical Studies*, vol. 19, no. 75, pp. 199–212.

Baron, Ava, 'Questions of Gender: Deskilling and Demasculinization in the US Printing Industry, 1830–1915', *Gender and History*, vol. 1, no. 2, Summer 1989, pp. 178–99.

Baron, Ava, and Klepp, Susan, ' "If I didn't have my sewing machine": women and sewing machine technology', in Jane Jensen and Sue Davidson (eds), *A Needle, a Bobbin, a Strike: Women Needleworkers in America*, Philadelphia, 1984, pp. 20–59.

Barrett, Michelle, and McIntosh, Mary, 'The Family Wage: some problems for socialists and feminists', *Capital and Class*, no. 11, 1980, pp. 51–73.

Barron, R. D., and Norris, G. M., 'Sexual divisions and the dual labour market' in D. Barker and S. L. Allen (eds), *Dependence and Exploitation in Work and Marriage*, London, 1978, pp. 47–69.

Bassett, J., 'Lyla Barnard: Khaki Girl', in M. Lake and F. Kelly (eds), *Double Time*, Ringwood, 1984, pp. 268–75.

Baudouin, T., Collin, M., and Guillerm, D., 'Women and immigrants: marginal workers?' in C. Crouch and A. Pizzorno (eds), *The Resurgence of Class Conflict in Europe since 1968*, vol. 2: *Comparative analysis*, London, 1978, pp. 71–99.

Baxandall, R., Ewen, E., and Gordon, L., 'The working class has two sexes', *Monthly Review*, vol. 28, no. 3, 1976, pp. 1–9.

Beechey, Veronica, 'Some problems in the analysis of female wage labour in the capitalist mode of production', *Capital and Class*, no. 3, Autumn, 1977, pp. 45–66.

——, 'What's so special about women's employment: a review of recent studies of women's paid work', *Feminist Review*, no. 15, Winter 1983, pp. 23–46.

Benjamin, Dorothy, 'The Discrimination Against Women and their Exploitation in the Clothing Trade during the Depression of 1929–1936, and the Police Role of the Victorian Amalgamated Trades Union', *Second Women and Labour Conference Papers*, 1980, vol. 1, pp. 316–26.

Bennett, Laura, 'The construction of skill: craft unions, women workers and the conciliation and arbitration system', *Law in Context*, no. 2, 1984, pp. 118–32.

——, 'Legal intervention and the female workforce: the Conciliation and Arbitration Court 1907–21', *International Journal of the Sociology of Law*, no. 12, 1, February 1984, pp. 23–36.

——, 'Job classification and women workers: institutional practices, technological change and the conciliation and arbitration system 1907–72', *Labour History*, no. 51, November 1986, pp. 11–23.

Benston, Margaret, 'The political economy of women's liberation', *Monthly Review*, no. 21, 1969, pp. 13–28.

Bland, L., *et. al.*, 'Women "inside and outside" the relations of production', in Women's Studies Group Centre for Contemporary Cultural Studies, *Women Take Issue: Aspects of Women's Subordination*, London, 1978, pp. 35–78.

Blau, Francine D., and, Jusenius, Carol L., 'Economists' approaches to sex segregation in the labor market: an appraisal', in Monica Blaxall and Barbara Reagan (eds), *Women and the Workplace*, Chicago, 1975.

Blewett, Mary H., 'Work, gender and the artisan tradition in New England shoemaking, 1780–1860', *Journal of Social History*, vol. 17, no. 2, Winter 1983, pp. 221–48.

Branca, Patricia, 'A new perspective on women's work: a comparative typology', *Journal of Social History*, vol. 9, no. 2, 1975, pp. 129–53.

Braverman, H., 'Two Comments', *Monthly Review*, vol. 28, no. 3, 1976, pp. 119–24.

Brennan, Theresa, 'Women and Work', *Journal of Australian Political Economy*, no. 1, October 1977, pp. 34–52.

Brenner, Johanna, and Ramas, Maria, 'Rethinking women's oppression', *New Left Review*, no. 144, March–April 1984, pp. 33–71.

Brighton Labour Process Group, 'The capitalist labour process', *Capital and Class*, no. 1, Spring 1977, pp. 3–26.

Brooks, Brian, 'Compulsory arbitration versus collective bargaining—the Australian experience', *International Business Lawyer*, vol. 13, March 1971, pp. 104–7.

Brooks, Raymond, 'The Melbourne Tailoresses' Strike 1882–3: An assessment', *Labour History*, no. 44, May 1983, pp. 27–38.

Bruegel, Irene, 'Women's employment legislation and the labour market', in Jane Lewis (ed), *Women's Welfare/Women's Rights*, London, 1983, pp. 130–69.

Buckley, Ken, 'Arbitration—its history and process', *Journal of Industrial Relations*, no. 13, March 1971, pp. 96–103.

Bulbeck, Chilla, 'Manning the machines: women in the furniture industry 1920–1960', *Labour History*, no. 51, November 1986, pp. 24–31.

Burawoy, M., 'Towards a Marxist theory of the labour process', *Politics and Society*, vol. 8, nos. 3–4, 1978, pp. 247–312.

——, 'Terrains of contest: factory and state under capitalism and socialism', *Socialist Review*, (USA), vol. 11, no. 4, 1981.

Butlin, N. G., 'The shape of the Australian Economy 1861–1900', in N. T. Drohan and J. H. Day (eds), *Readings in Australian Economics*, Canberra, 1965, pp. 143–68.

——, 'Some perspectives on Australian economic developments, 1890–1965', in C. Forster (ed.), *Australian Economic Development in the Twentieth Century*, London, 1970, pp. 266–327.

Butlin, N. G. and Dowie, J. A., 'Estimates of Australian workforce and employment 1861–1961', *Australian Economic History Review*, no. 9, 1969, pp. 138–55.

Chan, K., 'The origin of compulsion in Australia: the case of Victoria 1888–1894', *Journal of Industrial Relations*, no. 13, 1971, pp. 155–63.

Cochrane, Peter, 'Doing time', in V. Burgmann and J. Lee (eds), *A People's History of Australia since 1788*, vol. 2: *Making a Life*, Melbourne, 1988, pp. 177–93.

——, 'Company time: management ideology and the labour process: 1940–1960', *Labour History*, no. 48, May 1985, pp. 54–68.

——, 'Job security: the frontier of control', *Arena*, no. 64, 1983, pp. 121–30.

Cockburn, Cynthia, 'The material of male power', *Feminist Review*, no. 9, 1981, pp. 41–58.

Cohen, Jan S., 'Managers and machinery: an analysis of the rise of factory production', *Australian Economic Papers*, vol. 20, June 1981, pp. 24–39.

Cohen, Sheila, 'A labour process to nowhere?', *New Left Review*, no. 165, September–October 1987, pp. 34–51.

Collins, J., 'A divided working class', *Intervention*, no. 8, 1977, pp. 64–78.

Collins, John, 'Fragmentation of the working class', in E. L. Wheelright and K. D. Buckley (eds), *Essays on the Political Economy of Australian Capitalism*, Sydney, 1978, pp. 42–85.

Collins, Jock, 'Marx's reserve army of labour: still relevant 100 years on', *Journal of Australian Political Economy*, no. 16, March 1984, pp. 51–66.

Coombs, R., 'Labour and monopoly capital', *New Left Review*, vol. 107, January–February, 1978, pp. 79–96.

Curthoys, Ann, 'Women—a "reserve army of labour"?', *Refractory Girl*, 13, 1977–78.

——, 'The Sexual Division of Labour under Capitalism', in Norma Grieve and Patricia Grimshaw (eds), *Australian Women: Feminist Perspectives*, Melbourne, 1981, pp. 39–43.

——, 'The sexual division of labour: theoretical arguments', in N. Grieve and A. Burns (eds), *Australian Women: New Feminist Perspectives*, Melbourne, 1986.

Cuthbert, Catharine, 'Lesbia Harford and Marie Pitt: Forgotten Poets', *Hecate*, vol. VIII, no. 1, 1982, pp. 33–48.

Dabscheck, Braham, ' "The typical mother of the White Race", and the origins of female wage determination', *Hecate*, vol. 12, nos. 1–2, 1986.

Davies, Margery, 'Women's place is at the typewriter: the feminization of the clerical labour force', *Radical America*, vol. 8, no. 3, pp. 1–28.

Davies, M., and Brodhead, F., 'Labour and Monopoly Capital: a review', *Radical America*, vol. 9, no. 2, 1975, pp. 79–94.

Davis, M., 'The stop watch and the wooden shoe: scientific management and the Industrial Workers of the World', *Radical America*, vol. 8, no. 6, pp. 69–94.

Deacon, Desley, 'Political arithmetic: the nineteenth-century census and the construction of the dependent woman', *Signs*, vol. 11, no. 1, 1985, pp. 27–47.

Deery, Stephen, 'Dividing and ruling', in V. Burgmann and J. Lee (eds), *A People's History of Australia since 1788*, vol. 2: *Making a Life*, Melbourne, 1988, pp. 304–13.

De Garis, B. K., '1890–1900' in F. Crowley (ed.), *A New History of Australia*, Melbourne, 1971, pp. 216–23.

De Kadt, M., ' "Management and labour" review of Braverman', *Review of Radical Political Economy*, vol. 7, no. 1, 1975, pp. 84–90.

Dex, Shirley, 'Issues of gender and employment', *Social History*, vol. 13, no. 2, May 1988, pp. 141–50.

Dunkerley, David, 'Technological change and work: upgrading or deskilling', in Paul Boneham and Geoff Dow (eds), *Work and Inequality*, vol. 2, Melbourne, 1980, pp. 163–79.

Dunn, Michael, 'The Britannic question: the Empire and the Colonies, 1870–1910', *Bowyang: Work on Changing Australia*, vol. 1, no. 1, March 1979.

Edwards, R., 'The social relations of production in the firm and labor market structure', *Politics and Society*, vol. 5, no. 1, 1975, pp. 83–108.

———, 'Social relations of production at the point of production', *Insurgent Sociologist*, vol. 8, nos. 2–3, 1978.

Ehrenreich, B., and Ehrenreich, J., 'Work and consciousness', *Monthly Review*, vol. 28, no. 3, 1976, pp. 10–18.

Eisenstein, Z., 'Developing a theory of capitalist patriarchy and socialist feminism', in Z. Eisenstein (ed.), *Capitalist Patriarchy and the Case of Socialist Feminism*, London, 1979, pp. 5–40.

Elger, A., 'Valorisation and deskilling—a critique of Braverman', *Capital and Class*, no. 7, Spring 1979, pp. 58–99.

Elger, A., and Schwarz, B., 'Monopoly capitalism and the impact of Taylorism: notes on Lenin, Gramsci, Braverman and Sohn-Rethel', in T. Nichols (ed.), *Capital and Labour: A Marxist Primer*, London, 1980, pp. 358–69.

Feeney, J., and Smart. J., 'Jean Daley and May Brodney: Perspectives on labour', in M. Lake and F. Kelly (eds), *Double Time*, Ringwood, 1984, pp. 276–87.

Fisher, S. H., 'Sydney Women and the Workforce, 1870–1890', in M. Kelly (ed.), *Nineteenth Century Sydney: Essays in Urban History*, Sydney, 1978, pp. 95–105.

Forster, C., 'Economies of scale and Australian manufacturing', in C. Forster (ed.), *Australian Economic Development in the Twentieth Century*, Sydney, 1970, pp. 123–68.

———, 'Australian manufacturing and the war of 1914–18', *Economic Record*, XXIX, 1953, pp. 211–30.

———, 'Australian unemployment 1900–40', *Economic Record*, no. 41, 1965, pp. 426–50.

Frances, Raelene, ' "No more Amazons": Gender and work process in the Victorian clothing trades, 1890–1939', *Labour History*, no. 50, May 1986, pp. 95–112.

———, 'Harrison Ord', *Australian Dictionary of Biography*, vol. 11, 1988.

———, 'Robert Solly', 'Alfred Russell Wallis', *Australian Dictionary of Biography*, vol. 12, 1990.

Friedman, A., 'Responsible autonomy versus direct control over the labour process', *Capital and Class*, no. 1, Spring 1977, pp. 43–57.

Fry, Eric, 'Outwork in the Eighties', *University Studies in History and Economics*, vol. 2, no. 4, July 1956, pp. 77–93.

Gardiner, J., 'Women in the labour process and class structure', in A. Hunt (ed.), *Class and Class Structure*, London, 1977, pp. 155–63.

Garnsey, E., 'Women's work and theories of class stratification', *Sociology*, vol. 12, no. 2, 1978, pp. 223–44.

Hagan, J., 'An incident at the *Dawn*', *Labour History*, no. 8, May 1965, pp. 19–20.

——, 'Employees, trade unions and the first Victorian Factory Acts', *Labour History*, no. 7, 1964, pp. 3–11.

Hagan, J., and Fisher, C., 'Piecework and some of its consequences in the printing and coal mining industries in Australia, 1850–1930', *Labour History*, no. 25, November 1973, pp. 19–39.

Hall, A. R., 'Some long period effects of the limited age distribution of the population of Australia 1861–1961', *Economic Record*, no. 39, 1963, pp. 43–52.

Hartman Strom, Sharon, 'Challenging "Woman's Place": Feminism, the Left and Industrial Unionism in the 1930s', *Feminist Studies*, vol. 9, no. 2, Summer 1983, pp. 359–86.

Hartmann, Heidi, 'Capitalism, patriarchy and job segregation by sex', in Blaxall (ed.), *Women in the Workplace*, Chicago, 1976.

Hince, K., 'Wages boards in Victoria', *Journal of Industrial Relations*, no. 7, 1965, pp. 164–178.

Humphries, Jane, 'Women: scapegoats and safety valves in the Great Depression', *Review of Radical Political Economics*, vol. 8, no. 1, 1976, pp. 98–121.

——, 'The working-class family, women's liberation and class struggle: the case of nineteenth-century British history', *Review of Radical Political Economics*, vol. 9, no. 3, Autumn 1977, pp. 25–41.

——, 'Protective legislation, the capitalist state and working class men: the 1842 Miners Regulation Act', *Feminist Review*, no. 7, 1981, pp. 1–35.

Hunt, Felicity, 'The London trade in the printing and binding of books: an experience in exclusion, dilution and de-skilling of women workers', *Women's International Forum*, vol. 6, 1983, pp. 517–524.

Hyman, R., 'Trade unions, control and resistance', in G. Esland and G. Salaman (eds), *The Politics of Work and Occupation*, London, 1980.

Jacoby, R., 'Review of Braverman', *Telos*, no. 29, Autumn 1977, pp. 199–207.

Joyce, Patrick, 'Labour, capital and compromise: A reply to Price', *Social History*, vol. IX, no. 1, 1984, pp. 67–76.

Keeley, G. S., 'Work control, the labour process and nineteenth century Canadian printers', in C. Heron and R. Storey (eds), *On the Job: Confronting the Labour Process in Canada*, Kingston and Montreal, 1986, pp. 75–101.

Kelly, J., 'Useless work and useless toil', *Marxism Today*, vol. 26, no. 8, 1982.

Kessler-Harris, Alice, 'Where are the organised women workers?', *Feminist Studies*, no. 3, Fall 1975, pp. 92–110.

Kirkby, Diane, ' "Oh what a tangled web!". Labour, the state and the Australian arbitration system', in Verity Burgmann and Jenny Lee (eds), *A People's History of Australia*, vol. 2: *Making a Life*, Melbourne, 1988, pp. 253–66.

Lake, Marilyn, 'Socialism and manhood: the case of William Lane', *Labour History*, no. 50, May 1986, pp. 54–62.

——, 'Socialism and Manhood: a reply to Bruce Scates', *Labour History*, no. 60, May 1991, pp. 114–120.

Lamb, Lesley, 'Lesbia Venner Harford', *Australian Dictionary of Biography*, vol. 9, 1891–1939.

Lee, Jenny, 'A redivision of labour: Victoria's wages boards in action, 1896–1903', *Historical Studies*, vol. 22, no. 88, April 1987, pp. 352–72.

Lee, Jenny, and Fahey, Charles, 'A boom for whom? Some developments in the Australian labour market, 1870–1891', *Labour History*, no. 50, May 1986, pp. 1–27.

Lewis, Jane, 'The debate on sex and class', *New Left Review*, no. 149, 1985, pp. 108–20.

Linge, G. J. R., 'The forging of an industrial nation: manufacturing in Australia 1788–1913', in J. M. Powell and M. Williams (eds), *Australian Space Australian Time: Geographical Perspectives*, Melbourne, 1975.

Lockwood, David, 'Sources of Variation in Working-Class Images of Society', in M. Bulmer (ed.), *Working-class Images of Society*, London and Boston, 1975, pp. 16–34.

MacCarthy, P. G., 'Victorian wages boards. Their origin and the doctrine of the living wage', *Journal of Industrial Relations*, no. 10, 1968, pp. 116–31.

——, 'Employers, the tariff and legal wages determination in Australia 1890–1900', *Journal of Industrial Relations*, no. 12, 1970, pp. 182–93.

——, 'Wages in Australia 1891–1914', *Australian Economic Review*, X, 1970, pp. 56–75.

——, Labour and the living wages 1890–1910', *Australian Journal of Politics and History*, XIII, 1967, pp. 67–85.

McBryde, Theresa, 'Review of *The Sweated Trades: Outwork in Nineteenth Century Britain* by Duncan Blythell', *Journal of Social History*, vol. 13, no. 4, Summer 1980, pp. 660–1.

McGaw, Judith, 'Women and the history of American technology', *Signs*, vol. 7, no. 4, Summer 1982, pp. 798–828.

McDonald, Peter and Quiggan, Patricia, 'Lifecourse transitions in Victoria in the 1880s', in Patricia Grimshaw, *et al.* (eds), *Families in Colonial Australia*, pp. 64–82.

Maier, C. S., 'Between Taylorism and technology: European ideologies and the vision of industrial productivity in the 1920s', *Journal of Contemporary History*, vol. 5, no. 2, 1970, pp. 27–61.

Marglin, Stephen, 'What do bosses do? The origins and functions of hierarchy in capitalist production', in Andre Gorz (ed.), *The Division of Labor: the labor process and class struggle in modern capitalism*, Brighton, 1976, pp. 55–62.

McGregor, Lachlan, 'The development of manufacturing in Australia', in N. T. Drohan and J. H. Day (eds), *Readings in Australian Economics*, Canberra, 1965, pp. 300–16.

Melling, J., ' "Non-commissioned Officers": British employers and their supervisory workers, 1880–1920', *Social History*, vol. V, no. 1, 1980, pp. 193–221.

Middleton, C., 'Sexual Inequality and Stratification Theory', in F. Parkin (ed.), *The Social Analysis of Class Structure*, London, 1974, pp. 179–205.

Milkman, Ruth, 'Women's work and the economic crisis: some lessons of the Great Depression', *Review of Radical Political Economics*, vol. 8, no. 1, Spring 1976, pp. 73–97.

——, 'Organising the sexual division of labour: historical perspectives on women's work and the American Labour Movement', *Socialist Review*, vol. 10, no. 49, January–February 1980, pp. 95–150.

Modjeska, Drusilla, 'Introduction' to *The poems of Lesbia Harford*, D. Modjeska and N. Pizer (eds), North Ryde, 1985, pp. 1–39.

Monds, J., 'Workers' control and the historians: a new economism', *New Left Review*, no. 97, 1976, pp. 81–99.

Montgomery, David, 'The past and future of workers' control', *Radical America*, vol. 13, no. 6, 1979, pp. 7–24.

——, 'The new unionism and the transformation of workers' consciousness in America, 1909–1922', *Journal of Social History*, vol. 7, no. 4, 1974, pp. 509–29.

——, 'Workers' control of machine production in the nineteenth century', *Labour History*, no. 17, 1976.

Mulligan, William H. Jr., 'Mechanization and work in the American shoe industry—Lynn, Massachusetts 1852–1883', *Journal of Economic History*, vol. XLI, no. 1, March 1981, pp. 59–64.

Murray-Smith, S., 'Technical education in Australia', in E. L. Wheelwright (ed.), *Higher Education in Australia*, Melbourne, 1965.

Nichol, W., 'Women and the Trade Union Movement in NSW: 1890–1900', *Labour History*, no. 36, 1979, pp. 18–30.

Nichols, T., 'Review of Braverman's *Labour and Monopoly Capitalism*', *Sociological Review*, vol. 25, no. 1, 1977, pp. 192–4.

Oxnam, D. W., 'The relation of unskilled to skilled wage rates in Australia', *Economic Record*, XXVI, 1950, pp. 112–18.

Palloix, C., 'The labour process from Fascism to Neo-Fascism', in Conference of Socialist Economists (eds), *The Labour Process and Class Strategies*, London, 1976, pp. 4–25.

Palmer, B., 'Class, conception and conflict: the thrust for efficiency, managerial views of labor and the working-class rebellion, 1903–1922', *Review of Radical Political Economics*, vol. 7, no. 2, 1975, pp. 31–49.

Panzieri, R., 'Surplus value and planning: notes on the reading of *Capital*', in Conference of Socialist Economists (eds), *The Labour Process and Class Strategies*, London, 1976, pp. 46–67.

——, 'The capitalist case of machinery: Marx versus the "Objectivists" ' in P. Slater (ed.), *Outline of a Critique of Technology*, London, 1980.

Parsons, T. G., 'An outline of employer organisations in the Victorian manufacturing industries, 1879–1940', *Journal of Industrial Relations*, no. 14, 1972, pp. 23–8.

Phillips, Anne, and Taylor, Barbara, 'Sex and Skill: notes towards a feminist economics', *Feminist Review*, no. 6, 1980, pp. 79–89.

Power, Margaret, 'The Making of a Woman's Occupation', *Hecate*, vol. 1, no. 2, July 1975, pp. 25–34.

Power, Marilyn, 'From home production to wage labor: women as a reserve army of labor', *Review of Radical Political Economics*, XV, 1, Spring 1983, pp. 71–91.

Price, Richard, 'The labour process and labour history', *Social History*, vol. VII, no. 1, 1983, pp. 57–75.

——, 'Theories of labour process formation', *Journal of Social History*, vol. 18, no. 1, Fall 1984, pp. 91–110.

——, 'Conflict and co-operation: a reply to Patrick Joyce', *Social History*, vol. 9, no. 2, May 1984, pp. 217–24.

——, 'Working Women, Women's Work and the occupation of Being a Woman', *Women's Studies International Quarterly*, vol. 1, no. 2, Summer 1978.

Rabinbach, Anson, 'The European science of work: the economy of the body at the end of the nineteenth century', in S. L. Kaplan and C. J. Koepp (eds), *Work in France: Representations, Meaning, Organization and Practice*, Ithaca and London, 1986, pp. 475–513.

Radi, Heather, '1920–1929' in F. Crowley (ed.), *A New History of Australia*, Melbourne, 1974, pp. 357–414.

Ratner, Ronnie Steinberg, 'Unionization and social reform: To Them That Hath Shall Be Given', *International Journal of the Sociology of Law*, vol. 9, 1981, pp. 303–28.

Reekie, Gail, ' "Humanising industry": Paternalism, welfarism and labour control in Sydney's big stores, 1890–1930', *Labour History*, no. 53, November 1987, pp. 1–19.

Reid, D. A., 'The decline of Saint Monday 1766–1876', *Past and Present*, no. 71, 1976, pp. 76–101.

Rimmer, P. J., 'The boot and the shoe industry in Melbourne', in J. M. Powell (ed.), *Urban and Industrial Australia*, Melbourne, 1974, pp. 113–24.

Rose, Sonya O., 'Gender at Work: sex, class and industrial capitalism', *History Workshop*, no. 1, Spring 1986, pp. 113–31.

——, 'Gender antagonism and class conflict: exclusionary strategies of male trade unionists in nineteenth-century Britain', *Social History*, vol. 13, no. 2, May 1988, pp. 191–208.

Samuel, Raphael, 'The workshop of the world: steam power and hand technology in mid-Victorian Britain', *History Workshop*, no. 3, Spring 1977, pp. 6–72.

Scates, Bruce, 'A struggle for survival: unemployment and the unemployed agitation in late nineteenth-century Melbourne', *Australian Historical Studies*, no. 94, April 1990, pp. 41–63.

———, 'Socialism and Feminism, the case of William Lane: A reply to Marilyn Lake', *Labour History*, no. 59, November 1990, pp. 72–94.

———, 'William Arthur Trenwith', *Australian Dictionary of Biography*, vol. 12, 1990.

———, 'Socialism and Manhood: a Rejoinder', *Labour History*, no. 60, May 1991, pp. 121–5.

Schofield, Ann, 'Rebel Girls and Union Maids: the woman question in the journals of the AFL and IWW, 1905–1920', *Feminist Studies*, vol. 19, no. 2, Summer 1983, pp. 338–55.

Schwarz, B., 'On the monopoly capitalist degradation of work', *Dialectical Anthropology*, vol. 2, no. 2, 1977, pp. 159–67.

Scott, Joan W, and Tilly, Louise A., 'Women's work and the family in nineteenth-century Europe', *Comparative Studies in Society and History*, vol. 17, no. 1, January 1975, pp. 36–64.

Siltanen, J., 'A commentary on theories of female wage labour', in Cambridge Women's Studies Group (eds), *Women in Society*, London, 1981, pp. 25–40.

Simeral, Margaret H., 'Women and the reserve army of labour', *Insurgent Sociologist*, VIII, nos. 2 and 3, 1978, pp. 164–80.

Sinclair, W. A., 'The depression of the 1890s and 1930s in Australia: a comparison', in N. T. Drohan and J. H. Day (eds), *Readings in Australian Economics*, Canberra, 1965, pp. 85–92.

———, 'Aspects of economic growth, 1900–1930', in A. H. Boxer (ed.), *Aspects of the Australian Economy*, 2nd edn, Melbourne, 1969.

———, 'The tariff and manufacturing employment in Victoria, 1860–1900', *Economic Record*, XXXII, 1951, pp. 100–4.

———, 'The tariff and economic growth in pre-Federation Victoria', *Economic Record*, no. 47, 1971, pp. 77–9.

———, 'Women at work in Melbourne and Adelaide since 1871', *Economic Record*, vol. 57, 1981, pp. 344–53.

———, 'Women and economic change in Melbourne 1871–1901', *Historical Studies*, vol. 20, no. 79, October 1982, pp. 277–91.

Steedman, Mercedes, 'Skill and gender in the Canadian clothing industry, 1890–1940', in C. Heron and R. Storey (eds) *On the Job: Confronting the Labour Process in Canada*, Kingston and Montreal, 1986, pp. 152–76.

Stephen, Ann, 'Agents of consumerism: the organisation of the Australian advertising industry, 1918–1938', *Media Interventions*, Sydney, 1981, pp. 78–96.

Stiglet, G., 'The division of labour is limited by the extent of the market', *Journal of Political Economy*, vol. LIX, 1951, pp. 185–93.

Storey, J., 'The means of management control', *Sociology*, May 1985, pp. 193–211.

Taylor, Barbara, ' "The men are as bad as their makers . . .": Socialism, feminism and sexual antagonism in the London tailoring trade in the 1830s', in J. Newton, M. Ryan and J. Walkowitz (eds), *Sex and Class in Women's History*, London, 1983, pp. 187–220.

Thompson, A., 'The enigma of Australian manufacturing 1851–1901', *Australian Economic Papers*, no. 9, 1970, pp. 76–92.

Thompson, D., 'Women and Nineteenth-century Radical Politics: A Lost Dimension', in J. Mitchell and A. Oakley (eds), *The Rights and Wrongs of Women*, Harmondsworth, 1976, pp. 112–38.

Thompson, E. P., 'Time, work discipline and industrial capitalism', *Past and Present*, no. 38, 1967, pp. 56–97.

Tiffin, Susan, 'In pursuit of reluctant parents', in Sydney Labour History Group, *What Rough Beast? The State and Social Order in Australian History*, Sydney, 1982, pp. 130–50.

Tilly, L. A., 'Individual lives and family strategies', *Journal of Family History*, Summer 1979, pp. 137–52.

Traub, R., 'Lenin and Taylor: the fate of "scientific management" in the (early) Soviet Union', *Telos*, no. 37, 1978, pp. 82–92.

Wajcman, J., 'Work and the family: who gets the best of both worlds?' in Cambridge Women's Studies Group (eds), *Women in Society*, London, 1981 pp. 9–24.

Walsh, G. P., 'Factories and factory workers in New South Wales, 1788–1900', *Labour History*, no. 21, November 1971, pp. 1–16.

Whelan, Dominica, 'Women and the Arbitration System', *Journal of Australian Political Economy*, no. 4, March 1979.

Willis, Paul, 'Shop-floor culture, masculinity and the wage form' in John Clarke, C. Critchen and R. Johnson (eds), *Working-class Culture: Studies in History and Theory*, New York, 1979, pp. 185–98.

Wright, Andree, '*The Women's Weekly*: Depression and War Years, Romance and Reality', *Refractory Girl*, no. 3, Winter 1973, pp. 9–13.

Yelland, Sheryl, 'Adeline Lloyd: a biography of an unmarried woman', *Lilith*, no. 2, Winter 1985, pp. 42–78.

Zeitlin, Jonathon, 'Engineers and compositors: a comparison', in Royden Harrison and Jonathon Zeitlin (eds), *Divisions of Labour*, Urbana, Illinois, 1985.

——, 'Craft control and the division of labour: engineers and compositors in Britain, 1890–1930', *Cambridge Journal of Economics*, vol. 3, no. 3, 1979, pp. 263–74.

——, 'Social theory and the history of work', review article, *Social History*, vol. 8, no. 3, October 1983, pp. 365–74.

Theses and unpublished papers

Baldock, Cora, 'Technological Change and Skills of Women', Paper presented at Second International Interdisciplinary Congress on Women, Groningen, April 1984.

Baron, Ava, 'Technology and the Crisis of Masculinity: the Social Construction of Gender and Skill in the US Printing Industry, 1850–1920', Paper for 5th UMIST-ASTON Conference on Organisation and Control of the Labour Process, Manchester, England, April 1987.

Bennett, Laura, 'The 1972 Equal Pay Case: ideology and practice in the Conciliation and Arbitration Commission', Paper presented to Australian Historical Association Conference, Melbourne, 1984.

——, 'Women workers and the processes of the Conciliation and Arbitration System', LL.M. thesis, University of Melbourne, 1984.

Brown, Stephanie, 'Beyond Control: A Critique of Gender and Skill in the Organisation of the Meat Industry, Victoria 1930–1968', Paper presented to Australian Historical Association Conference, Melbourne, 1984.

Bulbeck, Chilla, 'The Labour Process, Technology and Worker Power', Paper presented to SAANZ Conference, University of New South Wales, 1982.

Campbell, Iain, 'Workers and Capital: the Development of a Real Subsumption', Paper presented to Australian Historical Association Conference, Melbourne, 1984.

Cutler, F. H., 'The Anti-Sweating Movement in Victoria 1873–1896', M.A. thesis, University of Melbourne, 1956.

Davey, P. R., 'Wages Boards in Victoria 1896–1920', Ph.D. thesis, University of Melbourne, 1975.

Deacon, Desley, 'Political arithmetic: the nineteenth-century census and the construction of the dependent woman', Seminar Paper, Department of Demography, RSSS, Australian National University.

Donnelly, L. P., 'International Capital Movements, the Terms of Trade and the Australian Economy, 1861–1929', Ph.D. thesis, Brown University, 1970.

Frances, Raelene, 'The Politics of Work: Case Studies of Three Victorian Industries, 1880–1939', Ph.D. thesis, Monash University, 1989.

French, Merryle, 'Women in the Workforce, Victoria 1881–1907', B.A. Honours thesis, History, University of Melbourne, 1984.

Fry, Eric, 'The Condition of the Urban Working Class in the 1880s', Ph.D. thesis, Australian National University, 1956.

Ingham, S. M., 'Some Aspects of Victorian Liberalism 1880–1900', M.A. thesis, University of Melbourne, 1950.

Jackson, E., 'Legislation to Protect Women in Industry: South Australia and Victoria, 1884–1904', M.A. Prelim. thesis, History, University of Melbourne, 1971.

Kelly, Farley, 'The "Woman Question" in Melbourne, 1880–1914', Ph.D. thesis, Monash University, 1982.

Maccarone, Elvira, 'The Impact of the Depression on the Labour of Australian Women', B.A. Honours thesis, History, University of Melbourne, 1981.

Moses, K., 'A Study of the effects of the Depression upon Women in the Workforce during the late twenties and early thirties in Victoria', B.A. Honours thesis, History, La Trobe University, 1980.

Nolan, M., 'Uniformity and Diversity: Female Shop and Office Workers in Victoria, 1880–1939', Ph.D. thesis, ANU, 1990.

Parsons, Leslie, 'The Quest for Lesbia Harford', B.A. Honours thesis, History, University of Melbourne, 1976.

Parsons, T. G., 'Some Aspects of the Development of Manufacturing in Melbourne, 1870–1890', Ph.D. thesis, Monash University, 1970.

Philipp, J. M., 'Trade Union Organization in New South Wales and Victoria', M.A. thesis, University of Melbourne, 1954.

Raymond, M., 'Labour Pains: Working-class Women in Employment, Unions and the Labor Party in Victoria 1880–1914', M.A. thesis, University of Melbourne, 1987.

Rich, Jeff, 'Engineers and Work in Victoria, c.1860–1890', B.A. Honours thesis, History, University of Melbourne, 1986.

Scates, Bruce, ' "Faddists and Extremists": Radicalism in the Labour Movement, South-Eastern Australia, 1886–1898', Ph.D. thesis, Monash University, 1987.

Stephen, E., 'Women or Workers: a Study of Female Trade Union Identity in the Clothing and Confectionery Industries in Victoria, 1912–1928', B.A. Honours thesis, History, University of Melbourne, 1981.

Williams, J., 'The Victorian Printing Industry and the Diffusion of New Technology, 1885–1905', B.A. Honours thesis, History, University of Melbourne, 1984.

Index

Abrahams, John, 105
accounting, 103, 165
Acme factory, 30
advertising, 116, 126
Age, 32, 33, 44, 61, 71
age:
  distribution, 18
  minimum working, 79
Ager, J. E., 155
alliances between workers and employers, 34, 41, 63, 68, 88, 122, 140, 145, 152, 154, 158
Amazons, 89, 191
American influences, 85, 102, 104, 183
  see also scientific management; United States of America
American loose-nailing machine, 103
anarchism, 10, 53, 192
  see also Chummy Fleming
Anderson, George, 176
anti-conscription, 95-8
anti-labour offensive, 109
anti-Semitism, 143
anti-sweating campaign, 42, 144
apprenticeship, 3, 17, 18, 21, 77-8, 187
  boot trade, 44, 46, 51, 109-13, 155, 158, 165, 167
  clothing trades, 31, 39, 145, 147-9
  printing trades, 58, 63, 68-71, 125-6, 133, 172, 177-8
  see also training
Apprenticeship Act, 113
arbitration awards, 137, 151-2, 155, 158-60, 169, 172-9
  consent, 151, 153
  enforcement, 134, 142-3
arbitration court, 80, 94-5, 108, 110, 113-14, 126, 133, 140, 151, 164-5, 187
  see also federal arbitration system
arbitration hearing, 1919, 86, 89
Argus, 61, 71, 97
artistic work, 25, 55, 67, 119, 126, 173
assembly lines, 84, 85
Australasian Manufacturer, 84
Australasian Typographical Association, 66, 68, 69, 71, 121, 126
Australasian Typographical Journal, 66, 69-70, 125
Australian Labor Party, 80, 109
Australian Leather Journal, 38, 43, 102-3, 112, 115, 158
automation, 165, 170
Aves, Ernest, 76, 99
awards, *see* arbitration awards

Babbage, Charles, 26
Baldock, Cora, 4
Ballarat, 28, 45, 48, 50, 56, 84, 90, 91, 96, 97, 113
  see also Busy Bee factory
band-knives, 31
Banks and Co., 35, 37, 40
Baron, Ava, 69, 127
Barry, Mrs, 119-20
Bartlett, Edward, 18, 40
basic wage, 126, 170

basket shoes, 164
Beath and Schiess, 30, 32, 35
Bedggood family, 154
Bedggood, John, 44
Bedggoods factory, 43-4, 105, 109
Beeby, George, 159, 165-7, 173, 176
Beeby, Miss, 166
Beechey, Veronica, 5, 8
benchwork, 16
Bennett, Laura, 170, 172, 177
Billson, J. W., 52-3, 105-6, 110, 113
Billson, Mrs, 108
blacklegs, 35, 97, 168
Black sole sewer, 45, 102
Blencowe, J. R., 26
Blomfield, Henry, 30, 38
Blythell, Duncan, 23
boards of conciliation, 46-7, 75
boards of health, 20
bonus systems, 96, 115
Bookbinders' Union, 61, 63, 120, 122, 171
bookbinding, women's sections, 117
Boomerang, 66
'Boomerang', 103-4
Boot Manufacturers' Association, 46-7, 114, 152-3, 155, 159, 163, 164
Boot Trade Union Federation, 151
Boot Wages Board, 57, 105
boot and shoe industry, 10, 16, 18-19, 72, 43-57, 100-15, 133, 136, 151-68, 180-92 *passim*
boot finishers, 45

bootmakers' strike and lockout, 1884, 46-9, 55
boy labour, 187, 189
    boot industry, 46, 50, 55, 107, 109-10, 112, 114, 154-5, 158, 161, 166-7
    printing industry, 60, 61, 68, 72, 125-6, 128
    see also juvenile labour
Braeside Shirt Factory, 25, 30
Braverman, Harry, 1, 4, 5, 9
breadwinners:
    female, 25, 67
    male, 66, 82, 136, 162, 175, 191
Brenner, Johanna, 25
Britain, 3, 16, 23, 55, 99
    see also England
Brodney, May, see Francis, May
Bryant, Mrs, 24
building industry, 15-19 passim
Bulbeck, Chilla, 4
Burawoy, Michael, 6, 111, 185
Burke, Frank, 120, 125, 171
Busy Bee factory, 29, 40
Butlin, Noel, 32

cabinet makers, 109
Cain, John, 96
Cairns, John, 56
Callard, Maurice, 146
capital, 2, 4, 30, 78, 191
capitalism, 2, 3, 5, 6, 10
Cardboard Box and Carton Employees Association, 122-4
Carter, Herbert, 86, 87, 89, 91, 95, 97, 138, 143-6
case-making machines, 61
certificates of discharge, 47, 48, 140
Chamber of Manufactures, 138, 140
Chief Inspector of Factories, 18, 23, 37, 61, 75-6, 89
children's shoes, 100, 156
Chinese labour, 66
civil servants, 76-7
Clark, John, 28
classification, 155-7, 160-1, 164-6, 170, 175, 179, 190
clerical work, 78, 103, 144
Clerks' Union, 79
Clickers' Union, 106
clicking, 17
cloth merchants, 26
clothing industry, 10, 15-16, 19, 20, 22-42, 82-99, 133, 136, 137-50, 167, 180-92
Clothing Manufacturers' Association, 33, 37
Clothing Trades Union, 86, 87, 93, 94, 95, 122, 138
Cochrane, Peter, 5, 78, 169
Cockburn, Cynthia, 9, 67
Cohen, Lewis, 93

Cohen, Sheila, 7, 71
coke ovens, 28
Collingwood, 45, 162
Collopy, Factory Inspector, 98
commercial employment, 79
commercial printing, 60, 71, 126
common rule, 134
Commonwealth Clothing Factory, 84, 94, 97, 98
Commonwealth Court of Conciliation and Arbitration, 11
    see also arbitration court
communism, 10, 145, 153, 164, 192
company managers, 75
company shares, 40
compositors, 4, 6, 58-72, 116-31, 169-79
compulsory unionism, 143
conception and execution, 2, 5, 85, 103, 104, 147, 148, 183
conditions of work, 20, 94, 98, 185-6
    boot trade, 50, 167
    clothing trades, 28, 87, 142, 145
    printing trades, 58, 125, 127, 128
    see also arbitration awards; health and safety; hours; wages
conference agreements, 152-3
consent awards, 151, 153
conscription, see anti-conscription
consumer industries, 1, 16-17, 19
consumer price index, 137
consumers, 15, 16
contagious effeminacy, 28
contracting, 25-7, 34, 143-3, 149, 164
control of labour, 2, 7
    versus exploitation, 7, 8, 38, 47, 69-71, 86, 145-6
Cookes, W. D., 154
Corbauld, William, 28
costing methods, 51
Court of Industrial Appeals, 80, 92, 134
craft exclusiveness, 37-8
craft unionism, 95
craft work, 1, 17, 26, 127, 145, 148, 169, 175, 177, 179
craftworkers, 19, 85, 116, 119, 125, 127-8
Cresswell, Ellen, 24, 32, 35, 37
crises of exploitation, 32, 187-92
crises of valorisation, 4, 32, 45, 51, 82, 187-92
Cross, Louisa, 120-4, 171
Curlewis, Judge, 159-60
Curthoys, Ann, 9
Cuthbertson, Margaret, 23, 24, 31, 77, 89, 124, 128
Cutters and Trimmers Union, 90
cutters: tailoring, 31, 39
    underclothing, 92
cutting, 26, 28
cutting machines, 28, 30, 38, 84, 85, 190

Daley, Jean, 123
dangerous work, 20, 21, 118, 127
daughters, 18, 26
Davis, Abraham, 92
Davison, Graeme, 16, 17
Dawn, 60
Defence Department, 94, 97-8
degradation of craft work, see deskilling
demographic features, 17, 21
Denton, George, 40
Department of Labour, 142
depressions:
    1890s, 5, 15-16, 20, 39-41, 44, 49, 51, 53-4, 56, 61, 68-9, 77, 91, 116, 185-7, 189
    1930s, 134, 136, 142, 153, 159, 163, 175, 176, 185-7, 189
deskilling, 1, 3-4, 8, 55, 86, 109, 112, 127, 145, 155, 180-92
Dethridge, Judge, 173-8
Detmold, William, 63
Detmolds factory, 60
dilution of skill, see deskilling; skill
discipline:
    market, 185
    factory, 40-1, 44, 47, 50, 53, 55, 103, 168, 183-4
division of labour, see sexual division of labour; subdivision of work
domestic production, 10, 16, 18, 22, 43
domestic work, 10, 17-18, 43
Don, Ellen, 162
Drake-Brockman, Judge, 143
drapers, 16, 25, 26, 29
Dress Wages Board, 92, 93, 96
Dressmakers' Union, 93
dressmaking, 17, 25, 35, 83, 89, 90, 149
dual labour markets, 6
dyeing and cleaning, 139
dynamic of work, 180-92 passim

Eckersall, Ellen, 82, 87
economies of scale, 29, 30, 78, 83
economy, general state, 15-16, 21, 77-9, 136
    see also depressions
education, see apprenticeships; technical education; training
Edwards, Richard, 6
eight-hour day, 47, 48
    see also working week
electric power, 82, 102, 190
Elger, Tony, 4
Ellinson Bros, 144
embroidering machines, 84
employers, 1, 5, 84
    attitudes to female labour, 28, 61, 69, 89, 107
    see also alliances between workers and employers
engineering, 15, 17, 19, 77

England, 26, 54, 65
  see also Britain
Equal Status Committee, 165
equal pay, 79-80, 133, 135, 188, 190
  boot trade, 107, 114, 155
  clothing trades, 83, 86, 91, 95-6, 143-4,
    148
  printing trades, 124, 178
ethnicity, 136, 138, 143, 164
excess capacity, 115, 163
Executive Council, 75
exports, 15, 45, 57, 78, 83, 100, 114, 189
Ezywalkin firm, 154

factories:
  American, 85
  backyard, 17, 26, 142-3, 145
  clothing and textile, 16, 18, 32
  co-operative, 48, 112
  primitive, 4, 51
  registered, 20, 41
  shirt and dress, 90
  see also names of specific factories
Factories Act, *see* Shops and Factories Act
Factories Commission, 1884, 18
Factories Office, 76, 94, 117
factory girls, stereotypes of, 36
Factory Inquiry, 1893, 40
factory inspection, 20-1, 125, 134, 142
Factory Inspector Bishop, 117, 119, 125
Factory Inspector Shay, 110
Factory Inspector Thear, 115
factory inspectors, 21, 76, 77, 93, 98, 110,
  115, 117, 119
factory legislation, 21, 34, 41, 54, 65, 68,
  77, 164, 185, 188
  see also Shops and Factories Act
factory system, 16
Fahey, Charles, 30
family:
  and work, 40-1, 44, 56-7, 108, 123-5,
    146-7, 162, 177, 184-5, 187-8, 191
  economy, 18, 19, 22, 23, 57
  defence of, 9
  under capitalism, 8, 9
  wage, 136
  see also gender ideology
farming, 15, 78
fashions, 29, 83, 169
federal arbitration system, 133-79
  see also arbitration court
federal council (of PIEUA), 170-1
Federated Clothing Trades Union, 91
federation, 77, 81, 83, 100, 104, 110
Felstead, Minnie, 89, 93, 120-1
Female Boot Operatives Society, 56, 108
female labour:
  cheaper, 84, 148, 155, 167, 189
  demand, 10, 78-9
  market, 18
  over-supply, 32

shortages, 18, 19, 78-9, 84, 98, 99, 104,
  115, 117, 136-8, 161, 168, 189, 190
supply, 10, 18, 19, 37, 56
  see also employers; girl labour
female suffrage, 80, 81
female workforce, 17
females:
  and male overseers, 7
  as bookbinders, 3, 58-72, 116-31,
    169-79
  as bootworkers, 48, 55-6, 106-8, 159
  as breadwinners, 25, 67, 162-3, 184
  as compositors, 58, 60, 66-7
  as percentage of workforce, 82
  as union organisers, 96, 121-3, 139,
    144, 165, 171
  attributes of, 4, 61, 104, 121
  see also women
feminine culture, 7
femininity, 10, 24, 35, 56, 67-8, 79, 190-1
feminisation, 4, 8, 16, 17, 79, 136, 182,
  188-90
  boot trade, 44, 107, 156, 166
  clothing trades, 26-9, 82
  printing trades, 179
  see also contagious effeminacy
feminism, 10, 60, 66-7, 80, 89, 95,
  119-20, 136, 192
feminist critique of Braverman, 8
fertility, 10
Ferguson, James, 46
finishing machines, 31, 38, 85, 86, 97
Firth and McCutcheon, 60
Fisher, Chris, 6, 127
Fisher government, 94
Fitchett Brothers, 61
flat irons, 28
flat rate margin, 155-6, 159-61, 167, 170,
  172
Fleming, Chummy, 44, 53, 106, 109, 111,
  192
folding machines, 58, 65, 118
food processing, 15, 16, 18, 77, 137
footwear industry, *see* boot industry
Ford, Henry, 85
foreign investment, 15
foremen, 104, 115
Fortuna skiving machines, 161, 156
40-hour week, *see* working week
Foy and Gibson's factory, 30, 98
fragmentation, 3, 39, 86, 104, 145, 177,
  180-92
Francis, May, 88, 92, 93, 95, 96, 138-9,
  192
Friedman, A., 5
Frieze Bros, 144
Fry, Eric, 36
Fry, Gordon, 171-2
fur work, 139

games at work, 6

  see also racing games
gas engines, 21, 30, 31, 38, 46, 55, 82,
  190
Gee, Walter, 117
Geelong, 28, 41, 51, 52, 109
gender and militancy, *see* men as unionists; women and industrial organi-
  sation/militancy
gender ideology, 10, 21, 135, 190-1
  boot trade, 104, 162-3, 168
  clothing trades, 22, 28, 32-4, 82, 147
  printing trades, 66-8, 121, 127-8, 169,
    174, 177
  see also male union culture; sex struc-
    ture of unions; sexual division of
    labour
gender orders, esp. 2, 190-1
girl labour, 92, 115
  see also juvenile labour
goldrush, 19, 37, 43
Goldstein, Vida, 95
Goodyear welter, 49, 100, 102, 113
Gordon, D., 6
Government Gazette, 75
government, 94-5, 99
  see also state
Greenwood, William, 105
guerilla warfare, 138, 147

Hagan, J., 6, 121, 127
Hammond, Prof., 75-6
Hancock, John, 66, 71
hand finishing, 16
handmade boots, 44
handwork, tailoring, 84
Harford, Lesbia, *see* Keogh, Lesbia
Harkness, T. Y., 109, 152, 154
Hattersley machine, 71
Heagney, Muriel, 144, 165
health and safety, 20, 50, 127, 145, 146,
  178, 186
heeling machines, 49
Hellings, Daniel, 152, 154
Herald, 71, 126
Higgins, H. B., 112, 133-4, 143, 145, 155,
  158, 160-1, 165, 170, 173, 178
High Court, 114, 134-5, 143
historical perspectives, 1-2
Hobsbawm, Eric, 5, 6, 39, 54
home production, *see* domestic production
Hotham boot factory, 52
hours of work, 20-1, 36, 48, 126, 185
  shorter, 86-7, 113, 127-8, 145, 152-3,
    165, 170, 178, 185
  see also eight-hour day; night work;
    Saturday morning work; working
    week
household economy, 10
  see also domestic economy
Hyams' factory, 106

Hyndman, Miss, 171
hysteria, 98

ideologies, radical, 10, 92
  see also anarchism, communism; feminism; Industrial Workers of the World; socialism
ideology of woman's place, see gender ideology
immigrants, 15, 37, 138, 142-3, 164
  see also goldrush
import-replacement industries, 15, 16
imports, 15-16, 29, 41, 43-5, 60, 72, 114, 165, 175, 189
indexing, 117, 124
industrial capitalism, 10
industrial efficiency, 145
industrial psychology, 5, 148
industrial revolution, 2, 16
industrial unionism, 80, 95, 121
Industrial Workers of the World, 96, 192
industrialisation, 15
inflation, 99, 128, 155
Internationalist, 36
interstate agreements, 157-9
interstate conferences, 151, 155, 160, 164
ironworking, 17
Italian workers, 143

Japan, 175
Jewish workers, 143
job control, 1-11, 183-6
Johnstone, David, 159
judges, 133-5, 143, 153, 159, 172-3, 177
justices of peace, 77
juvenile labour, 17, 19, 20, 187, 190, 192
  and militancy, 23
  boot trade, 46, 55, 107, 115, 155, 166
  clothing trades, 25, 30, 40, 82-4, 92, 142, 144, 147-9
  printing trades, 63, 116, 123-4, 174-5

Keleher, Mr, 98
Kelly, John, 180
Keogh, J., 105-6, 111
Keogh, Lesbia, 92, 95, 96, 192
Khaki Girls, 97, 98
Kingston, Beverley, 138
Knights of St Crispin, 44

Labor Call, 94, 135
Labor Members of Parliament, 110
  see also Pearce, Senator
labour:
  and capital, 7
  green, 155, 159
  real subordination of, 2
  reproductive, 191
  reserve army of, 9
  skilled, 78-9
  turnover, 24, 108, 123, 125, 148

  see also female labour; juvenile labour; male labour; sexual division of labour; work
labour market, 2, 31, 81, 78, 158, 188, 190
  see also female labour; juvenile labour; male labour
labour movement, 34
labour process debate, 1-11
labour-intensive industries, 25
lady inspectors, 76-7
  see also factory inspectors
Lane, William, 66
Lang government, 153
lasting machines, 49, 53
Laundry Workers Union, 87
Law, James, 84, 86, 87, 90, 96, 97, 140, 147, 148, 192
Lawson, Louisa, 60
learner system, 3
leased machinery, 190
  see also royalty system
Lee, Jenny, 30
left-wing politics, general, 80, 164
legal counsel, 133
legislation, 40
  see also factory legislation; protective legislation; names of specific acts
Leovold, Arthur, 120-1
letterpress machining, 175, 179
line of demarcation:
  bootmaking, 107, 156-7, 163, 166
  printing, 61, 63, 65, 124-5, 128, 175, 179, 189, 117
linotype machines, 61, 68-9, 71-2, 116, 126-7, 189-90
Littler, Craig, 5
Long, Arthur, 110, 113, 153-5, 161-2
long boom, 20
Lucas Girls, 97, 98
Lucas, E. and Co., 84, 90, 96, 184
Lukin, J., 153
Lyell, Andrew, 48

machine feeders, 58, 165
machine minders, 3
machine Telltales, 103
machinists and time work, 39
MacRobertson's factory, 181
Magrath, E. C., 171, 176, 179
Mair and Company, 47, 48
male labour, 19, 167
  see also boy labour; men's work
male union culture, 9, 79-80, 135, 188
  boot industry, 107-9, 159-65 passim
  clothing industry, 32-3, 37-8, 86, 89, 91, 96, 138-44
  printing industry, 65, 117-29, 171-2, 176
males:
  as bootmakers, 43-57, 71, 100-14,

151-68
  as breadwinners, 18, 22, 136, 162, 175, 191
  as entrepreneurs, 85
  as managers, 83
  as supervisors, 83
  as unionists, 123, 162
Maloney, J. J., 156, 151
management, 5, 7
  systematic, 110
  see also scientific management
Mann, Tom, 80, 110, 112
Mantach, Miss, 95
mantle manufacturing, 20, 29
manufacturers, divisions amongst, 34-5
manufacturing consent, 185
manufacturing industries, 20, 77
manufacturing investment, 78
margins for skill, 128, 135, 145, 147, 148, 155, 159-61, 165-7, 170, 172-9, 187
  see also flat rate margin
Maritime Strike, 15, 51
market:
  discipline, 185
  limitations, 22, 78, 115, 149, 167, 189
  see also labour market
Markey, Ray, 23
married women:
  and militancy/organisation, 124, 164, 184-5
  in paid workforce, 82, 135, 136, 164, 168
Marshall, William, 154, 158
Marshall's factory, 54
Marx, Karl, 2, 11, 158
masculinisation, 83, 156, 163, 182-3
masculinist political economy, 177
masculinity, 7, 10, 66, 67, 69, 119, 127-8, 155, 162, 190-1
mass production methods, 45, 84-5, 167, 191
Massina and Company, 60, 61, 68
Master Printers Association, 68, 71, 125-6
Mathews, John, 1
McDougall, James, 63
McGan's factory, 47
McKay, H. V., 98
McKay sole-sewer, 45
McLeod, Jane, 24, 37
McMahon, B., 126
mechanisation, 3, 8, 16-17, 81, 180-92 passim
  bootmaking, 43-5, 49, 53, 55, 102, 107, 110, 112, 114
  clothing industry, 25, 30, 38, 40, 82-3, 144, 146
  printing industry, 61, 65, 71, 117-18
  see also power-driven machinery; technology; names of specific machines
men's clothes, ready-made, 17
men's work, 4, 17, 19, 189-91

men's work (*cont*):
  bootmaking, 107, 156-7, 162, 166
  clothing industry, 26, 28
  printing industry, 63, 67-8, 72, 117, 127, 169, 175
  see also male labour; sexual division of labour
Mergenthaler machines, 71, 61
metal trades, 15
metalworkers' case, 176, 173
methods of payment, 6, 39-40, 71, 82, 110-11, 114-15, 147, 155, 167, 170, 184, 192
Meyer, Hinrich and Catherine, 23
middle-class women, in clothing industries, 23
middlemen, 34
Middleton, Richard, 67
migrant workers, *see* immigrants
Militant Minority Movement, 145, 164
Militant Propagandists of the Labor Movement, 95
Milliners Wages Board, 93
millinery section, 25, 31, 83, 89
minimum rates, 165, 170
  boot trade, 104, 106-7, 109, 114, 152, 159-60
  clothing trades, 87, 92, 93, 143
  printing trades, 117, 119, 126, 128
  see also wage rates
Minister for Labour, 75, 152, 158
Mirams, Mr, 48
Modern Printing Company, 171
Moore, Notley, 92
mothers, 18, 24
Muir, Sarah, 39, 89, 94
Mulcahy, Ellen, 89, 95, 119-20, 123-4
Murphy, Chief Inspector, 89
Myers factory, 139

national efficiency, 79
nature of work, factors determining, 1-11, 180-92
needlewomen, 16
needs doctrine, 175
New South Wales, 15, 66-7, 110, 122, 151-2, 156, 159-60, 165, 171, 175-6, 179
  government clothing factory, 94
  railway strike, 96
New Zealand, 68, 161
new industrialism, 90
new women, 35
newspapers, 60
  offices, 16, 71-2, 178
Niebert, Alice, 108
night work, 65, 68, 178
non-Labor politicians, 177
non-union labor, 51-2, 142
  see also blacklegs
North Melbourne, 92

Oldster, 44
Oliver, Edith, 89
One Big Union, 120, 124
Ord, Harrison, 23, 42, 76, 77, 92
Osborne, Ethel, 178
output regulation, 54, 111-12, 163
Outside Tailors Union, 38
outwork, 18-19, 21, 75, 77, 183, 188, 192
  boot industry, 45, 49, 52, 54
  clothing industry, 22-42 *passim*, 82, 86, 93, 142-3, 145-6
outworkers and industrial organisations, 22, 23, 46
over-production, 50
overlocking machines, 144, 150
overseas investment, 78
overtime, 142, 159
  bans, 48

Palmer, Bryan, 5
paper-bag industry, 117
Parry, John, 34
paternalism, 85, 90, 96, 140-1, 192, 184
patriarchal authority, 7
  see also family and work
patriotism, 96, 97, 98
payment:
  overaward, 161
  see also methods of payment; wages
Peacock, Alexander, 105
Pearce, Senator, 97, 98
Pearson, Law Company, 85
Pelaco factory, 84-7, 90, 141, 147-8, 183-4, 191
periodicals, 60
philanthropy, 90
Phoenix Clothing Company, 34
phrenology, 148
pickets, 35, 48, 52
piece rates, 82, 91, 110
  reductions, 46, 50, 52, 128, 142, 149, 187-8
piece work system, 20
  boot trade, 46-7, 53, 110-11, 114-15, 167
  clothing trades, 40, 84, 142, 144-5, 149
  printing trades, 120, 125, 176
platen machining, 179
police magistrates, 76, 77, 92
Polish workers, 143
Pollert, Anna, 7
Ponchard, Frank, 153
population ideology, 79, 121, 159, 178
Port Melbourne, 54
Powell, Mrs Margaret M., 89, 92, 98
power-driven machinery, 30, 45, 58, 59, 87
pre-industrial methods, 16
premiums, 25, 31
Pressers' Union, 39, 90
pressing machines, 84, 97

pressing, 26, 28
Price, Edward, 84, 85, 90, 96, 97
Price, Richard, 2
Printers Wages Board, 117, 120, 128
printing industry, 10, 15-16, 20, 58-72, 116-31, 169-79, 181-92
Printing Industry Employees Union of Australia, 120-4, 128, 170
Printing Trades Journal, 125
product market, 2, 61, 81, 187-8
  boot trade, 45, 60, 72, 100, 104, 152, 163-4, 167
  clothing trades, 29, 83, 84
  printing trades, 116, 169
product specialisation, 104
productivity bargaining, 99
professional employment, 79
Progressive Era, 3
Progressivism, 169
protective legislation, 9, 79, 178, 190-1
Provisional Board of Management, 121
publishing, 126

racial orders, 2, 138, 143
racing games, 111-12, 185
racism, 143, 164
Ramas, Maria, 25
rank and file organisation/militancy, 137-50, 153-4, 164
Reddin, Frances, 92-3
Reece trouser buttonholer, 149
Rees, Miss, 87
Reich, M., 6
reintegration of work process, 86
respectability, 24, 56, 89, 191
responsible autonomy, 5
retailers, 26, 88
Richards, Thomas, 51, 154
Richmond, 24, 43, 162
Robertson, Helen, 24
Round Table Conferences, 151-3, 155-6, 164
royalty system, 101, 187
  see also leasing
rule of thumb practices, 85

Sackville's factory, 144
safety regulations, 21
Saint Monday, 44
salaries, *see* wages
Samuel, Raphael, 29
Sands and McDougall's factory, 58-60, 61, 63, 72
Sargood, Butler, Nicol, Ewen, 28
Sargood, Frederick, 34
Saturday morning work, 86-7
Scates, Bruce, 66
scientific management, 2, 3, 4, 84-8, 90, 103-4, 115, 125, 145-8, 155, 167, 183-5, 188, 192
  see also Taylorism

seasonal fluctuations, 19, 20, 29, 36, 43, 50, 98, 189-90
self-measurement cards, 29
semi-skilled workers, 8
service industries, 20
sewing machines, 16, 17, 31, 36, 41, 87, 102, 144, 149-50, 167
sewing machinists, 127
sex structure of unions, 184-5, 192
    boot trade, 107-8, 161, 164
    clothing trades, 91, 95-6, 139
    printing trades, 120-3, 170-1, 176, 179
sexual division of labour, 4, 5, 8-10, 79, 136, 169, 184, 187, 188, 190
    boot trade, 45, 55, 107, 156, 114, 157, 163, 166, 168
    clothing trades, 22-3, 82, 169
    printing trades, 58-60, 61, 63, 65, 117, 124, 128, 175, 177-9, 189
    see also feminisation; masculinisation; men's work; women, work of; women's industries
sexual harassment, 92
Sharwood, J. H., 155
Sheridan case-maker, 63, 65
Shirt Wages Board, 92, 93, 87
shirt and whitework section, 25, 30, 82, 84, 90, 97, 140-1, 147, 149, 191
shop committees, 145, 164
Shops and Factories Acts:
    breaches, 107, 117, 134, 142-3, 151, 164
    1873, 20, 31, 41
    1885, 20, 41, 68
    1893, 21
    1896, 11, 21, 42, 55, 77, 82, 88, 91, 105, 106, 109, 164
Shops and Factories Commission, 1884-5, 33, 35, 67
Sinclair, W. A., 18, 19
single women:
    and militancy/organisation, 24, 57, 108, 123-4, 108, 164, 184-5
    as proportion of female population, 19
    in clothing industry, 23
    work of, 18-19
    workforce participation, 78-9
skill, 2-4, 180-92 passim
    and masculinity, 67
    boot trades, 109, 155, 158-60, 165-6
    clothing trades, 23, 86, 92-3
    dilution of, 117
    printing trades, 63-5, 67, 79, 116-17, 119, 124-7, 170, 172-9
    see also deskilling; labour, skilled; margins for skill
Slade, Mr, 94, 97
slipper making, 156, 163
slop garments, 26, 27, 34
slop-order garments, 29
Smalley and Harkness' factory, 49

Smith, Ted, 144, 147
smoking, 56, 103
Sniders, Barnet, 88
socialism, 10, 66, 95, 98, 119, 192
Solly, Mrs, 108
Solly, Robert, 53, 106, 110
South Melbourne, 94
specialisation, 3, 45, 127, 158, 165, 181-2, 186, 189
speeding-up, 81, 181, 188
    boot industry, 50, 53, 104, 110-11, 153, 163-4, 168
    clothing industry, 40, 84, 142, 144-5, 149
    printing industry, 120, 125, 176
St Crispin's Monday, 53
standardisation of tasks, 2
starching and ironing, 30
state, 2, 5, 180-92
    as employer, 84, 94, 97, 98
    wage-fixing, see arbitration; wages boards
    see also government
stationery industry, 175
steam engines, 16, 21, 31, 118, 190
Stellner, Maria, 89
straw hats, 83, 139
strike-breakers, see blacklegs
strikes:
    boot trade, 51-2, 56, 105, 113, 153-4, 156-7, 161, 163-5, 168
    clothing trades, 32, 94, 97-8, 137-8, 144-6, 188-9
    printing trades, 121, 124, 128, 134
    NSW railway, 96
    waterside workers, 134
strong boots, 43, 49, 52, 114
subdivision of work, 3, 8, 16-17, 19
    boot industry, 43-5, 49-50, 52, 54-5, 102-3, 155, 166-7, 169
    clothing industry, 26-30, 38-9, 82, 84, 86, 144-50
    printing industry, 68, 117, 123, 125, 175, 179
Summerfield, Rose, 56
Sunshine Harvester Works, 135
supervision, 7, 40, 104, 110, 115, 184
surplus value, 5, 8, 55
sweating, 21, 34, 41, 42, 47, 94, 106, 133-4, 137, 142, 143-4, 146, 148, 158, 164
Sydney, 15, 68, 96, 152, 153, 173
syndicalism, 10

table system, 39
tailoresses, 32-5, 37, 127
Tailoresses' Strike, , 1882, 24, 32-4, 188
Tailoresses' Union, see Victorian Tailoresses' Union
tailoring section, 17, 26-8, 82-4, 86, 148, 150

Tailors' Trade Protection Society, 38, 90, 91
tariffs, 15, 41, 44, 45, 52, 60, 71, 77, 83, 110, 114, 144, 165, 167, 190
task range, 3, 4
task system, 47, 53, 71, 82, 84, 99, 109, 111-12, 114, 149, 163
Taylor, Barbara, 24
Taylor, Federick, 2, 3, 85
Taylorism, 4, 5, 7, 85, 125, 167, 169, 191
team system 50, 54, 86, 89, 102, 104, 110, 144, 146, 166, 184
technical education, 71, 78, 126
    see also apprenticeship
technology, 1, 2, 10, 16, 17, 30, 38, 45, 49-50, 60-1, 71, 85, 97, 101, 112, 116, 140, 150, 169, 187, 190
    see also mechanisation
textile industry, 20, 77, 136, 137
30-hour week, see working week
Thompson, E. P., 185
Thompson, J. S. M., 109
Thompson, Mrs Tilly, 97
Thomson, Hugh, 105
Thomson's factory, 54
Tillett, Ben, 137
time and motion studies, 54, 85, 147, 148
time as a commodity, 39
time machines, 88
Tocsin, 87
toilets, 103
Trades Hall, 137
Trades Hall Council, 32-3, 105, 108, 110, 112, 122
    committees, 80, 95, 98, 109, 122
training, 3, 4
    flexible, 113, 145, 155, 158, 166-7, 181, 190
    see also apprenticeship; technical education
treadle machines, 25, 31, 38, 45, 84, 87
Trenwith, W. E., 46, 47, 52

umbrella making, 139
underclothing and whitework section, 83, 91-2
Underclothing Wages Board, 76, 89, 92
underemployment, 20, 38, 52, 61, 153, 162, 167, 185
underwear, ready-made, 83
unemployment, 17, 49-50, 61, 111, 113, 135, 145, 153, 156, 167, 185
Union Special Machine Company, 149
unions, 95, 121, 143
    amalgamations, 91, 93, 95, 97, 106, 108, 117, 120, 122-4, 128, 139, 179
    banners, 112
    federal, 95, 110, 113
    organisation, 19, 24, 37, 81, 88-9
    see also male union culture; victimisation of unionists

union officials, 1, 75, 188
  attitude to immigrant workers, 143, 164
  boot trade, 47, 105-7, 110, 113, 151, 153-5, 160-5
  clothing trades, 26-30, 38-9, 82, 84, 86, 144-50
  printing trades, 68, 117, 123, 125, 175, 179
United Shoe Machinery Company, 49, 100
United States of America, 3, 5, 8, 16, 69, 189
  see also American influences
upper-folding machine, 102

vertical integration, 30
victimisation of unionists, 51, 93, 96, 107, 140, 142, 144
Victorian Apprenticeship Commission, 155
Victorian Employers Federation, 109
Victorian Operative Bootmakers' Union, 44, 46-7, 103, 106-10, 114
Victorian Tailoresses' Union, 24, 32, 35-7, 39

wage rates, 15, 18, 20-1
  boot trade, 22, 56
  clothing trades, 25, 30-2, 36, 85, 87, 147, 185-6
  male, 9, 10
  printing trades, 65, 124, 128
  see also minimum rates; piece rates
wages:
  female, 84, 148, 155, 167, 189
  real, 20, 99, 128, 185-6
  reductions in, 32, 35, 54, 137-8, 145, 157, 187
  secondary, 172
  underpayment, 77
  see also arbitration awards; basic wage; equal pay; methods of payment; wage rates; weekly wage system
wages boards, 21, 75, 94, 100-15, 152-3, 158, 187
  chairmen, 75-6, 92-3, 105, 111, 124, 133, 135, 160
  determinations, (boot trade) 56, 82-3, 89, 105, 107, 109, 111, 117, 152, 155-6, 159, (clothing trades) 82, (printing trades) 126
  elections, 75

system of, 11, 75-7, 88, 91, 93, 99, 133-5, 178
Walkeley, Albion, 34
Walker, Thomas, 106
Wallis, Alf, 86, 89, 94-5, 98, 138-9, 142-7, 192
warehouses, 16, 25, 26, 34
Warsaw, Mrs, 24
Waterside Workers Federation, 134
web-rotary presses, 61
Webb, Deputy President, 172-9
Webber, Minnie, 89
weekly hiring, 159
weekly wage system:
  boot industry, 46-9, 52-5, 104, 110-11, 114-15
  clothing industry, 39-40, 82, 84
  printing industry, 71
welfarism, 5, 141, 184
Western Australia, 16, 105
wheat farming, 16
Whipp, Richard, 39
white supremacist political economy, 177
Whiteworkers Union, 94
Whiteworkers Wages Board, 94
Whitford, Lillian, 96, 139
Whitten's factory, 45, 56
wholesalers, 29, 88
Whybrow, Arthur, 44, 49, 52-4, 110, 154
Whybrow Case, 135
Whybrow's factory, 44
widows, 162
Williams, Jenny, 71
Williamson's factory, 88
Willis, Paul, 7
Wilson, Mr, 143
Wing, John, 37, 39
wives, 18, 26, 108
Woman's Sphere, 119
women:
  and arbitration system, 139
  and industrial organisation/militancy, 23-4, 33, 65-6, 80, 93, 95, 123, 138, 143-4, 161-4, 171, 184-5
  and reproduction, 9
  as dependents, 22, 82
  as unpaid housekeepers and care-givers, 8-10, 21-2
  in boot trade, 44-5, 48, 55-6, 106-8, 159
  in paid work, proportion of, 19
  in public sphere, 24, 32-4, 81, 188

in tailoring, 26
work of, 17, 79, 107, 137, 148, 156, 157, 166, 169, 177, 189, 175, (unhealthy) 28, (non-traditional) 135, (white collar) 135
  see also daughters; females; gender ideology; married women; mothers'; new women; single women; wives
Women and Girls' Advisory Committee, 122, 170
Women Bookbinders' Union, 117, 120, 121, 122, 124
women's industries, 177
Women's Political Association, 95
Wood, Stephen, 180
work, see conditions of work; dangerous work; deskilling; fragmentation; hours of work; labour; mechanisation; men's work; nature of work; scientific management; sexual division of labour; skill; subdivision of work; wages
workers:
  and new methods, 1, 5, 7, 85-8, 97, 125, 144-6
  apathy, 89
  consent, 6
  discretion, 4
  displaced by machines, 50, 51, 60, 97, 118, 170
  old and slow, 54, 111
  resistance to wage reductions, 33-9
  see also alliances between workers and employers
workflow, 104
Working Men's College, 126
working man's paradise, 20, 33
working-proprietors, 34, 40, 60
working week:
  30-hour, 153, 165
  40-hour, 165
  42-hour, 185
  44-hour, 128, 152, 158-9, 178, 185
  48-hour, 91, 185
  see also hours of work; night work; Saturday morning work
working-class, 5, 9, 23
workshops, 16, 31, 41, 44
World War I, 81, 84, 93-5, 97-9, 118, 120, 128, 152, 154, 158, 183, 187
Wyeth, James, 29

Yugoslav workers, 143